WAR CRIMES

WAR CRIMES

THE LEGACY OF NUREMBERG

Belinda Cooper
EDITOR

New York

Dedicated to the memory of
Telford Taylor

Publisher's Cataloging-in-Publication Data

War crimes : the legacy of Nuremberg / Belinda Cooper, editor ; foreword by Richard J. Goldstone. — 1st ed.
    p. cm.
    ISBN: 1-57500-009-1
    1. Nuremberg Trial of Major German War Criminals, Nuremberg, Germany, 1945–1946. 2. War crime trials—Germany—Nuremberg. 3. Trials (Crimes against humanity) I. Cooper, Belinda. II. Title: Legacy of Nuremberg.
    JX5437.8.C66 1998   341.69'0268
                                         QBI98–66767

The publisher has made every effort to secure permission to reproduce copyrighted material and would like to apologize should there have been any errors or omissions.

TV Books, L.L.C.
Publishers serving the television industry.
1619 Broadway, Ninth Floor
New York, NY 10019
www.tvbooks.com

Contents

Foreword

Justice Richard J. Goldstone

Most governments find it difficult to adapt to some of the consequences of our shrinking world—globalization, as it is usefully called. Scientific and technological advances have, in some respects, made a mockery of national borders, currency restrictions, and control of what people may say, hear or even see. In the developed world, many adaptations have already been accomplished and others are on the way. Modern travel, the Internet, the use of outer space, health hazards, drug trafficking, money laundering are the subject of hundreds of meetings, seminars, and conferences.

Yet until the Security Council established the International Criminal Tribunal for the former Yugoslavia in May 1993, there had been an irrational, almost perverse, neglect by the international community of one of the most serious and growing problems facing our world—the increasing frequency of the commission of crimes such as genocide, crimes against humanity and war crimes like grave breaches of the Geneva Conventions. These are crimes of a magnitude difficult for the mind to comprehend—designed as they are to exterminate whole peoples, to compel members of this or that ethnic, religious or political group to leave the places where their families have lived for centuries. The cost in human and financial terms is incalculable.

Since World War II there have been more than one hundred wars, for the most part civil conflicts. In those conflicts, millions of people have been slaughtered, raped and forced to flee their homes and their countries. The fact that wars may be internal is cold comfort to neighboring countries which, willingly or not, become havens for millions of refugees. In many cases the refugees not only tax the resources of the countries granting them a haven, but also create political instability. The Rwanda genocide of 1994 has thrown the whole Great Lakes region of Central Africa into turmoil. The wars in the former Yugoslavia have created huge refugee problems in Europe. Germany alone has over 300,000 Yugoslav refugees. Civil wars are no longer only the concern of the countries in which they are waged.

Despite numerous instances of horrendous human rights violations as a result of these conflicts over the decades, be they in Cambodia, Mozambique, Iraq, or any other country which could be cited, never, before the establishment of the Yugoslav tribunal, did the international community respond by establishing an institution to punish those responsible for human rights violations. What, then, prompted such action by the international community in the case of the former Yugoslavia? I would suggest that a combination of factors compelled the international community to take action. The end of the Cold War, the fact that the offenses were reminiscent of those committed in the Nazi era, and crucially, the almost instant images of the horrors of the war transmitted to hundreds of millions of television viewers worldwide, all combined to impel a shocked international community to take action through the Security Council. The international media was in this case instrumental in galvanizing the conscience of the international community.

But just as the modern media played an important role in exposing the atrocities committed in the former Yugoslavia, so it also was instrumental in inciting and instigating their commission. I would suggest that the growing frequency with which horrendous war crimes are committed is yet another consequence of globalization. Modern means of communication and the dissemination of venomous propaganda (the hand-maiden of genocide and crimes against humanity) now also assist evil politicians to achieve their nefarious ends.

It was the scale and horror of the Nazi war crimes that led the victorious Allied powers to put the German leaders on trial at Nuremberg. An important legacy that came to us from Nuremberg was the recognition of a universal jurisdiction in respect of crimes against humanity and, later, genocide. The ambit of international law and humanitarian law was considerably extended by this recognition. It is a matter for deep regret that this legacy did not resonate for almost fifty years. The zeal with which nations have protected their sovereignty has unfortunately extended to the protection of the perpetrators of egregious war crimes. What else could explain the almost universal reluctance, until recently, to establish a permanent international criminal court?

Where there is an outbreak of criminal activity in any national state there is an inevitable response from government—policing is increased and every attempt is made to apprehend criminals. Penalties often become harsher and the criminal justice system is made more efficient. Yet, in the face of the escalation of war crimes and their disastrous consequences for the international community, no equivalent steps have been taken by that community to apprehend perpetrators of gross human rights violations, bring them to justice and punish them. With a few recent and notable exceptions, the most powerful nations in the world, in particular the United States of America, have thus far refused to order their well-armed troops to arrest war criminals indicted by the Yugoslav tribunal—a tribunal they themselves established. This has largely been motivated by a fear of the political fallout that would result if their troops were injured or killed as a consequence of making such arrests. Yet even in the grief over the loss of a child, a mother or father feels the pride of sacrifice in protection of one's own people. Should a mother or father of a soldier, or the American people for that matter, be less proud of a similar sacrifice in consequence of the apprehension of someone wanted for the murder and rape of thousands of innocent human beings, even if they are many miles away in a foreign country? That pride was palpable during two world wars, when the United States sent its armies to protect the human rights of people on a distant continent.

As events unfold in Bosnia, it becomes more and more apparent that the successful implementation of the Dayton Peace Accord depends upon the apprehension and transfer to the tribunal of indicted war criminals whose continued obstructive presence threatens to unravel the whole peace process. It is not too late for the international community to take appropriate action. Increased political pressure should be placed on governments in the region to compel them to carry out the arrests necessary to ensure the effective functioning of the tribunal. In the absence of state arrests, those international troops enforcing the peace in Bosnia must be instructed to take active steps to make arrests. These troops have both a clear right and, in fact, a legal duty to do so under the Dayton Accord. Although in recent months we have seen some effort to apprehend certain indictees, there has been no sustained policy in this regard, and many key indictees remain at large, flouting the provisions of the accord.

It is widely acknowledged that the performance of the Yugoslav and Rwanda tribunals will have consequences for the establishment of a permanent international criminal court—a matter which is now seriously on the agenda of the United Nations. It is in the foregoing context that this collection of essays is particularly welcome. When, and I like to say when and not if, a permanent International Criminal Tribunal is established, the authors of this volume will be able to consider themselves amongst those experts and advocators of international justice whose work contributed significantly to the realization of what was once but a mere ideal.

Introduction

A little over half a century ago, the horror of Nazi atrocities, brought home to a wider public with a new immediacy through the medium of newsreel footage, shocked the world. Yet remarkably, the response to this horror was not brute revenge. Instead, the scale of the atrocities, the desire to find a way to prevent such carnage in the future and the spirit of international cooperation that followed the Allied victory led the victorious powers to attempt an approach to postwar justice based, at least in theory, on the rule of law rather than the rule of strength. The International Military Tribunal (IMT) at Nuremberg, made up of representatives of the four victorious Allied powers, introduced the novel concept of individual legal accountability before an international body for atrocities committed in wartime. Not the German government, but individual Germans—twenty-one of the most important Nazi leaders, plus one in absentia—stood trial for these atrocities. Nineteen were convicted of war crimes, crimes against humanity, or crimes against peace, twelve were sentenced to death, and the world had a new catchword: "Nuremberg."

But over the fifty years that followed, realpolitik seemed to negate the principles of responsibility and accountability declared at Nuremberg. Cold War political maneuvering became the order of the day, and international cooperation to enforce norms against war crimes and other violations of humanitarian law seemed little more than a utopian notion. Even as recently as the late 1980s, it seemed the world might never unite to repeat the achievement of the Nuremberg trial; aside from lip service to Nuremberg, there was little effort to punish those guilty of atrocities in places like Vietnam, Algeria, Biafra, Cambodia and Afghanistan.

Yet pressure to establish principles of accountability in international law never entirely ceased. On the international level, this was mirrored in the ratification of a variety of international instruments—the 1948 Genocide Convention, the 1949 Geneva Conventions and many others. Though they often had little practical effect, their existence and acceptance by the international community left open the possibility that they might someday be given more substantive content. On another level, social and cultural attempts to grapple with the consequences of World War II were changing the way people thought, altering their view of the place of individuals and states in the international system and of the responsibilities of the international community toward individuals.

The end of the Cold War created a setting in which these changes could begin to bear more practical fruit, simultaneously clearing away ideological obstacles to international cooperation and loosing forces that

made such cooperation more crucial than ever. The appearance of devastating ethnic conflict in Yugoslavia and Rwanda—once again broadcast with horrifying clarity into people's living rooms—this time shocked
an international community that seemed incapable of taking concrete
action to head off disaster.

Despite—or perhaps because of—their exposure to this international
inability to unite politically to prevent catastrophe, the terrible conflicts
in Yugoslavia and Rwanda catalyzed renewed efforts in the international
legal arena. Two war crimes tribunals—the International Criminal Tribunal for former Yugoslavia (ICTY), in the Hague, and the International
Criminal Tribunal for Rwanda (ICTR), in Arusha, Tanzania—were created by the UN Security Council to take up the Nuremberg project, prosecuting those suspected of committing wartime atrocities. They grant us
the unprecedented opportunity to observe the Nuremberg legacy in action, compare and contrast the different frameworks in which war crimes
prosecution can occur, and consider the strengths and weaknesses and
the possible long-term impact of the latest trials. The purpose of this volume, originally inspired by a 1996 Court TV documentary commemorating the fiftieth anniversary of the Nuremberg Tribunal, is to assist in
understanding the substance of the trials and the issues and controversies
surrounding them.

In keeping with the universality of the issues raised by the Nuremberg
tribunal and today's war crimes tribunals, the contributors to this volume
come from a variety of fields; they are international lawyers, historians,
policy experts and journalists, each bringing the particular perspective of
his or her discipline to the subject. Because the issues transcend the trials themselves, many of these contributions go beyond the mechanics of
international adjudication to consider the historical, political and moral
implications of Nuremberg's legacy. What is the nexus between justice
and politics, and do international tribunals truly represent the former or
simply the latter? What are the goals of international adjudication? Is a
trial, on its own, enough to resolve the issues arising out of dictatorship
and war? Do such tribunals lead the guilty to repent, do they ease the
pain of the injured, do they deter atrocities in the future—or are they
simply a way to soothe the conscience of a world that seems unable, and
often unwilling, to find political solutions to its most terrible conflicts?
Are they the best way to move a society from violence to peace, or are
domestic prosecutions, or even nonlegal remedies, more effective? These
and similar questions are more significant than ever today, at a time
when so many societies are emerging from periods of strife, when our interdependency has grown to the point that we can no longer simply re-

treat into isolationism, and when, therefore, we need more than ever to find mechanisms to smooth such transitions and prevent future conflict.

The book is divided into three main sections. Section I focuses on the Nuremberg tribunal, both its achievements and its weaknesses. Section II considers Nuremberg's legacy as the international community confronts war crimes and crimes against humanity today; it looks first at the background, contexts and ongoing process of the international criminal tribunals for the former Yugoslavia and Rwanda, then at the functions of, and alternatives to, such international tribunals for societies attempting to free themselves from the legacies of war and violence. Section III looks to the future, particularly the proposed permanent international criminal court, placing this court in its context as the culmination of a process begun at Nuremberg. The appendix contains some relevant background materials on the tribunals.

Since work began on this book, the international tribunals for Rwanda and Yugoslavia have surprised skeptical observers by overcoming many of their original difficulties; they now have significant numbers of important suspects in custody, have held trials and handed down verdicts, and are becoming respected and accepted institutions of international law. The statute for a permanent international criminal court was adopted in the summer of 1998, and the court is likely to become a reality in the near future. Thus Nuremberg's legacy endures.

Because the events discussed in this book are in constant flux, certain factual details may have changed by the time of publication. Up-to-date information on the ICTY, ICTR, and the permanent international criminal court can be found at their websites, at www.un.org/icty, www.un.org/ictr, and www.un.org/icc.

Acknowledgements

Thanks are due to a number of people and institutions without whom this compilation would not have been possible. Court TV provided generous access to its materials and resources. The World Policy Institute, its former acting director, Mira Kamdar, and its present director, Stephen Schlesinger, contributed logistical aid, inspiration and a working home. Ian Cuthbertson and Peter Kaufman gave me the idea for, and the opportunity to compile, this book and the moral support necessary to complete it. Megan Dieter contributed research assistance at the start, succeeded later in the project by Amy Frumin. Mary Albon contributed her excellent editing skills. Donna Axel came on board as the book was taking shape, and her enthusiasm, friendship, and organizational skill were invaluable in carrying it through to the end. My parents, as usual, bore with me throughout. My work on this book was inspired throughout by my father, Victor Cooper, who survived the Holocaust.

Belinda Cooper
December 1998

PART I

Nuremberg:
The Precedent

Introduction

The International Military Tribunal at Nuremberg (IMT) is considered the modern precedent for holding individual war criminals responsible for their crimes in an international forum. Its attempt to create accountability for wartime violence through legal process was a remarkable historical development. Those most directly involved in the tribunal, and the twelve American trials that followed it, believed firmly in the importance of countering atrocity and brutality with legality, in contrast to many on the side of the victors who would have preferred more traditional executions without trial.

Nuremberg was groundbreaking in many respects, though it was neither a perfect trial nor a perfect precedent. Given the context, guilt was in a sense presumed, but the outcome was not predetermined; the defendants were given every opportunity to present their case, and several were acquitted. Nuremberg established, for the first time, the crucial international legal principle that following orders was not a defense, and it changed the focus of international law and accountability from governments to individuals. Perhaps most important, some feel, Nuremberg established an indisputable historical record of the Nazi atrocities.

But Nuremberg also had significant shortcomings. The trial was seen as little more than victors' justice by many on the losing, and even on the winning, side. The presence of the Soviet Union on the judges' bench, despite its own responsibility for massive crimes against humanity, detracted from the tribunal's credibility; in fact, war crimes by all but the losing side were ignored. Nuremberg was accused of imposing ex post facto justice, since there were no codified international laws forbidding the acts it punished. The predominance of the Anglo-Saxon legal system at the trial placed the defense, accustomed to the civil law system, at a disadvantage, and the conspiracy charge so central to the prosecution did not exist on the Continent.

These and other issues are addressed, with differing emphasis and from differing points of view, in the essays that follow. Bernard Meltzer, a member of the prosecution team at Nuremberg, provides both personal recollections of the trial and an overview and analysis of the IMT. He describes the tribunal's background and discusses the controversies surrounding it, particularly the issues of retroactive law and victors' justice. Benjamin Ferencz, a prosecutor at the American trials that followed the International Military Tribunal, also looks back upon his own experience. Ferencz describes the hopes invested in the trials by those most directly involved—the hope of "moving toward a more humane and

rational order." He offers a positive assessment of Nuremberg's legacy in
the context of subsequent advances in international law, while arguing
passionately for a more effective system of international humanitarian
law and enforcement mechanisms to carry on the Nuremberg legacy. Associate Supreme Court Justice Stephen Breyer praises the vision of the
chief American prosecutor at the IMT, Robert Jackson, also a Supreme
Court Justice; he emphasizes the trial's representation of the human striv-
ing for justice, its value as precedent, and its achievement in recording
for all time the horrors of the Holocaust.

Law professors Ruti Teitel and Edward Wise consider the legacy of
Nuremberg as a sea change in the way we view responsibility for international crimes. Teitel describes four dualities central to Nuremberg and the
conceptual shifts that emerged out of them: politics versus individual legal
accountability; collective versus individual responsibility; national versus
international jurisdiction over war crimes; and laws governing international armed conflict versus humanitarian laws that apply to internal conflict and times of peace. Wise concentrates primarily on the reasons for the
importance of the aggressive war charge to prosecutors at Nuremberg and
its far lesser significance in discussions of the legacy of Nuremberg today;
he describes this as a paradigm shift in which international law was recon-
ceptualized to focus on the individual rather than the state.

Although they discuss the shortcomings of Nuremberg, all of these authors ultimately view Nuremberg's problems as less significant than its
contributions to advancing the international rule of law. The next two
chapters, by historians Peter Maguire and Jörg Friedrich, are less san-
guine. From an American and a German perspective, they follow the immediate legacy of Nuremberg—the rapid sacrifice of the tribunal's lofty
principles to the exigencies of the Cold War and German integration
into the Western alliance, and Germans' corresponding refusal to recognize the validity of the judgments handed down at Nuremberg. Maguire
describes the origins of the American clemency boards that released most
of those convicted in the twelve American successor trials only a few
years after they were sentenced. Quoting numerous American politicians
and policymakers of the postwar period, he shows how public outrage
over war crimes soon gave way to the political wooing of Germany. Not
even the perpetrators of the massacre of American soldiers at Malmedy
could be kept in prison, it seemed, once political realities made a strong,
well-disposed German ally desirable to U.S. policy makers.

Friedrich sets the trials within the context of the Allies' political goal
of transforming Germany and bringing it into the Western alliance. He
emphasizes German resentment of Nuremberg's retroactive justice
(something which, as Bernard Meltzer suggests in his contribution, may

have been especially sensitive to Germans accustomed to the codifica-
tions of civil law rather than a constantly evolving common law).
Friedrich describes a German population largely resistant to the salutary
influence of Nuremberg and a German legal system that succeeded in
nullifying the Nuremberg judgments.

These chapters raise questions about the actual, as opposed to theoretical, significance of international legal principles, and about the relationship between politics and justice, that are also relevant to today's tribunals
for former Yugoslavia and Rwanda. It is true that the negotiators of the
Dayton Accord that ended the war in former Yugoslavia refused, at least
in principle, to conform to the Cold War model described by Maguire;
rather than bowing to the supposed exigencies of practical politics, which
might have dictated a sacrifice of principle for the sake of securing an
agreement, the accord at least barred war criminals from participation in
the political process. But the day-to-day realities in former Yugoslavia tell
a different story, as indicted war criminals continue to exercise influence
while the world community stands by. In such a situation, the significance
of a tribunal seems less apparent. Does the development of shared humanitarian legal principles by an international body have any meaning if
politics prevents them from being consistently applied?

Additionally, despite the fundamental changes in the political con-
stellation since the postwar period, we must still ask what actual impact
these trials will have on the citizens of the countries for which they are,
at least in part, being held. Friedrich's evidence of German refusal to recognize war crimes judgments suggests that legal structures may be less effective tools of change than other developments—such as education,
social and political reform, and the natural change in generations—that
have allowed Germans to face their past as honestly as they do today.

Finally, directly addressing the question of the relationship between
politics and law and revealing the complexities of that relationship, law
professor Diane Orentlicher approaches the issue of victors' justice from
a very different perspective. She argues that it was precisely the Allies'
action against Hitler that gave them the moral authority to prosecute
German leaders. This authority is lacking in an international community
that failed to intervene in Bosnia; in her view, prosecution of those responsible for the crimes in Bosnia and Rwanda is necessary if that moral
authority is to be recovered.

Remembering Nuremberg[1]

Bernard D. Meltzer

Fifty years ago, Justice Robert Jackson, on leave from the United States
Supreme Court, and serving as chief of the United States Prosecution,
delivered his magnificent opening statement in the trial before the International Military Tribunal in Nuremberg. The trial, because of the
horrors it addressed and the purposes it sought to accomplish, has been
viewed as the greatest in this century, if not in history. The road back to
"Nuremberg"—which means both a trial and a place—is, of course, well
travelled. Nonetheless, there are reasons, in addition to its recent fiftieth
anniversary, for another trip. Nuremberg seems relevant—alas, too relevant—because of the atrocities, the grim clichés, of our own time, such
as so-called ethnic cleansing in the former Yugoslavia and Rwanda and
mass rape as an instrument of terror and territorial expansion. Finally, the
memory of Nuremberg is also evoked by the rise of neo-Nazism in Germany and the United States, as well as by the preachers of bigotry and
separatism everywhere. And so I hope here initially to sketch the trial's
purposes, its limitations, and the principal criticisms surrounding it.

The way for the trial was paved by Germany's unconditional surrender
on May 7, 1945, and by the Allies' capture of the major surviving leaders
of the Nazi regime. On November 20, 1945, a little over six months after
the surrender, the trial of the "Major War Criminals of the European
Axis" before the International Military Tribunal opened at the Palace of
Justice in Nuremberg, with the reading of the hundred-page indictment.
In the courtroom were twenty-one defendants—the surviving major leaders of the Nazi regime, such as Goering, Ribbentrop and Hess. All of the
defendants pleaded not guilty. Seeing them in the dock, stripped of their
medals and insignia of power, one could scarcely believe that these men
had dominated much of the world and had terrified most of it.

The International Military Tribunal had been established under the
so-called London Charter agreed to by the major Allies, that is, the
United States, the United Kingdom, France, and the Soviet Union. Two
of the principal authors of the charter, representing the United Kingdom
and the United States, as had been anticipated, served as chief prosecutors for their governments. The Soviet draftsman later served as a member of the tribunal. The French brought new people into those posts. The
charter set forth the law that was to govern the trial.

Each of the major Allies appointed one judge and an alternate to this
military tribunal, although all except the Soviet judges were civilians.

The British judge, Sir Geoffrey Lawrence, was elected the tribunal's president by the other judges; he announced its decisions on procedural matters. His election was apparently designed to play down the numerical dominance of the Americans; our legal staff, I believe, was larger than the three other prosecution staffs combined.

Incidentally, the international trial is to be distinguished from so-called "subsequent proceedings," that is, later trials held at Nuremberg by only the U.S. government; other trials were also held elsewhere before other national tribunals.[2]

The choice of the Nuremberg Palace of Justice as the situs of the trial of the Nazi leaders surely meshed with a justice of retribution. The Nuremberg Laws of 1935 had been part of a series of anti-Semitic measures that had stripped German Jews of their citizenship and their property and had excluded them from the government, the armed forces, and other important areas of economic and cultural life. Beginning in 1934, during Nazi party rallies in Nuremberg, Hitler sought to seduce, deceive, and terrorize his potential adversaries and to fire up his followers. When the trial began, Nuremberg was a pile of rubble; but the Palace of Justice and the prison adjacent to it had not suffered any substantial damage. Albert Speer, a convicted defendant, wrote in his diary that he could not help thinking that there had been a deeper meaning to this almost miraculous survival of the Palace of Justice.[3]

In describing the international indictment, which in general tracked the London Charter, I will oversimplify a bit. The first count charged a common plan or conspiracy to commit crimes against peace as well as war crimes and crimes against humanity. The second count charged the actual commission of crimes against peace, namely, preparation and waging of aggressive wars, which were also in violation of international treaties. The third count alleged certain specified war crimes. The fourth count alleged crimes against humanity, namely, extermination, enslavement or other inhumane treatment of any civilian population either before or during the war or persecution on political, racial or religious grounds.

The London Charter rejected certain defenses, such as acts of state and superior orders, which in combination might have immunized all the defendants. Furthermore, in the trial of any individual member of an organization, the charter authorized the tribunal to declare organizations, such as the SS, illegal. About those organizational provisions, I will say only that they created overwhelming practical and moral problems and were of little use.

The most criticized provisions of the charter were those making aggressive war an international crime and providing for individual punishment of those guilty of that crime. Critics challenged that approach as incompatible with the principle that punishment should not be imposed on the basis of standards or penalties retroactively defined. Before examining that criticism, it is useful to recall the context out of which the London Charter arose. Before Germany's surrender, this is what reliable evidence had shown:

- Ruthless pre-war Nazi assaults on the Jews, the churches, independent labor unions and dissidents in Germany, as the Nazis achieved and consolidated their power.
- Deliberate and indisputable German aggression against Czechoslovakia, Poland, most of the rest of Europe, and then against the USSR and the United States.
- As a result of those wars, the systematic and massive pillaging, plundering and devastation of a continent, and the deportation of millions of slave laborers, all centrally organized.
- The deliberate mistreatment and execution of prisoners of war, the murder of millions of Jews, Slavs, Gypsies and dissidents. The murder of Jews had occurred on so large a scale that it was then uncertain how many millions had been exterminated. But the vast scope and general consequences of the Nazis' Final Solution and the unspeakable horrors that had attended it were known before the war ended.[4]

World War II has understandably been called "the largest single event (and the Holocaust the greatest crime[5]) in human history."[6] It has been estimated that the war killed nearly fifty million, and, for millions more, destroyed their towns and cities and left them wounded in mind and body.

Many of those horrors had, of course, been war crimes, which for a long time had led to individual punishment. But given the human misery resulting from Nazi aggressions, Jackson, among others, found such charges, based only on how the war had been conducted, insufficient. It was necessary also to impose individual punishment for the Nazis' aggressive wars, the supreme evil and the generating cause of most of the other offenses and their attendant agonies. Jackson urged, moreover, that the principles against retroactive punishment, properly understood, did not preclude punishment in the circumstances present.

Those principles are designed to avoid punishing one who, when he acted, had no reasonable warning that his conduct was culpable. That rule was manifestly inapplicable to the Nazis. They knew of the Kellogg-Briand Pact,[7] which had outlawed war except in self-defense, and which had been signed by an earlier German government. They were aware of an impressive list of other international formulations explicitly or implicitly condemning aggressive war as an international crime. They knew that, given modern technology, the launching of such a war was a terrible act. Not even Hitler had been prepared to claim publicly the right to do so. Thus, after the attack on Poland, Hitler, in a speech to the Reichstag, contended that the Poles had launched a war of aggression and that the Nazis had acted only in self-defense. Hitler's aggressive "Poles" had been concentration camp inmates forced into Polish uniforms—a mordant bit of irony.

As Justice Jackson urged, the character of international law precluded the strict and automatic application of the rule against retroactivity. That rule has flourished in comparatively well-developed legal systems, but not in primitive or immature ones. Thus, during the early development of our common law, offenses like killing and robbery that had shocked the moral sense of the community had been retrospectively transformed into crimes for which individual punishment was exacted. Similarly, individual punishment for war crimes had become an established feature of international law without any express provisions for individual punishment in organic documents such as the Geneva Convention. International law was at best a primitive system, lacking a legislative body and, like the early common law, dependent on case-by-case development. The strict and automatic application of the principle against retroactivity in such a system would have created too large a gap between the law and the developing moral sense of the world community. Without going into the more intricate arguments about the ex post facto label, the key argument is that the principle against retroactivity was a principle of justice and the reasons behind it were totally inapplicable to the Nazi leadership.

I was once convinced that the foregoing considerations trumped the ex post facto objection, but I am now doubtful about that conclusion. It was undermined by the pre-1945 practices of nations.[8] The most troubling events were the Soviet aggressions against Poland, the Baltic states, and Finland. Furthermore, the French, stressing the ex post facto objection, resisted, even though they ultimately acquiesced in, the inclusion of crimes against peace. Like most European lawyers, they relied on a tradition of a code or a statute, which tended to be less flexible and open-ended than the common law tradition.[9] To be sure, the idea of "crimes against peace" met the emotional needs of the time, but it also cast a shadow on the trial.

Incidentally, the London Charter and the indictment raised another independent question of retroactivity by appearing to include, within "crimes against humanity," governmental persecution and extermination of civilian populations in Germany before the outbreak of the war. The tribunal ducked that question by folding crimes against humanity into war crimes or into crimes against the peace, thereby eroding any independent legal significance for crimes against humanity.

Concerns about retroactivity seemed to sharpen the question of whether judicial procedures should have been used to determine guilt and impose punishment. For a time the United States and the Soviet Union had flirted with the idea of executive punishment, which had been pressed by the British. The British had proposed that the Allies would identify, let us say, twenty-five or one hundred leading Germans whose offenses had been serious and obvious and shoot them, out of hand. Stalin, who was said to have been pulling Churchill's leg, had raised the ante to 50,000 Germans. But the Allies ultimately decided to grant the defendants a hearing—a decision explained by Jackson with characteristic power early in his opening statement. He declared:

> That four great nations, flushed with victory and stung with injury, stay the hand of vengeance and voluntarily submit their captive enemies to the judgment of the law is one of the most significant tributes that Power has ever paid to Reason.[10]

He added:

> It may be that these men of troubled conscience, whose only wish is that the world forget them, do not regard a trial as a favor. But they do have a fair opportunity to defend themselves—a favor which these men, when in power, rarely extended to their fellow countrymen.[11]

Nonetheless, some critics condemned the use of judicial procedures to determine guilt and impose punishment, emphasizing that to do so would turn a court into a political instrument by which the victors exercised their power to punish the defeated. Thus, as Dennis J. Hutchinson has recently reported, then-U.S. Chief Justice Harlan Stone privately labeled the trial as a "high class lynching party."[12] These critics urged that avowedly political means—that is, summary executions by executive fiat—rather than ostensibly judicial means should be used for political punishments.

But that position ignored or dismissed the risk of error involved in summary action, whether it is based on "principles of law" or executive fiat. That position was in essence an argument against due process. Had it prevailed, it would no doubt have triggered an outcry against the risks of prosecutorial error aggravated by denial of the right to make a defense. The acquittal of three Nuremberg defendants is a powerful reminder of such risks. Indeed, it would not be pleasant to defend today the summary execution of individuals chosen on the basis of incomplete evidence, untested by an adversary proceeding.

A trial, moreover, would respect the needs of history and provide a record of the Nazi affronts to civilization—a record that might serve an educative and reformative role for the generation of 1945 and beyond, in and outside of Germany. Such a record might also, as Jackson urged, both foreclose responsible denial and avert martyrdom for the major leaders of the Nazi regime. The evidence of the Holocaust was so strong and palpable in 1945 that I doubt that anyone then foresaw the so-called Auschwitz lie—the recent denials that the Holocaust actually happened. But the trial record surely serves as a corrective to such fantastic revisionism.

What I have said so far does not, of course, deal with what was the central difficulty of the trial. The governing law was not applied equally. The standards of guilt were applied only to the losers. For example, the Soviets, who sat on the tribunal, were not forced to answer for Soviet aggression against Poland, the Baltic states, or Finland. Nor were the United Kingdom and the United States required to face the questions raised, for example, by the bombings of Dresden and Hiroshima. To some, the unequal application of the law, compounded by the Soviet presence on the Nuremberg Tribunal, fatally compromised the morality of the trial. To others, the Nazis' monstrous barbarities and the fact that it was their aggression that precipitated the ensuing horrors warranted the apparently unequal application of the law.

Furthermore, Nuremberg merely reflected the troubling inequality. It did not produce it. It was the product of an undeveloped and fragile international system. Long before Nuremberg, the victor had applied an unequal standard, for example, in dealing with traditional war crimes. The victor punished the misconduct of the enemy; similar conduct by his own forces largely went unpunished. Unless the Allies had been prepared to comb their own ranks for violators of the rules of war, the logic of the inequality argument would have required us to give the Nazis complete immunity for all their crimes, war crimes as well as crimes against the peace. Even the critics shrank from that position. We were, I believe, justified in rejecting it, because of the overwhelmingly greater depravity of the Nazis and because they had launched wars of aggression.

I want now to turn from those large legal questions to narrower problems regarding the content of the London Charter, the indictment and the conduct of the trial. One set of problems arose from the need to mesh different legal and political cultures. For example, the French were puzzled by the concept of a common plan or conspiracy but acquiesced reluctantly in its inclusion in the charter.[13] The Soviet negotiator at first insisted that aggressive war should be made a crime only when committed in the past by the Nazis. Jackson held out for and secured a more expansive prohibition—one addressed to the future as well as the past. There were also differences among the Allies on the role of the indictment, the role of the lawyers and the importance of cross-examination. The Soviets were used to much more specificity in an indictment; in crimes against the state, at least, the evidence set forth in the indictment was not expected to be challenged but to be received as the truth by the tribunal, and, as we know, often accepted by the accused as well. The French and Germans were accustomed to an active judge who did much of the investigating and questioning of witnesses. Perhaps as a result, the French and German lawyers were not skillful cross examiners; nor were the Soviets. These and other differences were bridged by workable compromises and by recognizing, within broad limits, the discretion of each prosecuting team to follow its own style.

There were also lively disagreements among the U.S. prosecutors on issues of trial policy. The most important issue was whether to rely primarily on documents without much live testimony. Some argued that live witnesses in the prosecution's case-in-chief would spice up the proceedings. Jackson, however, decided to rely primarily on documentary evidence. Documents, although drabber, would be free from the problems that live witnesses would entail—bad memory, susceptibility to pressure, currying favor, or turning the tables and making Nazi propaganda. Because of Jackson's policy, the case against the defendants was proved by documents of their own making, the authenticity of which was challenged only once or twice. Fortunately, the German obsession for record keeping made our case.

The defendants were afforded adequate opportunity to challenge and meet the evidence offered against them. They were allowed to pick their lawyers from the German bar, or they could have German counsel appointed for them. After some logistical difficulties were resolved, their lawyers received a copy, in German, of all the documents put into evidence and could and did have witnesses and documents subpoenaed. The defendants could and did in most cases take the stand. Even critics of the idea of a trial or of some provisions of the charter generally applauded the fairness of the trial.

In the end the Nuremberg Tribunal acquitted three defendants and sentenced twelve to die by hanging and seven to prison terms ranging from ten years to life. Only one defendant, Rudolf Hess, was convicted only of crimes against peace. The others were also convicted of war crimes or crimes against humanity. (Of course, their convictions for crimes against peace might have affected the sentences imposed on them.) The USSR dissented from all the acquittals but dissented from only one sentence, life imprisonment rather than death for Hess.

Nuremberg, in its condemnation of aggressive war, focused not only on the offenses of these defendants but also on establishing a precedent designed to punish and deter aggression in the future. But to my knowledge, at the time the prospects for such deterrence had not been closely analyzed. No one, of course, expected aggressive war to be completely exorcised by the trial. The hope seemed to be that the condemnation of aggression would bite into the culture, affect public opinion and constrain aggression by governments because of concern for domestic and foreign criticism or sanctions against an offending nation, as well as individual punishment. But the significance of those considerations for shaping official decisions about aggression—especially by totalitarian governments—was far from clear. In any event, after Nuremberg, there were plenty of aggressive wars—Korea, Afghanistan and the Persian Gulf, to mention but a few wars for which no individual punishment was imposed. Nuremberg may, of course, have helped keep the number down and was invoked to justify and organize resistance to the Korean and Gulf aggressions. But the incidence of aggression in the subsequent decades has been high enough to raise questions about Nuremberg's deterrent effect—questions that are sharpened by the difficulties of enforcing the proscriptions of Nuremberg. Furthermore, it is arguable that once an aggressive war breaks out, the aggressors' fear of punishment might encourage them to make a gambler's throw and to prolong the war even when the probability of their winning is low.

I am going to leave those questions to others more adept in speculating in futures and turn to my own past—my work in Nuremberg. Before I get to my own work, let me explain the general order of proof. First, the prosecution introduced evidence of the Nazis' commission of crimes alleged in the indictment. The responsibility for introducing such evidence was divided among the four Allied prosecutors, not without some overlap. After the prosecution had introduced proof of general criminality, it focused on proof connecting each defendant with the substantive crimes involved. Then the defendants submitted their evidence.

My own work dealt primarily with what was called "the economic case." The economic case included, first, crimes against peace by defendants who had financed the building of, or had built, the German war machine with knowledge of Germany's aggressive purposes; and second, war crimes and crimes against humanity resulting from the systematic plundering and pillaging of occupied territories and the deportation and exploitation of millions of slave laborers.

I coordinated and reviewed the work of a group of lawyers who assembled the evidence and prepared trial briefs on the various aspects of the economic case. Some of our briefs related to pillaging and plundering in the East. After those subjects had been allocated to the Soviets, we gave them our briefs. Disclosure was, however, a one-way street.

The Soviets' disinclination to share information reminds me of a story about Justice Jackson. At a birthday party for him, he was given a Swiss watch, the best of our PX's meager supply. After graciously conveying his thanks, Justice Jackson asked: "Where did it come from?" Before giving you the answer, I want to remind you that Soviet soldiers loved a watch with Mickey Mouse on its face even more than vodka. So a wag's answer to the Justice was "from the Russians." The Justice quickly replied: "That's fine, that's fine. Up to now I haven't been able to get even the time of day from them."

I also was responsible for preparing and presenting to the tribunal the case against defendant Walter Funk, who had been charged under all four counts of the indictment. Funk had joined the Nazi party in 1931, and, as the tribunal found despite his denial, he had soon become one of Hitler's personal economic advisers. Later, in March 1933, he had become the undersecretary of the newly established Ministry of Propaganda, headed by the notorious Joseph Goebbels, who had remained faithful to Hitler until they both committed suicide. As a propagandist, Funk had played a significant part in stimulating the persecution of Jews and other minorities. He had succeeded Schacht as minister of economics and plenipotentiary general for the war in 1938, and as head of the Reichsbank, in January of 1939—three jobs crucial to war finance. Funk had also been involved with, although he had not played a major role in, agencies that determined the number of slave laborers required for German industry and called on others to produce them. He had headed the Reichsbank when it had become the storehouse for the gold fillings, jewelry, eyeglass frames, and other valuables stripped from the corpses of concentration camp victims. Funk wept when confronted with this evidence before the trial and claimed that he had known nothing about that ghoulish traffic. The tribunal concluded that he had known or had not wanted to know.

By trial time, Funk was in poor health; he wept frequently as evidence of Nazi horrors piled up. His apparent weakness as a man seemed to serve him well as a defendant. The tribunal noted that he had been subject to the supervision of Goering and found him not guilty under count one (the conspiracy count), but guilty under the other three counts and sentenced him to life imprisonment. He was released from Spandau Prison in 1957 because of ill health (after serving only ten years) and died three years later.

In connection with my work on Funk and on economic crimes, I interrogated Goering and lesser figures before the trial. Of those I met face to face, I found Goering the most interesting and most diabolical. As Hilary Gaskin put it, he had the "charisma of evil."[14] He was intellectually quick, verbally nimble, and always wily. He often sensed the ultimate purpose of a question as soon as it was put. Incidentally, he did very well on an IQ test, which all the defendants took, ranking just below Schacht. Goering was completely unrepentant and gloried in his role as second to Hitler and the first of the named defendants. He assumed the responsibility for defending the Nazi regime while attacking the laws of war as obsolete. During the trial, he outmaneuvered Justice Jackson during the latter's cross-examination of him—a notorious defeat for Jackson. In the end, Goering also managed a small triumph. He cheated the hangman by swallowing cyanide.

In addition to the economic case, I was quite unexpectedly given another assignment that highlighted both the horrors of the concentration camps and the Germans' obsession with records. About ten days before the concentration camp case was to be presented to the tribunal, I was asked to work on that presentation, which had been the responsibility of a U.S. Army team whose circuits had apparently been overloaded by mountains of evidence. I couldn't read German, so I got help from two lawyers who could. We had seven days to prepare the principal part of the case that was, for many, the mark of the Nazi regime. Other evidence of the pervasive role of the camps had emerged or would do so in separate presentations concerning the Nazi attacks on, for example, the Jews, labor unions, churches and Gypsies. Indeed, the movies that Allied troops had taken showing the horrors of the camps when they had been liberated had been presented to the tribunal earlier—out of order—as relief, if that is the word, from the tedium of documentary evidence. Anyhow, my partners ran through the files, fired up evidence, and I wrote as fast and slept as little as I could. The evidence was a lawyer's dream and a humanist's nightmare. It included two *Totenbücher*—deathbooks—that recorded approximately 300 deaths at the Mauthausen camp, deaths recorded as having occurred in alphabetical order, at brief intervals of time, and in each case because of heart disease. I still recall the hush in the courtroom when those books were put into evidence.

Let me turn from evidentiary details to a brief assessment of the legacy of Nuremberg.

First, the law of the London Charter has been absorbed into international law. Nuremberg has also helped promote the development of what is now called humanitarian law, embodied in such instruments as the Genocide Convention. Enforcement is, of course, a different matter.

Second, the trial was an important part of the closure of World War II, validating the casualties and devastation that the Allies had suffered and inflicted; satisfying, in part at least, the demand of the peoples of the occupied countries for a judgment concerning, and punishment for, the crimes inflicted on them; and helping, it appears, to reintegrate Germany into Europe. Finally, although the law of the trial has been generalized beyond the Nazi defendants, the trial has remained essentially a product of its special time and circumstances.

The trials relating to the former Yugoslavia, which have been so much in the news, arise from vastly different circumstances. I can mention only some of the major differences. The Balkan indictments are based on the authority of the UN Security Council, and they charge not aggressive war but only violations of humanitarian law. They certainly do not constitute victors' justice. Indeed, Radovan Karadzic and Ratko Mladic, the leaders of the Bosnian Serbs, apparently the big territorial victors, have been the subjects of two indictments. But in the absence of the right kind of undisputed victors, there may be no justice. Unlike the situation in Nuremberg, key defendants and suspects are not in custody but in power. Furthermore, even though the Bosnian Serbs seem to have been the worst offenders, none of the parties or forces involved appears to have clean hands.[15] Under all the circumstances, vigorous prosecution may be seen as an obstacle to peace rather than as part of a process leading to a durable peace. But Judge Richard Goldstone, the former chief prosecutor of the Balkan trials, has argued that genuine peace is not possible unless the key suspects are handed over for trials. He maintains that otherwise the victims and their survivors will consider whole groups collectively guilty, and that there will be no end to the cycle of violence.

Whatever the ultimate outcome of the Balkan indictments, the prosecutors and staff of the tribunals have, I believe, earned our gratitude for their skill, energy and tenacity. For they and their supporters have shown their awareness of a charge not made at Nuremberg but resonating from it—the charge, as Elie Wiesel has reminded us, of the crime of silence and indifference. In remembering Nuremberg, it is right that we remember that charge—perhaps above all others.

Notes

1. A version of this chapter originally appeared as Bernard D. Meltzer, "Remembering Nuremberg," University of Chicago Law School Occasional Paper no. 37 (1995).
2. See generally, Telford Taylor, "The Nuremberg War Crimes Trials," International Conciliation, no. 450 (April 1949): 243, 277.
3. See Albert Speer, Spandau: The Secret Diaries (New York: Macmillan, 1976), 52.

4. See generally Martin Gilbert, "Final Solution," in *Oxford Companion to World War II* (New York: Oxford University Press, 1995), 364. He states that six million Jews were murdered (p. 371); see also J.A.S. Grenville, *A History of the World in the Twentieth Century* (Cambridge: Belknap Press, 1994), 284, arguing that historians cannot tell for certain to the nearest million the huge number of Jews murdered; David S. Wyman, *The Abandonment of the Jews* (New York: Garland Publishers, 1984), chapters 2–4.

5. See, e.g., Leopold Gratz (president of the Austrian Parliament), quoted in Arthur Spiegelman, "Head of Austrian Parliament Meets Jewish Leaders," The Reuter Library Report, September 28, 1987, available in Lexis News Library, World Library, Allnws File.

6. See John Keegan, *The Second World War* (New York: Viking, 1990), foreword.

7. The International Treaty for the Renunciation of War as an Instrument of National Policy, signed in 1928 and commonly known as the Kellogg-Briand Pact, was ultimately accepted by forty-four nations, including most of the great powers, though not the Soviet Union.

8. See George A. Finch, "The Nuremberg Trial and International Law," *American Journal of International Law* 41 (1947): 20; Robert K. Woetzel, *The Nuremberg Trials in International Law* (New York: Praeger, 1962), 166–69.

9. See Telford Taylor, *The Anatomy of the Nuremberg Trials* (New York: Alfred A. Knopf, 1992), 65–66, 628, 629.

10. See Robert H. Jackson, *The Nürnberg Case* (New York: Alfred A. Knopf, 1947), 31.

11. Ibid., 34.

12. Dennis J. Hutchinson, "Justice Jackson and the Nuremberg Trials," (forthcoming).

13. See Taylor, *The Anatomy of the Nuremberg Trials*, 80, 550–553 581, 628, 629.

14. See Hilary Gaskin, *Eyewitness at Nuremberg* (London: Arms & Armour, 1990), xix.

15. See Charles Boyd, "Making Peace with the Guilty," *Foreign Affairs* (September/October 1995): 22.

Nuremberg:
A Prosecutor's Perspective[1]

Benjamin Ferencz

I would like to describe what Nuremberg meant to us at the time, what it has meant in the interim, and, as I look back upon it, what its significance is today. My involvement began before the war. One of the things I did to work my way through law school was to do research for one of my professors who was writing a book on war crimes. As soon as I got out of the Harvard Law School, I enlisted as a private in the artillery, and fought in all the campaigns in Europe. As we began to invade Germany and France, I was sent to General Patton's headquarters to help set up a war crimes division. Soon, my assignment was to go into the concentration camps as they were being liberated, in order to try to capture the criminals or collect evidence for subsequent trials. This experience has had an impact on everything that I have done since then.

When the war was over and the Nuremberg trials began, I was recruited to go back as a civilian with the Department of the Army and help in the war crimes prosecutions. I became the chief prosecutor of the largest murder trial in history. It was the trial of the *Einsatzgruppen*—we could not translate their name—the special extermination squads that had murdered over one million people. They were 2,000 men who, for about two years, did nothing else but march their victims out into the woods and machine gun them and drop them into a ditch, with the help of the local militia, the Latvians, the Lithuanians, the Ukrainians and the local police. We captured their daily reports. We picked twenty-two defendants out of the 2,000 or so who were engaged in those mass murders and put them on trial.

The *Einsatzgruppen* case was one of the so-called subsequent trials. Nuremberg did not consist only of the International Military Tribunal; there were a dozen trials at Nuremberg subsequent to that, at which we tried the next echelon of German government—the SS, the generals and industrialists, the doctors and lawyers—and other leaders.

What were we trying to do? Was it a matter simply of punishing the guilty? In that case, to pick out twenty-two would have been rather absurd. We had something more in mind. First, of course, we wanted to establish a historical record. I should say that the very question of whether we should have trials was a major issue. At one time, the British, noted for their fair play, decided that instead of trials it would be better to just take the German leaders out and shoot them. The Russians, of course, would have gone along with that very eagerly, because they never did quite understand why we needed trials. At one time, even Roosevelt had agreed to that.

But subsequently, under the influence of some very good lawyers, the United States was persuaded to take the position—which finally came to be accepted by all the powers—that we should have trials. If you decide to shoot people, the question becomes, Whom are you going to shoot, and when do you stop shooting? It was decided that we would give the accused, as Justice Robert Jackson, the chief American prosecutor, said, "the kind of trial which they, in the days of their pomp and power, never gave to any man." And we did. The courtroom was open to the world. Every word that was said in that courtroom was open to the world. Every word that was said in that courtroom was recorded in German and English, and everyone could watch.

My instructions were, and my practice was, to give every single piece of evidence that I had to the defense counsel—and the defense counsel outnumbered us twenty to one—so that they could prepare for trial. It was the fairest possible trial. Some have raised the question about trying persons for crimes that were legislated ex post facto, and some have also noted that this was the first time that there was a trial by the victors over the vanquished. These are fair questions. But if you study the development and evolution of the law of war crimes, you will see that it was not the first time that these issues had been faced. These issues were faced after World War I, and at that time the same debate took place: Will there be an international trial, and who will try the accused? After World War I, it was decided not to try the German head of state because aggression had not yet been declared a crime and he had not yet been warned that he might be put on trial for that offense. But, the Germans were warned, the next time around it would be different. There were also a number of warnings given in the course of the earliest days of World War II, when the heads of state of all the Axis powers were told that they would be brought to justice. So it was not quite as ex post facto as it would seem to someone unfamiliar with the history or the evolution of the problem.

The question remains: Why a trial by the Allies? It is regrettable that there was no real choice. It would have been preferable had there been an international tribunal of persons who were completely neutral. But it was very difficult in those days to find anybody who was completely neutral, and politically it was quite impossible. So we did the best we could. It was imperfect, but in many ways it was quite remarkable because these great powers "stayed the hand of vengeance," in Justice Jackson's words, and put their enemies on trial despite the enormity of the crimes that had been committed. That is perhaps the most important thing that came out of Nuremberg: the recognition that your enemy, no matter what his crimes, is entitled to as fair a trial as you can give him.

But we wanted something more than that. We felt that the time had come "for the law to take a step forward," in the words of Justice Jackson, who represented the United States. It was declared in the Nuremberg Charter of the International Military Tribunal—which was drawn up by the four victorious powers speaking, in fact, for the so-called civilized world—that there would be a punishable offense known as the "crime against peace." In the future, anyone who started a war of aggression would be guilty of a crime. Why should one murder be considered a crime and one million murders be considered something other than a crime? So, the law took a step forward and declared that aggressive war was a punishable crime.

Another step forward was the concept of "crimes against humanity." The concept of "war crimes" was an old, well-established one under customary law. But the concept of crimes against humanity was something new. In the past it had been the practice, when acts of genocide were committed against minorities, that only diplomatic intervention was permissible. Governments could send a note of protest saying, "You know, we have heard that Armenians are being slaughtered in your country. We would deplore that action should it be true." That was the limited nature of the permissible intervention by the international community. At Nuremberg, we said that that time was past.

When crimes reach such a magnitude that they offend all of humankind, they are crimes not merely against the state but against humanity. And every nation has a right to intervene and insist that those who are responsible, those who have committed these crimes and their accomplices, be held accountable in a court of law. That was another great step forward that we thought we were taking at Nuremberg. We were beginning a process, a legal process, of moving toward a more humane and rational order. That, at least, was our aspiration and our dream at the time. As a young fellow assigned to prosecute this biggest murder trial in history (it was, incidentally, my first case), I was confronted with the problem of what penalty to ask for. One million people had been murdered in cold blood; there was clear documentary evidence and no dispute about the facts. I had dug many bodies out of mass graves with my own hands. What punishment should I ask for? How could I balance one million deaths against twenty defendants—should I ask that they be chopped up in pieces? You can never really balance the punishment and a crime of such magnitude. I wanted the trial to take law and humanity a step forward.

My opening statement was made on September 29, 1947. In the opening paragraph, I said, "We ask this court to affirm by international penal actions man's right"—by that I meant women as well—"to live in peace and dignity regardless of his race or creed. The case we present is a plea of humanity to law." I think that that reflects what we were trying to do. It was a plea of humanity to allow all people, regardless of their race or creed, to live in peace and dignity. That is what Nuremberg was all about. It was the planting of a seed of what we hoped would be an evolutionary process for a more humane and just society.

To what extent has Nuremberg achieved its goals? Let me begin, first, with the negatives, because it is quite obvious that Nuremberg did not put an end to genocide or genocidal acts. It is obvious that we do not yet have an international criminal court. Nuremberg was the beginning. Some might say Nuremberg was only "victors' justice," and was therefore unfair; nations engage in wrongful discrimination continually, yet no one brings the offenders to trial because there are no victors to try the vanquished. I understand that point of view. I have only one thing to say about it: it is wrong. Nuremberg did not achieve all of its goals, but there are certain things it did do, and we must not forget these, because if we forget, we lose hope. We become cynical. In a cynical world, nothing works; everything is seen to be fake. We need hope because without it we will not have the strength to do all the things that we must do if we are going to make a better world.

Is there a basis for hope? Let us look at the positive side. The outrage that was evoked by these trials immediately brought forth the Convention on Genocide in the United Nations. The UN General Assembly unanimously accepted the principles of Nuremberg: that aggressive war is a crime, that there are crimes against humanity, that "superior orders" is not a good defense, and that even the head of a state is responsible under the law. These were the evolving principles we were trying to articulate and confirm at Nuremberg. The United Nations confirmed these principles and immediately appointed a committee to codify them and to articulate a code of offenses against the peace and security of humankind.

Conventions on human rights began to appear. The Universal Declaration of Human Rights was adopted. Courts of human rights were created. There is a Court of Human Rights at Strasbourg, which hears complaints of citizens against their own governments, and other similar international tribunals. And there is the court of the European Communities; it functions very well and settles disputes that used to lead to war between the nations of Europe. This is a very great and important step forward.

The United Nations passed many resolutions and conventions advancing international law. For many years, it worked on a definition of aggression. The absence of an agreed-upon definition served to postpone work on an international criminal court. Eventually, the UN did agree upon the consensus definition of aggression. It took them about fifty years; it could have been done faster. It was not a very good definition, but there it was. The United Nations adopted a Convention Against Terrorism; it condemned apartheid as an international crime; it condemned the crime of genocide.

All of these efforts to enact or improve international law had their defects. The definition of aggression was defective. The Convention Against Terrorism was defective—it was more an invitation to terrorism than a prohibition of it, because the definition of terrorism left large loopholes.

We did not realize all of our dreams. We were trying to create a more orderly and humane world, but the world as I see it now is neither more orderly nor more humane in many ways. The things we tried to stop at Nuremberg—aggression, crimes against humanity—have not been stopped. But even though many of the efforts of the United Nations were not very effective, they represented a step forward. There was, in fact, an awakening of human conscience. Nuremberg set in motion an evolutionary process that we have since advanced. We planted seeds of hope and seeds of a future legal order based upon a humanitarian consideration of all people as fellow human beings, entitled to equal dignity and to peace.

Despite these advances, the first forty years after Nuremberg were a period of slow progress in developing international criminal law. The ten years since then, however, have witnessed great changes. The Nuremberg trials established that all of humanity would be guarded by an international legal shield and that even a head of state would be held criminally responsible and punished for aggression and crimes against humanity. The right of humanitarian intervention to put a stop to crimes against humanity—even by a sovereign against his own citizens—gradually emerged from the Nuremberg principles affirmed by the United Nations. Traditional notions of sovereignty began to be challenged. It was increasingly recognized that in a democratic society it is the individual who should be served by the sovereign and not vice versa. It was slowly being recognized that accepting binding rules of the road serves everyone's interest and that human rights must prevail over human wrongs.

To be sure, this awareness of the inadequacy of the law and the willingness to do something to enforce such new principles were slow in coming. The failure of the international community to develop binding norms of international criminal law was glaringly illustrated by the snail's pace of various UN committees charged in 1946 with drafting both a code of crimes against the peace and security of mankind and the statutes for an international criminal court. While the law limped lamely along, international crimes flourished. Nations were accused of aggression in Korea, Czechoslovakia, Hungary, Vietnam, Cambodia, Afghanistan,

Iran, Iraq, Grenada, Nicaragua, Cuba, Panama, the Middle East, Africa and other parts of the world. Millions of innocent people were killed in such conflicts, which frequently violated established laws of war with acts such as illegal use of poison gas, genocide, terrorism and similar atrocities. Idi Amin of Uganda and Pol Pot of Kampuchea were denounced, but never tried, for murdering millions of their own people. All of these terrible crimes—despite Nuremberg—went untried and unpunished—to the everlasting shame of the international legal community!

The sleeping giant of international law began to stir when the armed forces of Iraq, led by its dictator Saddam Hussein, launched an unprovoked attack against its peaceful Arab neighbor, the sovereign state of Kuwait, in August 1990. The Security Council of the United Nations responded promptly with a barrage of resolutions, followed by action under Article VII of the UN Charter authorizing the use of military force to expel Iraq and restore peace. An allied coalition led by the United States immediately began to bombard Iraqi troops. Within 100 hours, the Iraqi army was in complete rout. Military action, authorized by the Security Council, brought a halt to Saddam's aggression. But no legal action was taken to put the aggressor on trial.

It should have been no surprise when Saddam began to slaughter Iraqi citizens who were Kurdish guerrillas and Shiite Muslims opposed to his tyrannical regime. No international court existed to condemn his terrible crimes against humanity. Those who had the power to act chose, for their own political reasons, not to turn to the Nuremberg principles and the enforcement of international law. It was sadly ironic that a great military victory won by brave young people fighting in distant lands would be followed by a great human rights disaster and a lack of legal courage by political leaders back home. There is always a price to pay for such timidity and vacillation.

The end of the Cold War opened the door to further progress. In 1991, when violence erupted among ethnic groups in former Yugoslavia, graphic reports of "ethnic cleansing," including mass rapes, appeared on worldwide television. Public opinion was outraged. Nations that had been unwilling to intervene to block the carnage now recognized that some action was essential. For the first time since Nuremberg, a new international criminal tribunal was quickly put in place on an ad hoc basis by the UN Security Council. Under the impetus of shocked public demand, it became possible for the UN Secretariat to draft the statutes for the International Criminal Tribunal for former Yugoslavia (ICTY) in about eight weeks—the same time it had taken to agree upon the charter for the International Military Tribunal at Nuremberg. The ICTY began functioning in 1994. It led to the speedy creation of a similar ad hoc tribunal to deal with genocide and crimes against humanity in Rwanda. The existence of these two tribunals demonstrates that—where the political will is present—it is possible to create a fair international criminal tribunal in a matter of weeks. But law is not a one-way street. What is needed is a permanent international criminal court to punish such crimes wherever and whenever they occur. That's what Nuremberg was all about.

The International Law Commission (ILC), a body of distinguished legal experts acting at the request of the UN General Assembly, completed its draft statute for a permanent international criminal court in 1994. In 1996, the ILC finally completed its draft code of crimes against the peace and security of mankind. This new momentum reflected widespread agreement that an international criminal court, with fair trial for the accused, should be created as an essential component of a just world order under law. The technical legal problems of form, substance and procedure were debated at a conference of diplomats in 1998 that drew up a treaty establishing the first permanent international criminal court since Nuremberg.[2] This treaty attempted to reconcile major differences among many nations on many problems.

The views of all nations must be respected, but we must not forget that the goal is to close an existing gap in the international legal order as quickly as possible. In the last analysis, it will depend upon the will of the public. If the leaders will not lead, it is up to the public to lead and the "leaders" will follow. The most important immediate problem is to make sure that the two existing ad hoc criminal tribunals created by the Security Council succeed in their mission. These tribunals will need all of the help they can get, from both the UN and the public. Indicted suspects, no matter how high their rank or station, should not be allowed to flout the will of the international community—as they are now doing. All nations must honor their legal commitment to support Security Council decisions.

An international criminal court is a vital component of a rational and more humane world order. But it is only *one* component. We also need clearer laws, a world court with compulsory and binding jurisdiction, and a system of effective law enforcement. The United Nations is the only agency accepted by 185 member states to organize a more rational world. But its charter purposes must be respected and its members must provide the UN with the rules and the tools to do its job. Disarmament under effective international controls is vital, for as long as we spend enormous resources on weapons of mass destruction, there will never be enough money left to meet legitimate social needs that give rise to unrest. Revolting conditions inspire revolt. Social justice—economic, environmental and human—is an equally important requirement for a peaceful world. As we move toward the next millennium, diplomats and decisionmakers must demonstrate that they care enough and dare enough to move courageously toward a new world order of peace under law for all of humankind. That would be the enduring legacy and greatest tribute to the work done at Nuremberg many years ago.

Notes

1. This is a revised and updated version of a talk given at the conference "Nuremberg Forty Years Later: The Struggle Against Injustice in Our Time" at the McGill University Faculty of Law, November 1987. The conference proceedings, and a 1993 retrospective, may be found in Irwin Cotler, ed., *Nuremberg Forty Years Later: The Struggle Against Injustice in Our Time* (Montreal: McGill-Queen's University Press, 1995).
2. See Part III of this volume.

A Call for Reasoned Justice[1]

Stephen G. Breyer

Fifty years ago, another member of the court on which I sit, Justice Robert Jackson, joined representatives of other nations as a prosecutor at Nuremberg. That city, Jackson said, though chosen for the trial because of its comparatively well-functioning physical facilities, was then "in terrible shape, there being no telephone communications, the streets full of rubble, with some 20,000 dead bodies reported to be still in it and the smell of death hovering over it, no public transportation of any kind, no shops, no commerce, no lights, the water system in bad shape." The courthouse had been "damaged." Its courtroom was "not large." Over one door was "an hour glass." Over another was "a large plaque of the Ten Commandments"—a sole survivor. In the dock, twenty-one leaders of Hitler's Thousand Year Reich faced prosecution.

Justice Jackson described the Nuremberg Trial as "the most important trial that could be imagined." He described his own work there as the most important "experience of my life, infinitely more important than my work on the Supreme Court, or...anything that I did as Attorney General." Speaking as an American Jew, a judge, a member of the Supreme Court, I should like briefly to explain why I think that he was right.

First, as a lawyer, Robert Jackson understood the importance of collecting evidence. "Collecting evidence?" one might respond. What need to collect evidence in a city where, only twenty years before, the law itself, in the form of the Nuremberg Decrees, had segregated Jews into ghettos, placed them in forced labor, expelled them from their professions, expropriated their property, and forbidden them all cultural life, press, theater and schools. "Evidence," one might then have exclaimed. "Just open your eyes and look around you."

But the Torah tells us: There grew up a generation that "knew not Joseph." That is the danger. And Jackson was determined to compile a record that would not leave any other future generation with the slightest doubt. "We must establish incredible events by credible evidence," he said. And he realized that, for this purpose, the prosecution's thirty-three live witnesses were of secondary importance. Rather, the prosecutors built what Jackson called "a drab case," which did not "appeal to the press" or the public, but it was an irrefutable case. It was built of documents of the defendants' "own making," the "authenticity of which" could not be, and was not, "challenged."

The prosecutors brought to Nuremberg 100,000 captured German documents; they examined millions of feet of captured moving picture film; they produced 25,000 captured still photographs, "together with Hitler's personal photographer who took most of them." The prosecutors decided not to ask any defendant to testify against another defendant, lest anyone believe that one defendant's hope for leniency led him to exaggerate another's crimes. But they permitted each defendant to call witnesses, to testify in his own behalf, to make an additional statement not under oath, and to present documentary evidence. The very point was to say to these defendants: What have you to say when faced with our case—a case that you, not we, have made, resting on your own words and confessed deeds? What is your response? The answer, after more than ten months and 17,000 transcript pages, was, in respect to nineteen of the defendants, that there was no answer. There was no response. There was nothing to say.

As a result, the evidence is there, in Jackson's words, "with such authenticity and in such detail that there can be no responsible denial of these crimes in the future and no tradition of martyrdom of the Nazi leaders can arise among informed people." Future generations need only open their eyes and read.

Second, as a judge, Robert Jackson understood the value of precedent—what Benjamin Cardozo called "the power of the beaten path." He hoped to create a precedent that, he said, would make "explicit and unambiguous" what previously had been "implicit" in the law, "that to persecute, oppress, or do violence to individuals or minorities on political, racial, or religious grounds...is an international crime...for the commission [of which]...individuals are responsible" and can be punished. He hoped to forge from the victorious nations' several different legal systems a single workable system that, in this instance, would serve as the voice of human decency. He hoped to create a "model of forensic fairness" that even a defeated nation would perceive as fair.

Did he succeed? At the least, surveys at the time indicated that three-quarters of the German nation found the trial "fair" and "just." More important, there is cause for optimism about the larger objectives. Consider how concern for the protection of basic human liberties grew dramatically in the United States, in Europe, and then further abroad in the half-century after World War II. Consider the development of what is now a near consensus that legal institutions—written constitutions, bills of rights, fair procedures, an independent judiciary—should play a role, sometimes an important role, in the protection of human liberty. Consider that, today, a half-century after Nuremberg (and history does not count fifty years as long), nations feel that they cannot simply ignore the most barbarous acts of other nations; nor, for that matter, as recent events show, can those who commit those acts ignore the ever more real possibility that they will be held accountable and brought to justice under law. We are drawn to follow a path once beaten.

Third, Jackson believed that the Nuremberg trials represented a human effort to fulfill a basic human aspiration—"humanity's aspiration to do justice." He enunciated this effort in his opening statement to the tribunal. He began: "The wrongs which we seek to condemn and punish have been so calculated, so malignant, and so devastating, that civilization cannot tolerate their being ignored, because it cannot survive their being repeated. That four great nations, flushed with victory and stung with injury, stay the hand of vengeance and voluntarily submit their captive enemies to the judgment of the law is one of the most significant tributes that Power has ever paid to Reason."

To understand the significance of this statement, it is important to understand what it is not. Nuremberg does not purport to be humanity's answer to the cataclysmic events the opening statement goes on to describe. A visit to the Holocaust Museum in Washington, DC—or, for some, to the corridors of memory—makes clear that not even Jackson's fine sentences, eloquent though they are, can compensate for the events that provoked them. But that is only because, against the background of what did occur, almost any human statement would ring hollow. A museum visit leads many, including myself, to react, not with words, but with silence. We think: There are no words. There is no compensating deed. There can be no vengeance. Nor is any happy ending possible. We emerge deeply depressed about the potential for evil that human beings possess.

It is at this point, perhaps, that Nuremberg can help, for it reminds us that the Holocaust story is not the whole story; it reminds us of those human aspirations that remain a cause for optimism. It reminds us that after barbarism came a call for reasoned justice.

To end the Holocaust story with a fair trial, an emblem of that justice, is to remind the listener of what Aeschylus wrote 2,500 years ago, in his *Eumenides*—where Justice overcoming the avenging furies, humanity's barbaric selves, promises Athens that her seat, the seat of Justice, "shall be a wall, a bulwark of salvation, wide as your land, as your imperial state; none mightier in the habitable world." It is to repeat the Book of Deuteronomy's injunction to the Jewish People: "Justice, justice shall you pursue."

And if I emphasize the role of Nuremberg in a story of the Holocaust, that is not simply because Justice Jackson himself hoped that the trial "would commend itself to posterity." Rather, it is because our role—the role of almost all of us—today in relation to the Holocaust is not simply to learn from it, but also to tell it, and to retell it, to ourselves, to our children, and to future generations.

Those who were lost said, "Remember us." To do that, to remember and to repeat the story, is to preserve the past; it is to learn from the past, it is to instruct and to warn the future. It is to help future generations understand the very worst of which human nature is capable. But, it is also to tell that small part of the story that will also remind them of one human virtue—humanity's "aspiration to do justice." It is to help us say, with the psalmist, "Justice and Law are the foundations of Your Throne."

Notes

1. This chapter is an edited version of a speech made by Justice Stephen G. Breyer in Washington, DC, on Holocaust Memorial Day, April 16, 1996 and published as Stephen Breyer, "Crimes Against Humanity, Nuremberg, 1946," *New York University Law Review* 71 (1996): 1161. Reprinted with permission of the *New York University Law Review*.

Nuremberg and its Legacy:
Fifty Years Later

Ruti Teitel

Fifty years ago, the Nuremberg trials were convened to bring to justice those who had masterminded the terror of World War II. Even as the international community commemorates these trials, we have embarked on two contemporary efforts at international criminal justice: war crimes tribunals to prosecute violations of humanitarian law in former Yugoslavia and the attempted genocide in Rwanda. These new tribunals raise the question: What is the ongoing legacy of Nuremberg?

Nuremberg established the principle of individual criminal accountability for human rights violations perpetrated against civilians in wartime, making it clear that certain crimes are so heinous that they violate the "law of nations" and may be prosecuted anywhere. The twentieth century has witnessed the commission of many terrible atrocities: Turkey's massacre of the Armenians; Bangladesh; the Pol Pot regime in Cambodia; Iraq's brutal campaign against its Kurds; the more recent Hutu-Tutsi massacres in Rwanda; and the crimes of war torn Yugoslavia. Nevertheless, half a century after Nuremberg there have been few attempts to enforce international accountability. The twentieth century's record is one of state persecution and impunity, keeping alive the question of the meaning of rule of law when states turn on their citizens.

Thus there is a puzzling aspect to the question of Nuremberg's significance. The Nuremberg trials were intended as a precedent for the future. They were expected to teach individual responsibility for crimes of aggressive war and crimes against humanity, so that such crimes might never again be perpetrated. Nevertheless, it would be a full half-century before another international tribunal would be convened to bring individuals to justice for human rights abuses in times of conflict. Yet despite the general record of failure of criminal accountability and the Nuremberg Tribunal's anomalous nature, we have a sense that Nuremberg's impact transcends this anomaly and has acted as a guiding force in the latter half of this century.

In fact, the force of the Nuremberg legacy lies in the way it has constructed our understanding of state injustice, as well as the normative response to it. Its impact is evident in its domination of the legal culture of international human rights.

Exploring the significance of Nuremberg requires recognition of the diverse implications of the precedent, which may be understood in a number of ways. We might distinguish the actual fact of the tribunal and its proceedings from the tribunal's broader precedential value. In terms of the tribunal and its proceedings, Nuremberg was deliberately and self-consciously styled as the first of the postwar trials. That was how the architects of Nuremberg understood what they were doing. Thus there was precedential value in both the convening of the international tribunal and the standards and principles contained in the tribunal's judgment. Nuremberg would be foundational in terms of the law applied, the weight of the judgment and the related doctrinal principles ratified after the war.

A number of features of Nuremberg have played a significant role in defining the way we think about state persecution and the responses to such persecution—our sense of what is justice. The points of categorical change set in motion by Nuremberg can usefully be thought of in terms of a series of dualisms, which might be considered the Nuremberg categories of justice. These categories have largely defined the way in which we structure successor justice following state persecution in the late twentieth century.

I will discuss four central Nuremberg constructions: first, judgment and accountability; second, the conceptualization of responsibility, individual versus collective; third, the impact of Nuremberg on notions of military or civilian legal order, the move away from the laws of war to the laws of peace, and related developments regarding the relation between war crimes and human rights violations; and finally, the question of sovereignty and jurisdiction, the sense in which post-Nuremberg accountability is international, transcending national borders. There may well be other points to make about Nuremberg, but these are the features that remain central because of their precedential impact; they are the features or dualisms that define the Nuremberg paradigm.

Judgment and Accountability

To begin, there is the perhaps obvious, yet often elided, point that Nuremberg stands for postwar judgment—the notion that the manner of warmaking would be subject to judgment. The accountability sought is neither political nor moral, but legal. Judgment is where the rule of law and politics meet. At Nuremberg, even the war could be adjudged unlawful. Aggression would be deemed the "supreme" crime. Moreover, Nuremberg stands for the proposition that the appropriate form of judgment is the trial, and the appropriate forum for judgment the International Military Tribunal. The International Military Tribunal was intended to establish the wrongdoing underlying individual judgment, as well as to apportion punishment.

Judgment after war takes the form of individual rather than collective accountability. The judgment at Nuremberg represents the belief that despite the pervasive nature of totalitarian criminality, the correct response is to hold individuals accountable. As early as the St. James Declaration,[1] issued during the war, the Allies made clear their intent to renounce vengeance and collective sanctions, and instead to pursue a policy of punishing the guilty. The significance of this punishment policy can best be understood in a historical light, in the context of past postwar justice. The trials at Nuremberg were convened in the shadow of post-World War I justice. The general understanding was that Versailles and Germany's trial policy after World War I stood for impunity for persecutions committed in wartime. This failure to apportion individual responsibility was believed to represent the failure of Versailles. The course of past postwar justice thus led to the primacy of the principle of individual accountability at Nuremberg.

The move toward legal judgment would distinguish the Nuremberg Tribunal's work from politics as usual. Accordingly, it was critically important that the tribunal adhere rigorously to the forms of procedural justice—to legality. Legality requires individual trials for specific charges to be proven on the basis of evidence, with full opportunity for the accused to offer evidence in defense or mitigation. Allied traditions were blended in the relevant procedures. Nuremberg was not a show trial, not in the ordinary sense of a preordained result. Right to counsel was guaranteed, along with the presumption of innocence.

Further, there was no difficulty establishing the necessary historical record at Nuremberg. The evidence underlying the charges was so massive that the defenses at Nuremberg were mainly defenses of law, involving the nature of the charges and the extent of individual responsibility. The Nuremberg trial would generate a record of twenty-two volumes that would become the record for future proceedings, as well as for later historical study of the period. The accuracy of this record has never been questioned, and it constitutes a form of accountability in and of itself.

Nevertheless, though the trials largely adhered to accepted criminal procedures, the tribunal ran into problems of legality where its operation appeared, paradoxically, to collide with adherence to the rule of law. The fundamental challenge was the ex post facto nature of the Nuremberg charges, raising the issue of retroactivity.[2]

This conceded retroactivity was in tension with the tribunal's legality. Retroactivity was apparent in the extraordinary character of the proceedings and the nature of certain charges in the Nuremberg Charter, such as "crimes against peace" and "crimes against humanity." The trial attempted to carve out a postwar rule of law; given the unprecedented nature of such a trial, much of it was ad hoc, a mingling of various national procedures, creating a new criminal procedure that represented a compromise. Nevertheless, the retroactivity of the charges—for example, regarding crimes against the peace or aggressive war—was indeed problematic. No firm consensus existed on the definition of unjust war, or the distinction between such wars and others advancing political aims. Holding individuals responsible for such offenses, not previously codified, thus also raised questions of fundamental fairness.

The tension between political justice and the rule of law emerged in particular in connection with the "crimes against humanity" offense. At Nuremberg, the offense of "crimes against humanity" was codified for the first time to clearly distinguish rule of law from political justice. Perpetrators of "crimes against humanity" were conceived of as the equivalent of pirates of old, enemies of the world. Invoking "humanity" is understood as an attempt to place this offense outside the parameters of permissible war—but also outside politics. The notion of the offense against humanity is another place where Nuremberg tried to move beyond political justice and attempted to construct a transcendent, normative order.

Reconstructing Responsibility after Totalitarianism: The Individual and the Collective

Nuremberg raised the problem of how to prosecute totalitarian crime, the massive systemic crimes of the modern bureaucratic state. Who is responsible? What does accountability mean? Accountability, Nuremberg suggested, should be enforced through individual prosecutions. In the shadow of Versailles, Nuremberg took an important step away from collective guilt and the notion of state or collective responsibility. Though at Nuremberg, individuals would be convicted and Nazi organizations declared criminal, Germany as a whole would not be held accountable. Instead, at Nuremberg, for the first time, individuals were held responsible for what was arguably state policy. This was an enormous departure from prevailing law, which viewed states as the relevant subjects of international norms.

But Nuremberg did not merely contemplate prosecuting individuals; organizations would also be declared responsible. Thus Nuremberg was predicated upon a fluid understanding of individual and collective responsibility. (Six organizations were alleged to have been "criminal," and three would be so held: the Gestapo, the SS and the Leadership Corps.)[3] Nuremberg's innovation, based on the American law of conspiracy, was a mechanism that linked individual to organizational responsibility. The idea was to determine the criminality of organizations making up the Nazi regime through a single set of proceedings. At Nuremberg, only the leadership stood trial; but in the follow-up trials, these precedents would be used to bootstrap individuals into convictions based only on membership in groups adjudged to be "criminal." This idea, where applied, would have affected two million people, all members of organizations judged in this way. However, the subsequent American trials convened under Control Council Law No. 10[4] limited the strategy's reach. Membership would serve as grounds for prosecution only where it had been clearly voluntary and where the person involved had knowledge of the organization's criminal objectives.

The impact of the Nuremberg conception of criminal responsibility is evident in the many subsequent postwar trials held in Germany, as well as in the former occupied countries. Implicit in Nuremberg was a radical reconceptualization and expansion of the understanding of individual responsibility for state persecution. Responsibility for state wrongdoing transcends official state action.[5] In the trial of the major war criminals, Nazi officials were held responsible. But the American follow-up trials after Nuremberg moved away from the high political echelons to encompass the elites supporting the Nazi regime, such as the business sector and the professions. In this respect, Nuremberg set the tone for the many subsequent national trials of collaborators throughout the formerly occupied countries. While these follow-up trials were taking place, responsibility was also being defined in terms of collective categories of membership in criminalized organizations. Nuremberg's easy attribution of collective, organizational guilt was reflected in widespread denazification policies purging those supportive of the prior regime everywhere in the region.[6]

Nuremberg's affirmative conception of individual responsibility was codified after the trial in the United Nations General Assembly's Nuremberg principles. The significance of the Nuremberg conception of responsibility was apparent in these principles, for the expansion of individual responsibility meant eliminating two central defenses to culpability: the act of state and due obedience defenses. Removing the act of state defense would change the prevailing international law understanding of responsibility, particularly regarding the responsibility of the prior regime, while eliminating the due obedience defense would change the understanding of the military order and its chain of command. Rejection of these defenses against individual responsibility at Nuremberg has had an enduring effect on our understanding of individual responsibility for violations of the laws of war, as demonstrated in the follow-up trials.[7] Acceptance of this understanding of broader responsibility is also seen in German denazification, where categories ranged from "major offenders" to "followers,"[8] as well as in Germany's subsequent national war crimes trials, where the defense of obedience was never accepted or raised.[9]

But this is not the only place where Nuremberg has had an effect; the Nuremberg principles have had an impact on human rights trials held decades later, such as in Argentina in the aftermath of the military dictatorship.[10] Indeed, the ongoing precedential value of the Nuremberg privilege of individual responsibility has been evident in the contemporary International Criminal Tribunal for former Yugoslavia convened in the Hague, where top Serbian leaders, such as Radovan Karadzic and Ratko Mladic, as well as low-level guards and members of paramilitary forces, have been indicted for atrocities in the region.[11]

Making Accountability Real:
The Questions of Sovereignty and Jurisdiction

Putting into practice the above principles of accountability for grave human rights violations raises the question of sovereignty, as well as the problem of jurisdiction. At Nuremberg, war crimes were not tried in military court martial proceedings, but at an international tribunal. The convening of the International Military Tribunal was based on the legal premise that the implicated crimes could be considered crimes everywhere; thus the Nuremberg Charter refers to these crimes as "offenses" without "geographic location." They were considered so overarching that they could not be said to have occurred in one place. They defied the ordinary criminal jurisdiction principle of territoriality, and therefore were considered appropriate to the jurisdiction of an international military tribunal.

Though there have been isolated attempts to hold individuals accountable for violations of international humanitarian law, Nuremberg's precedent of holding individuals accountable within international jurisdiction has hardly been followed. But it would be a mistake to conceptualize the understanding of Nuremberg as jurisdictional precedent as synonymous with the Nuremberg Tribunal. For Nuremberg did not contemplate exclusive international jurisdiction. In this regard, the Nuremberg precedent is compatible with more traditional jurisdictional principles, such as that of territoriality. Here, the Nuremberg precedent goes beyond the fact of the proceedings convened at the Military Tribunal, because as the charter explicitly provides, Nuremberg contemplated further national trials for similar violations.[12] Thus Control Council Law No. 10 was the basis for war crimes trials held at Nuremberg after the International Military Tribunal. Thousands of follow-up trials were held under Nuremberg, in the sense that they followed its guiding view of individual responsibility for persecution. Further war-related national trials include those convened by Germany (to this day), Holland and France.[13]

Since Nuremberg, the substantive definition of rights violations has been inextricably linked to the question of jurisdiction. State-sponsored persecution could no longer be confined to national, political borders. In the post-Nuremberg understanding, violations of the "law of nations" could be prosecuted by any state, under universal jurisdiction. "Universal" is a jurisdiction that lies outside traditional political parameters. Like the construct of "crime against humanity," the construct of "universality" demonstrates international law's attempt to move beyond political justice. Perhaps the most notable example of the construction of universality was the trial of Adolf Eichmann, which took place in Israel, a nation-state that did not exist as such at the time of the crimes. The precedential force of the concept of universal jurisdiction can be seen today in more contemporary prosecutions for genocide and crimes against humanity, such as those relating to war crimes in Bosnia.

There is another sense in which Nuremberg has transformed our understanding of jurisdiction—a more profound way, as it relates to our conception of criminal accountability. It is the belief, widely shared today, that a state's persecution of citizens is not confined within national borders, but is an international, even universal matter. Despite the absence of a real codification of international criminal violations or of substantial progress in the establishment of an international tribunal, there nevertheless exists a widely shared view of international accountability that has been reflected not in enforcement through trials, but rather through more pervasive forms of enforcement, in exposure and censure and through representation of human rights issues in the media. Because of the media, contemporary persecution knows no borders. Moreover, the international response of exposure and condemnation shares affinities with punishment in its normative force.

From the Laws of War to the Laws of Peace

Beyond the reconceptualization of accountability, there has been a reconceptualization of those offenses that entail state injustice. In this part I turn to the substantive charges at Nuremberg, in order to explore the transformation they engendered in our understanding of injustice.

At first, Nuremberg was intended to send a message about unjust war and designed to vindicate Allied military policy regarding the war. This concept of the unjust war was reflected in the charges. The idea of such war related to the way it was initiated and waged; thus at Nuremberg, the central offense was "aggression" or "crimes against the peace." The significance of this charge is evident in the way the prosecution was divided, with the United States responsible for prosecuting the aggression charge.

The injustice of the war centered on its initiation. Aggression exists where there is no provocation or military necessity for invasion. Thus much of the judgment at Nuremberg was devoted to explaining when these initiatives were unjust. Aggressive war was considered the "supreme" crime because of its "totality," as it was believed to include all other offenses.[14] Initiation of unjust war was considered to predicate all violations occurring in the waging of that war.

The charge of aggressive war was a controversial aspect of the Nuremberg judgment, and turned out to have lesser precedential force. Despite its centrality at Nuremberg, the offense of aggressive war had rarely been enforced prior to the trials; thus the notion of prosecuting individuals for waging aggressive war was novel, and was felt to challenge the rule of law. Insofar as aggression could be separated out from other war crimes prosecuted at Nuremberg, this aspect of the tribunal's judgment was generally considered to be a case of political justice. The task undertaken by the tribunal, to distinguish between belligerence and hostility, was extraordinarily different in its various political ramifications from that of an ordinary court; therefore, this aspect of the precedent has hardly taken hold. In the trials under Control Council Law No. 10, individuals were tried for waging aggressive war, but war crimes trials grounded in this offense have been rare. Despite numerous instances of aggression, recognized as such by the United Nations Security Council, military intervention has not been followed by legal action as at Nuremberg. Moreover, with technological advances, the line between aggressive wars and wars of self-defense appears increasingly blurred.[15]

Still, the idea of the unjust war underlies all the offenses prosecuted at Nuremberg. The charter's second charge, violations of the "laws and customs of war," included war crimes codified since the Hague Convention. Violations of the laws of war, including genocide, were considered to be related to armed conflict. As such, at Nuremberg genocide was prosecuted as a violation of customary international law. After the war, the precedential impact of the Nuremberg concept was seen in the Genocide Convention, which codified the Nuremberg ideas. Similarly, war crimes—"willful killing, torture or inhuman treatment"—were codified as "grave breaches" of the Geneva Convention of 1949, and included mistreatment of prisoners of war and civilians.

In the contemporary International Criminal Tribunal for violations of humanitarian law in the former Yugoslavia, genocide is being prosecuted for the first time since Nuremberg in an international tribunal, pursuant to the postwar convention, as "[an] act of intent to destroy, in whole, or in part, a group." This imposes a difficult burden of specific intent; moreover, as at Nuremberg, the Hague Tribunal still considers the perpetration of the offense of genocide within the context of armed conflict. In this contemporary instantiation of genocide prosecution, Nuremberg casts a long shadow.

The greatest force of the Nuremberg categories over time is seen in the convergence of the area of humanitarian law applicable in times of armed conflict with human rights law applicable in peacetime. Many norms re-lating to the law of armed conflict have been extended to internal conflict and to peacetime, demarcating a broader area of human rights norms.

The "crime against humanity," defined as a separate charge in the charter, was a statement of new positive law at Nuremberg. Here, again, there was a nexus to war. Though the Nuremberg Charter would have al-lowed prosecution of offenses occurring before the war,[16] the tribunal limited its enforcement powers to crimes against humanity committed during the war. This was done as a prudential matter to avoid ex post facto challenges to the tribunal's charges, because of the sense that crimes against humanity constituted a new charge.[17] Thus conceptual-ization of crimes against humanity was narrowed at Nuremberg, setting a precedent that crimes against humanity required a nexus to war.

In the contemporary war crimes trials before the International Crimi-nal Tribunal for the former Yugoslavia, the offense of "crimes against hu-manity" still bears a nexus to conflict. The statute regarding Yugoslavia specifically contemplates "armed conflict," though it may be either "in-ternational" or "internal" in character. Yet, insofar as "crimes against hu-manity" are still predicated upon conflict, conceptualization of this crime is, to some extent, still guided by the Nuremberg precedent half a cen-tury after the postwar trials.

Finally, perhaps the most significant feature of crimes against human-ity codified at Nuremberg was their definition as crimes that could be committed by a state against its own citizens. The Nuremberg Tribunal defined these violations as "murder, extermination, enslavement, depor-tation and other inhumane acts committed against *any civilian* popula-tion" [emphasis added], or persecutions on political, racial or religious grounds "whether or not in violation of the domestic law of the country where perpetrated."[18]

This may seem unremarkable today, but the central change after Nuremberg was the rethinking of the offense of state persecution, ren-dering a state's treatment of its own citizens an international matter. This transformed conception would spur subsequent prosecutions in other countries by successor regimes for attacks committed by the prior regime against its own civilians. But most significant was that it would forever penetrate internal sovereignty, imposing a limit, even if honored more in the breach, upon the behavior of states towards their citizens, standing for a principle against persecution and similar systematic abro-gations of equality. This notion of limits would become a significant part of the normative understanding of what constitutes liberal democracies in the late twentieth century.

Conclusion

No trials or war crimes tribunals similar to Nuremberg have been held until the present day. There is still no permanent international criminal court or criminal jurisdiction in the International Court of Justice. Nevertheless, the impact of Nuremberg on the way we think of state injustice and the response to it extends far beyond its facts.

The force of the Nuremberg legacy can be seen in the many ways the Nuremberg ideas have constructed our understanding of state evil and, relatedly, our responses to such wrongdoing in this century. The Nuremberg paradigm created fundamental alterations in our view of the rule of law as accountability; in the reconceptualization and shift of responsibility from the collective to the individual; in the reconceptualization of jurisdiction, from national to international; and finally, in the reconceptualization of humanitarian law violations pertaining to the law of armed conflict to include persecution even in times of peace. Over time, the force of the Nuremberg legacy has only increased, transcending the particular circumstances that engendered it, to play a constitutive role in contemporary international human rights. The rhetoric of Nuremberg has a powerful influence on our human rights discourse. Nuremberg gave us nothing less than a new vocabulary for thinking and talking about responsibility for state wrongdoing. Perhaps the greatest legacy of Nuremberg is that, after this precedent, the question of accountability for atrocities or persecutions committed within a state would never again be confined within national borders, but would reach beyond such boundaries to become a matter of international human rights import.

Notes

1. The St. James Declaration, signed in 1942 in London by nine Nazi-occupied countries and the United States, the United Kingdom and the Soviet Union, announced Allied intentions to punish crimes against civilians following the war.
2. The dilemma raised at Nuremberg relating to the rule of law catalyzed a debate on the nature of international norms and the extent to which these could be considered consistent with positive law. Ultimately, Nuremberg would imply a move away from support of positivist principles of interpretation and towards an endorsement of natural law principles. For an exploration of this issue see Quincy Wright, "Legal Positivism and the Nuremberg Judgment," *The American Journal of International Law* 42 (1948): 405.

3. For discussion of the approach at Nuremberg to the responsibility of Nazi organizations, see Robert H. Jackson, "The Law Under which Nazi organizations are Accused of being Criminal," *Temple Law Quarterly* (19): 371.

4. Control Council Law No. 10 provided the legal basis for the subsequent American trials. It delineated the crimes that could be prosecuted under the heading crimes against peace, war crimes, and crimes against humanity.

5. Compare articles 6(a) (b), and (c) of the charter.

6. Denazification in Germany through the U.S.-imposed "Law of Liberation." For an account, see John Herz, *From Dictatorship to Democracy: Coping with the Legacies of Authoritarians and Totalitarians* (Westport: Greenwood Press, 1982).

7. See Telford Taylor, *The Anatomy of the Nuremberg Trials* (New York: Alfred A. Knopf, 1992).

8. See Law for Liberation from National Socialism and Militarism, March 5, 1946.

9. See Adalbert Ruckerl, *The Investigation of Nazi Crimes, 1945–1978: A Documentation* (Hamden: Archon Books, 1980).

10. See "Trial of Former Military Commanders," Federal Criminal and Correctional Court of Appeals, *Human Rights Law Journal* No. 2–4 (Buenos Aires, 1987).

11. See "Full Picture of OTP's Strategy," International Tribunal for the Former Yugoslavia, Office of the Prosecutor, press release, July 25, 1995: 3; see also statement by Justice Richard Goldstone, April 24, 1995.

12. According to the Nuremberg Charter, Article 6: "Nothing in this Agreement shall prejudice the jurisdiction or the powers of any national or occupation court established or to be established in any allied territory or in Germany for the trial of war criminals." See also Article 10 of the charter, providing for follow-up trials in national, military or occupation courts.

13. See Ruckerl, *The Investigation of Nazi Crimes*. The subsequent non-national French trial of Klaus Barbie was based on a scene of the crime or territoriality principle of jurisdiction.

14. See Taylor, *Anatomy of the Nuremberg Trials*.

15. See Michael Walzer, *Just and Unjust Wars* (New York: Basic Books, 1977).

16. Compare Article 6(c) of the Nuremberg Charter, which provided that persecution was punishable only if perpetrated "in connection with any crime within the jurisdiction of the Tribunal," with Article 6 of the charter, referring to acts committed "before or during the war."

17. See Judgment of the International Military Tribunal, p. 41. For discussion, see Taylor, *Anatomy of the Nuremberg Trials*.

18. See Nuremberg Charter, Article 6(c).

The Significance of Nuremberg[1]

Edward M. Wise

Three kinds of crimes were prosecuted before the International Military Tribunal at Nuremberg—four if one includes the catch-all conspiracy charge contained in Count One of the indictment.

First, crimes against peace. These were defined in Article 6(a) of the tribunal's charter as encompassing the "planning, preparation, initiation or waging of a war of aggression, or a war in violation of international treaties, agreements or assurances, or participation in a common plan or conspiracy" to do any of these things.

Second, war crimes (in the technical or narrow sense of the term). These included, in the words of Article 6(b) of the tribunal's charter, "violations of the laws or customs of war" such as "murder, ill-treatment or deportation to slave labor or for any other purpose of civilian population of or in occupied territory, murder or ill-treatment of prisoners of war or persons on the seas, killing of hostages, plunder of public or private property, wanton destruction of cities, towns or villages, or devastation not justified by military necessity."

Third, crimes against humanity. These were defined in Article 6(c) of the charter as comprehending "murder, extermination, enslavement, deportation, and other inhumane acts committed against any civilian population, before or during the war, or persecutions on political, racial or religious grounds in execution of or in connection with any crime within the jurisdiction of the Tribunal, whether or not in violation of the domestic law of the country where perpetrated."

Prosecution of war crimes in the technical or narrow sense of the term was not particularly novel. Well before Nuremberg, it was generally accepted that one side in a war can put captured enemy prisoners on trial for precapture violations of the laws and customs of war. Previously the laws of war had been enforced in this way only against soldiers or officers of low and middling rank. Nuremberg reached higher, to the top of the German hierarchy, and thus posed other problems; but, at least so far as substantive charges of war crimes were concerned, the one objection to which the Nuremberg trial was not open was that the relevant norms had been freshly minted for the particular occasion.

Prosecution both of crimes against peace and of crimes against humanity at Nuremberg represented, however, a dramatic innovation; it is these two charges that have largely inspired complaints about the ex post facto or retroactive character of the law applied at Nuremberg. Whether or not these complaints are valid, whether or not it matters whether or not they are valid, it certainly is the case that, before the Nuremberg proceedings, no one ever had stood in the dock charged with crimes against peace or with crimes against humanity as such.

Crimes Against Peace

To some extent, the concept of crimes against peace was anticipated in the idea which emerged during World War I of punishing Germany, as it were, in the person of the Kaiser and imposing penal responsibility on Wilhelm II for starting an unjust war. "Hang the Kaiser" became a popular slogan, the subject of songs and cartoons, and a campaign pledge in the British elections of December 1918, a month after the armistice. The difficulty, as legal experts pointed out, was that, in 1914, international law did not prohibit starting a war. In the end, Article 227 of the Versailles Treaty provided that the Kaiser would be tried, not precisely on a criminal charge, but for "a supreme offense against international morality and the sanctity of treaties." To everyone's relief, the Netherlands, where he took refuge at the end of the war, refused to surrender him.

The notion of imposing criminal responsibility on those who had initiated the war reemerged during World War II. In 1919, the best that could be said was that initiating war should be treated as a crime in the future, even if it was not then a crime. The question was whether this situation had been significantly altered by the condemnation of war contained in the Kellogg-Briand Pact of 1928. The question was controversial. A substantial body of opinion favored the view that there was no basis in international law for punishing anyone for starting World War II. This position, however, did not prevail within the United States government, nor ultimately with the Nuremberg Tribunal. The view that ultimately prevailed was that the Kellogg-Briand Pact of 1928, along with the cumulative effect of various international pronouncements in the interwar years denouncing aggression as an international crime, made starting war not only illegal as a breach of treaty, but criminal (in more than a metaphorical sense), so that individual government leaders could be punished for starting a war of aggression.

Crimes Against Humanity

How far the concept of crimes against humanity represented an innovation in 1945 depends on distinguishing two kinds of activity that fall under that heading.

On the one hand, certain crimes against humanity are also war crimes (in the narrow sense), and vice versa. There is considerable overlap between the two categories. War crimes include murder, ill-treatment and deportation of civilian populations in occupied territory; crimes against humanity include murder, deportation and inhumane acts against any civilian population. In large part, the difference seems to be one of scale or magnitude. In other words, certain war crimes are atrocities committed on such a vast scale that they also constitute crimes against humanity. Yet insofar as crimes against humanity are nothing but aggravated war crimes, they did not really amount to an innovation in 1945.

On the other hand, the definition of crimes against humanity contained in the Nuremberg Charter referred to inhumane acts committed against any civilian population, and so included atrocities committed against a state's own nationals as well as those committed against civilians in occupied territory. This was a tremendous innovation. There was absolutely no precedent for outsiders actually imposing criminal responsibility on members of a government who persecuted or exterminated their own nationals.

The germ of the phrase "crimes against humanity" is to be found in the Martens clause (named for the Russian jurist, Fyodor Martens, who drafted it) that appears in the rules of land warfare appended to the Fourth Hague Convention of 1907. The Martens clause states that in cases not covered by Hague rules, "inhabitants and belligerents remain under the protection of and subject to the principles of the law of nations as established by usages prevailing among civilized nations, by the laws of humanity, and by the dictates of the public conscience." In the Commission on Responsibility, which was part of the Paris Peace Conference after World War I, it was proposed that the reference in the Martens clause to "laws of humanity" as supplementing the laws of wars made the "laws of humanity" a basis of penal responsibility apart from the laws of war, and that this would permit prosecution for atrocities, such as the Armenian massacres of 1915, not clearly covered by traditional laws of war. Indeed, in a Declaration of May 28, 1915, issued on the initiative of the Tsarist foreign minister, the major Allied powers (France, Britain and Russia) had condemned the massacres of Armenians as "crimes against humanity and civilization for which all members of the Turkish Government will be held responsible together with its agents implicated in the massacres." Nothing came of this declaration at the time (although after the war the Turks themselves did try some of their wartime leaders); nothing came of the proposal at the Paris Peace Conference to treat the laws of humanity as a basis of penal responsibility supplementary to the laws of war, until 1945 when Article 6(c) of the Nuremberg Charter gave the tribunal jurisdiction over "crimes against humanity" as well as traditional war crimes. (The phrase "crimes against humanity" itself, as a rubric for large-scale atrocities, is said to have been suggested to Justice

Robert Jackson by the British jurist Hersch Lauterpacht during the conference in London that drew up the charter of the Nuremberg Tribunal.)

Fifty years later, the primary significance of the Nuremberg trial is
generally supposed to lie in the fact that it was the first prosecution ever
for the kinds of systematic persecution and barbarity against a state's
own nationals that we have come to call (using the very words of the
Nuremberg Charter) "crimes against humanity." Fifty years later, the
prosecution of crimes against humanity is perceived to be the "moral
center" of the Nuremberg trial, its crowning moral and legal achievement; the chief "legacy" of Nuremberg is supposedly the precedent it set
for the international criminalization of atrocities against civilians, wherever and whenever they occur.

At the time, however, the central charges at Nuremberg were supposed
to be those of crimes against peace and conspiracy to wage aggressive war.
These were characterized by one of the U.S. prosecutors (Sidney Alder-
man) as "the heart of the case." In the very first words of his eloquent
opening statement, Justice Jackson referred to "the privilege of opening
the first trial in history for crimes against the peace of the world...." For
Jackson and others, the decisive accomplishment, the principal legal construct, of the Nuremberg trial was the criminalization of aggressive war.
Aggression, said the tribunal's judgment, picking up this theme, is "the
supreme international crime." Insofar as Nuremberg was supposed to set a
precedent, it was to be a precedent that condemned, with penal sanctions,
recourse to aggressive war as an instrument of national policy.

In other words, there has been, since 1946, a sea change in thinking
about the significance of the Nuremberg trial: it is no longer seen as a
proceeding concerned primarily with the outlawry of aggressive war. For
us, if Nuremberg stands for any one thing, it stands for the condemnation
of genocide and other crimes against humanity. It is this aspect of the
"legacy" of Nuremberg that is invoked in discussions of the ad hoc tribunals set up to prosecute "war crimes" (in the large sense) committed in
the former Yugoslavia and Rwanda.

In 1995, Court TV showed footage of the Nuremberg trial to whet
viewers' appetites for its upcoming broadcast of the Tadic trial before the
International Criminal Tribunal for former Yugoslavia in the Hague. A
comment by Alex Ross on *The New York Times* television page, echoing a
criticism that historians of the Holocaust have voiced about Nuremberg,
noted that, "At the start, Nuremberg was weighted down by idealistic
plans to prohibit unjust war...Understanding the Holocaust did not always fit the agenda...The Nuremberg prosecution was on the right track
with its idea of a conspiracy. It would have succeeded if it had concentrated on the horror of the Holocaust and put a different array of actors on

trial."[2] The gist of this criticism is that Nuremberg was mainly supposed to be about crimes against humanity, but somehow got them out of focus.

Yet in fact, it is our focus that is different from that of the organizers of the Nuremberg trial. In part, the difference has come about because we have a more coherent notion of what the Holocaust involved than was possible in 1945. In part, it may stem from our greater disillusionment with efforts to ban aggression and treat it as a crime. (These efforts have not been a total failure; the example of Nuremberg has reinforced the inhibitions represented by the principle stated in Article 2(4) of the United Nations Charter, which requires member states to "refrain in their international relations from the threat or use of force" against other states; these inhibitions, in turn, have influenced consciousness regarding what is proper in international relations, even if they have not influenced conduct as much as one might desire.)

Protecting Individuals against Governments

If one has to say, however, what real difference Nuremberg has made in the world, it has made a difference not primarily because it stands as a precedent for punishing those who start aggressive wars, but because it marks the beginning of the great movement of our times to protect individuals against oppression by their governments—a movement which has come to fruition in the development of international human rights law and of international humanitarian law and in the blending of the two in an emergent international criminal law.

We see Nuremberg in a way that was not possible in 1946 because we exist in a different conceptual universe, which is a product of developments not so much begun as given added momentum by Nuremberg, and whose full consequences are only being realized with the end of the Cold War. It is a universe in which it is taken for granted that gross violations of human rights, including the mass murder of civilians and other crimes against humanity, are properly a matter of international concern, even if something is not always done about them; it is a new international order of which a basic tenet is the cosmopolitan principle that international law can properly concern itself with the treatment of individual human beings, even at the hands of their own government.

At the time of Nuremberg, it was a cardinal principle of international law that how a state treats it own nationals or citizens is not properly a matter of international concern. The international legal universe of 1945 was a state-centered universe in which international law was supposed to be a law between states, and states alone and exclusively.

In some ways, the aggressive war charge fit more easily with the basic premises of this universe than the charge of crimes against humanity.

There is nothing worse in a state-centered universe than interference with another state's sovereignty. Initiating war against another state represents quite considerable interference. It violates the principle of respect for other states' sovereignty, which is a main prop of a society composed exclusively of states; thus criminalizing aggressive war is not a departure from, but a vindication of, the premises on which a state-centered universe is constructed. By contrast, condemning a state's treatment of its own nationals contradicts the principle of respect for state sovereignty that is a basic premise of that universe. In this regard, inclusion of crimes against humanity in the Nuremberg Charter was a greater innovation than the inclusion of crimes against peace: it was less easy to assimilate into the existing system of international law, as it fit less easily with the prevailing paradigm of what international law was all about.

In consequence, while the concept of crimes against humanity figured in the proceedings at Nuremberg, it was sometimes in contexts or with restrictions that now seem curious, even obtuse. Let me just mention a few items at random.

First, there was the persistent insistence by the American prosecutors on including a wide-ranging conspiracy charge in the indictment.

The conspiracy charge was the brainchild of Colonel Murray Bernays, head of the special projects branch of the Intelligence Division of the U.S. Army General Staff, who was assigned to come up with a War Department answer to the Morgenthau plan to reduce Germany to a deindustrialized, agricultural state. The plan Bernays devised was, perhaps, the single most important source of the ideas that shaped the Nuremberg Tribunal. It included both the idea of prosecuting Nazi organizations and the idea of bringing a conspiracy charge. Bernays was particularly preoccupied with the problem of reaching atrocities committed in Germany itself before the war. These were not war crimes in the traditional sense of the term, but they involved brutalities he believed could not be left unpunished. Drawing on his experience as a lawyer with cases charging conspiracy to commit securities fraud, Bernays came up with a solution: a charge alleging that the whole Nazi regime constituted a criminal conspiracy to achieve its ends by illegal means. To prove this charge, he suggested, everything done in furtherance of the conspiracy from the time of its inception would be admissible, including domestic atrocities committed within Germany before the war. This idea caught the imagination of U.S. Secretary of War Henry Stimson, who first made his legal reputation prosecuting antitrust conspiracies as United States Attorney in New York during Theodore Roosevelt's administration. Stimson later said that the principal defect of the judgment of the International Military Tribunal was that it downplayed the conspiracy charge.

During the negotiations in London that produced the Nuremberg Charter, the French were genuinely shocked by the peculiar common-law concept of a conspiracy, viewing it as a barbarous legal anachronism. The Russians, when they grasped the unfamiliar idea, were said to be envious. At any rate, at the London Conference (and later in the reactions of defense counsel and in the deliberations of the International Military Tribunal), it was apparent that European lawyers were quite uncomfortable with the concept of a criminal conspiracy.

In London, the result was a curious compromise in the tribunal's charter, which allowed prosecution for conspiracy to wage aggressive war, but not for conspiracy to commit war crimes or crimes against humanity. (The last clause of Article 6 did provide that anyone participating in a common plan or conspiracy to commit any offense within the jurisdiction of the tribunal would be responsible for "all acts performed by any persons in execution of such plan," i.e., it made co-conspirators liable as accomplices to each other's criminal acts. It did not, however, make conspiracy itself a distinct substantive crime.) It has been suggested that Justice Jackson accepted this compromise because he regarded the charge of aggressive war as central to the trial and was not particularly concerned about whether the charter would cover prewar persecutions and atrocities.

Yet, despite this compromise, Count One of the indictment, drafted by the American team headed by Jackson, alleged a general conspiracy to commit all of the crimes defined in the charter—not only crimes against peace but war crimes and crimes against humanity as well. Everything the Nazi regime did was alleged to have been done, from the beginning, with the intent of carrying out a conspiracy or common plan to subjugate the European continent. In other words, the indictment went beyond what the charter authorized and embodied the original American idea rather than the letter of the charter. It amounted to an end run around the limited notion of conspiracy contained in the charter.

Ultimately, this end run was unsuccessful. The tribunal's judgment held that, to be a separate criminal offense for which the charter permitted conviction, conspiracy must consist of a specific concrete plan to wage aggressive war. Charges of conspiracy to commit war crimes or crimes against humanity were rejected; allegations pertaining to prewar persecutions were disregarded.

Second, there is the fact that, at the Nuremberg trial, incidents in the "war against the Jews" figured mainly as war crimes, not as crimes against humanity. Similarly, the term "genocide" is used only once in the indictment, again in connection with war crimes, not in connection with crimes against humanity. Perhaps this should not occasion surprise. The term "genocide" was coined during the war by the Polish jurist Raphael

Lemkin. Later, in 1948, Lemkin was largely responsible for pushing the Genocide Convention, which he had drafted, through the United Nations General Assembly. But when the term first appeared, it was in Lemkin's book *Axis Rule in Occupied Europe* (1944), which focused on German occupation policies. The term "genocide" was devised to refer not only to annihilation of Jews, but more broadly to the effort to reconstruct social and economic structure, to Aryanize and destroy a sense of separate national identity in all German-occupied countries.

Then there is the curious episode of the semicolon that shrank to a comma. Article 6(c) of the Nuremberg Charter specifies that crimes against humanity include (1) "murder, extermination, enslavement, deportation, and other inhumane acts committed against any civilian population, before or during the war" and (2) "persecutions on political, racial or religious grounds." Then it says: "in execution of or in connection with any crime within the jurisdiction of the Tribunal [crimes against peace or war crimes], whether or not in violation of the domestic law of the country where perpetrated." Does this last clause modify (1) and (2), or only (2)? The answer depends on whether a comma or a semicolon divides the first two clauses. The English text drafted at London had a semicolon; the Russian text, a comma. A protocol replaced the semicolon with a comma in all versions. As a result, the requirement that crimes against humanity be connected to some other crime within the jurisdiction of the tribunal became a limitation on all forms of crimes against humanity, not just on persecutions on political, racial or religious grounds. It is not entirely clear whether the protocol represented a change of position or a recognition of an earlier punctuation error in drafting. (Complicating the picture is the fact that Control Council Law No. 10, adopted after the Nuremberg Charter, did not require linkage between crimes against humanity and war.)

Finally, in line with the idea that everything the Nazis did was part of one large conspiracy, the prosecution's case at Nuremberg at times verged on presenting persecution simply as a measure of preparation for war. For instance, there was the showing in court on November 29, 1945, of the film *Nazi Concentration Camps*.[3] Even the defendants (except Goering) were horrified by what the film showed. Yet the prosecution went on to argue as if these horrifying images were mostly about perverted militarism, not genocide.

A number of explanations have been advanced for this dogged focus by the prosecution on conspiracy to commit aggressive war, and the subordination of everything else in the case to that. It has been said, for instance, that Jackson was worried that the United States might relapse into isolationism and sought to head off that possibility by reassuring

Americans that they had been right to resist aggressors; that World War II had been fought by the United States in a wholly just cause; that the war from the first had been one of aggression by Nazi Germany. It has been suggested, less charitably, that Jackson's main concern was to vindicate the opinion he had expressed as Attorney General in favor of the validity of the destroyer-bases deal and of lend-lease; if it could be shown that Germany from the outset had been engaged in a criminal war of aggression, then the morality as well as the legality of aiding Britain would be demonstrated once and for all.

But to put sole emphasis on this kind of explanation neglects the limitations imposed by the theory or paradigm of international law and relations that was dominant fifty years ago—one in which acts of a state that affected only its own nationals were of no proper concern to other states.

At the London Conference, Justice Jackson argued that all charges involving prewar crimes within Germany had to be tied to the crime of waging aggressive war. Otherwise, there would be no basis for international concern with them; otherwise, condemning a government for how it had treated its own nationals would amount to intervention in the domestic affairs of another country, and Americans were opposed to that: we had no intention, he said, of letting foreign nations meddle in our own domestic racial policies. The only reason, he argued, "that this program of extermination of Jews becomes an international concern is this: It was part of a plan for making an illegal war. Unless we have a war connection, I think we would have no basis for dealing with the atrocities . . . committed inside Germany." In Justice Jackson's world, crimes against humanity had to be tied to other crimes in order to be matters of international concern.

In our world, fifty years later, that is no longer so, at least in principle. (There is a controversy, reignited by dicta of the Yugoslavia Tribunal's appeals chamber in the Tadic case, about whether crimes against humanity, in the sense of the Nuremberg Charter, can be committed in peacetime. In principle, there is no reason why they cannot be, and there is no doubt that genocide can be: the Genocide Convention says that genocide can be committed in peacetime, and was meant in this regard to rebuke the judgment of the Nuremberg Tribunal.)

If, to us, the emphasis at Nuremberg on the criminality of aggressive war seems to get things out of focus, to paint a picture of the Nazi era that seems slightly askew, it is because we live in a conceptual universe, shaped by law, which is different from the universe that existed at the time of Nuremberg, but which has, in large part, been made possible by Nuremberg.

The greatest significance of the Nuremberg trial lies in its contribution to the development of a different view of international relations, to a change in the way in which international law is conceptualized. International law is no longer regarded as a body of rules concerned only with relations between states. It is a body of law in which individuals have a place and in which human rights can be asserted on the world stage over and against the claims of the state.

What Nuremberg contributed to this shift was not only the concept of crimes against humanity. Equally, perhaps more significant, was the imposition of direct individual responsibility under international law, extending to the highest levels of government. This, too, was an innovation. Older international law acknowledged only the responsibility of states, not that of individuals. It allowed states to prosecute individuals for war crimes; it did not itself necessarily hold war criminals directly responsible for a breach of international law. In turn, the assertion, dramatically affirmed at Nuremberg, that individuals can be held directly responsible for breaches of international law concedes that international law can apply to individuals as well as to states; and once individuals are recognized as persons who can be held responsible under a system of law, it is a short step to recognizing them as persons who are entitled to protection under that law. (Biblical scholars have made the point that when Deuteronomy 22:22 provides for stoning the woman as well as the man caught committing adultery, it represents, in a way, a landmark in the development of women's rights, since it treats the erring wife as a legal person rather than as an object to be dealt with as her husband chooses. Similarly with the imposition of international penal responsibility on individuals, which represents the recognition that individuals are legal persons, however inconvenient that recognition may be for the individuals who first achieve it.) Thus, Nuremberg was crucial in subverting the paradigm that sees international law as exclusively a law between states and in affirming the possibility of an international legal universe in which individual human beings are the ultimate participants.

The term "paradigm" was popularized in Thomas Kuhn's influential book, *The Structure of Scientific Revolutions*.[4] Critics have noticed that it is not always clear what Kuhn means by a paradigm; but, roughly speaking, the term seems to designate the general picture or way of seeing the world prevalent among a community of scientists; for instance, the Copernican or Keplerian view of the solar system as opposed to the earlier Ptolemaic picture in which the earth stood at the center of a system of fixed stars and moving planets. In Kuhn's view, successive paradigms supplant each other completely, which is what happened in the history of astronomy. In his view, the history of science is punctuated by revolutions in which this kind of paradigm shift has occurred.

In international relations, paradigms do not seem to supplant each other with the definitiveness that Kuhn finds in the history of science.

Different paradigms coexist as competing traditions of thought: partial, incomplete, complementary, mutually limiting, as if, even after Copernicus or Newton, Ptolemeic astronomy or Aristotelian dynamics still had adherents and, more important, still had explanatory power.

One can multiply variations, but there seem to be three basic views or paradigms of international relations: (1) the so-called "realist" view, which depicts international relations as taking place in a Hobbesian state of nature in which politics among nations is ultimately a war of all against all; (2) the view that underlies classical international law and that pictures the world as a stage on which nation-states are the principal actors and sees international law as doing nothing more or less than setting basic ground rules by which independent and otherwise absolute sovereigns can coexist in the same social space; and (3) the cosmopolitan view, which depicts the people of the world as comprising a genuine planetary community and sees international law as concerned with promoting cooperation to achieve common ends having to do with the well-being and welfare of the human beings of whom that community is ultimately composed.

In our own time, we are witnessing a transition from a situation in which (1) or (2) more nearly represents reality to a situation in which (3) more nearly is predominant, although not entirely so. Where international law traditionally has been the law governing only relations between sovereign nation-states, it is becoming the law of a planetary community of which all human beings are members. People who believe in "states' rights" are uncomfortable with the consequences of this transition to an inclusive world community; and, indeed, it is not without its drawbacks and dangers. But it definitely is taking place, albeit slowly, and sometimes with retrograde movements, and Nuremberg played a crucial role in opening up this new conceptual universe—one in which it actually is possible to think of ourselves as inhabiting a genuine global community in which the individual human being rather than the state stands (to adapt a phrase of Hersch Lauterpacht's) "in the very centre of the [moral] constitution of the world." Yet precisely because it played that role, what happened at Nuremberg is destined, from our point of view, to seem somewhat out of focus.

Notes

1. An abbreviated version of this chapter was delivered as a talk at an international conference to commemorate the 50th anniversary of the Nuremberg trials, sponsored by the Cohn-Haddow Center for Judaic Studies, Wayne State University, Detroit, Michigan, on October 14, 1996.
2. *The New York Times*, November 12, 1995.

3. This is discussed in an article by Lawrence Douglas, "Film as Witness: Screening Nazi Concentration Camps Before the Nuremberg Tribunal," *Yale Law Journal* 105 (1995): 449.

4. Thomas Kuhn, *The Structure of Scientific Revolutions*, 2nd ed. (Chicago: University of Chicago Press, 1970).

Nuremberg:
A Cold War Conflict of Interest

Peter Maguire

I.

> People insist that, in conflicts between states, the conqueror should
> sit in judgment upon the conquered, moral code in hand, and inflict
> punishment upon him for what he has done.... This is an altogether
> unreasonable demand. Punishment and revenge have nothing to do
> with policy. Policy must not meddle with the calling of the nemesis,
> or aspire to exercise the judge's office.
>
> Otto von Bismarck[1]

With the exception of five *Einsatzkommando* members hanged in 1951, the vast majority of war criminals convicted by American courts in postwar Germany were quietly released by 1955. Because U.S. leaders never unambiguously determined whether the war crimes trials were acts of politics or acts of law, two contradictory American war crimes policies emerged. This served to undermine both the controversial American war crimes program and the legacy of Nuremberg.

The first American war crimes policy was a decidedly legalistic approach to conflict resolution. Henry Stimson and his team of War Department lawyers conceived of two international trials for major Axis war criminals and twelve American trials for German civilian, military and political leaders. The International Military Tribunal (IMT) was a legal and political success.

Because the international trial was held under quadripartite control, any attempt to tamper with the prisoners' sentences required the consent of the French, the British and, most important, the Soviets. As a result of these constraints, the prisoners served out their sentences and the rulings of Nuremberg's International Military Tribunal were upheld. The same cannot be said for those convicted by American courts in the western zone of occupation. The subsequent American trials proved far more complicated.

A parole process was created by the Americans that was designed to release what the State Department described as the "hardcore" German war criminals long before their sentences had expired. In April 1958, an Allied parole board released the final four war criminals in Western captivity. Three of the four had been *Einsatzkommando* members originally sentenced to death by an American tribunal at Nuremberg in 1948. Adding insult to injury, in the Paris Treaty reestablishing West German sovereignty, drafted in 1952 and ratified in 1955, the Federal Republic of Germany explicitly refused to affirm the validity of the sentences of any of the Allied war crimes tribunals in postwar Germany. The abandonment of America's radical and controversial war crimes policy coincided with West German rearmament and reopened the question the Americans had brushed aside in 1945. Rather than admit outright that the war crimes trials were political acts, U.S. leaders chose to manipulate the judicial machinery, tacitly demonstrating to Germans that they had been correct all long—that the treatment of the vanquished was, and had always been, a political act.

The first phase of American war crimes policy (1946–1949) followed the stern guidelines of denazification, deindustrialization, and reeducation set down in Joint Chiefs of Staff Directive 1067, signed by President Franklin Roosevelt in 1945. Although Roosevelt halfheartedly lent his name to the Nuremberg idea, there was never a broad base of support for the War Department's novel judicial approach to conflict resolution. Because of the vague policy guidelines for occupying two countries, early American war crimes policy possessed a strong ad hoc character; theater officials were often forced to interpret ambiguous directions. What emerged was a hydra-headed approach; on the one hand, high-ranking Axis leaders were given elaborate trials in Nuremberg and Tokyo, while lesser offenders were tried by military commissions with few legal pretenses. Only German and Japanese leaders were confronted with the War Department's novel legal constructions.[2]

The only other courts to employ the novel aggression and conspiracy charges created for the IMT were the twelve American trials conducted under Brigadier General Telford Taylor at Nuremberg. Justice Robert Jackson, the U.S. chief prosecutor, did not consider the job complete after Nuremberg's international trial; a number of high-level Nazis remained in Allied captivity. In the summer of 1946, five additional courtrooms were added to the Palace of Justice in Nuremberg, and between 1947 and 1949, twelve tribunals composed of conservative American judges tried 184 defendants. One hundred forty-two faced sentences ranging from death (twenty-four) to prison terms (twenty life sentences).

These subsequent proceedings provided the most strenuous field test of Nuremberg's new laws (now embodied in Control Council Law No. 10).[3] Industrial leader Alfried Krupp, diplomat Ernst von Weizsäcker, and bureaucrat Hans Lammers could not be handed over to the military; businessmen, diplomats and judges cannot be tried under the traditional laws of war (the Hague and Geneva Conventions). The subsequent proceedings thus faced a problem: if a court rejected Nuremberg's expanded definition of international criminality, this would remove the heart from a number of cases. The trials featured doctors, judges, *Einsatzkommando* members, concentration camp administrators, generals, diplomats, industrialists and government officials.[4] The decisions of eleven of the twelve courts were reviewed and confirmed by legal staff of the U.S. Military Government.

Standing in stark contrast to the sophisticated political justice of the Nuremberg trials were the U.S. Army trials at Dachau, which represented more typical victors' justice. Most of the 1,672 defendants in these 489 proceedings had been concentration camp guards or personnel at Buchenwald, Flossenburg, Mauthausen, Nordhausen and Mühldorf. They were tried for violations of the laws of war. The most infamous defendants at Dachau were Joachim Peiper, Sepp Dietrich and the soldiers accused of the Malmedy Massacre of American soldiers. The other large group (600) were accused of murdering American pilots. U.S. Army and Navy military commissions tried 1,400 Japanese in Asia and the Pacific.[5]

The U.S. Army's military commissions were not up to the standards of the Nuremberg courts; they were more in keeping with the tradition of vindictive successor trials. But because U.S. leaders had loudly and conspicuously committed themselves to higher standards, all of the American cases would be measured by those standards. The most infamous case of victors' justice occurred in the Philippines in 1945, where General Douglas MacArthur evened the score with his former adversaries Tomoyuki Yamashita and Masaharu Homma. MacArthur selected a five-man commission to try the generals. None of the officers were lawyers, and they were not "bound by technical rules of evidence."[6] The prosecution even produced a mock documentary movie as "evidence." It showed an American soldier removing a piece of paper from the pocket of a dead Japanese soldier; the paper read (in English) "Orders from Tokyo." The narrator broke in: "We have discovered the secret orders to destroy Manila." On December 7, 1945, the fourth anniversary of the Japanese attack on Pearl Harbor, MacArthur's legal commission found that the atrocities had been methodically supervised by the Japanese officers and noncommissioned officers. Tomoyuki Yamashita was sentenced to death and hanged.[7]

The *Yamashita* case was an example of more traditional postwar military justice. The conquered had no choice but to submit to the judicial fiat of the victors. In MacArthur's eyes, Yamashita had violated old and sacred norms: "The soldier, be he friend or foe, is charged with the protection of the weak and unarmed. It is the very essence and reason for his being. When he violates his sacred trust, he not only profanes the entire cult but threatens the very fabric of international society."[8] Yamashita and Homma were hanged, but not before the U.S. Supreme Court was brought into the case. Although the majority dodged the substantive legal questions, Justices Rutledge and Murphy issued strong dissenting opinions.[9] MacArthur's treatment of his former foe, although abhorrent when measured by the progressive standards of the War Department, was consistent with both history and the *vae victis* (woe to the conquered) tradition. The Japanese and Germans understood and accepted this, because harsh occupation measures were part of their military tradition.

Of all the Army proceedings in Germany, the military trials against Sepp Dietrich, Joachim Peiper and the soldiers accused of committing the Malmedy Massacre were the most symbolically important because the crimes had been committed by elite Waffen SS units led by two of Hitler's most decorated officers, Peiper and Dietrich. Seventy-two Americans had been killed, execution style, during the Battle of the Bulge in December 1945. In 1946, the Army identified the 500 most likely suspects and transferred them to a century-old prison in Bavaria. Army interrogators threatened and beat prisoners. The suspects were separated and subjected to macabre mock trials, during which hooded "defendants" were given an opportunity to confess. These confessions gave the prosecution enough evidence to begin their trial. On May 16, 1946, the Army charged seventy-three Waffen SS soldiers with various violations of the laws of war.[10]

After a five-week trial at Dachau, the military commission sentenced Peiper, Dietrich and forty-two other men to death and twenty-two others to life in prison. Peiper's attorney petitioned the U.S. Supreme Court. Although the court refused to rule on the case, the legal maneuvering took time, and American foreign policy was changing dramatically.[11] In the minds of many American statesmen, the crimes of the Nazis had been eclipsed by the perceived threat of the Soviet Union. American policy toward Germany began to reflect this change as early as 1947.

II.

I personally considered that it would have been best if the Allied commanders had standing instructions that if any of these men fell into the hands of Allied forces they should, once their identity had been established beyond doubt, be executed forthwith. But to hold these Nazi leaders for public trial was another matter. This procedure could not expiate or undo the crimes they had committed.

George F. Kennan (1945)[12]

George Kennan was a consistent and vociferous critic of the American legalists' reform efforts. He attacked these policies on the grounds that they tarnished American foreign policy with hypocrisy. To Kennan, reeducation policies were an example of "moralistic-legalistic" foreign policy at its worst. Nothing was to be gained from sharing the judges' bench with the Soviet Union: "The only implication this procedure could convey was...that such crimes were justifiable and forgivable when committed by the leaders of one government, under one set of circumstances, but unjustifiable and unforgivable, and to be punished by death, when committed by another set of government leaders under another set of circumstances."[13]

Kennan even argued that the crimes of the Third Reich were simply the "customs of warfare which have prevailed generally in Eastern Europe and Asia for centuries in the past, they are not the peculiar property of the Germans."[14] When it came to actual Nazi atrocities, he proved, as the Germans say, "blind in one eye." He candidly admitted that Nazi atrocities were a subject he chose not to examine too closely: "If others wish, in the face of this situation, to pursue the illumination of those sinister recesses in which the brutalities of war find their record, they may do so, the degree of relative guilt which such inquiries may bring to light is something of which I, as an American, prefer to remain ignorant."[15] As early as 1947, many in the State Department considered moral commitments such as denazification and war crimes trials a burden that would inhibit America's range of foreign policy motion.

U.S. Military Governor for Germany Lucius Clay remained convinced that cooperation with the Soviets was possible. However, Washington was moving in a different direction. As the State Department became more involved with the affairs of Germany, General Clay felt less and less comfortable with American policy. Clay halfheartedly attempted to resign in July 1947. In a letter to General Eisenhower, he wrote: "I feel that the State Department wants a negative personality in Germany. As you know, I can carry out policy wholeheartedly or not at all and there is no question left in my mind but that my views relative to Germany do not coincide with present policies."[16] Eisenhower convinced his old friend to stay on. According to Jean Smith, editor of General Clay's papers, "Clay got the message; henceforth, he realized that U.S. policy in Germany would march to a different drummer."[17]

Stephen Chamberlin, the director of U.S. Army intelligence, met with General Clay in Berlin in early 1948. Years later, Clay recalled the conversation: "General Chamberlin came to see me in Berlin in late February [1948]. He told me that the Army was having trouble getting the draft reinstated, and they needed a strong message from me that they could use in congressional testimony. So I wrote out this cable. I sent it directly to Chamberlin and told him to use it as he saw fit."[18] Clay's cable was rather vague, yet the tone was very serious:

> For many months, based on logical analysis, I have felt and held that war was unlikely for at least ten years. Within the last few weeks, I have felt a sudden change in Soviet attitudes which I cannot define but which now gives me a feeling that it may come with dramatic suddenness. I cannot support this change in my own thinking with any data or outward evidence other than to describe it as a feeling of new tenseness in every Soviet individual with whom we have official relations.[19]

General Clay was shocked when Chamberlin leaked his cable to the media. He later recalled: "I assumed they would use it in closed session. I certainly had no idea they would make it public. If I had, I would not have sent it."[20]

The shift away from the punitive occupation policies of the early occupation period was not without impact on American war crimes policy. As early as 1948, the State Department was attempting to temper what it saw as the excesses of the American legalists. The Policy Planning Staff was beginning to echo the views of George Kennan. In the 1948 "Review of Current Trends in American Foreign Policy," the Policy Planning Staff deemed the first phase of American war crimes policy a failure:

> Next, we must recognize the bankruptcy of our moral influence on the Germans, and we must make plans for the earliest possible termination of those actions and policies on our part which have been psychologically unfortunate.... Secondly, we must terminate as rapidly as possible those forms of activity (denazification, re-education, and above all the Nuremberg Trials) which tend to set us up as mentors and judges over internal German problems.[21]

III.

> I desire to say that what is taking place in Nuremberg, Germany, is a disgrace to the United States.... A racial minority, two and a half years after the war closed, are in Nuremberg not only hanging German soldiers, but trying German business men in the name of the U.S.
>
> Representative John Rankin

These war-trials were decided on in Moscow and they were carried on under Moscow principles. These trials were essentially the same as the mass trials held in the 1930s by Stalin when Vyshinsky used treason trials to liquidate his internal enemies. At Nuremberg the Communists used the war crimes trials to liquidate their external enemies. It is the Communist's avowed purpose to destroy the Western World which is based on property rights.

Senator William Langer[22]

The year 1949 was a transitional one for Germany, as the civilian U.S. High Commission for Germany (HICOG) replaced the U.S. Military Government (USMG). The State Department was now in charge, and it sought to ease the level of external control the Allies exercised over the Federal Republic. John McCloy was named high commissioner and inherited the legacy of the controversial trials that he had helped create.[23] McCloy's relationship with the German war criminals was much more complex than it had been in 1944, as the punitive policies of the occupation period were not compatible with the new American program for Germany.

There was growing dissatisfaction in Germany over the continued incarceration and pending executions of war criminals. Many West Germans, their leaders included, found the Nuremberg manner of punishment and parole confusing, unprecedented and ultimately illegitimate. This was especially true among veterans and the professional military, two segments of the population whose support was now vital.

The absence of an official appellate or review court provided a loophole that the United States used to speed the releases of German war criminals without calling into question the validity of their original sentences. The sentences of the International Military Tribunal could not be revised without the consent of the other three powers. In the American cases, however, the judicial machinery was tailored to mirror contemporary strategic interests. Initially, McCloy considered having one board review both the American Nuremberg trials and the Army trials. Secretary of State Dean Acheson expressed his doubts about having a single board review all the sentences:

Army cable to CINCEUR [Commander in Chief in Europe] suggests that same individuals deal with both the Nuremberg and Dachau death sentences. This seemed undesirable in view of different nature of trials.... Boards of the caliber you suggest would be bound to attract attention and might tend to create impression that legal basis and procedure of Nuremberg trials under review, or at least be construed as indication of doubt.[24]

Acheson recognized that widespread sentence reviews and subsequent mass paroles would cast a pall of doubt over the already controversial Nuremberg decisions.

In the end, two review boards were established, one for the American Nuremberg trials and one for the Army's trials at Dachau. McCloy's three-man panel was composed of State Department legal advisor Conrad Snow, former State Supreme Court Justice David Peck, and the chairman of the New York Board of Parole, Frederick Moran. Although they read the judgments in all twelve of the American Nuremberg trials, they could not possibly consider the wealth of documentary evidence or the actual trial transcripts. The transcripts in the *Ministries* case alone ran to 28,000 pages, with 9,000 documentary exhibits.[25]

The review board was not allowed to raise sentences or challenge the basis of the convictions. They could only lower or, to use their own euphemism, "equalize" sentences. Some of the original decisions were very lenient, and the McCloy panel used these courts' decisions as their legal point of reference. Fifty lawyers, representing most of the prisoners, were brought before the board. Although the three men likened themselves to an American parole board, they did not follow standard operating procedure. Not only were the judges and prosecutors who had tried the cases conspicuously absent, but they did not know that their sentences were being reviewed.

The Peck Panel presented its final report to the High Commissioner in August 1950. When McCloy's trusted legal advisor Robert Bowie read the report, he objected:

> The reductions recommended are excessive. I have serious doubts as to the validity of the 24 recommendations of the Board which seem to me to fail to give sufficient recognition to the seriousness of the crime for which the individuals concerned were sentenced by Tribunals. Moreover, certain statements of the Board suggest that they have striven to be as lenient as possible and I am concerned lest the report as a whole create the impression of a repudiation of the Nuremberg trials.[26]

Bowie shared Acheson's view that sentence reviews that led to mass paroles would call into question the validity of the Nuremberg trials.

On January 31, 1951, McCloy announced his decisions when the final report, entitled *Landsberg: A Documentary Report*, was made public. The high commissioner followed most of the board's recommendations and one-third of the Nuremberg convicts were immediately freed.[27] Most conspicuous was the decision to free all the businessmen and industrialists tried in the *Farben*, *Flick*, and *Krupp* cases. Due to a 1949 U.S. Senate investigation by William Langer of abuses in the Malmedy trials, General Clay had been unable to execute the final thirteen men on Landsberg Prison's death row. McCloy upheld five of the death sentences, and on June 11, 1951, a U.S. Army hangman carried out the final executions of war criminals on German soil. In the Army cases, General Thomas Handy's clemency board was less lenient. However, he did commute all the Malmedy death sentences to prison terms, because "the crimes are definitely distinguishable from the more deliberate killings in concentration camps."[28]

John McCloy has become a convenient scapegoat for the failings of American war crimes policy. His greatest shortcoming was a failure to recognize the power of impressions in international politics. Pedantic distinctions between "sentence review" and "sentence equalization" were eclipsed by the release of Alfried Krupp and the restoration of the Krupp fortune.

The high commissioner's use of the parole and clemency process was in fact conservative when compared to the actions of his successors. However, it is difficult to overlook the poor job the high commissioner did in defending his actions. Initially, McCloy claimed that no reviews had been conducted. This was simply untrue. General Clay's legal staff had reviewed nearly ninety percent of the sentences and all of the death sentences. At the time of his reviews, Clay wrote:

> When you have the responsibility of whether someone is going to die, before you sign a paper you worry about it an awful lot. And I never signed any of those papers without going through the trial record from A to Z. And if there was any doubt, *any doubt*, I commuted the sentence.[29]

The irritation with John McCloy grew over the years, as did his insistence that these were apolitical, "legal" decisions. But ultimately, it was John McCloy who best described the American legalist mindset: "I saw my public service in terms of getting things done.... I never considered myself a politician, but rather a lawyer, so the question I asked myself in the various jobs I had was 'What should we do to solve the problem at hand?', then I tried to solve the problem."[30]

IV.

The Cold War produced an American James Bondism based on the thesis that Communist disrespect for international law and accepted

standards of behavior could only be countered by an even more san-
guinary immorality on the part of the United States.

John Kenneth Galbraith [31]

In 1952, the clemency loophole began to widen. In the Paris Treaty,
which reestablished West German sovereignty, Allied leaders created a
second clemency and parole board. This process coincided with West
German remilitarization and was of great symbolic importance. Many
Germans found it ironic that the United States was now eagerly preparing to rebuild the Wehrmacht while many of its leaders (List, Kuntze,
Reinecke, Hoth, Warlimont) remained in prison.

On July 14, 1952, over two million German veterans adopted a resolution calling for an amnesty for war crimes. Retired admiral and Chairman of the Union of German Ex-Soldiers Gottfried Hansen appealed to
U.S. General Mathew Ridgway:

> In March this year I made bold to address a reasoned request to
> General Eisenhower, asking him to use his influence in order to
> bring the "war criminals" problem to a speedy and satisfactory solu-
> tion by having a general amnesty granted to the prisoners. . . . But
> what is oppressing humanity as a whole now is the curse called
> down at Tehran, Yalta, and Potsdam. It . . . is against this curse that
> the western world is struggling. Are Nuremberg and all that fol-
> lowed to become a similar curse? Is this curse to stand in the way of
> the western forces being welded into one true force of defense,
> united by comradeship and respect?[32]

On December 22, 1952, the high commissioner (now James Conant)
received a report from the State Department's office of political affairs.
The report outlined the ways in which continuing to hold war criminals
could adversely affect American policy in Germany: "(1) It will affect the
political strength of the Chancellor and his party and thus the chances for
continuation of present German foreign policy course; (2) it will affect the
development of the EDC [European Defense Community], both in terms
of German popular support, and the more specific problem of recruiting
experienced officer material for the German contingent of the EDC." The
final recommendation of the report was neither new nor groundbreaking:
"We would suggest further that a more lenient system of reduction of sentence and parole be adopted. . . . An alternative which is posed for possible
consideration is the use of a large scale clemency device."[33]

John Auchincloss of the State Department's office of German political
affairs objected strongly to the proposal contained in the memo. He con-

sidered it a political solution to what he saw as a judicial question: "The paper advanced a political solution of the war crimes problem, and it might be well to point out certain objections which would apply to any solution of that kind." Auchincloss, like Acheson and Bowie, argued that a political solution would have a corrosive effect on the legacy of Nuremberg:

> There is so much background to this question—the Moscow Declaration of 1943 issued by President Roosevelt, Mr. Churchill, and Stalin; the trials themselves, with the wide expectation that they would serve the ends of justice and also create new principles of law; the international acceptance of these principles by the adherence of other nations to the Charter of the International Military Tribunal, and by the General Assembly resolution of December 11, 1946 affirming the principles of international law recognized by the Charter of the Nurnberg Tribunal and the judgment of the Tribunal—that an American yielding to a German demand for the release of war criminals would be a concession of uncommon significance.[34]

The State Department officer warned that it would be a monumental error to cloak political action in judicial robes. He wrote that "any political solution will be attended with great difficulty; the particular vice of the one recently suggested is that it is a political solution which pretends to be something else." Auchincloss was prophetic, given the final outcome of American war crimes policy: "I believe this is one subject on which we have no chance of fooling other people, and we had better not try, or we shall fool only ourselves."[35]

German Chancellor Konrad Adenauer traveled to the United States in April 1953 to discuss rearmament. The State Department knew that Adenauer intended to press for the release of more war criminals. In a confidential, preconference memo, the State Department conceded that "the lessons of Nuremberg" had been lost on the majority of Germans: "The German attitude towards the war crimes trials and the confinement of criminals has constituted a problem of continuous difficulty ever since the trials were held. The Germans have not accepted the underlying principles of the trials and do not believe in the guilt of those who have been convicted."[36] According to a HICOG public opinion survey of October 1952, sixty percent of Germans questioned disapproved of the Allied handling of the war crimes question, while only ten percent approved.[37]

In the first meeting with American leaders, Adenauer "pointed out that there were considerable psychological and public opinion problems in Germany connected with the war criminal issue."[38] In the second meeting, American leaders made major concessions to the German leader's demands: "Ambassador Conant said that the US would hope to have either a mixed board or some new procedure... in the near future, and certainly before the September elections in Germany. He suggested that little publicity be given to these plans and that public references be made in only general terms."[39] Secretary of State John Foster Dulles went even further; he "reiterated to the Chancellor that the U.S. would review the policies of its military authorities with a view to a more liberal treatment of war criminals.... Returning to the parole board question, he reassured the Chancellor that we anticipated the establishment of the joint parole board or commission prior to general EDC ratification."[40]

Above all, the White House and Konrad Adenauer wanted a new parole board before the 1953 elections in Germany. In June 1953, James Riddleberger advised U.S. Secretary of State John Foster Dulles of the political importance of the war crimes question in Germany:

> German resentment over the trial and continued confinement of war criminals has been causing difficulty in Allied-German relations for several years. It would help the Chancellor greatly if some way could be found to improve this situation before the elections in Germany this autumn.... Consideration has, therefore, been given to the institution of a parole system for prisoners tried and held by the United States. This possibility was discussed with Adenauer in Washington, and he is strongly in favor of it.[41]

On October 20, 1953, the Interim Mixed Parole and Clemency (IMPAC) Board was established to rule on American war crimes cases until the treaties establishing the mixed board were ratified. The IMPAC Board consisted of two Germans and three Americans. The chairman was an attorney from Boston (Henry Lee Shattuck); the other two Americans were an Army major general (Joseph Muller), and a career State Department officer (Edwin Plitt). Both German representatives (Emil Lersh and Hans Meuschel) were former high court judges. Parole standards were further eased; credit for time served was increased, and the parameters for medical paroles were also broadened. Eligibility for parole for those with life imprisonment and death sentences was reduced to fifteen years from the day of arrest.

John Auchincloss of the State Department continued to argue against the use of parole for political purposes. In a secret memo to Geoffrey Lewis at the U.S. Embassy in Bonn, he described the damaging effect that a political solution would have on the Nuremberg Principles: "The appearance of a political solution would have, in effect, the same disadvantages of a real political solution, and we should not underestimate what these disadvantages would be. The United States would have put itself in the position of disregarding the principles involved in the original trials, and this would undermine, in retrospect, the entire war crimes program."[42]

John Auchincloss rejected simple legalism and raised the question of principle: "More important than any of these is the question of principle, and I do not think we should hesitate to raise it, even if some people are uncomfortable." He considered wide ranging paroles, under any pretext, to be both an abandonment of and an affront to the original decisions: "The men now serving sentences for war crimes are doing so because we believed at one time that they deserved to be punished for what they did. Do we still believe this, or do we not?" The secret memo asked that John Foster Dulles discuss the matter with Secretary of Defense Wilson so that they might "put the matter before the President, in order to obtain his authorization for a proposal in which he will be interested, and which has been the subject of doubt and misunderstanding that he can properly be asked to resolve."

Above all, Auchincloss sought a clarification of America's rapidly changing war crimes policy: "We should reexamine our basic position in order to see whether we believe in what we have done, before we proceed to undo it. If we believe in it, we should stick to it, for to act against it would be cynical, if our purpose were to gain a political advantage, or weak, if our purpose were to avoid political pressure." This advice was not heeded; between 1953 and 1955, the population of Landsberg Prison was reduced from 318 to forty-one prisoners. Parole eligibility for those with life imprisonment and death sentences was cut again, from fifteen to ten years.[43]

A major crisis over war criminals erupted in November 1955 when word of the release of the infamous Malmedy convict Sepp Dietrich leaked out. Dietrich had originally been sentenced to death for his role in the Malmedy Massacre. In bending over backwards to appease the Federal Republic with his release, the United States outraged many Americans, especially veterans. On November 4, Senator Estes Kefauver described the release as a "serious error" and called for a Senate investigation of American war crimes policy.[44] Ambassador James Conant wrote the Secretary of State the same day to warn him of the implications of an investigation: "US public reaction Re [sic] Dietrich case has reached a point where it may endanger American-German relations to such a degree that I am bringing the matter to your personal attention. Any Senate investigation of this case, which would necessarily bring into question Allied policy on war criminals, could do great damage." Conant suggested that "a full message be sent to Senator Kefauver."[45]

Veterans of Foreign Wars Commander Joseph Lombardo called for an investigation: "It is the thought of this office that the reasons of the American member of the Mixed Board for voting favorably on the release of the Hitlerite Killer should be investigated and his resignation immediately forthcoming to wipe out the dishonor to the memory of our murdered comrades at Malmedy."[46] On November 28, American Legion National Commander J. Addington Wagner called for the resignation of the American board member, Edwin Plitt.

The controversy continued to swirl throughout December 1955 and into January 1956 as the State Department refused to release the details of the board's decision. On January 6, 1956, Senator Hubert Humphrey called upon Secretary of State John Foster Dulles to explain why the U.S. government had not prevented the release of Dietrich. Humphrey wrote: "Surely, few instances in military history have been more enormous in criminality than the massacre of 142 American prisoners at Malmedy by Dietrich and Peiper."[47] It was becoming increasingly clear that fine legalistic distinctions, such as that between the forgiveness inherent in clemency and the acknowledgment of guilt that preceded parole, were lost on both American and German critics. American critics were temporarily appeased on January 24, 1956, when the State Department announced that Edwin Plitt would be replaced by Senator Robert Upton of New Hampshire. The presence of a prominent jurist like Upton would help bolster the mixed board's credibility. However, the action had an opposite effect in Germany, where Edwin Plitt was highly regarded by his German colleagues.

Although the Allies had granted broad concessions to Chancellor Adenauer on the war crimes question, he was still not content. Between August 31, 1953, and August 1, 1955, the United States released eighty-two percent of the convicts in Landsberg Prison. By 1956, only forty-one "hardcore" war criminals remained. Yet prior to the German Chancellor's visit to Washington in June 1956, the State Department reported a conversation with German Foreign Minister Born, who informed them that the Chancellor wanted the United States to "speedup releases from Landsberg and (2) Relaxation conditions [sic] those now on parole."[48] Born "mentioned the shock felt German Circles when Plitt removed; thought Plitt's government should have supported him; said removal under pressure home politics had seriously undermined confidence in independence of Board."[49] It was now clear that German authorities would not rest until all war criminals in Western captivity had been released. Minister Born warned: "German authorities gravely concerned slow progress Mixed Board; at present rate problem will last many years."[50]

The mixed board considered the application of Sepp Dietrich's equally infamous comrade, Joachim Peiper, on April 16, 1956. Peiper failed to receive the unanimous vote required for parole; the vote was five to one, with the lone dissenting voice coming from the American representative, Robert Upton. In his minority recommendation, Upton wrote: "In my opinion Col. Peiper must be held primarily responsible for the violations of the laws and customs of warfare committed by his combat group. Consequently I am convinced that his release on parole at this time would be premature." Upton expressed his dissatisfaction with the mixed board's view of the parole process: "A majority of the board apparently are disposed to hold that on applications for parole by a war criminal eligible for ... parole the nature of the offense is not to be considered in determining whether ... the applicant would have been sufficiently punished."[51]

Robert Upton made it clear that the State Department's comparison between the mixed board and a traditional parole board was inaccurate: "These members hold that, if eligible for parole, a war criminal has expiated his crime. This is contrary to the procedure of Parole Boards generally." Upton observed: "In Germany the Board has come to be regarded as an instrumentality for the release of war criminals rather than an agency for the exercise of clemency or parole in deserving cases." After serving for less than four months, Senator Robert Upton announced that he would resign on June 30, 1956. In a letter to the State Department, he wrote: "I left with feelings of regret, but I would not choose to continue as a member of the Mixed Board reviewing the same cases again and again, especially as the work would lose interest for me."[52]

Robert Upton was replaced by Spencer Phenix of the State Department. In December 1956, the mixed board voted unanimously to release Joachim Peiper. As of February 1, 1957, only twenty-three prisoners remained in Landsberg Prison. On February 8, 1957, Phenix offered two plans to help speed the release of the remaining "hardcore" war criminals. Again, parole standards would be further eased. Phenix wrote State Department legal advisor John Raymond: "I should be glad if, while in Washington, I could be given an informal indication that the procedure I have suggested ... is not unacceptable per se or inconsistent with the Department's basic policies. ... I hope I can answer all your questions and that between us we can reach substantial agreement on what can and should be done to get this bothersome problem quietly out of the way where it will no longer complicate international relations."[53] By the spring of 1958, only four "ultra hardcore" prisoners, in Phenix's words, remained in Landsberg Prison.

On May 6, 1958, the State Department announced that the final four prisoners in Allied custody would be released. Three of the four men had been *Einsatzkommando* members. During their trial at Nuremberg in

1948, the prosecution had taken only two days to present its case. Martin Klinghoffer's report from the Soviet Union was typical of the evidence offered: "Nebe ordered me to go from Smolensk to Tatarsk and Mstislavl to get furs for the German troops and liquidate part of the Jews there. The Jews had already been arrested by order of Hauptsturmfuehrer Egon Noack. The executions proper were carried out by Noack under my supervision."[54] On April 14, 1948, Biberstein, Klinghofer and Ott had been sentenced to death. The Peck Panel had decided to spare their lives in their 1951 review of the *Einsatzgruppen* case. On May 9, 1958, the gates of Landsberg prison swung open one last time as they were released on parole. On May 13, 1958, Spencer Phenix reported to State Department legal advisor John Raymond: "It is only fair to say that circumstances played a more significant part than I did. In any case it is pleasant to feel that this diplomatic pebble has been removed from the State Department's shoes."[55] A few weeks later, John Raymond offered Phenix "his sincere congratulations on the very capable manner in which you have discharged an exceedingly difficult and delicate assignment."[56]

By the early 1950s, American leaders felt bridled by the weight of prior moralistic/legalistic entanglements. Was pardoning the sins of the worst sinners an amoral act? Good policy? Or simply in keeping with tradition? More than a century earlier, Bismarck had found himself in a dominant position over France. In the Chancellor's eyes, strategy and necessity overruled popular passions and morality. Asked Bismarck, "Which of the two would be more useful to us—a badly-used Napoleon, or a well-used Napoleon?"[57]

Notes

1. Moritz Busch, *Our Chancellor*, vol. 1 (New York: Scribner and Sons, 1884), 99.
2. Kurt Tauber, *Beyond the Eagle and the Swastika: German Nationalism Since 1945* (Middletown, CT: Wesleyan University Press, 1967), 26.
3. Control Council Law No. 10 was a mandate to take up where the International Military Tribunal had left off. It was intended to "give effect to the terms of the Moscow Declaration...and the London Agreement...and Charter...in order to establish a uniform legal basis in Germany for the prosecution of war criminals." The text of C.C. 10 is contained in Telford Taylor, *Final Report to the Secretary of the Army on the Nuernberg War Crimes Trials* (Washington, DC: U.S. Government Printing Office, 1949).
4. For a case-by-case breakdown see Telford Taylor, *Final Report.*
5. Robert Wolfe, ed., *Americans as Procounsels: United States Military Government in Germany and Japan, 1945–1952* (Carbondale, IL: Southern Illinois University Press, 1984), 288.

6. Lawrence Taylor, *Trial of the Generals: Homma, Yamashita, MacArthur* (South Bend, IN: Icarus Press, 1981), 163. See also Richard Lael, *The Yamashita Precedent: War Crimes and Command Responsibility* (Wilmington, DE: Scholarly Resources, 1982), 79–95. For the account of Yamashita's counsel see A. Frank Reel, *The Case of General Yamashita* (Chicago: University of Chicago Press, 1949); William Manchester, *The American Caesar* (Boston: Little and Brown, 1978), 486. General MacArthur considered the rules of evidence "obstructionist." Article 13 of General MacArthur's "Special Proclamation" stated: "The Tribunal shall not be bound by technical rules of evidence. It shall adopt and apply to the greatest possible extent expeditious and non-technical procedure, and shall admit any evidence which it deems to have probative value" (p. 137).

7. Philip Piccigallo, *The Japanese on Trial: Allied War Crimes Operation in the East 1945-1951* (Austin: University of Texas Press, 1979), 53-54. See also Taylor, *Trial of the Generals*, 168.

8. Manchester, *American Caesar*, 488. Manchester traced MacArthur's view of war back to more chivalrous times.

9. America's highest court had been conspicuously silent on the question of war crimes until Frank Reel, attorney for General Tomoyuki Yamashita, appealed to the U.S. Supreme Court for a writ of *habeas corpus*. In February 1946, the court upheld Yamashita's death sentence. The majority based their ruling on the 1942 decision in the Quirin case that authorized Congressional passage of the articles of war and sanctioned the use of military tribunals to try war criminals. This allowed the court's majority to avoid the substantive legal questions. Not all of Stone's Supreme Court brethren were willing to take such an easy way out: Justices Murphy and Rutledge issued dissenting opinions. Both dissenters were outraged by the military commission's inability "to demonstrate that Yamashita had committed or ordered the commission of war crimes" (p. 105).

10. James Weingartner, *Crossroads of Death: The Malmedy Massacre* (Berkeley: University of California Press, 1979), 95–96.

11. Thomas Schwartz, "From Occupation to Alliance," Ph.D. dissertation, Harvard University, 1985, 42. Also see Frank M. Buscher, *The U.S. War Crimes Trial Program in Germany, 1946-1955* (New York: Greenwood Press, 1989), 109. Cold War historians agree that Secretary of State James Byrnes' Stuttgart speech on September 6, 1946 "renounced the more retributive elements of JCS 1067 and began to relax the external controls of occupation." Hans A. Schmitt, ed., *The U.S. Occupation in Europe after World War II* (Lawrence, KS: Regents Press of Kansas, 1978), 93.

12. George Kennan, *Memoirs* (Boston: Atlantic Monthly Press, 1967), 260.

13. Ibid.

14. Ibid.

15. Ibid.

16. Letter from Clay to Eisenhower, July 28, 1947, *The Papers of General L.D. Clay 1945–1949*, vol. 1 (Bloomington, IN: Indiana University Press), 389–90.

17. Jean Smith, "The View from USFET: General Clay's Interpretation of Soviet Intentions in Germany, 1945–1948" in Schmitt, *U.S. Occupation in Europe*, 73.

18. Jean Edward Smith, *Lucius D. Clay: An American Life* (New York: Henry Holt, 1990), 75–76.

19. Ibid., 76.

20. Ibid.

21. Thomas H. Etzold and John Lewis Gaddis, eds., *Containment: Documents on American Policy and Strategy, 1945–1950* (New York: Columbia University Press, 1978). The Policy Planning Staff saw their objective as returning Germans to self-government: "Thirdly, we must have the courage to dispense with military government as soon as possible and to force the Germans to accept responsibility once more for their own affairs. They will never begin to do this as long as we will accept that responsibility for them" (p. 120).

22. Both quotes in Robert Conot, *Justice at Nuremberg* (New York: Carroll and Graf Publishers, 1983), 517. Langer quote dated December 18, 1949.

23. Etzold and Gaddis, *Containment*.

24. Dean Acheson to John McCloy, February 5, 1950, RG 466, U.S. High Commission for Germany, Security-Segregated General Records 1949–1952, Box 28, 321.6, War Criminals File, NA.

25. There were death sentences in the American Nuremberg trials' *Medical* case (seven), *Pohl* case (three), and the *Einsatzgruppen* case (thirteen). For a case by case breakdown, see Telford Taylor, *Final Report*, and John Alan Appleman, *Military Tribunals and International Crimes* (Westport, CT: Greenwood Press, 1971). The American courts provided a voluminous documentary record. However, due to the size of this record, the clemency review board faced an impossible physical task. See also Buscher, *U.S. War Crimes Trial Program in Germany*, 65–66.

26. Robert Bowie to John McCloy, October 31, 1950, National Archives [NA], RG 466, box 28.

27. *Landsberg: A Documentary Report* (Washington, DC: U.S. Government Printing Office, 1950) (hereinafter cited as *Landsberg Report*).

28. *Landsberg Report*, p. 5. This was the first official pronouncement of the high commissioner's decisions regarding clemency for German war criminals. The *Report* was included in the February 1951 issue of the high commissioner's "Information Bulletin." Senate Subcommittee on Armed Services, Investigation of Army Action with Respect to Trial of Persons Responsible for the Massacre of American Soldiers, Battle of the Bulge, near Malmedy, Belgium, December, 1944, p. 102. The Langer resolution read: "I have introduced Senate Resolution 39 for Congressional investigation of administration of military justice by American courts and legal representatives in

occupied countries. I trust that until this matter is reviewed you will use your influence to order further executions or hanging of condemned prisoners stopped" (*The Congressional Record*, December 18, 1949 [Washington, DC: U.S. Government Printing Office, 1950], 16708).

29. Jean Edward Smith, ed., *The Papers of General L. D. Clay, 1945-1949* (Bloomington, IN: Indiana University Press, 1978), 1012.

30. John McCloy obituary, *The New York Times*, March 12, 1989.

31. John Kenneth Galbraith, "The Sub-Imperial Style of American Foreign Policy," *Esquire Magazine* 77 (1972): 79.

32. Gottfried Hansen to General Mathew Ridgway, September 6, 1952. RG 59, LFN 57D, box 29, National Archives, College Park, MD.

33. "War Criminal Question," classified report written by various staff members of the High Commissioner's Office of Political Affairs, December 22, 1953, RG 466, NA.

34. John Auchincloss to Brewster Morris, director of the State Department Office of German Public Affairs, January 9, 1953, RG 59, box 17, NA.

35. Ibid.

36. Extract from Bonn despatch 3041, April 1, 1953, RG 59, D609, box 17, NA.

37. Ibid.

38. *The Foreign Relations of the United States: Germany and Austria 1952–1955*, (Washington, DC: U.S. Government Printing Office), 434, 442–3.

39. Ibid.

40. Ibid.

41. James Riddleberger to Secretary of State, June 15, 1953,RG 59, box 18, NA.

42. This and following Auchincloss quotes from "War Criminals" memo by John Auchincloss, March 31, 1953, RG 59, D 609, box 17, NA.

43. "Statistics on German War Criminals," June 29, 1953, RG 59 D609 box 17, NA and Colonel Howard Levie to Brigadier General George Gardes, 5 March 1956, RG 338, NA.

44. Estes Kefauver to John Foster Dulles, November 8, 1955, RG 59, box 18, NA.

45. Confidential memo from James Conant to John Foster Dulles, November 4, 1955, RG 59, box 18, NA.

46. Joseph Lombardo to Charles Wilson, November 8, 1955, RG 59 box 18, NA.

47. Enclosure to Despatch No. 1471 from American Embassy, Bonn, January 7, 1956, RG 59, D609, box 19, NA.

48. Memo from American Embassy in Bonn to the secretary of state, June 9, 1956, RG 59, D609, box 19, NA.

49. Ibid.

50. Ibid.

51. Robert Upton to John Raymond, July 30, 1956, RG 59, box 19, NA.

52. Robert Upton to John Raymond, September 7, 1956, RG 59, box 19, NA.
53. Spencer Phenix to John Raymond, February 8, 1957, RG 59, D609 box 19, NA.
54. *U.S. v. Ohlendorf* (Washington, DC: U.S. Government Printing Office, 1949), p. 558. Gustav Nosske, commander of Einsatzkommando 12, summarized his group's activities from August 12, 1942, to September 5, 1942: "The Jewish question is at present being solved in Nikolaev and Kherson. About 5000 Jews were rounded up in each town." *U.S. v. Ohlendorf*, p. 529.
55. Spencer Phenix to John Raymond, May 13, 1958, RG 59, LN59, D609, box 9, NA.
56. John Raymond to Spencer Phenix, June 23, 1958, RG 59, box 19, NA.
57. Moritz Busch, *Our Chancellor*, vol. 1 (New York: Scribner and Sons, 1884), 99.

Nuremberg and the Germans

Jörg Friedrich

Resentment

The Germans learned from posters on the street that their former leaders had been hanged at Nuremberg. In the last three months of war, more than 700,000 German soldiers and civilians had lost their lives. Now people crowded around the pillars on which the posters hung, reading in silence that ministers, field marshals and police chiefs had also died. There were no signs of remorse. In Wuppertal, schoolgirls dressed in black on the morning of the execution; in Hamburg, people whispered that the British leaders responsible for the bombing of the city also deserved to hang. Among the 43,000 who had died in the June 1943 air raid, 8,000 had been children younger than fourteen. Nearly all large and medium-sized German cities lay in ruins, charred and exploded into rubble by aerial warfare. In February 1945, in the Baltic port of Swinemünde, a hospital city, more than 20,000 sick, exhausted refugees from eastern Pomerania had been killed in bombings. German settlements in and beyond the eastern and southeastern borders had been purged, in the course of which 1.5 million people perished. In Yugoslavia, 98,000 ethnic Germans were killed or starved to death, one in five members of the population. Two million women were raped by the invading Red Army. None of this was justified by international law, nor by justice, nor by humanity. It was brute revenge.

The Germans understood this perfectly. Reprisals had been their customary method of occupation. Moreover, Nazi propaganda chief Josef Goebbels had announced that the Allied forces, if successful, would destroy the vanquished. So the public regarded the International Military Tribunal as the Allies' way of eliminating an enemy, just as trials had been used in the Third Reich. The fact that the Soviet Union, an aggressive and genocidal state, was participating in a legal proceeding strengthened this belief. The masters of the gulag would convict the masters of Auschwitz for crimes against humanity. Whatever crimes the victors had committed were justified, rationalized or conveniently deemed "irrelevant" to the present case.

The Soviet Union lived up to expectations by accusing the defendants of its own massacres—the annihilation of the Polish officers corps, carried out in part in the Belorussian forests of Katyn. The western Allies, who knew the truth from Poland's government in exile, tolerated this transference of guilt. The Soviets believed the court would simply rule as the prosecution demanded. They, too, understood justice in terms of their own legal system. Some villain had to be held responsible for the evils of the time; as they considered the trial a political act, proof was secondary.

The Soviets had argued beforehand for special laws applicable only to the Nazis. Why, then, did Justice Robert Jackson, a major architect of Nuremberg, establish a set of international laws with general authority to prosecute governmental crimes around the world? If he believed his own rhetoric, the Soviet victors would also have been placed in the dock for their attack on eastern Poland in September 1939. Moreover, the atrocities Soviet troops committed in occupying the territory had been carried out in close cooperation with SS and Gestapo officials. But indicting the Stalinist leadership would have required, as with Hitler, a forcibly obtained unconditional surrender. This was clearly infeasible, and thus, in all probability, so was Jackson's entire concept of international criminal law. Despite his consistent attempts to contain Soviet efforts to turn Nuremberg into a show trial, Germany's legal professionals contemptuously held him to be a hypocrite.

In the German legal debate, the majority of commentators criticized the trial for being exactly what the Soviet Union was trying to make it: a continuation of political warfare in judicial robes. Yet in fact, the Soviets failed in this aim. The court at Nuremberg avoided addressing the Soviet Union's counterfeit Katyn case and even acknowledged, without further examining, the German-Soviet alliance during the Polish campaign. Nevertheless, curiously, German critics ignored—and continue to ignore—some distinctive characteristics of Nuremberg, such as due process of law.[1] They glossed over the sober presentation of abundant evidence of German atrocities. Instead, they insisted Nuremberg was legally flawed, with the reservation that the major Nazis deserved what they got. In their view, the other side also deserved punishment, but escaped unscathed. The common refrain was that the verdicts depended on the military outcome. To enforce the novel Nuremberg laws, the world would have to go to war constantly; losers can be punished, winners cannot.

As law should, theoretically, apply to everyone equally, there was some logic to German resentment of the new norms of international justice. But whose justice would the losers have preferred? In 1945, any law, except Hitler's laws, would have been victors' justice. Whether by revolution or occupation, the existing legal system had to be replaced by force. If Hitler had not been vanquished from within or without, his law would have prevailed and, applied to the criminals, would have provided protection. Under its provisions, after all, their actions were justified—they were not criminals at all. Under the victorious law, however, their actions were not justified, although those laws were not valid within Germany at the time the crimes were committed, though perhaps abroad. Even there, they may have been moral standards rather than laws actually in effect, cherished in theory but not in practice.

The criminals' complaints of victors' justice essentially recognized the ephemeral nature of law. Laws came into force and were defeated, no longer providing shelter to those who had acted on the basis of those cruel orders and decrees. Alien lawyers appeared, declaring which eternal principles and international treaties should have been known, respected and followed. Hitler's orders, formerly pronounced by native judicial authorities to be the supreme source of law, became at best waste paper, at worst a criminal conspiracy.

Faced with these double standards, caught in legal schizophrenia, Germans abandoned considerations of legal guilt and asked a fundamentally emotional question: who actually deserved punishment? In the German mind, their defeat was undeserved. Germans had fought well, but were unable to stand against the entire world. The men responsible for leading them into this desperate situation deserved the worst. By thus acknowledging the need to punish the major war criminals—the defendants at the first Nuremberg trial, the International Military Tribunal (IMT)—Germans joined the winning side; together they were setting the record straight. In this view, however, any further prosecutions were undeserved, because the victims of criminals cannot be their accomplices. Yet accomplices were precisely what the Nuremberg project considered many Germans to be.

Purge

Aside from the top Nazis, certain mass organizations, such as the SS, the Gestapo and the Nazi party, also stood trial. They were convicted as criminal gangs and their members as gangsters, to be sentenced without delay. Over one million people were affected by this procedure. Like the trial program, denazification became a form of political purge that involved the entire population. Nazi supporters were sought out and subjected to a variety of punishments, including fines, confiscation of property, dismissal from public service and loss of businesses.

The third weapon for denazifying the country was social reeducation. All media were subject to censorship; the German mind was to be exorcised by "right-thinking" newspapers, books and films. The purpose of this triad of criminal justice, political purges and reeducation was the rebirth of a society freed from a leadership of convicted murderers. Those with noxious political biographies were ostracized through social discrimination, while their ideology was declared to be evil and done with.

Such legally imposed treatment had no basis in international law. The Hague rules of land warfare do not authorize an occupier to undertake any such interference in the enemy's domestic affairs. According to the Hague rules, an occupier can replace national authorities in the territory conquered during the course of hostilities; it can interfere with the existing legal system only in order to secure its military position. The western Allies took this further, detaining 300,000 people in camps for three years to prevent uprisings and partisan activities.[2] The internees were not criminal suspects; they were seized collectively as security risks, having served as mayors, Hitler Youth leaders and the like. There were no trials, no individual interrogations, no reasons given.

This exceeded military custom (except that of Hitler and Stalin), though perhaps not the letter of the Hague rules. Screening the entire population and imposing sanctions for political behavior in the years prior to the outbreak of war, however, was unprecedented. Since occupation law lacked any authorization for such policies, the Allies simply pretended they were not occupying powers. They instead declared themselves to be the German government, since the preceding government had been overthrown, sentenced, hanged or imprisoned.

The German people, left without governing authorities, were forbidden to constitute new ones. They had been spoiled by twelve years under authoritarian rule; its psychological burdens could be overcome only by another authoritarian system. This came in the guise of the Allied military government, which controlled the police, courts, prisons, traffic, information and secret services. On paper and in theory, the Nuremberg Tribunal appeared to be a pioneering use of international justice; in fact, however, it was an instrument of a successor regime that had taken power in a revolutionary coup in the form of a world war.

The purpose of the Nuremberg trials was to destroy the ruling elites, whose grip on the country had been broken once Allied tanks entered the cities. The vanquished rulers had turned out to be genuine criminals, and since criminals were inappropriate rulers, their removal legitimized the Allied seizure of power; the Allies filled the vacuum left by these former leaders. The military government offered itself as a trustee for the incapacitated Reich administration, promising to step down and allow itself to be replaced after several years of intense purging and brainwashing. Power was slowly transferred to the military government's own hand-picked trustees, who functioned first as deputies, later as officials of a sovereign power and partner.

The entire punishment, purge and reeducation program was a weapon with which Allied leaders reconstructed the country by installing new rulers, new elites and a new ideology. The establishment of a global system of international penal law was merely a pretense. No one had ever tried anything similar to the system of military rule in postwar Germany; the aim was to change not international law, but Germany's legal system. (Proof of this surfaced when the two-step transition of power in Germany was accomplished. Once power had changed hands successfully, from Hitler to the military governors and then from them to the Bonn leadership, the legacy of Nuremberg was immediately erased, as discussed below.)

The political transformation by way of war crimes trials between 1946 and 1948 succeeded on a technical level thanks to two assets that only a national authority could provide. Ninety percent of the Nuremberg evidence consisted of the Third Reich's governmental files. Conquering archives means conquering power. No government in office will hand over its foreign policy papers, military documents, police and banking records, economic figures and judicial files to an international institution. By confiscating these papers as booty, the invading army indicated it was taking over the government. According to Article 53 of the Hague regulations, an occupier may seize state property only for military purposes. But since the Allies seized the state for political purposes, its property belonged to them. Oral evidence was gathered in similar ways. Some of it was provided by victims under the protection of the military government, who were willing to risk testifying for this reason. Some testimony was drawn from former colleagues and subordinates of defendants, who were arrested and subjected to discreet pressure and therefore obeyed the authorities.

To the German public, the harsh trial and purge treatment meted out by the occupation forces was as impressive as it was reprehensible. Impressive, because it was familiar to them; their soldiers and police officers had recently ruled the continent in accordance with Hitler's motto, "brute force convinces." Reprehensible, because it was directed equally toward those whom they felt deserved it and those who did not.

Yet the transition of power was a fact; the top Nazis had lost power. Faced with ruined cities, torn families, shattered economies and pure exhaustion, people were prepared to trade their old commanders for new ones. Not since Napoleon had Germany experienced warfare on its own soil or lived under a conqueror. People were used to following leaders, not resisting them, whoever they might be. The Allies, having witnessed the German army's stubborn, if hopeless, resistance in 1945, awaited similar partisan resistance, led by Prussian colonels and fueled by tough Ruhr industrialists. But nothing of the sort materialized. Military and civilians alike had followed Hitler's orders to the very last. Having suffered tremendous losses, they lacked any disposition to fight on their own account, now that the state they had defended was gone. They were prepared to accommodate.

To deflect Allied distrust, people retroactively denazified themselves. Hitler had coerced and deceived them, they insisted. For twelve years, they had secretly undermined his policies, saving some Jews, attending churches, all with one foot in the concentration camps. Apparently, decency, democracy and peace, the ideals implanted by the occupiers, had secretly been cherished by nearly everyone under the Nazi dictatorship. Therefore, they deserved not punishment, but trust and assistance.

Elites

But the Nuremberg prosecution program marched in the opposite direction. German democrats in exile had explained to the British and Americans why the Weimar Republic of 1919–1933 had failed: the elites of the defeated empire had remained in office and conspired against democracy. The lessons of history taught that these elites must be removed once and for all. So the Americans staged a series of twelve follow-up trials at Nuremberg, going beyond the political leadership to include the military and industrial establishment, judges, doctors and high officials of the interior, justice and foreign ministries.

In their defense, these people argued that they had seemed to obey orders while secretly sabotaging them. They had trusted in Hitler's lies, misunderstanding their participation in genocide. Judges had, apparently, sentenced innocent people to death in order to assure them of judicial proceedings, though Hitler would have preferred naked killings by police. Diplomats had deported foreign Jews because they did not want the Nazis to suspect them of subversion and undermine their position in clandestine peace talks. Nazi doctors had conducted deadly experiments on camp inmates, who would have died anyway, and had thereby contributed to science and the welfare of humankind. Industrialists had used slave labor because people who work cannot be gassed. Generals had annihilated Bolsheviks to protect Christianity and civilization. Aside from the fact that they lied to the courts, those who offered such testimony demonstrated their submission to the victors' value system, exhibiting retroactive opportunism.

The Nuremberg prosecution, well supplied with documentary evidence, succeeded in refuting these nonsensical excuses and winning convictions. However, the public was not won over. In order to remove the old elites, those elites had to be detached from the social network through proof of their culpability. Yet although their guilt was proven beyond a reasonable doubt, the public simply chose not to believe it. The wedge of criminal guilt that was meant to be a wedge between the public and the defendants turned out to form a link between them.

Accommodation does not function by revealing truth, but by burying it. Like the defendants, people willing to change their minds and memories took refuge in these new lies. Those who offered these excuses shared a desire to forget what was wrong and confirm what was right. And sooner or later, Allied politicians had to agree that flexibility in the "right" direction deserved not punishment, but encouragement. It was not the consistent German lying and veiling of the past that was wrong, but the merciless attempt to unveil the fact that people had been Nazis when they desperately wished they had not been.

The first notables to lobby for these converted sinners were Catholic and Protestant clergymen. The churches had collaborated heavily with the Nazi government, though to Hitler's great displeasure; he was suspicious of any other ideology in his Reich and tried, cautiously but steadily, to limit their influence. Despite their institutions' subservience, however, many priests and bishops had been individually persecuted for their integrity. Now the military governors, eager for local partners untainted by Nazism, conferred some credibility on the compromised churches by calling them resistance movements. And in order to bolster this credibility with the public, the churches promptly offered resistance to the denazification and trial programs.

There was a strange irony in Germans lobbying for war criminals. At the time of their crimes, the Nuremberg defendants had nurtured a profound contempt for legal concerns, feelings of mercy, God's commandments and secular ethical values. They took pride in their toughness and ability to massacre the defenseless, punish the innocent, plunder the poorest and attack the harmless. They ardently overcame what might have caused hesitation in the ordinary person, because of what they saw as their special insight into the course of history, their deeper devotion to their country and their clear-cut vision of their ends. They strove for true greatness by freeing themselves from traditional customs, convictions and laws; they wished to be judged by their own laws and principles, still alien to mankind, but sure to triumph in the future.

The moment these ideologues lost and had to stand trial, however, they insisted on application of all the norms upon which they had formerly trampled. On no account did they wish to be judged by their own standards or treated according to their own methods. They insisted there be no punishment without trial and no indictment under laws not in force at the time of the crime; that only judges of spotless neutrality were acceptable; and that sanctions against political views were impermissible.

This newfound German legalism was a curious, if understandable, phenomenon. No major Nuremberg defendant would have been surprised at being stood against a wall and shot by a Jewish execution squad; that is what they expected, and it would have fulfilled Hitler's prophecies. But of course, this was not what they asked for. They fought for their lives or their freedom, a right no one can be denied. The German defendants chose legality and morality as their battleground, though they viewed legal and moral concerns as expressions of weakness. Because such concerns were their enemies' Achilles heel, however, the defense lured the Allies into a battle over their own respect for law and fair trials. Having been reeducated to adopt this view, Germans demanded the highest standards from their educators.

Defense lawyers brought the episcopate in to argue their case, and the clergy protested the trials' legal shortcomings and the undue harshness of prison conditions. The same bishops who had witnessed the murder of more than 4,000 priests and nuns by Nazi courts and kept silent about the deportation and gassing of Jewish converts[3] now felt the need to confront the occupation authorities with biblical rigor. They harangued military governors about the imperfections of war crimes tribunals, the innumerable violations of human rights and the duties of a God-fearing ruler. They complained that the Allies had used the testimonies of homosexuals and communists against the oaths of decent officers. They argued that witnesses had been influenced or threatened and that defense lawyers had been handicapped by inadequate access to files, small offices and low pay. Trials against generals and field marshals had been held under civilian judges, though military personnel should have been entitled to trial by their peers. Guilt had been proven for violating laws that had not existed before the trials began and had been unknown to the defendants. The victors had neither confessed to, nor even mentioned, their own sins during the war. Prosecutors accused citizens of following their superiors' orders instead of the guidelines of international law—a highly debatable issue. The military governors talked about reestablishing justice, but continued to play power politics, and as a result, the German people were growing desperate. Young people hoping to start a new life were disappointed. Demoralization was inevitable.

The military governors soon realized that these bishops, briefed by defense attorneys, lacked concrete knowledge of the reasons the prisoners had been sentenced in the first place. Nevertheless, the pleas of the clergy, one of the few groups virtually untainted by genocide, atrocities and persecution and surely not steeped in Nazi doctrine, could not fail to impress the wider population. The clergy's appeal for heightened legal and moral standards in the occupied zones indicated that some ground had been laid for spiritual renewal.

Two of their rebukes might even have been well-founded. First, the clergymen demanded a court of appeal, clearly a basic right, though not in military proceedings. Second, they argued an issue also considered critical by Allied commanders: a soldier's duty to obey superior orders. The Nuremberg courts had limited this duty of obedience to legal orders, much to the displeasure of the British and American armed forces. Obedience is the essence of military discipline, discipline is the flip side of command, and command is absolutely essential in warfare; the field is no place for arguments about the legality of orders. In fact, war crimes in actual combat usually involve not obedience to superior orders, but violations of military discipline and excesses in the heat of battle.

Allies

The Nuremberg sentences threatened to undermine the efficiency of the Prussian military, the model of the modern army. Most of the crimes dealt with by Nuremberg courts had been committed within the chain of command by either army or SS and police units. Convictions were generally for giving orders, not executing them. But all orders beneath the level of the commander in chief, Adolf Hitler, were suggested, encouraged or approved by him. The chain of command must be unbreakable, and it relies on mutuality. The commander, expecting obedience to his orders, obeys the commander in chief. If discipline toward Hitler had broken down, it would have broken down all along the line.

Thus by punishing the iron discipline of German soldiers, the preeminent fighters in World War II, Nuremberg set a precedent that was unlikely to be respected by the military leadership of any country. As it is unwise to establish legal principles that nobody will follow, Allied leaders saw a need to review the Nuremberg sentences. So a variety of political visitors, American congressional delegations and military government commissioners set out to investigate the treatment of what had been branded as criminal, inexcusable and unforgivable.

Meanwhile, while the legal issues surrounding total warfare were restricted to Nazi brutalities at the 1946 trial, the 1948 proceedings against the German high command and leadership of the Russian campaign took place during the Soviet blockade of Berlin. The judges correctly applied the norms that had been developed over the previous two years, but the sense that they were anachronistic grew day by day. In 1947, the Soviets had succeeded in overthrowing the Czechoslovak Republic. They had inherited Hitler's empire in central and southeast Europe, and with the help of Hitler's scientists, had tested the atomic bomb. If they managed to conquer Hitler's possessions in the western and northern part of the continent, the same power bloc would emerge that the Führer had narrowly missed.

European nations could not and would not defend themselves. They had failed miserably in the fight against Hitler and were divided and undermined from within by strong communist factions, just as fascist factions had demoralized resistance in 1940. All Europe's political instincts leaned toward neutrality and collaboration. Even had this not been the case, they had been ruined and plundered during the German occupation and could not have fought the highly trained, well-equipped and spirited battalions of the Red Army.

In 1949, the communists took over China; Chiang Kai Chek's corrupt forces were unable to defend the nation. In June 1950, communist North Korea invaded the southern half of the country. Stalin, marching his puppets, crossed the global dividing lines drawn at the Yalta conference. Once again, a shrewd aggressor was assembling an empire because of the lack of both will and decisive force to confront and deter him.

In interpreting their situation, the United Kingdom and the United States could not but be reminded of the political pattern that had prevailed in Europe between 1938 and 1941. Hitler had rolled across the continent with the backing of Soviet friendship and supplies. The defenders of democracy had failed because they would not recruit Stalin as an ally. He would certainly have been a strange bedfellow, after annihilating more than five million of his countrymen in 1939 and enslaving twelve million more in the gulags; but when Churchill, after Germany's surprise attack on Russia, brought Stalin into the anti-Hitler alliance, he said that he would march with the devil to fight National Socialism. In retrospect, it must also be said that no one but the devil of the Kremlin could have worn down the tremendous fighting machine that was the German army. What democracy in the world would sacrifice fifty million lives to drive back an invader?

The decision to be made in 1950 was the same as the one that should have been taken in 1939, was actually made in 1941, and ultimately succeeded in 1945. This time, the devilish fighting forces of the Wehrmacht were necessary to contain the Red Empire. There was no other alternative. Had the West abstained from cooperating with Germany, the East would undoubtedly have invited all of Germany to join it. The Soviets had already recruited Hitler's chemists and bacteriologists for arms development, men wanted by the Americans for their participation in deadly human experiments. They were now militarily important precisely because of their unique knowledge.

German reunification, which would have required a neutral stance toward the Soviet Union on Germany's part, was considered by most German patriots to be a national duty. West German support for an anti-Soviet alliance might be the cornerstone of European defense policy, but it would be fatal to national unity.

The German people were tired of war, strategies, politics, friends and foes. They were eager to restore home, family, business and the joys of life.

Though some U.S. analysts opined that Germans longed for nothing so much as to don a uniform and march eastward seeking revenge, this was not true. The existing situation, however, reassured them in a different way; they were no longer the scum of the earth, the objects of penalties, purges and reeducation by unyielding benefactors. By 1950, Germans were needed and respected for their soldiering, and they now had a response to allegations of political immaturity. They had been the first to recognize the Soviet threat; now the West, too, had caught up to the point at which, in 1941, the German army had begun defending Christian civilization.

The preventive attack for which defendants had been executed at Nuremberg was now recommended by U.S. strategists on a daily basis. The stern response to Bolshevik partisan tactics for which Wehrmacht generals had been convicted by the Allies was actually copied by U.S. generals in the Korean jungle. What civilian lawyers in the Nuremberg courtrooms had deemed war crimes proved to be appropriate counter-measures. Only German officers, unsuccessful earlier because of U.S. support for Stalin, could judge how to confront Soviet-style warfare. With their credibility enormously improved, Germans fought the Nuremberg sentences, calling them undeserved, unjust and illegal. In fact, it did not matter; they had become irrelevant.

Failure

The Nuremberg trials had originally served to weaken, embarrass and delegitimize a vanquished but still vigorous enemy. There had been no further political use for the German Reich. For security reasons, it had to be incapacitated and placed under surveillance. But now—also for security reasons—it had to be cast in an opposite role. The defense of freedom no longer required Germany's legal consciousness and moral remorse, but its old vigor, fighting expertise, innovative science, artful weapons design and dynamic industry. All these virtues, which had served Hitler against the world for half a decade, had to be mobilized to contain Stalin, his rival and spitting image.

This was a risky maneuver. Political allies had been exchanged; social elites had to be rehabilitated for reuse. They were kept in check by their leaders, now sworn democrats, who had been installed by military governors and had enjoyed semiautonomy since 1949. But no military strategy could survive as long as those groups whose utter loyalty was required were kept under constant and hostile surveillance. No Atlantic or European defense alliance would rely on the staffing and training of officers whose former commanders were serving criminal sentences in their new partner's jails. They could not be allies and prison guards at the same time. There was no choice but to pardon and integrate the convicted.

This in itself, however, was not out of keeping with the common practice of criminal justice. Clemency is a normal part of legal systems, following legally recognized judgments. Prisoners convicted by the Nuremberg and other war crimes tribunals were constantly being pardoned by the Allied powers, their sentences commuted, their properties restored. Accompanied by waves of public cheers and tears, cannon king and slaveholder Alfried Krupp went free in 1950.

Five death sentences, however, were upheld and had to be carried out. They involved members of SS units who had slaughtered tens of thousands of Jews. This, admittedly, had nothing to do with fighting communism. Nevertheless, German political and church leaders, columnists and veterans joined together to save their countrymen. Here and there, it was mentioned that bloody crimes had been committed and punishment merited, but as the convictions dated back years and the German constitution forbade the death penalty, the protesters regarded executions as immoral and a threat to partnership. Yet the time lag between sentence and execution had been caused by constant German pleas for review and delay, and at the time of the Nuremberg trials there had been no German constitution.

Germans attempted to block the legal consequences of the trials through superior reasoning, by casting doubt on the evidence, by appealing to human rights and by objecting to the shortcomings of the trial; by criticizing their hypocrisy and questioning their political usefulness, praising the virtue of forgiveness, invoking the final judgment of God and recommending that a better path to perfect justice lay in refraining from enforcement.

The Americans nevertheless executed the mass executioners in June 1951. This, however, was their final pièce de résistance. The uproar over the hanging of these bloodstained—and publicly despised—butchers underlined Nuremberg's failure. Law is something that must be generally acknowledged, but after five years of reeducation, Germans refused to make any practical distinction between the treatment of those who deserved and those who did not deserve punishment. The distinction they did make was purely theoretical, allowing them to argue that those who had been punished by no means deserved it. Thus the public called not for clemency and reintegration, but for amnesty and rehabilitation.

U.S. foreign policy experts[4] recognized that Germans had never accepted the legal basis of the tribunals; they were highly emotional on the issue and immune to arguments or empirical evidence. Germans strongly believed that war criminals were soldiers convicted for doing their duty, that they had been illegally detained as prisoners of war, and that they could only be freed through a show of solidarity. The government paid their lawyers and sustained their families, priests held masses and rang church bells for them, and veterans vowed never to pick up a rifle as long as comrades remained in jail.

Konrad Adenauer, who became the first postwar German chancellor in 1949, was far ahead of his people in his willingness to offer rearmament in exchange for complete national sovereignty. They are natural twins; a nation that defends itself belongs to itself. The Allies saw this in much the same way, with the caveat that the Federal Republic had to join the Western defense alliance. This accorded with Adenauer's wishes; he was, after all, an inveterate Rhinelander, with some reservations about the Prussian military and its traditional hegemony over the German states.

The German public, especially after the outbreak of the Korean war, feared an attack by the Red Army at the Elbe River demarcation line. To prevent this, western Germany could either be fortified as an outpost of the Western world or neutralized to appease the Soviet Union. There was widespread fear among the socialist opposition, and even here and there in the governing coalition itself, that German military genius joined with American capabilities might panic Stalin into a preemptive strike on the country. Adenauer had only a tiny majority, if any, for his western course. The United Kingdom and the United States knew that this 74-year-old man was their one true asset. He had to be backed by any means necessary.

Surrender

Preparatory talks on handing over sovereignty to the Federal Republic began in May 1951. The most contentious point, the war criminals, was initially kept to one side, as the Americans, British and French agreed with Germany on most basic issues. In gaining full control of the country, the Germans would also take over the prisons. Three of them— Landsberg, Werl and Wittlich—held war criminals, approximately 1,300 people.

John McCloy, the U.S. high commissioner, saw four possible ways of handling the issue, each one worse than the last. The first was to transport the prisoners to Allied countries, which would raise a huge outcry in Germany. As a second option, they could be imprisoned in Germany under the supervision of neutral powers. But this would reward those countries that had done nothing to overthrow Hitler. Moreover, neutrals would prefer to remain neutral rather than interfere in such delicate matters. Third, the Allies could reserve authority over war criminals in Germany, thus making a mockery of German sovereignty; fourth, prisoners could all be handed over to the Federal Republic, which would instantly set them free. German lawyers and lobbyists for the criminals campaigned for this latter plan, which would transfer the right of clemency to the president of the German republic. He would then pardon the war criminals one by one, which would amount to an amnesty. A last resort was a mixed clemency board of former victors and vanquished under a neutral chairman whose vote would be decisive. Germans knew from experience that they could rely on the neutral Swiss or Swedes.

Parliamentary spokesmen for the officers' corps announced a clear-cut ultimatum: either the West declared an amnesty, or no treaty or alliance was negotiable. On one point, all Germans were unanimous: under no circumstances would the Nuremberg judgments be recognized as valid legal acts. This position had been maintained since 1946 and would not be sacrificed now.

In December 1951, Adenauer paid his first state visit to the United Kingdom, where Winston Churchill, Nazi Germany's most steadfast adversary, had just been reelected prime minister. British Foreign Office analysts had already drawn the line; the Federal Republic had to be treated more favorably than Japan. Under Article 11 of the peace treaty with Japan in September 1951, that country had agreed to recognize the validity of the Tokyo war crimes trials and enforce prison sentences for those in its custody. However, Germany was in a completely different situation. It was expected to contribute troops to an alliance army, providing Bonn with a formidable bargaining chip.

On December 4, Churchill proposed a handover of imprisoned war criminals to the Germans. He assured Adenauer that Germany, unlike Japan, need not recognize the validity of their sentences. The release procedure could be handled by a mixed clemency board under a neutral presidency. Churchill had never advocated war crimes tribunals, confidentially joking that in case of Allied defeat, he certainly would have been hanged for his aerial bombardments. As the role of the devil passed from Hitler to Time Magazine's 1943 Man of the Year, "Uncle Joe" Stalin, the foolish discrimination against Nazi generals weakened the West's already shaky defensive position in Europe.

Returning to Bonn, Adenauer informed McCloy on December 21 of Britain's generous offer. He insisted to the high commissioner that invalidating the judgments was of major importance. McCloy, astute lawyer that he was, noted that the chancellor had not recognized the significance of accepting custody of the prisoners. He was apparently prepared to do so without realizing that enforcing a sentence implied accepting its validity.

That problem, however, had already been debated by Bonn's legal experts in July 1951. They found themselves on the horns of a nasty dilemma. Germany could either imprison its generals itself in order to gain control over their pardon and release, in the process automatically acknowledging the verdicts' validity; or it could renounce its right to carry out the sentences as well as this acknowledgment, thus losing leverage for an amnesty. The administration decided in favor of custody of the prisoners. If the neutral president of a clemency board would provide for quick releases, forfeiture of the German legal position had to be swallowed. What does the validity of a judgment matter if its enforcement is annulled?

The Allies had changed policy dramatically since the end of the war. The fearsome German army had to be revived and certain trouble spots in the free world needed to be pacified. What had to be concealed, however, was the wreckage of the old policy. Hitler's evil empire had been defeated and punished with armies of the dead. As Nuremberg prosecutor Telford Taylor put it in 1945, the validity of their sacrifice was linked with the validity of Nuremberg. War had been waged to protect countries from unspeakable crimes. If war crimes convictions were invalid, these crimes had not been crimes.

When former enemies become friends, when criminals serve their sentences and start anew, it is moving. It is quite a different spectacle when criminals maintain they have never been criminals, shake off the injustice done to them, pardon their prosecutors and march off with them, hand in hand.

The Allies tried to hide the more squalid dimensions of this spectacle. In February 1952, they proposed an article on war crimes as an annex to the Paris treaties that would end occupation law and introduce military partnership. This article contained three main provisions: first, a mixed clemency board would be established to review sentences, but with no authority to question their validity. This, however, sounded like something it was not, serving to protect Allied sensibilities. It did not make a difference to the German government whether some board could or could not raise questions. The second provision empowered Germany to take custody of war criminals, which they were prepared to do. Churchill had not succeeded in achieving a neutral presidency with a deciding vote for the clemency board: under the third provision, it could order clemency only by unanimous vote. Adenauer agreed to this.

Back in Bonn, Adenauer met with stiff resistance from bureaucrats, parliamentarians, coalition partners and veterans. They would never stoop to helping carry out the victors' revenge. The German public had heretofore regarded the sentences as captivity. Locked up in native jails, however, the convicts would appear to be ordinary criminals. Germans had endured a great deal of humiliation; such is the nature of defeat. But they would not humiliate themselves. No government dependent on elections could steer a course against these emotions.

In the turmoil, something happened that Adenauer had long awaited. On March 10, 1952, Stalin fired off his tempting offer. To keep the Federal Republic out of the Western alliance, he proposed German unification after free elections and deployment of a national army. There was one restriction: Germany had to remain neutral toward East and West.

The political class was electrified. Whether Stalin was serious about national unity remained to be explored, but chaining Germany to the Western bloc seemed unwise in such a flattering situation. Both factions of the former enemy were now rivals for the hand of a resurrected Germany, and the stakes had to be raised.

Adenauer saw his majority to ratify the Paris treaties in parliament melting away. On April 28, he told McCloy that anything that might offend German patriots in the signed package should be deleted. The worst offense of all was the acceptance of the validity of the Nuremberg verdicts implicit in handing over their enforcement to Germans; German critics preferred to curtail the country's sovereignty by tolerating Allied penitentiaries on German soil. As a result, Section 11 was added to the war criminals article, Article 6, of the Convention on the Settlement of Matters Arising Out of the War and the Occupation, one of the series of treaties reestablishing German sovereignty. In it—quietly, discreetly, and by mutual consent, in barely comprehensible wording, virtually screened off from the eyes of the world—Nuremberg was surrendered. Because of "matters arising out of the war and [seven years of] occupation," policies had to be changed and justice sacrificed. Under the settlement in Section 11, none of the war crimes convictions were deemed valid.[5] This nonvalidity applies only in Germany, of course. But it is against the criminal that law must be enforced—and that duty was abandoned.

Because of Franco-German differences, ratification of the Paris treaties was delayed until 1955. In three years, the last of the Western Allies' prisoners had been pardoned by the mixed clemency board. The surviving defendants convicted by the International Military Tribunal, the first Nuremberg trial of Hermann Goering et al.—those who, in German eyes, deserved what they got—were jailed in Berlin's Spandau prison, under four-power administration, with Soviet participation. Some of them were released because of ill health, but none for political reasons. The German government denied the legal validity of their punishments as well. Today, they have no criminal records in Germany.

Documents

1. **Convention on the Settlement of Matters Arising Out of the War and the Occupation, formulated in May 1952, signed at the Paris Conference in October 1954, went into force in 1955 (note the exception in Article 6 (11)—emphasis added):**

ARTICLE 6

(1) There is hereby established a Mixed Board (referred to in this Article as "the Board"). The task of the Board will be, without calling into question the validity of the convictions, to make recommendations for the termination or reduction of sentences, or for parole, in respect of persons convicted by a tribunal of an Allied Power of crimes against humanity or against the law and usages of war or of crimes committed during the war, commonly referred to as "war crimes," and confined by the Three Powers in prisons in the Federal Republic on the entry into force of the present Convention.

(2) The Board shall consist of six members, of whom one shall be appointed by the Government of each of the Three Powers and three by the Federal Government. The members of the Board shall be independent persons not exercising other official functions except as a judge or university teacher and not subject to instructions of the appointing Governments in formulating their recommendations. No person may be appointed who has participated in any manner in any war crimes trial....

(11) *The provisions of Article 7 of this Chapter shall not apply to the matters dealt with in this Article.*

ARTICLE 7

(1) All judgments and decisions in criminal matters heretofore or hereafter rendered in Germany by any tribunal or judicial authority of the Three Powers or any of them shall remain final and valid for all purposes under German law and shall be treated as such by German courts and authorities....

2. **Annex 4 to Drucksache no. 3500 of German Bundestag, first electoral period *(I. Wahlperiode), Begründung zum Vertrag über die Beziehungen zwischen der Bundesrepublik Deutschland und den Drei Mächten,* commenting upon the above Convention during the parliamentary ratification process, sentences 1-3 *(the article of the German constitution mentioned in this excerpt, Article 103, deals with prohibition of retroactive laws and punishments)*:**

...ART. 6

The attempt in Art. 6 to resolve the so-called "war criminals issue" aims to resolve, within the framework of what is politically attainable, an issue that has strained relations between the Federal Republic and the Powers, or at least to moderate its weight. The treaty arrangement has been formulated so thoroughly, due to its political significance, that it hardly needs additional explanation.

It was not possible, especially taking account of the provisions of Art. 103 of the constitution, for the Federal Republic to recognize the judgments by taking over their enforcement. . . .

3. **Article 7 of the [European] Convention for the Protection of Human Rights and Fundamental Freedoms, 213 U.N.T.S. 222, which entered into force September 3, 1953. The Convention was ratified by Bonn in December 1952, with the exception of Article 7 (2)** *(this exception was necessary in order to justify Bonn's refusal to execute the judgments, as set out above)*:

ART. 7

1. No one shall be held guilty of any criminal offense on account of any act or omission which did not constitute a criminal offense under national or international law at the time when it was committed. Nor shall a heavier penalty be imposed than the one that was applicable at the time the criminal offense was committed.

2. This Article shall not prejudice the trial and punishment of any person for any act or omission which, at the time when it was committed, was criminal according to the general principles of law recognized by civilized nations.

4. **Excerpts from two decisions by the highest German appeals court, the BGH, interpreting the meaning of Articles 6 and 7 of the Convention on the Settlement of Matters Arising Out of the War and the Occupation:**

(Decision of January 16, 1959) . . . the Federal Republic did not want to recognize the judgments on crimes against humanity and war crimes because it had legal reservations about the way in which some of these judgments had come about and because of the substantive law upon which they were based. . . .

(Decision of September 9, 1958) . . . Art. 7 (1) provides that "All judgments and decisions in criminal matters heretofore or hereafter rendered in Germany by any tribunal or judicial authority of the Three Powers or any of them shall remain final and valid for all purposes under German law and shall be treated as such by German courts and authorities."

However, this recognition by the Federal Republic did not apply to decisions of occupation courts through which sentences were imposed for crimes against humanity or war crimes. This follows from Art. 6 (11): "The provisions of Article 7 of this Chapter shall not apply to the matters dealt with in this Article."

The expression "matters" ("matters" in the English text, "questions" in the French) does not refer, as the trial court, the federal prosecutor, and the Schleswig Appeals Court... believe, only to details of the enforcement of occupation sentences for crimes against humanity or war crimes and the creation and operation of the Mixed Board. Rather, the judgments themselves are excepted from the recognition supplied by Art. 7 (1)...

This interpretation, which is at least not contradicted by the wording of Art. 6 (11), arises from the fact that Articles 6 and 7 contain a compromise between the three former Western occupation powers and the Federal Republic.... Essentially, both sides were interested in the lasting effectiveness of occupation judgments and their continued enforcement...

However, judgments for crimes against humanity and war crimes formed a special group. There were reservations against them on the German side, mainly because of the way in which many of them had come about and because of the substantive law on which they were based. This was Control Council Law No. 10, which German courts had already ceased to apply since Decree No. 234 of August 31, 1951..., which was enacted at German instigation. For all these reasons, the Federal Republic was not prepared to recognize these judgments as effective under German law. On the other hand, the former occupying powers did not refrain from executing them. They thus retained their responsibility for this. The Federal Republic had to accept this. It was able to assure German influence only on the practice of clemency in the Mixed Board, which, however, under Art. 6 (1)(2), could not question the validity of the judgments. This restriction in itself indicates that the Federal Republic did not want to recognize the judgments themselves and, as expressed in Section 11 of the same Article, in fact did not recognize them.

Notes

1. On the legal debate at the time, see generally Hans-Heinrich Jescheck, *Die Verantwortlichkeit der Staatsorgane im Völkerstrafrecht* (Bonn: 1952); August von Knieriem, *Nürnberg, Rechtliche und Moralische Probleme* (Stuttgart: E. Klett, 1953); Wilhelm G. Grewe, "Nürnberg als Rechtsfrage (1947)," in Wilhelm G. Grewe, *Machtprojektionen und Rechtsschranken. Essays aus vier Jahrzehnten über Verfassung politischer Systeme und internationale Strukturen* (Baden-Baden: 1991).

2. See generally Lutz Niethammer, *Die Mitlauferfabrik: die Entnazifizierung am Beispiel Bayerns* (Berlin: Dietz, 1982); Clemens Vollnhals, *Entnazifizierung, Politische Säuberung und Rehabilitierung in den Vier Besatzungszonen 1945-49* (Munich: Deutscher Taschenbuch Verlag, 1991); Heiner Wember, *Umerziehung im Lager: Internierung und Bestrafung von Nationalsozialisten in der britischen Besatzungszone Deutschlands* (Essen 1991).

3. On the role of the churches in the Third Reich, see generally R. P. Ericksen, *Theologians under Hitler: Gerhard Kittel, Paul Althaus and Emanuel Hirsch* (New Haven: Yale University Press, 1985); Wolfgang Gerlach, *Als die Zeugen schwiegen: Bekennende Kirche und die Juden* (Berlin 1987); Georg Denzler and Volker Fabricius, *Christen und Nationalsozialisten: Darstellung und Dokumente* (Frankfurt/Main: Fischer Taschenbuchverlag, 1993).

4. For some of the reactions of American policymakers at the time, see Peter Maguire, "Nuremberg: A Cold War Conflict of Interest," in this volume.

5. The legal technique employed in the convention to circumvent the judgments, the explanation supplied by the German government during the parliamentary ratification process, and confirmation of the sense and meaning of Articles 6 and 7 by the Federal Supreme Court of Appeals (the *Bundesgerichtshof* or BGH), are found in the documents at the end of this chapter.

A Half Century of Silence:
The Politics of Law[1]

Diane F. Orentlicher

Introduction

The title of the panel at which I first presented these remarks—"A Half Century of Silence: The Politics of Law"—seemed to be freighted with implied claims. Its key premise was that political factors, above all, account for the world's failure to convene an international tribunal for world-class criminals in the half-century following Nuremberg. My aim in this essay is twofold: first, to explore the political dynamics that prevented international prosecutions of war crimes for almost fifty years; and second, to assess the prospects for such an enterprise in the closing years of the twentieth century.

The timeliness of these issues speaks for itself: with the recent establishment of two United Nations tribunals to prosecute war crimes committed in Bosnia-Herzegovina and Rwanda, international society has, for the first time since the postwar years, shown itself willing to bring to justice those responsible for monstrous crimes. Both the crimes that can be prosecuted before the two tribunals and the United Nations' action in creating them are timely in a larger sense as well: they are emblematic of a singular moment in post-Nuremberg history—the end of the Cold War. One of the hallmarks of this period has been an explosion of ethnic violence, at times entailing crimes against humanity. In the vacuum left by communism's collapse, ethnic mobilization has at times inflated to perilous, even lethal proportions. At the same time, the end of the Cold War also opened the way to superpower cooperation to establish tribunals that can punish epic crimes.

Law and Politics

Since I will be addressing the interplay between law and politics, it may be useful at the outset to make explicit several claims concerning the nature of that relationship. First, although law and politics are commonly seen as the antithesis of each other, at one level the judicial process is, in Judith Shklar's words, "just one form of political action."[2] Shklar was, of course, using the term "political" in a broad sense. So, too, was Otto Kirchheimer when he wrote, "Something is called political if it is thought to relate in a particularly intensive way to the interests of the community."[3] To the extent that trials confirm and enforce core community values, they are political in a sense that is, far from the antithesis of justice, indispensable to public perceptions that justice has been rendered.

But if law by its nature reflects and confirms the deepest values of political community, some forms of politicization of legal process are anathema to common conceptions of justice. Shklar captures "the real horror" of political justice when she writes of "the politics of persecution which political trials serve...."[4] Kirchheimer similarly regarded the use of courts to eliminate a political adversary as a classic paradigm of "political justice," especially when the outcome of such trials is predetermined.[5]

The inverse of that paradigm—a government's *failure* to bring to justice those deserving punishment for reasons relating to their political power—is, it hardly needs to be said, another pernicious form of political justice. It is this paradigm that is especially pertinent to the subject of my remarks.

In sum, then, community perceptions of justice are scarcely offended by trials that are political in the sense that they express, affirm and reinforce core social values. On the contrary, impunity for crimes that breach core values of community conscience is a demonstrable failure of justice. In contrast, justice is surely subverted when trials are used to persecute political enemies or when their principal or ostensible aim is to consolidate a shift of power between political rivals.

The Politics of Nuremberg

Viewed in light of these distinctions, the Nuremberg trial was political in rather complex ways. The censure captured in the phrase "victors' justice" derives in large measure from the Allies' resolve to sanction only the defeated nation's crimes, leaving their own possible war crimes beyond the reach of universal law.

But if its one-sided nature is at the root of the claim that Nuremberg embodied "victors' justice," the critique may have drawn additional force from the Allies' prosecution of some defendants on the charge of crimes against peace. However deserving of punishment, the crime of aggression—which was scarcely well established in international law at the time of Nuremberg—seemed redolent of political calculations and power politics. Prosecution of this crime was therefore peculiarly likely to invite charges that the Allies used Nuremberg as a vehicle for confirming their conquest of a political enemy.

In contrast, the Allies' prosecution of German officials for crimes against humanity, in Otto Kirchheimer's words, "defined where the realm of politics ends or, rather"—Kirchheimer catches himself here—"is transformed into the concerns of the human condition...."[6] Prosecution of crimes against humanity at Nuremberg was thus a deeply principled instance of political justice; it confirmed the most profound values of political community.

Through Nuremberg, then, we can find a morally nuanced understanding of political justice: prosecution of those who commit crimes against universal conscience is a legitimate—indeed, morally *necessary*—form of political justice. When, however, trials are tainted by the perception—justified or not—that they are a device for confirming the defeat of a political adversary, they are liable to be faulted as "political justice." By equal measure, when relations of power between international society and those who escape judgment account for failure to prosecute epic crimes, the resulting impunity embodies another pernicious form of political justice—or, more accurately, a politically driven failure of justice.

The Politics of Silence

By common wisdom, the impunity that so often has been enjoyed by individuals responsible for monstrous crimes has been a function of precisely this brand of power politics. Khmer Rouge leaders responsible for at least one and a half million deaths during their murderous reign in Cambodia, for example, are widely believed to have escaped prosecution by virtue of their patronage by China, as well as the fact that they were the proverbial enemy of the enemy (Vietnam) of the leading superpower.

In a complicated way, Nuremberg itself might have contributed to states' longstanding reticence to bring to justice those responsible for universal crimes. By linking prosecution of crimes against peace—crimes that, however deserving of punishment, could not have been prosecuted but for Germany's military defeat—with prosecution of crimes against humanity, Nuremberg may have helped forge a lasting association between punishment even of the latter with the notion of vanquishing political enemies. After Nuremberg, transnational efforts to bring delinquent officials to book would be even more likely than before to be construed as hostile action; a measure of political enmity. Even so, as I will argue shortly, the Allies' defeat of Hitler on the battlefields of Europe, far from diminishing their moral authority to punish Nazis for offenses against the laws of humanity, bolstered their standing to do so.

A second component of the standard account of international society's acquiescence in massive crimes is that the alternative—bringing criminals to the bar of justice—would radically diminish time-honored prerogatives of state sovereignty. Time and again, states contemplating initiatives that might result in prosecutions before a global court have been brought up short by the prospect of the resulting precedent—one that would entail yet another incursion into the jealously guarded province of state sovereignty. Nor would major powers trust the authority of a global prosecutor as long as the Cold War endured.

While these standard accounts are persuasive, there is also a deeper explanation—one that helps explain the international community's failure to intervene to stop genocide in Bosnia and Rwanda as well as its general reluctance to establish international institutions of criminal law enforcement. It has to do with the responsibility that the concept of crimes against humanity engages—a responsibility from which most are inclined to shrink. Hannah Arendt captured the point when she wrote that people instinctively feel that

> the idea of humanity . . . implies the obligation of a general responsibility . . . . For the idea of humanity, when purged of all sentimentality, has the very serious consequence that in one form or another men must assume responsibility for all crimes committed by men and that all nations share the onus of evil committed by all others.[7]

That the world shrank from assuming responsibility for the onus of evil committed in Bosnia, and then Rwanda, remains one of the signal failures of our time. Among its costs have been a hollowing out of our own morality and a betrayal of those who believed that the vow "Never Again"— a vow enacted into international law and inscribed on the conscience of mankind—meant that the world would not stand by in the face of genocide. I believe that that failure has also had an insidious effect on public support for the work of the two tribunals created to punish crimes that the world lacked the resolve to stop—and, as I will elaborate, has ironically induced a certain nostalgia for "victors' justice."

When the United Nations established the International Criminal Tribunal for the former Yugoslavia, supporters of the tribunal hailed the fact that the context surrounding its creation—those most liable to prosecution held the upper hand in what was still an ongoing conflict—meant that this time the international community had escaped Nuremberg's taint of victors' justice. Yet an unacknowledged sense of nostalgia for victors' justice seems to pervade discussions of the tribunal's merit and prospects. This ambivalent attitude lies just beneath the surface of the oft-stated view that prosecutions before the Hague Tribunal are a poor substitute for more forceful action by the international community to stop "ethnic cleansing" in Bosnia. This assertion plainly reflects a sense of unease about the international community's standing to prosecute crimes it did not undertake to suppress. By what moral authority do we judge those whom we judged it beyond our interest to stop when they were practicing genocide, gruesomely portrayed in the daily media?

In contrast, the Allies' defeat of Hitler on the battlefields, far from diminishing the legitimacy of their prosecution of German leaders for war crimes, helped clothe them with the moral authority to do so. Reconsidered through a contemporary lens—one whose moral focus has been sharpened by the world's failure to respond adequately to the epic crimes of "ethnic cleansers"—the victors' justice of Nuremberg takes on a new cast.

The daunting challenges confronting the Hague Tribunal are rendered more complex still by the inherent paradox surrounding its creation: It is at once the most ambitious global effort since Nuremberg and Tokyo to subordinate lawless power to the rule of international law and to moral principle, and yet, at the same time, it is a project instituted by states that stunningly failed in other respects to arrest the behavior they now claim authority to judge. For three and a half years, the United Nations Security Council produced scores of resolutions on the conflict that raged across Bosnia. Many of these resolutions seemed to inscribe new principles of moral responsibility into international law, affirming the right of states to intervene on behalf of imperiled civilians. Yet, throughout that same period, the daily headlines told a much different story, one of a colossal failure of will to enforce those principles.

But if past failures somehow diminish the authority of the Hague Tribunal, they also make its work all the more imperative; perhaps redemptive in the sense evoked by Justice Robert Jackson in his closing argument at Nuremberg: "Goaded," he said, by the barbaric facts that were the subject of the Allies' prosecution, "we were moved to redress the blight on the record of our era."[8] His words echo across generations, exhorting us not to let past failures in respect of Bosnia and Rwanda diminish our will to bring to justice those who were responsible for the grand evil those nations endured.

Beyond the moral challenges bound up in the work of the Yugoslavia and Rwanda tribunals, eminently practical obstacles to their effective operation have contributed to the new nostalgia for victors' justice. Among other things, the Allies' victor status enabled them to gain ready custody of most of the men whom they sought to prosecute, as well as vast amounts of incriminating documents. In contrast, among the most difficult challenges confronting the Yugoslavia Tribunal have been gaining physical custody of indicted suspects and obtaining evidence against them. Yet its failure to prosecute the chief authors of "ethnic cleansing" would tarnish the tribunal's authority, transforming it into a universal symbol of "political justice" in the most pernicious sense of the term.

Far more than symbolism is at stake in the tribunal's ability to meet these challenges. As David Rieff has observed, where genocide used to be exceptional, it may now be emerging as the paradigmatic means of waging war in the post-Cold War period[9]—a period in which the vast majority of conflicts are not wars between states, but wars within states. Those wars, as the daily headlines attest, are increasingly waged, with unfettered savagery, along ethnic lines

In this setting, the cost of failure is unbearable. To paraphrase Sir Hartley Shawcross in his closing argument at Nuremberg: "And in their graves, crying out, not for vengeance but *that this shall not happen again:* hundreds of thousands who might be living in peace and happiness at this hour... civilians killed in battles that ought never to have been."[10]

Notes

1. A version of this chapter was originally presented on April 2, 1995, at a conference on "Judgments on Nuremberg: The Past Half Century and Beyond" at Boston College.
2. Judith N. Shklar, *Legalism: Law, Morals, and Political Trials* (Cambridge, MA: Harvard University Press, 1986), 143.
3. Otto Kirchheimer, *Political Justice* (Princeton, NJ: Princeton University Press, 1961), 25.
4. Shklar, p.145.
5. See generally Kirchheimer, pp. 46–47, 49–50.
6. Ibid., p. 341.
7. Hannah Arendt, "Organized Guilt and Universal Responsibility," in Larry May & Stacey Hoffman, eds., *Collective Responsibility: Five Decades of Debate in Theoretical and Applied Ethics* (Savage, MD: Rowman & Littlefield, 1991), 282.
8. *Trial of the Major War Criminals Before the International Military Tribunal at Nuremberg*, Vol. XIX, Proceedings 19–29 July 1946 (Nuremberg: The Tribunal, 1948), 398.
9. See David Rieff, "The Rwanda Crisis: History of a Genocide," *The New Republic*, January 29, 1996.
10. *Trial of the Major War Criminals Before the International Military Tribunal at Nuremberg*, XIX, Proceedings 19–29 July 1946, 433 (Emphasis added).

PART II

The Legacy:
The International Community
Confronts War Crimes

Introduction

Faced with "ethnic cleansing" and genocide in former Yugoslavia and Rwanda, the United Nations Security Council decided in 1993 and 1994 to establish international tribunals to prosecute those responsible. Neither tribunal has been uncontroversial. Both courts have been seen by some critics as little more than a sop to the conscience of a world that did little to stop the wars and genocide in the two countries. The tribunal in the Hague certainly cannot be accused of victors' justice, since some of those most responsible for atrocities in former Yugoslavia, such as Radovan Karadzic and Ratko Mladic, continue to operate largely unmolested by international forces. In Arusha, the tribunal for Rwanda was plagued early on by corruption charges and a lack of resources.

Yet over time, the tribunals have gained a measure of credibility as they have begun to operate more smoothly. At the time of this writing, in late 1998, the Hague tribunal has completed three trials, with several more in progress, and three trials are proceeding in Arusha. Each tribunal has over twenty suspects in custody, including not only "small fish," but also higher-level perpetrators. Cooperation with the tribunals has grown; in addition to the willingness of countries such as Zambia, Cameroon and Kenya to transfer captured suspects to Arusha, Croatia's unexpected transfer of ten indicted war criminals to the Hague in fall of 1997, and the surrender of three Serbs in February 1998, NATO forces in Bosnia appear to be taking a firmer line against indicted war criminals, taking several into custody during 1997 and 1998. In a very different vein, a perverse incident—the televised "war crimes trial" of Pol Pot by his erstwhile Khmer Rouge comrades in 1997—suggests that war crimes tribunals may have already gained a surprisingly firm foothold in the vocabulary of international behavior, leading even criminals to turn to them when seeking international approval.

The first part of this section looks at the background and mechanics of the tribunals and the processes governing them. William Horne, a former editor of *The American Lawyer* magazine, describes the background of the first case heard by the Yugoslavia tribunal, that of Dusko Tadic, with emphasis on the personal and institutional factors involved in its evolution. Alison Des Forges, an expert witness at the Rwanda tribunal, sheds light on the types of crimes being tried before the tribunals; she supplies documents constituting something of a "paper trail" of genocide in Rwanda, revealing the involvement of the government and the (non)response of the outside world. Unlike the perpetrators in former Yugoslavia, and more like the Nuremberg criminals, Rwanda's leaders left bureaucratic traces of their crimes. Des Forges's contribution makes it clear that there is no dearth of material upon which to base trials, and she indirectly illuminates one main function of such tribunals, often discussed in connection with Nuremberg: establishing a record of the atrocities before the world and before history.

Though legal procedure tends not to be the stuff of headlines, the international tribunals have quietly been breaking new legal ground. Diane Orentlicher, an expert on international law and advisor to the tribunal in the Hague, explains one of the most important decisions by the tribunal's Appeals Chamber—the decision to apply the laws of war to domestic as well as international conflict, making prosecution easier in a situation like that of former Yugoslavia where international boundaries are unclear. This very significant shift reflects the change, described in greater depth in Part I, from a focus on states to a concern with individuals in international law, making the domestic or international nature of a conflict less crucial than the fact that human rights are being violated. Patricia Viseur Sellers, gender advisor to the prosecutor at the tribunal in the Hague, looks at the crimes of rape and sexual violence, which, despite their traditional use as a weapon in war and conflict, have only recently become a focus of international legal attention. She provides a history of international laws on sexual violence, culminating in the emphasis on prosecution of rape in the Hague and Arusha—a crucial development at the two trials that demonstrates the increasing influence of women, and sensitivity to women's human rights issues, in the international arena.

The second part of this section looks more closely at the purpose and functions of international tribunals and contrasts them with other ways of coping with the consequences of war and violence outside of the international courtroom. These chapters also focus more directly on the needs of both the victims and their societies.

Neil Kritz of the U.S. Institute of Peace considers the role of war crimes prosecutions in helping piece back together societies shattered by war and violence, comparing international and domestic prosecutions and the different ends they can serve. His analysis clarifies some of the basic issues underlying the call for war crimes prosecutions. Bill Berkeley, a journalist and eyewitness to the genocide in Rwanda, provides a concrete background to any analysis of international tribunals with his sweeping picture of the interplay between anarchy and tyranny in Africa, which has made it so difficult to achieve peace and justice there. Berkeley argues that violence in Africa is not the chaos that outsiders often imagine it to be, but rather involves orchestrated attacks by the strong against the weak that can and should be subject to legal sanction, and he describes ways that African societies have begun holding individuals accountable both in and outside of international fora.

Madeline Morris, an advisor to Rwanda's domestic war crimes trials, illuminates Neil Kritz's arguments on domestic and international trials with a study of Rwanda's program to prosecute thousands of war criminals domestically. She explains the concept of and problems with "stratified concurrent jurisdiction," under which the ICTR prosecutes leaders while domestic courts try lower-level defendants. She also describes the concrete ways in which Rwanda is dealing with the enormous problems inherent in the effort to prosecute tens of thousands of suspected war criminals in a social and legal system shattered by war and genocide, and highlights some of the issues that arise when domestic and international prosecutions proceed simultaneously.

Approaching the issue from a different perspective, that of the victims, Julie Mertus, who has worked with survivors of ethnic cleansing in Bosnia, questions whether trials are of any use at all to survivors of war and violence. Discussing the possible functions of the tribunals for various actors, she concludes that victims require more than legal remedies to deal with their experiences.

Tim Phillips and Mary Albon of the Project on Justice in Times of Transition discuss situations in which prosecutions, whether international or domestic, may not be possible or desirable. They describe alternatives to prosecution—such as truth commissions—that have been attempted in various parts of the world that, like Rwanda and former Yugoslavia, have found themselves on the road from violence to peace.

International tribunals are still relatively untried instruments of justice, and domestic prosecutions of war crimes in societies only just recovering from violence will be shaky. Given these drawbacks, some victims and their advocates are attempting to utilize a more established judicial system: in this section's final chapter, law professor Beth Stephens and Jennifer Green of the Center for Constitutional Rights outline the effort to bring Radovan Karadzic to trial in the United States and the jurisprudence that may allow his victims to gain justice in this country. These efforts highlight the way in which international human rights norms have begun to be integrated into domestic law and judicial proceedings in the United States—another legacy of Nuremberg.

THE INTERNATIONAL TRIBUNALS FOR FORMER YUGOSLAVIA AND RWANDA:
Background and Process

The Real Trial of the Century[1]

William W. Horne

Graham Blewitt—with twenty-nine years' experience as a federal prosecutor in Australia—is not given to exaggeration or emotional outbursts. As chief of an Australian Nazi war crimes investigations unit from 1989 to 1994, Blewitt thought he knew all there was to know about genocide, war crimes and crimes against humanity. When he joined the new International Criminal Tribunal for the former Yugoslavia in the Hague, the Netherlands, in early 1994 as its deputy prosecutor, he thought it would just be more of the same. It wasn't.

"I still shake my head when I come across these stories of these seemingly normal people murdering their neighbors," said Blewitt in a 1995 interview, his voice uncharacteristically choked up. "I can't imagine sitting there at a barbecue drinking a beer or two with your neighbor one day and then the next day you're murdering or treating that person in the worst way."

The fury of the neighbor-on-neighbor violence—perpetrated largely by the Bosnian Serbs against Muslims as part of a campaign of "ethnic cleansing"—was one of the mysteries of the Bosnian conflict for international spectators. Even the Nazis, Blewitt pointed out, killed their victims in a cold, efficient manner; rape and torture were the exception, not the rule: "But the atrocities here, this is blood lust."

For four years, Serbs thumbed their noses at international attempts to resolve the war on their Muslim neighbors. The world powers wrung their hands, their peacemaking and diplomatic efforts in the former Yugoslavia not only failing to end conventional war-making—armed soldiers killing armed soldiers on a battlefield—but failing also to deter the commission of war crimes. The Serbs, by far the biggest perpetrators, were not forced to answer for these crimes, and so they did not. But in May 1996, after three years of battling its United Nations paymaster for funding and overcoming the nightmarish logistics of collecting evidence in a war zone, the tribunal commenced proceedings against its first defendant, Bosnian Serb Dusko Tadic, in front of three judges and a worldwide television audience.

It may have been the most important criminal trial in this century. Not because the alleged crimes—132 counts related to rape, murder and torture—were necessarily worse than those committed by the hundreds of war criminals who now range freely in Tito's former domain. And not just because the case forged new international legal precedents. Tadic's trial may have been the most significant criminal trial in this century because it was a chance, finally, for the world to redeem the international rule of law and prove it learned something from the horrors of World War II.

When the war was in full swing from 1992 through 1995, most of us grew accustomed to, even bored by, that far-off conflict between Serbs and Bosnian Muslims and Croats. The daily tales of atrocities were just that—too daily, too regular to sink in. That apathy—that conclusion that war, murder, rape, even genocide are out of our control—is why the Tadic trial was so important.

No peace will last unless the victims see that some form of justice is meted out to the perpetrators. And if the prosecutors were even half right, Dusko Tadic was a perpetrator of the worst sort. Tadic, a former café owner in the Prijedor *opstina*, or district, in northeastern Bosnia, was charged with committing war crimes and crimes against humanity for the part that prosecutors said he played in thirteen deaths and several torture incidents in Bosnia and Herzegovina in May through August 1992. Among his more gruesome alleged exploits: forcing one prisoner to bite off the testicle of another, who subsequently died as a result.

Most of the allegations against Tadic, including the castration charge, related to his activities at the now notorious Omarska concentration camp, where hundreds if not thousands of the Bosnian Serbs' prisoners— nearly all Bosnian Muslims, civilians and soldiers, men and women— were horribly abused and often killed by their captors. What made Tadic's crimes even more heinous, if true, is that he was neither a commander nor a guard at the camp; he was one of what prosecutors at the war crimes tribunal call "camp visitors," outsiders who only visited the camps to participate in and direct the sadistic treatment of the prisoners—many of them their former neighbors.

Tadic pled not guilty and claimed he was not at the camps when the crimes were committed. With the trial in the Hague, the world had a chance to find out if he was telling the truth. Generally, those proceedings went slowly but smoothly, with well-prepared advocates from both sides appearing before experienced judges in a gleaming new courtroom—the epitome of smooth-running international justice. In the end, a verdict was rendered, Tadic vowed to appeal, and the wheels of justice revolved onward.

But the road to the Tadic trial was a rocky one. For those at the tribunal who made the journey, making personal and professional sacrifices in an attempt to bring the rule of law back to Bosnia, Tadic represented the end of a tortuous odyssey. "There's always been a great sense of urgency, [a sense] that the tribunal's future depended on getting results," said Blewitt.

End-Running the UN

The International Criminal Tribunal for the former Yugoslavia is based in a four-story sand-colored building in a quiet suburb of the Hague. A yellow brick drive sweeps past a reflecting pool dotted with modern sculpture, its surface mirroring the crescent-shaped tribunal building. Only a tiny sign confirms the tribunal's existence. From the outside, little activity was apparent on a midsummer's day in 1995.

Inside, it was a different story. Nine teams, each with four to seven experienced lawyers and investigators, were working furiously to put together cases and indictments. In the course of five days of interviews at the tribunal in late June 1995, then chief prosecutor Richard Goldstone and his deputy, Blewitt, were everywhere, poking their heads into offices, buttonholing people in the hallways, rushing off to strategy sessions. (Goldstone returned to South Africa in October 1996 to serve out his term on its highest court; he was replaced by Canadian jurist Louise Arbour.)

With twenty-one indictments issued in February and March 1995 and the Tadic trial looming, the tribunal had suddenly become a factor in the Bosnian quagmire. Would the prosecutors' actions affect the peace process? Were they prolonging the war or shortening it?

The war crimes prosecutors didn't care about those issues. In late July 1995 they raised the stakes even higher by indicting Bosnian Serb leader Radovan Karadzic and his army commander, General Ratko Mladic, for genocide and crimes against humanity "arising from atrocities perpetrated against the civilian population throughout Bosnia-Herzegovina, for the sniping campaign against civilians in Sarajevo, and for the taking of UN peacekeepers as hostages and their use as human shields," according to a tribunal press release. They also indicted Croatian Serb leader Milan Martic for ordering the shelling of Croatia's capital, Zagreb; fifteen guards, camp commanders and visitors to the Luka and Keraterm concentration camps; and six local Serb politicians and paramilitary leaders for directing the ethnic cleansing of a town called Bosanski Samac. The tribunal's spate of pretrial proceedings, indictments and deferral proceedings appeared to be the result of a coordinated, well-funded effort by the UN and the tribunal staff. The prosecutor chases, catches and tries the bad guys, just as prosecutors do the world over.

But those highlights could not obscure the tribunal's painful road to maturity. After all, the crimes with which Dusko Tadic was charged were allegedly committed in the spring and summer of 1992, three and a half years before he went to trial. The United Nations and international community had been well aware from press reports that summer that war crimes were being committed in the Bosnian conflict and that concentration camps had reappeared in Europe for the first time since 1945.

From the beginning, however, the international response was anemic; it took a handful of determined people to push toward a fully operational international war crimes tribunal.

The first was law professor Cherif Bassiouni of Chicago's DePaul University. In October 1992, the UN Security Council established a five-member commission of experts to collect evidence of alleged atrocities in the former Yugoslavia. It was a meager start: The UN paid only the salary of the chairman and five staff members and the expense of travel to the former Yugoslavia. The UN did not cover the enormous cost of conducting on-site investigations and collecting and recording that evidence in a central database.

But it was a start, and Bassiouni, an international law expert who was a member of and later chaired the UN commission, worked tirelessly to collect evidence while it was fresh, recruiting scores of volunteers and experts lent to the commission by the governments of such countries as Canada, Norway and the Netherlands, and private groups like Physicians for Human Rights. The governments of Austria, Germany and Sweden interviewed dozens of refugees in those countries on behalf of the commission, and the commission itself conducted thirty-five field investigations.

Bassiouni said that from the beginning it was obvious to him that certain powerful member states of the UN, such as the United Kingdom and France, had no appetite for pursuing war criminals. "But I found a way to end-run the pattern of delay the UN was engaging in," he said. When the UN declined his request to establish a database collection operation in Geneva, he set one up right at his own university in Chicago. When funding dried up, he drummed up more by convincing certain countries to kick in to a voluntary trust fund he says the UN created at his behest.

Even at this early stage, the alleged deeds of Dusko Tadic did not escape the attention of the war crimes investigators. On October 18, 1992, *New York Newsday* published a story by Roy Gutman—one in a series that won a 1992 Pulitzer Prize—on the notorious Omarska death camp. Among the dozens of survivors' stories Gutman recounted was one involving the castration of a man named Emir Karabasic. Prosecutors would later determine that the victim's name was Harambasic, but the facts alleged were the same. According to Tadic's February 1995 indictment, "The group of Serbs, including [Dusko] Tadic, severely beat the prisoners with various objects and kicked them on their heads and bodies. After Fikret Harambasic was beaten, two other prisoners, 'G' and 'H,' were called out. A member of the group ordered 'G' and 'H' to...sexually mutilate Fikret Harambasic. 'H' covered Fikret Harambasic's mouth to silence his screams and 'G' bit off one of Fikret Harambasic's testicles....Harambasic died from the attack."

Press reports were an important source of information for the commission. That castration-murder described in Newsday was entered into Bassiouni's growing database—an incident that would later be cross-referenced to dozens of others involving Tadic, a café owner and karate teacher turned alleged camp terrorist. Tadic had become an important blip on the embryonic tribunal's radar screen.

Eleven Judges, No Prosecutor

The Security Council officially established a war crimes tribunal for the former Yugoslavia on May 25, 1993, shortly after the UN had received the expert commission's first interim report. It took another four months for eleven judges to be confirmed by the UN: three from Asia, two from Europe, two from Africa, two from North America—including one of only two women on the panel, former Houston federal district judge Gabrielle Kirk McDonald, who later heard the Tadic case—and one each from Latin America and Australia. Italy's Antonio Cassese was elected by his fellow judges as the tribunal's president, or chief judge. He administered the chambers, including assignment of judges to cases, and was himself the head of the five-judge appeals chamber. (There are two trial chambers and one appeals chamber at the tribunal.)

Interviewed in his football field-sized office at the tribunal in mid-1995, Cassese, then fifty-eight, was a small, expressive man who took his job seriously. Should he lapse into lightheartedness, he had only to glance up at his walls; four large color photos depicted the dead and walking wounded in the former Yugloslavia, and a fifth was of wasted, hollow-cheeked inmates at Omarska. But don't all these photos of Muslim victims give the appearance of anti-Serb bias? "No, no, no," he exclaimed, his hands chopping the air for emphasis. "It doesn't matter to me what side of the conflict they are on. These are just to remind me of the job we have to do here."

When he arrived at the Hague to be inducted as a judge in November 1993, Cassese, an international law professor at the University of Florence who has written extensively on war crimes, was stunned by what he found. "There was zero!" he shouted. "Nothing! We had four secretaries, a few computers, and the UN had rented a meeting room and three small offices in the Peace Palace. The rent was paid for two weeks."

Eager to fulfill his mandate, Cassese convened the first working session of the tribunal shortly after the judges' induction ceremony. He has apparently never let up. "Some of us were saying, 'Let's go slow,'" recalled U.S. tribunal judge McDonald. "But to be frank, [Cassese] wanted us to accomplish something quickly."

The criminal procedure rules were hashed out in two plenary sessions that resulted in a first draft in February 1994. (By contrast, it took a committee of American judges and law professors four years to draft the federal Rules of Criminal Procedure in the early 1940s.) Since most of the judges and the acting prosecutor were from common law countries, the code is skewed toward that adversarial model, but it has clearly defined elements from civil jurisdictions as well, such as allowing judges to call and question witnesses of their own accord.

Next, unperturbed by what had already become a fiscal tug of war with his UN masters, Cassese found bigger, more expensive space to house the tribunal—its prosecution office, chambers and a courtroom. He commissioned construction of a custom-designed, state-of-the-art courtroom. An expert on detention, Cassese toured several prisons to determine the most humane, sophisticated design, then oversaw the construction of a modern twenty-four-cell detention center for the tribunal's accused that was built in the center of a Dutch prison in the Hague, where the prison courtyard once was. Prisoners have their own TV, radio and shower, but security is extremely tight. Visitors, for example, must go through first the Dutch prison's checkpoints and then the UN's before reaching the cells housing suspected war criminals. By May 1994 the court had also issued comprehensive rules governing the detention of accused war criminals and the assignment of defense counsel. "We had to invent and take a fresh approach to everything," Cassese recounted.

Despite Cassese's forceful leadership, a key component of the tribunal was still missing: a chief prosecutor. The Venezuelan who had been appointed in October 1993, Ramón Escobar-Salom, quit in February 1994 to take a position as minister of interior relations with his government.

We have a Pope!

Fortunately, a thousand miles away, Graham Blewitt was casting about for a new position. After twenty-four years as a prosecutor, Blewitt had spent the last five as the director of the Nazi war crimes investigation unit of the Australian equivalent of the FBI. Blewitt remembered the chill he felt upon reading of Serbian "ethnic cleansing" in 1992. That precise term had been used by the Nazi-backed Croats in their vicious campaign against Serbs during World War II. Blewitt's war crimes investigations had required him to travel to the former Yugoslavia to interview witnesses and to Ukraine to exhume graves. Now the witnesses were young and the graves fresh. He sent a query letter to the United Nations in early 1994, interviewed with Escobar, and was offered the job of acting deputy prosecutor a few days after he returned to Australia.

When Blewitt joined the tribunal in late February 1994, "there were hundreds of applications from people volunteering their services," he said. To his chagrin, however, while there were many lawyers eager to join the tribunal as either prosecutors or investigators, few veteran investigators had applied, and they were crucial to the next stage of the tribunal's work. The massive final report of Professor Bassiouni's commission of experts was due to arrive in late April, including 68,000 pages of documentary evidence and some 300 hours of video evidence. Using that report as a "blueprint," explained Blewitt, investigators could begin to develop the tribunal's cases.

Blewitt said he started calling potential investigators throughout the world and over the next two months convinced a handful to come. Fate intervened at that point: the United States lent twenty-two lawyers, prosecutors, FBI agents and other experts on its payroll directly to the tribunal for as long as they were needed. "It's worth saying that without that contribution at that time we wouldn't have started to investigate as soon as we did," commented Blewitt.

Meanwhile, the UN Security Council continued its search for a big-name prosecutor who could lead the tribunal toward indictments and trials. It was a ridiculous effort that highlighted the council's inability to act on crucial global issues. According to Professor Bassiouni—who was nominated by UN Secretary General Boutros Boutros-Ghali in August 1993 but failed to get enough votes in the Security Council—it was individual member states of the council that caused the delay in appointing a prosecutor.

The council considered, both formally and informally, half a dozen candidates for the office between August 1993 and the summer of 1994. Some didn't want the headache of the job; others were nixed by Security Council members (a single member could veto any candidate). Cassese said he grew desperate; the rules of procedure specified that only the prosecutor was authorized to conduct investigations and file indictments: "I was so dejected I said, 'Why don't we resign en masse to show the public we cannot go on?'" Instead, he took matters into his own hands. Throughout June he called lawyers and judges around the world whom he knew from his years on international commissions and human rights organizations, soliciting candidates. One name popped up more than once: South African judge Richard Goldstone, darling of the anti-apartheid forces. Goldstone had just completed his work as chair of the so-called Goldstone Commission, a massive, controversial three-year probe into the causes of the South African political violence that had left scores of black South Africans dead or wounded since 1991. On July 4, 1994, Cassese informally approached Goldstone. Would he take on the job as the tribunal's chief prosecutor?

Goldstone said he was interested but was concerned about leaving South Africa at "an exciting and important time in its history." When he first consulted with the new South African minister of justice, the difficulty of his decision was compounded: he was told that he was one of four judges who soon would be unanimously appointed to South Africa's new eleven-judge Constitutional Court. By taking the two-year stint as prosecutor, Goldstone would lose the opportunity to participate in seminal cases in South African constitutional history.

However, Nelson Mandela, South Africa's newly elected president, had a solution: Goldstone would do both. "President Mandela thought it was important for South Africa to accept the first prominent international job offered to a South African since our readmission to the world," recounted Goldstone. In fact, George Bizos, Mandela's personal lawyer, said Mandela felt indebted to the United Nations for its role in obtaining his release from prison. So it was set: Goldstone would go to the Hague tribunal and Mandela, by pushing through a constitutional amendment, would hold open Goldstone's spot on the high court until his return (Goldstone returned in October 1996 to serve out the five years remaining in his seven-year term).

For two days, said Cassese, he tapped his fingers and paced, waiting for an answer. On July 6 he had it: Goldstone accepted. An ebullient Cassese rushed out faxes to the tribunal judges with a traditional message from the Vatican heralding papal succession: "Habemus papum!" We have a pope!

The Pope Arrives

Richard Goldstone is a charming, thought-provoking conversationalist and host. He is well-traveled, reads prodigiously—favoring thick biographies of politicians, lawyers and civil rights leaders—frequently dines out (as in South Africa, with a squad of bodyguards poised nearby), and is a world-class wine connoisseur. But when it comes to his work, Goldstone, a short, stern-faced man with a piercing gaze and an unflappable demeanor, is all business.

In fact, Goldstone's straightforward style was probably the perfect counterbalance to that of more emotional members of the tribunal, notably Cassese. Upon arriving in the Hague in mid-August 1994, Goldstone recognized that his was a big-picture diplomatic role and that the hands-on prosecution work could be pushed down to experienced prosecutors and investigators like Blewitt, at least for the time being. "I felt that my first goal was to turn around the credibility crisis," recalled Goldstone in a 1995 interview. "The international media had become very antagonistic because of the delays in getting going. They had determined there was some sort of conspiracy, that the UN set up the tribunal only as a conscience salver, as a bargaining chip in the peace process."

Goldstone said he gave two dozen interviews and press conferences during his first month at the tribunal. He got out the message that the tribunal was in business and was not conspiring to dawdle while the war criminals got away with murder. It was a comfortable role; after all, Goldstone had made daily appearances on South African TV while he chaired the eponymous commission that routed out the causes of South African violence and paved the way for the 1994 elections there. Still, the media and some experts continued to question the delays, and Goldstone, recognizing that good press required tangible results, began his own push for progress. The tribunal was still operating on a quarterly budget; every three months it had to reapply to its UN paymaster for the next quarter. "Imagine how hard it is to attract good people with that kind of job security," said Blewitt. And new hires were subjected to the UN's time-consuming, paper-intensive vetting process.

Goldstone made numerous calls and two trips to New York in the fall of 1994, ingratiating himself with the various UN policy wonks who controlled funding, working the maze of power and pettiness. He said he discovered that the UN had not been consciously tugging at the new court's purse strings. "It took a while to sort out," he related, "but it was not a question of the UN's ill will. They simply had great difficulty fitting a judicial body into the UN structure." A senior UN official concurred with Goldstone's assessment, adding that the General Assembly has made "a real effort" to accommodate the tribunal's financial needs: "We won't pretend this was all done impeccably, but this is the first time anything like this has been done."

Goldstone managed to convince the UN funding committee to give his new hires guaranteed one-year contracts, allowing him nearly to double the tribunal from 45 to 80 employees by the end of 1994; by December 1997 the staff had grown to 367. (In 1994 the tribunal's budget was $11 million. It had grown to approximately $64 million by 1998.)

Goldstone also played diplomat, forging critical relationships with the UN High Commissioner for Refugees (UNHCR), the International Committee of the Red Cross (ICRC) and the UN Protection Force in Bosnia (UNPROFOR). The UNHCR and ICRC monitored the shifting Muslim and Serb populations in the wake of the Serbs' ethnic cleansing campaigns and interviewed victims and witnesses to alleged atrocities. UNPROFOR, among other things, maintained reports on the shelling of civilian targets, conducted its own investigations of alleged war crimes, and provided protection and access to the tribunal's investigators when they conducted investigations in the former Yugoslavia. "Without our own police force we must convince others to perform forensics tests, etc., for us," said tribunal investigator J.J. Du Toit, a prosecutor who worked for the Goldstone Commission before joining the tribunal. "[Goldstone] opened the doors to get that information back to the tribunal."

All this shuttle diplomacy to New York, London and Geneva took Goldstone away from the tribunal during his first two months on the job. But it was worth the payoff. "He ensured the tribunal's survival," said senior prosecuting trial attorney Grant Niemann, the veteran Australian prosecutor who later prosecuted Tadic. With money and staffing concerns allayed, Goldstone turned next to the tribunal's mandate, prosecuting war criminals. With no potential defendants in custody, Goldstone considered the next best possibility, an indictment.

No Nuremberg

As with everything having to do with an international tribunal that attempted to meld people from twenty-nine different cultures into a single cohesive unit, putting together a simple indictment could take ages. The lawyers were dealing with unfamiliar crimes committed in a foreign country, interpreting a brand-new code of evidence, working with unfamiliar people. Their primary targets—the Bosnian Serbs—were the victors rather than the losers of the conflict until the peace accord was signed. And the Serbs, unlike the meticulous Germans in the last world war, kept no detailed accounts of their deeds. So suspects and evidence were hard to come by. "There's no question that this is no Nuremberg," conceded senior prosecuting trial attorney Minna Schrag in mid-1995 (Schrag has since returned to legal practice in New York).

When Goldstone started looking for someone to indict in the fall of 1994, the office's best evidence concerned Serbian ethnic cleansing activities in the Prijedor district in northeastern Bosnia, where the Keraterm, Trnopolje and Omarska concentration camps were located. The commission of experts report had concentrated on that region, concluding that its prewar population of some 53,000 non-Serbs had been reduced to approximately 2,500 by May 1994 through forcible eviction. But was there enough evidence to indict? It depended on whom you asked. Tribunal investigator Jean-Pierre Getti, a well-known French investigating judge who conducted the war crimes investigation of former Nazi collaborator Paul Touvier, recalled that a healthy debate broke out at the tribunal over the standard for indicting.

The civil law view, Getti explained through an interpreter, is to require "serious and corroborated" evidence, while the common law interpretation is stricter: evidence sufficient to establish a *prima facie* case—i.e., evidence that, if uncontested, meets the criteria for a guilty verdict. The prosecutors went with the more conservative common law interpretation, delaying the first three indictments somewhat, Getti said. For the last five indictments, the prosecutors settled on a standard somewhere between the two interpretations.

The cultural clash over evidentiary standards was hardly the first dispute among the tribunal's disparate, polyglot assemblage of lawyers, investigators, and judges. (French and English are the official languages of the tribunal; English is the de facto working language.) Even the smallest details continue to be debated—and slow the pace of the proceedings. "What form should the interviews [of witnesses] take?" queried prosecutor Minna Schrag. "What should an indictment look like? None of the indictments we've issued has looked the same, and the next indictment won't look like any of the previous indictments."

Another member of the tribunal defends its deliberative style. Interviewed in 1995, Patricia Viseur Sellers, a former Philadelphia public defender, is the prosecutor's legal adviser on gender-related crimes, namely rape. (Rape has long been categorized as a war crime or crime against humanity under the Geneva Conventions. While a rape charge against Tadic was dropped on the eve of trial, prosecutors have charged other alleged war criminals in the Bosnian conflict with rape, marking one of the first times that rape, used as a systematic tool of terror and intimidation against a civilian population, is being prosecuted internationally as a war crime.) Sellers asserted that prosecutors simply wanted to do things right the first time around because they "know every step might be historically important, that they are on a world stage."

Nonetheless, by September 1995, through a process of trial and error, the kinks had—for the most part—been eliminated from the tribunal's system of investigations and indictment, which worked something like this: the nine investigation teams assembled proof of the underlying crimes—evidence that included depositions, reports by military observers, press reports, photographs, maps, charts, autopsy reports, etc. Each team had a data analyst to organize and ensure the chain of custody of evidence. The teams or portions of the teams travelled to the former Yugoslavia and other countries to depose witnesses and victims and collect other evidence both as to the alleged crimes and on any suspects that have emerged. (In 1994, twenty three-member teams conducted field investigations; forty-five teams conducted such investigations in 1995, each for an average of two weeks per month.)

The legal adviser assigned to each group worked with one of the three senior prosecuting trial attorneys to determine under which article of the tribunal's authorization each alleged crime fell. A rape, for example, may be a crime against humanity (Article 5) and a war crime (Article 3). An indictment was then crafted by those attorneys, tying the acts alleged to the charge under the statute. Commander William Fenrick, a Canadian expert on the laws of war, was often consulted at that stage about the finer points of fitting the alleged acts into a military context. Those preliminary indictments and the offers of proof—often hundreds of pages of documents and testimony—were then reviewed by Deputy Prosecutor Blewitt, who in turn forwarded it to then Chief Prosecutor Goldstone for final approval.

While the system sounds simple, even the smallest detail took—and continues to take—far more time and resources than would be necessary, for example, in a federal criminal investigation in the United States. Consider a simple victim or witness statement, as described by American prosecutor Schrag. First investigators must locate a witness to a particular crime. Many witnesses are in refugee camps or otherwise transient and difficult to reach. Once the witness is contacted, he or she has to agree to speak against the perpetrator. Many with families in occupied areas fear retaliation and will not testify; others, particularly victims, are too scarred by their experiences to do so. "These are badly damaged people," said Tadic prosecutor Niemann.

If they do agree to speak, an interpreter and two investigators must travel from the tribunal to wherever in Europe the witness is located. As one investigator questions a witness, the interpreter translates the Serbo-Croat into English and vice versa while another investigator takes notes. Those notes are later typed up into a statement in English that is then read back to the witness in Serbo-Croat for oral approval. The witness makes adjustments, and then the final statement, in English, is signed by the witness.

In spite of these logistical obstacles, the tribunal rumbled along through the fall of 1994 and finally, on November 7, Goldstone issued his first indictment, of Susica camp commander Dragan Nikolic.

Potemkin Tribunal?

Nikolic was probably not the best choice for the first indictment. He had some command responsibility for a small group of guards, and had allegedly participated in multiple murders and torture. But he could not be charged with genocide, the crime of crimes, and was not accused of rape—a little prosecuted international war crime that prosecutors hoped to showcase at the tribunal as a crucial means of deterring more rapes from being committed while the conflict still raged. He was not even within the investigators' main region of concentration, the Prijedor district. He also was not in custody.

Did that first indictment relieve the pressure on the tribunal to get results? "Not very much," Goldstone admitted. "Even after you achieve something, people just want more."

More, however, was just around the corner.

In February 1994, German police had arrested Dusko (also known as "Dusan" or "Dule") Tadic in Munich, where he had been hiding out at his brother's apartment. Refugees from the Serbian death camps now living in Germany had spotted their tormentor and identified him to German authorities as a Bosnian Serb who participated in a series of horrific crimes against his former Muslim neighbors in the Prijedor district of Bosnia. Germany arrested and charged Tadic under international war crimes laws with aggravated assault and murder, or crimes against humanity, as well as genocide.

On November 8, 1994, the day after Nikolic was indicted, Goldstone formally asked Germany to defer prosecution of Tadic to the tribunal. (In addition to the practical effect of granting the tribunal exclusive jurisdiction, deferral proceedings are a potent public relations tool, permitting the prosecution to air unsubstantiated charges against individuals prior to their indictment and signaling the tribunal's imminent indictment of those accused in local war crimes proceedings.) The tribunal supported its request with thirteen pieces of documentary evidence—such as maps, newspaper clippings and photographs—and nineteen statements from witnesses scattered throughout Germany, the Netherlands, Norway, Sweden and Switzerland. But it took nearly six months for the German parliament to pass a law permitting the transfer of the case to the tribunal.

Meanwhile, pressure on the prosecutors to act came from a surprising new quarter: the tribunal judges. On February 1, 1995, President Cassese issued an odd press release on the judges' behalf in which they "wished to express their concern about the urgency with which appropriate indictments should be issued," and that went on to state that the judges "were anxious that a programme of indictments should effectively meet the expectations of the Security Council and of the world community at large." The release is pure Cassese: prickly, brazen, impassioned. But it also betrays Cassese's civil law roots, where the prosecutor and the judges are often more or less on the same side, as well as perhaps the hubris and inexperience of a law professor turned judge.

Prosecutors who had been in the trenches for months weren't pleased. "They were impatient and frustrated," said Blewitt. "But we were already aware of the urgency of getting some results. We thought it was a useless statement." Indeed, two other judges, McDonald and Malaysian judge Lal Vohrah—both from common law countries—said they do not believe it is their role to tell the prosecutor how to do his job. "We want to work, to try cases," said Vohrah, a thoughtful, articulate jurist who gave up a spot on what is now Malaysia's highest court to join the tribunal. "But who is to be prosecuted is not our responsibility."

Cassese made no apologies. "Nikolic was small fry," he contended. "Allegedly he killed a few people. Minor thugs who rape or kill, without command responsibility, should be [handled] by the state courts." (The indictment does specifically refer to Nikolic's command responsibility as camp commander, and includes eight counts of murder.) Whether or not it was Cassese's doing, the tribunal did blast into action shortly after this intramural spat.

The Turning Point

On February 13, 1995, the tribunal indicted Tadic and his twenty death camp colleagues—the commander, guards and several Serb visitors to Omarska. In April of that year, Germany turned Tadic over to the tribunal in the Hague, where he became the sole occupant of Cassese's twenty-first–century detention center. The tribunal finally had a defendant in custody.

In May 1995, Goldstone dropped two bombshells. First, he expanded the tribunal's prosecutorial scope by requesting that Bosnian authorities cease their own prosecution in the Lasva River Valley investigation. That investigation—into the April 1993 slaughter of some 114 Muslim women, children and old men from the village of Ahmici, Bosnia, in front of scores of survivors and other witnesses—targeted Bosnian Croats. Previously, all twenty-one of those indicted by the tribunal were Bosnian Serbs. It was a carefully calculated move by Goldstone: "It's crucial that the mechanism is perceived as fair by all sides" to the conflict, he explained, in order to "break through the endless cycle of atrocity and revenge." Goldstone had again taken a page from his South African experience investigating the causes of political violence. "He recognized that the credibility of the tribunal depended on demonstrating we would go after Croats, Serbs and Muslims alike," said deputy prosecutor Blewitt.

Then, a week after the Lasva Valley deferral application, Goldstone filed a controversial deferral application with the Bosnian war crimes commission related to the Bosnian Serb leadership—namely Karadzic, General Mladic and former police chief Mico Stanisic. (Bosnia has set up its own war crimes commission and was then in the process of investigating the Bosnian Serb leadership.) The application specifically mentioned investigating their command responsibility for "genocide, other serious offenses against civilians, and destruction of cultural and historical monuments," as well as the "protracted siege of Sarajevo and the unlawful attacks upon civilian members of humanitarian agencies, members of the United Nations peacekeeping forces, aid convoys, and aircraft at Sarajevo."

The peace negotiators instantly expressed their distress at Goldstone's timing. "This decision could damage the peace efforts in the Balkans," warned a spokesman for the Russian Foreign Ministry. A cease-fire was on the verge of expiring; negotiators now faced the prospect of making a new deal with named war crimes suspects. To add insult to injury, Goldstone announced that the suspects would likely face indictments by the end of the year. At an April 24 press conference, according to a wire report from Agence France-Presse, Goldstone had a simple response to the supposed political inconvenience of his announcement: "We're not politicians, we're lawyers."

With the Tadic arraignment, the deferral applications, and nine investigation teams churning toward more indictments, the image of the tribunal as a do-nothing Security Council lapdog was finally vanquished. Even skeptics such as Cherif Bassiouni, former head of the commission of experts, voiced cautious optimism on the future of the tribunal: "I think there is a momentum building in world public opinion, a moral drive by the media, [the human rights] community, and scholars to give legitimacy and credibility to this tribunal."

In the early Tadic proceedings, in fact, the tribunal experienced enough success to keep up a steady trickle of good press. In summer 1995, it heard and dispensed with a variety of procedural motions.

On July 25, 1995, the tribunal indicted the Bosnian Serb leadership, Karadzic and General Mladic, for their command responsibility for the commission of genocide, war crimes and crimes against humanity. Still, by the end of 1996 Karadzic, Mladic and some sixty-four other war crimes indictees were still at large in Serbian-held areas of Bosnia or Croatia. New indictments were later issued against Karadzic and Mladic for their part in the alleged extermination of thousands of Muslim men by Serb forces in Srebenica in July 1995. Not surprisingly, neither Mladic nor Karadzic recognized the tribunal's competence. With only a handful of suspects in custody, prosecutors resorted to filing Rule 61 proceedings against some of those indicted, including both Karadzic and Mladic.

Rule 61 of the tribunal's code of criminal procedure is the common law answer to trials in absentia. It permits the prosecutor, after trying and failing to get jurisdiction over an indictee, to put on his or her entire case against that suspect, in public, before the tribunal. Witnesses may be called and evidence entered. If there are reasonable grounds for concluding that the accused committed the crimes indicated, the tribunal says so and issues an international arrest warrant. "It literally turns those indicted into international fugitives," according to Goldstone. If a UN member state refuses to turn over the subject of the arrest warrant, the matter is referred to the Security Council, which may consider imposing sanctions against the offending state.

The net effect of Rule 61 is to air allegations and, more importantly, to restrict the accused to their own country. If they travel to or through any of the 185 UN member states, they are subject to arrest. "Sooner or later we will [get custody of more alleged war criminals]," said Minna Schrag, the American prosecutor. "Because we keep getting information on people who travel." But meanwhile, the tribunal had a far more interesting proceeding to pursue: the Tadic trial.

Alleged Blood Lust

Dusko Tadic would have been cut from the first casting call to play a war criminal in the 1961 movie *Judgment at Nuremberg*. The somber, shifty-eyed man in the dock during the pretrial proceedings (a Dustin Hoffman look-alike) looked more like an insurance or car salesman than a war criminal. Yet court papers, press reports and, later, testimony painted a picture of Tadic as a thuggish part-time karate instructor and café owner in the town of Kozarac, who rose to power in the local Serbian Democratic Party as pan-Serb nationalism exploded in late 1991. Even the photographs of Tadic taken prior to his arrest suggested a burlier, more dangerous person than the cowed man in the button-down shirts now appearing at the tribunal.

He was described by one Muslim refugee as an arrogant, vengeful man who liked to show off his martial arts skill. "He was known around Kozarac as gratuitously violent, ready to beat up those who had slighted him," *The New York Times Magazine* reported in October 1994. "And he was financially vulnerable, in debt to Muslim acquaintances."

The stage was set, then, for Tadic to strike back at his perceived enemies when the Serbs seized control of Kozarac and other towns in the Prijedor area in early 1992. According to the declaration that war crimes prosecutor Michael Keegan filed in Tadic's November 8 deferral proceeding (which summarized the testimony of dozens of witnesses and several documents), "although [Tadic] had very good relations with the Muslim population prior to 1992, at the start of the tensions in the area, he banned Muslims from his café."

When the policy of ethnic cleansing was instituted to rid the Prijedor region of non-Serbs, Tadic became one of its chief proponents. "Eyewitness accounts identify Tadic as being personally involved in the forced removal of Muslims from the Prijedor area and the looting and destruction of Muslim homes," Keegan attested. Prosecutors claimed Tadic, a married father of two, became his former Muslim neighbors' worst nightmare.

According to Keegan's declaration, Tadic had served as a local police-man and was an officer in the reserve militia. After the conflict broke out, he assisted local Serb commanders who were compiling a death list of the area's intellectuals, civic leaders and prominent Muslims. When the concentration camps like Omarska began operating in early 1992, many of their first prisoners were on these lists and were allegedly killed or have since disappeared.

In May 1992, according to Tadic's indictment, Serb forces rounded up all Bosnian Muslims and Croats in the Kozarac area and marched them into the city of Prijedor, where they boarded buses for the various camps that had been set up in the Prijedor region. In a similar incident in June, 1992, Tadic allegedly forcibly removed thirteen unarmed non-Serb men from their homes, made the victims "lie on the ground, beat them with thick wooden sticks, kicked them, and then took them from the village to an unknown location," according to the indictment.

The Keegan declaration alleged that the worst of Tadic's sadistic ac-tivities took place at the Omarska death camp, which he visited "almost daily (or nightly)." Omarska was an abandoned iron ore complex. The 5,000 prisoners who reportedly passed through lived in inconceivably inhumane conditions. Many were held in an open ore pit, with no shel-ter, no toilets and little food or water. Tadic held no rank in the Bosn-ian Serb army and was not part of the camp's Serbian staff. Yet he allegedly often wore a camouflage uniform (and occasionally a black mask) and directed the activities of the men who accompanied him and the camp guards. "Tadic was also seen in the presence of the camp com-mander, giving directions to camp staff on the arrival of new prisoners," alleged Keegan.

The Keegan declaration claimed that Tadic "beat and tortured prison-ers on a daily basis and is personally responsible for the murder of more than ten prisoners...." The indictment zeroed in on six incidents in which Tadic was accused of raping one woman, murdering thirteen men, and torturing those men and scores of others. And then, of course, there was the alleged castration incident.

Tadic pled not guilty to all charges and claimed all these accounts of his activities were untrue, a case of mistaken identity. The prosecutors, led by senior prosecuting trial attorney Grant Niemann, put dozens of witnesses on the stand who testified otherwise.

Post-Tadic?

Grant Niemann was well-suited to prosecute the first international war crimes case in fifty years. One of the first prosecutors to arrive at the tribunal, in June 1994, he immediately began working on the prosecution of ethnic cleansing and the war crimes committed in the Prijedor section of Bosnia, where Tadic allegedly committed his crimes.

A stocky, ruddy-complexioned Australian with wavy white hair tucked back behind his ears, Niemann comes off as a pugnacious prosecutor but also a compassionate advocate for the war crimes victims. That soft center is perhaps unsurprising for a lawyer who spent his early years representing aboriginals in their land claims against the Australian government. And the gruff exterior can likewise be traced to his past: as a federal prosecutor in Adelaide from 1985 to 1994, Niemann tried two Nazi war crimes cases and assisted on a third.

According to Niemann, the decision to try Tadic was, in one respect, an easy one. In stark contrast to other indicted war criminals, Tadic was in custody. It didn't hurt that the Tadic files were fairly complete. "The Germans had done a very good and very thorough investigation themselves and turned their material over to us," said Niemann. Still, Goldstone repeatedly said that the tribunal's resources did not permit it to go after low-level players. Where did Tadic fit into that grand scheme?

Goldstone admitted the obvious: you have to start somewhere. "Witnesses can only implicate those they came into contact with on a local level," he explained. "Some of the leaders are saying that the events were random and unplanned. We need to establish a pattern of activity." And, he added, to go after people involved at a local level, like Tadic.

The Tadic case, Goldstone and Niemann acknowledged, might not exactly open the judicial floodgates. And the trial of a single man is, of course, only a small step toward justice and accountability in the Balkans.

But the Tadic trial is important even on its own. At the very least, "we expose those who committed the crimes to public scrutiny," explained tribunal president Cassese. "And with the international community so totally impotent to deal with these crimes otherwise, this result is not so meager."

And more important, the Tadic trial, beamed throughout the world by satellite, could send a message to the Serbs, Croats and Bosnians—and for that matter, to citizens of every country—that war crimes will not be tolerated, that whether it is next week or ten years from now, those who step over the bounds of acceptable behavior may end up being held accountable for their actions. As Judge McDonald succinctly puts it: "We are here to tell people that the rule of law has to be respected."

Epilogue

On May 7, 1997 the Hague Tribunal—after poring over some 7,000 pages of testimony from 125 witnesses—found Dusan Tadic guilty of eleven of the thirty-one charges then remaining against him. In its 300-page opinion, the three-judge panel found Tadic guilty of ethnic persecution, including beatings, torture and slitting the throats of two Muslim policemen. Though Tadic was found guilty of the umbrella crime against humanity that encompassed ethnic cleansing, the tribunal did not find sufficient evidence to link Tadic to any of the nine specific charges of murder with which he was ultimately charged. On July 14, 1997, Tadic was sentenced to a twenty-year prison term. As of autumn 1998, the tribunal had publicly indicted fifty-six men for war crimes; twenty-seven were in custody.

Notes

1. Adapted from a background article on the Hague tribunal that appeared in the September 1995 issue of *The American Lawyer* magazine.

Documenting Horror: The Administration of the Rwandan Genocide

Alison Des Forges

The organizers of the genocide in Rwanda engineered a killing campaign remarkable not just for its horror but also for the scale and speed of the slaughter. They mobilized the killers through three separate but connected hierarchies: the armed forces, the political parties and the administration. In most cases, particularly those of large-scale massacres, soldiers, national policemen (a force integrated into the Rwandan Armed Forces) and communal[1] policemen initiated and directed the killings. Militia—armed irregulars recruited and trained through two extremist political parties—backed up the soldiers and police and also launched attacks on their own. Ordinary citizens by the thousands joined in the genocide, under the orders of local government officials. For decades, government administration had been remarkably intense in Rwanda, with local officials and agents supervising units as small as groups of ten to twenty households. In conjunction with soldiers and political party leaders, these government agents led Hutu under their authority in slaughtering their Tutsi neighbors.

Sowing Fear and Hatred

Rwandan President Juvenal Habyarimana, in power for nearly two decades, was losing popular support at the end of the 1980s because of growing corruption and repression by his regime. At the same time, he faced an invasion by the Rwandan Patriotic Front (RPF), a guerrilla movement made up mostly of Tutsi who had been living in exile—some of them for nearly thirty years—after having fled a revolution that had overthrown a Tutsi-dominated state. Habyarimana and his immediate circle scapegoated Tutsi inside Rwanda in hopes of rebuilding their eroding power base among the Hutu, who had once supported them by an overwhelming majority. Right after the RPF attacked Rwanda in October 1990, extremist Hutu newspapers began spewing forth propaganda against the invaders, and also against Tutsi living within Rwanda, who were said to be "accomplices" of the RPF. Although the journals purported to be independent, many were linked to the highest circles of government.[2] They taught that Tutsi were aliens who had no right to be in Rwanda, a misreading of the history of the settlement of the region. Recalling the time when Tutsi ruled the country, the propagandists insisted that Tutsi intended to take control of Rwanda once again, and that they would do so by massive slaughter of Hutu. As early as several months after the start of the war, the Hutu extremists were warning that the Tutsi intended to carry out a genocide of the Hutu.

In mid-1993, businessmen, government and military officials, and even clergy close to President Habyarimana, established a radio station, RTLM, to deliver the message of hate more directly and to a wider audience. Among the founders were André Ntagerura, the minister of telecommunications, and Georges Rutaganda, the vice president of the *Interahamwe*, the militia of Habyarimana's political party. The director of the radio was Ferdinand Nahimana, who headed the national radio when it incited massacres of the Tutsi in 1992. Rutaganda, Ntagerura and Nahimana have all been indicted by the International Criminal Tribunal for Rwanda. Rutaganda's trial began in early 1997. Ntagerura and Nahimana, arrested by Cameroon, were handed over to the tribunal in early 1997.

Although RTLM purported to be an independent, private station, it broadcast a part of each day on the same frequencies as the official national radio, an arrangement that led listeners to see RTLM as the voice of the government. RTLM also used equipment belonging to government ministries.[3] In the months before and during the genocide, it broadcast the message that Tutsi were devious, dangerous, cruel—and that they meant to destroy the Hutu. It spread the word that the "enemy" had infiltrated among ordinary civilians, and during the genocide the station even directed listeners to attack particular individuals or neighborhoods. Killers manning the barricades often had radios tuned to RTLM at their sides, and those who set off to hunt Tutsi did so with the songs of RTLM on their lips.

Among the evidence available to the tribunal are the legal document establishing RTLM, with an attached list of its founders and financers, and tape recordings of the following RTLM broadcasts:

(Extracts from tape recordings of RTLM. The name *Inyenzi*, literally "cockroach," was used to refer to the RPF and to Tutsi in general. *Inkotanyi*, a more respectful name taken from a nineteenth-century military regiment, was used by the RPF to describe itself.)

Radio announcer Valerie Bemerki, June 3, 1994:
So you understand that the cruelty of the *Inyenzi* is irreversible, the cruelty of the *Inyenzi* cannot be cured except by their total extermination, by putting them all to death, their total extinction...."

Radio announcer Kantano Habimana, July 2, 1994:
Well, those *Inkotanyi* who used to telephone me, where are they now?

Huh? Oh!... they must surely have been exterminated... they must have been exterminated.... So let's sing. [He began a triumphant tune from the days when Habyarimana first came to power.] "Let us rejoice, my friends! The *Inkotanyi* have been exterminated! Let's rejoice, friend. God can never be unjust!"... Indeed God cannot be unjust... these criminals... these suicide commandos... without any doubt, they have been exterminated.... I myself saw their bodies yesterday spread out there at Nyamirambo... and that was just for a single day, yesterday....[4]

Preparing for War

From October 1990 through mid-1993, the war in Rwanda continued, with periods of active combat alternating with periods of cease-fire and negotiation. In August 1993, the RPF controlled a substantial part of northern Rwanda, and the Habyarimana government was burdened with a demoralized army, near bankruptcy and the withdrawal of support by the French, its chief foreign backers. After a year of negotiations and under heavy pressure, the Habyarimana government agreed to a final peace treaty, the Arusha Accords, on August 4, 1993. But Habyarimana and a number of his supporters intended to resume combat as soon as they had secretly strengthened their position. In late 1992 and early 1993, the Habyarimana regime had carried out massacres that killed several hundred Tutsi. The RPF had then violated a cease-fire agreement, using as a pretext the need to stop the slaughter of the Tutsi civilians. As the extremists prepared for a new round of war, they organized for more and larger-scale killings of civilians, knowing this would once more draw the RPF into battle.

The preparations included the distribution of weapons to civilians known to be sure supporters of the regime. Local and international human rights organizations, various other nongovernmental organizations and churches publicized and protested against this distribution, underlining the risks of arming civilians in communities where massacres of Tutsi had already taken place. A news release by the Bishop of Nyundo, a diocese in northwestern Rwanda, is an example of these protests:

(Excerpt from a one-page press release issued by the Bishop of Nyundo and the clergy of his diocese, December 28, 1993.)

...As for the question of security, criminals armed with guns and grenades have caused trouble in all parts of the diocese of Nyundo for some time. But now, the fear of people is growing because weapons have been distributed in certain communes. We earnestly implore all security agencies to prosecute unauthorized persons carrying firearms and to explain clearly to the public the use of the weapons that have been distributed recently.

In 1992, Habyarimana's political party, the Republican Movement for Democracy and Development (MRND) and its ally, the Coalition for the Defense of the Republic (CDR), had organized militias to counter the growth of rival political groups. In 1993 and early 1994, Rwandan soldiers and national police trained these militias to kill. The instruction was carried out as discreetly as possible, usually in forests or game parks distant from the capital. Nevertheless, information about the training spread and occasioned protests from human rights groups and others.

To assist in implementing the Arusha Accords, the United Nations had agreed to place a force of peacekeepers, known as the United Nations Assistance Mission to Rwanda (UNAMIR), in the country during the transition period when elections for a new government were being organized. Rwandans brought information about the distribution of weapons and the training of militias to UNAMIR officers. The commanding officer, General Romeo Dallaire, sent a cable to his New York headquarters on January 11, 1994, describing information about the militia training and distribution of arms.

The Language of War

A plane carrying President Habyarimana was shot down on April 6, 1994, and Colonel Theoneste Bagosora took command. The Presidential Guard promptly slaughtered the prime minister and other members of the government, making it possible for Bagosora and others to install a civilian government that would do their bidding. As Rwandan soldiers, police, militiamen and civilians carried out genocidal massacres of the Tutsi, the RPF resumed combat with the Rwandan army. The authorities defined Tutsi civilians as part of the "enemy" force, "accomplices" who were to be attacked as part of an effort at "self-defense." In official pronouncements on the radio and in countless meetings around the country, authorities insisted that Hutu were justified in killing Tutsi in order to protect themselves. The terms of the discourse were set at the top (see letter from Kambanda, below)[5] and disseminated through the agents of local administration (see letter from Kabayiza, below). Under this continuing pretext of self-defense, the roles of aggressor and victim were inverted. In official correspondence (see letter from Ntaganzwa, below), the massacre of civilians in a church, for example, became a battle in which the refugees were said to have attacked the commune.

(Excerpt from first page of a four-page letter from Interim Prime

Minister Jean Kambanda[6] to the prefects of all the prefectures, April 27, 1994.)

On April 6, 1994, the airplane transporting our chief of state, His Excellence Major General Juvenal Habyarimana and His Excellence Cyprien Ntaryamira, the President of the Republic of Burundi, as well as the delegations they were heading, was shot down by enemies as they were returning from a peace mission to Dar-es-Salaam, Tanzania. The Rwandan Patriotic Front, ignoring the Arusha Accords, began the war again and attacked the positions of the Rwandan Armed Forces. Their soldiers who were guarding the leaders of the *Inkotanyi* even came out of the CND building [where they were quartered] and spread out throughout the city of Kigali and began massacres while also trying to occupy the military camps of the Rwandan Armed Forces.

The terrible news of the death of the President of the Republic and of the renewal of combat by the RPF spread quickly throughout the whole country and troubles broke out immediately pretty much everywhere, destroying much property. Innumerable persons lost their lives and many others were chased from their homes.

Seeing this, the Rwandan Armed Forces quickly got themselves together and fought the enemy, meanwhile also doing everything possible to assure security to persons and their property.

The five parties that formed the government, that is, the MRND, the MDR, the PL, the PSD, and the PDC, learned of the death of the President of the Republic and became aware of the death of the Prime Minister as a victim of these troubles. They met to discuss how the country could escape from the institutional vacuum created by the death of its highest leaders.

(Letter from Andereya Kabayiza, burgomaster of the commune Mugusa, to the prefect of Butare Prefecture, May 18, 1994, followed by first page of an attached speech.)

I am pleased to send you the attached copy of a speech which will show you the message that the Burgomaster delivered to all the residents of Mugusa commune in all the sectors, at meetings run by the sector councilors assisted by members of the security committees.

In the course of these meetings, the residents elected security committees for the level of the cells.

Citizens,

Since April 6, 1994, Rwanda has been in mourning following the un-

timely death of our head of state, His Excellency, President Juvenal Habyarimana, killed when his airplane crashed at Kanombe airport on the
evening of his return from Dar-es-Salaam where he had been meeting to
discuss the problems of Rwanda and Burundi.

The horrible news of this death was followed by troubles caused by the
distress that some people have shown. Some important people, including
the Prime Minister, Her Excellency Madame Agathe Uwilingiyimanya, lost
their lives.

It was imperative and urgent to put a new government in place to represent Rwanda and to continue putting into effect the Arusha accords, on
which Rwandans have placed great hopes for getting out of the situation of
uncertainty in which we have been living for the past few days.

These troubles have irritated the RPF which then started the war again,
so that they are now fighting against the Rwandan Armed Forces.

Administration of the Genocide

The slaughter was carried out in a variety of ways. The first killings in
the capital of Kigali and elsewhere targeted leading Tutsi and Hutu members of moderate political parties who would have opposed the genocide.
Soldiers, police, militiamen, and bands of civilians led by former soldiers
went from one house to the next, sometimes using lists to identify their
victims. In some cases, they shot people in their homes; in others, they
transported them elsewhere for execution. A second stage of slaughter
involved attacking the homes of Tutsi and making the houses uninhab-
itable, either by burning them down or by destroying the roof, doors and
windows. Government officials directed Tutsi made homeless or those
frightened by attacks to gather in local churches, schools or communal
offices. These sites, which sometimes grouped thousands of people, were
then attacked by hundreds or thousands of assailants, commanded by soldiers, police or former soldiers. They usually assaulted the site with
grenades and gunfire and then completed the killing with machetes, nail-
studded clubs or other homemade arms. Following the massacre at
Cyahinda church in the southern commune of Nyakizu, the communal
council declared a communal work obligation for residents in order to
clean up the "filth"—that is, the bodies—left by the slaughtered Tutsi:

(Letter from Ladislas Ntaganzwa, burgomaster of the Commune
Nyakizu, to the subprefect of Busoro, May 10, 1994. From April 15
to April 19, the people of Nyakizu, under the direction of Ntaganzwa and soldiers, police and former soldiers, slaughtered thousands of civilians who had sought refuge in the church at Cyahinda.

It is this massacre of civilians that Ntaganzwa describes as the "bat-tle of Cyahinda." The document also demonstrates the extent to which people believed themselves to be following the orders of the government. It records the decision to require residents to con-tribute their labor to a communal clean-up to get rid of the bodies left from the massacre.)

> On April 28 we held a meeting at the Nyakizu communal office at-tended by all the councilors, representatives of the political parties, and members of the cell committees to examine together the situation follow-ing the war at Cyahinda.
>
> We exchanged ideas about how this had all come about and about the current climate in the commune and we discussed two principal ques-tions:
>
> 1. Ways and means to win the war initiated by the *Inkotanyi*
>
> 2. How to protect our economic development projects.
>
> Concerning the first point, we agreed after exchanging views that we will win this war if we respect the orders given by the government and in this regard, we made the following decisions:
>
> To do patrols to guard all the places where the enemy could pass
>
> To avoid difficulties among people and abusive acts against others
>
> To select ten young men to receive military training so that they can defend the sectors and their commune....
>
> ...Since the people who took refuge at Cyahinda have left behind a lot of filth, the participants in the meeting asked that communal work be re-quired to clean up the place.
>
> Since the *Inkotanyi* have often bragged about taking our commune, they clearly have plans to attack us again and therefore we must be vigi-lant.
>
> Keep your eyes open.

Killers also used roadblocks and foot patrols to apprehend Tutsi who were trying to flee. In some cases, the persons manning the barriers or carrying out the patrols recognized the Tutsi as local residents; in other cases, they identified them by checking their identity cards, which car-ried their ethnic classification along with other data. Patrols often ar-rived to search houses where Tutsi might have sought refuge, on the pretext that arms or enemy soldiers had reportedly been seen there. They also organized searches of forested areas, sometimes clearing the brush by cutting or burning it, to trap Tutsi who were hiding there. These activi-ties were organized by security committees at the various levels of local administration, from the prefecture down through the communes, the sectors and the cells. These committees, all of which saw themselves as implementing orders from above, took minutes of their meetings, which they then passed up the administrative hierarchy (see below, minutes of meeting in Bwakira and letter from Kabasha). The civilians charged with hunting Tutsi could and did call upon the armed forces when they needed assistance to complete their "work," as they called it (see below, note from Ndahimana). Hutu who refused to participate in the communal "security" activities were labeled traitors and risked being attacked themselves (see below, letter from Kabasha).

(Notes from a meeting to improve the functioning of a roadblock in the commune of Bwakira, May 17, 1994.)

Minutes of the meeting of people in charge of the Roadblock near Trafipro

The meeting was held on Tuesday, May 17, 1994 chaired by Apollinaire Nsengimana. About twenty-five people participated in the meeting, all of whom had been assigned to guard this roadblock.

The meeting discussed these issues:

1. How to improve the functioning of the roadblock.

2. How to make everyone who works there feel responsible and not expect others to work for them.

3. Other general problems.

On the first issue, the participants were asked to be more vigilant and not to be corrupted by people who offer them money because this would allow the enemy to infiltrate. At the roadblock, they must:

Check identity papers

Search luggage, baggage and vehicles

Ask everyone where he is going (hill, sector, cell) as well as the names of the people he knows there. If he answers wrongly, he is suspect and must be handed over to the authorities.

On the second issue, it has become clear that some people expect others to do their jobs, that there is disorder at the roadblock (drunkenness, assaults on other passers-by) and that no one makes decisions and settles disagreements. To avoid such disorder, the meeting decided to create teams with a leader for each team. The leader will be answerable for whatever happens at his roadblock. He will be responsible for the success of the patrol. Every team will have its own patrol day.

The participants expressed the wish that the commune provide them with weapons and, if this is not possible, that a communal policeman to be assigned to them. They also asked for the help of the rest of the population: checking on people is not an easy matter since some evade the roadblocks. Everyone should take responsibility for checking the papers of unfamiliar people, wherever they see them, even in local bars.

After the discussion, the teams were created. It was decided to mix workers and non-workers on the same teams.

These are the teams:

(Page 2 of this document lists the teams according to the following categories: Team Number, Names, Day. The days of the week begin with Wednesday, then Thursday, Friday, Saturday, Sunday, Monday, Tuesday.)

(Note from Mathieu Ndahimana, a medical assistant in the commune Ntyazo, addressed to Adalbert Muhutu, deputy in the national parliament.)

Monsieur Muhutu A.

Député

We have a lot of Tutsi at Karama (sector headed by Councilor Kanamugire). We have tried to fight them but they have turned out to be stronger than we had expected. We ask you to intervene again; send us some national policemen and also four other communal policemen to help our people who are fighting with bows and arrows.

N.B. We have guns and grenades.

Mathieu

April 27, 1994

(Letter from Tharcisse Kabasha, burgomaster of the commune Bwakira, to councilors of all sectors.)

Bwakira, June 20, 1994

No. 354/04.09.01/4

To All Sector Councilors

Mr., Ms. Councilor,

I am writing to say that some of you are behaving as if we were not in the midst of a war.

Given the circumstances, I give you the following directives:

You have primary responsibility for supervising roadblocks in your sectors. Make sure that there are at least four people at each barrier during the day and at least eight at night. Roadblocks must be closely guarded.

You must search the brush [around settled areas] every day. If necessary, the bushes must be cut down or burned.

Night patrols must be organized in all sectors and those who refuse to
participate must be punished.

You must follow these orders and remember that we are in the midst
of a war. Check what is going on in your sectors every day. Establish a security committee composed of cell leaders and former soldiers (if you have
any) and meet with them at least once a week to see what can be done
to defeat the enemy.

> Burgomaster of
> Commune Bwakira
> Tharcisse Kabasha

As the violence spread, the accusation of being "Tutsi," whether true
or not, meant death. Some who were falsely labeled Tutsi or whose family members had been so labeled appealed to local authorities for the confirmation of Hutu identity needed to assure their safety. Because the
detailed population records kept at the communal level included the ethnic identity of each resident, local administrators were in a position to resolve all such questions and thus held the power of life and death over
persons under their sway.

(Letter from Burgomaster Kabasha to the sector councilor informing him that certain children are in fact Hutu, as shown by communal records about their great-grandfather, and should not be
killed.)

> Bwakira, June 21, 1994
> No. 0 359/04.03/3

To the Councilor of Shyembe Sector
Mr. Councilor,

I am writing regarding the complaint of Mujawashema about people
who want to kill her children because they are Tutsi.

I have just checked the file of Kanyetambi, Nsengiyumva's grandfather,
which was completed on April 16, 1948. I see that Kanyetambi was Hutu.
Therefore, those children should be left in peace.

> Burgomaster of
> Commune Bwakira
> Tharcisse Kabasha

The Self-Defense Program

In 1991, Rwandan military authorities had established a form of "self-defense" program in communes bordering combat zones. Local civilians, trained by and under the command of soldiers, patrolled in search of infiltrators. In early 1993, Colonel Bagosora and a secret group of extremist military officers who called themselves AMASASU, the Kinyarwanda word for bullets, proposed creating units of young men throughout the country who would be trained and commanded by former soldiers who lived in the community. Some were to be armed with guns, others with machetes and other such weapons. Although the program was not formally established throughout Rwanda when the genocide began, it served as the model for attacks carried out by civilians under the direction of local former soldiers. Authorities then speeded up the implementation of the self-defense program, beginning training in arms almost immediately in some areas (see below, letter from Kayishema). In some places, young men trained under the program replaced untrained civilians in manning the barriers and carrying out patrols. The national authorities gave detailed instructions on implementing the "self-defense" effort (see below, letter from minister of the interior).

(Letter from prefect of Kibuye ordering burgomasters of all communes to recruit young men to be trained as part of the civilian "self-defense" program. Dr. Kayishema is on trial before the International Criminal Tribunal in Arusha.)

Kibuye, April 30, 1994
No. 0281/04.09.01

To all Burgomasters

Re: Civil defense of the population

Mr. Burgomaster,
    Given the security situation in the country, the Rwandan government has decided to organize civil defense for the population.
    The people themselves will do this civil defense in the cells and sectors and will help particularly in:
    • Organizing and supervising patrols and roadblocks
    • Maintaining vigilance especially against infiltration by the *Inkotanyi* through regular checking on hidden paths.
    Because of this, you are asked to urgently recruit the people to be trained. The recruitment should be directed especially at people:

• who are physically and morally in good shape
• known to be upstanding
• who have a certain credibility among the rest of the people.

The training will be carried out by former soldiers that you will identify in your communes. There will be meetings to explain all this after the recruitment is done.

Given the importance of maintaining order and peace in the country, this requires urgent action.

Prefect of Prefecture Kibuye
Dr. Kayishema Clément

Copy to the Subprefect of Subprefecture Birambo

(Letter from the Minister of the Interior and Communal Development to all prefects, giving orders for setting up the civilian self-defense program.)

Kigali, May 25, 1994
To all Prefects

Re: Putting into effect the
Prime Minister's orders on
self-organization of Civil Defense

To put into effect the prime minister's orders on civilian self-defense, I ask you to put to work all necessary mechanisms to get the following done immediately:

• Establishment of coordinating committees for civilian self-defense;
• Making lists of all former soldiers or national policemen residing in the communes;
• Informational and mobilization meetings for police and former soldiers at the subprefectures;
• Identification of key people who can form the core members for the political and ideological aspects of civilian self-defense;
• Defining objective criteria for selecting young men for training;
• Selecting young men by sectors to be trained;
• Setting up training sessions (handling arms, contra-guerrilla tactics and resistance, ideological and moral training);
• Inventory of all firearms in the hands of the population, in view of a possible redistribution;

• Defining the ways of managing and using the weapons distributed;

• Identifying the material available in neighborhoods that could be used collectively for civil self-defense;

• Listing the names of people who have received or who should receive firearms, indicating their family names, first names, their cells and sectors, their status (civilian or former soldier), their usual jobs and/or in the context of the strategy of civilian self-defense. Those who receive weapons should sign next to their names after receiving the firearm.;

• Publicity asking people to get their own traditional weapons (bows and arrows, spears . . .);

• Identifying and choosing ways to signal [the arrival of] the enemy, for group members to recognize each other, and of gathering these members together;

• Publicity campaign;

• Frequent and regular visits to supervise and evaluate the roadblocks guarded by civilians;

• Publicity meeting with the people about the importance of the roadblocks and the patrols for civilian self-defense and directions about activities to be carried out within this program;

• Summary evaluation of local authorities and identification of those who could possibly hinder putting the strategy of civilian self-defense into effect;

• Finding places in cells and sectors where civilian self-defense groups can gather;

• Census of all displaced young adults, by sector and by commune, so they can be trained in the techniques and operation of self-defense and then can return home with their families to their own property;

• Establishing functioning and complementary mechanisms of contact and collaboration between administrative and military authorities in charge of civilian self-defense.

We must stress that for this operation to succeed, information channels should be carefully controlled to avoid scattering efforts and to avoid infiltration by elements working for the enemy cause.

In order to do this, we must be sure from the start that everyone called to play whatever role in the civilian self-defense fight with conviction for the cause of the Republic and Democracy.

Minister of the Interior and Communal Development
Edouard Karemera

Copy for information:
His Excellence the President of the Republic

His Excellence the Prime Minister
The Minister of Defense
The Coordinator of National Civilian Defense

Dividing the Spoils

Most Rwandans live in great poverty. Before the genocide, one expert estimated that, even in the best of years, one-third of all Rwandans were ordinarily below the minimal nutritional standards set by international authorities. In the period right before the genocide, food production fell, in part because of poor climactic conditions, in part because of the disruptions of war. Rwandans, some 90 percent of whom are farmers, are also always short of land. Before April 1994, Rwanda was the most densely populated country in Africa.

Assailants joined in the attacks for different reasons: some from genuine fear of Tutsi, some from fear of harassment from fellow Hutu, some for material gain. Authorities recognized that conflicts over pillaged goods and, even more important, over the control of the land of victims, could divide the forces responsible for the genocide. In late April and early May 1994, authorities began establishing regulations for the distribution of the booty and for the use of land and crops of the victims. They directed local officials to make detailed inventories of property left by the Tutsi. Many lists of Tutsi killed and their property were found in government offices.

(Final note on letter from Joseph Kanyabashi, burgomaster of the Urban Commune of Ngoma, informing councilors of a meeting about security to take place at the commune at 9:00 a.m. on June 9, 1994.)

N.B. Those who come are asked to bring with them the inventory of the property of those people who have disappeared.

Denial of Guilt

Civilian and military authorities in power in Rwanda during the genocide continue to justify their actions under the cover of self-defense. The general staff of the Rwandan army in exile has produced a long document for the International Criminal Tribunal denying its guilt and accusing the RPF of having committed genocide against the Hutu that killed many times more Hutu than the number of Tutsi killed during this period.

(Excerpt from first page of "Contribution des Far a la Recherche de la Verite sur le Drame Rwandais" by the high command of the

Rwandan Armed Forces in exile, a document prepared in December 1995 for submission to the International Tribunal.)

Concerning the description of the violations, the FAR (Forces Armées Rwandaises) believes that the reports provided by human rights organizations and that underlay the creation of the International Tribunal for Rwanda are faulty in their partiality in introducing the idea of genocide. This description seems more emotional than legal. Indeed, it is based on the scale and nature of the massacres, thus on the reality and not on the intention of the crime.

The RPF has described the interethnic massacres as a genocide of Tutsi by the Hutu as a deliberate way of turning attention aside and so covering the genocide of the Hutu that was meticulously prepared by the RPF, before and during the war and [that continues] even now, but about which the international community says nothing.

The FAR also believe that during the troubles and during the war, the Hutu massacred by the RPF are many times more numerous than the Tutsi. Besides, the Tutsi who perished were victims of the situation of civil war set off in the country by the one who attacked Rwanda and who killed President Habyarimana and not [victims] of any intention or global will of the Hutu to decimate the Tutsi. In the absence of this intention, the genocide of the Tutsi proclaimed by the RPF far and wide is nothing but a purely gratuitous claim.

Notes

1. Rwanda's units of territorial administration are the prefecture, commune, sector and cell.
2. Jean-Pierre Chrétien et al., *Rwanda, Les médias du génocide* (Paris: Editions Karthala, 1995), 45.
3. Jean-Marie Higiro, "Distorsions et Omissions dans l'ouvrage *Rwanda, Les médias du génocide,*" *Dialogue*, no. 190 (April-May 1996): 161.
4. This document and those following were located and catalogued by a research team sponsored by Human Rights Watch and the International Federation of Human Rights Leagues.
5. Chrétien et al., Rwanda, *Les Médias du génocide*, 204–105.
6. In early 1998, Kambanda pleaded guilty to charges of genocide before the International Criminal Tribunal for Rwanda.

Internationalizing Civil War[1]

Diane F. Orentlicher

On October 2, 1995, the Appeals Chamber of the International Criminal Tribunal for the former Yugoslavia rendered one of the most important rulings on war crimes since the Nuremberg Judgment. At the time of the Nuremberg trial, the laws of war applied almost exclusively to wars between states. If governments went to war against their own citizens, international law would look the other way, however gruesomely the battles were waged. No longer. In a decision on its jurisdiction, the Appeals Chamber of the Yugoslavia Tribunal ruled that some atrocities committed in internal conflicts are universal crimes—crimes for which an international court can summon individuals to account.

This ruling reflects a profound change in the nature of armed conflict since World War II, and a corresponding evolution of the laws of war. As the decision notes, that law long enforced a "stark dichotomy," elaborately regulating wars between states while shielding the conduct of civil wars from the scrutiny of global conscience. But the dichotomy has gradually broken down, the chamber noted, in part because the "state-sovereignty-oriented approach" that relegated internal conflicts to the province of domestic jurisdiction "has been gradually supplanted by a human-being-oriented approach."

At the same time, civil wars have become both more frequent (one study has identified ninety-four armed conflicts during a recent six-year period; of these, only four were classic interstate conflicts) and more savage, often entailing violence on a scale so vast that their effects reverberate across an increasingly interdependent world. In consequence, the Appeals Chamber concluded, "the international community can no longer turn a blind eye to the legal regime of such wars."

No case better illustrates the point than the one that gave rise to the judgment. The decision arose out of a challenge to the tribunal's jurisdiction by its first defendant, Dusko Tadic, a former café owner and karate instructor in the Prijedor district of northwestern Bosnia. His crimes are emblematic of the depravity with which contemporary ethnic conflicts have been waged. When I visited a refugee camp in Croatia in 1993, relief workers told our delegation about a recent arrival from Bosnia who was experiencing extreme trauma. The refugee, who had been detained at the notorious Omarska camp in Prijedor, had been forced to bite off the testicle of another detainee, who is thought to have died of his injuries. Tadic was charged with—and later found guilty of—

participating in this incident, along with a grim litany of other crimes committed during the armed conflict in Bosnia.

At one time Tadic's depredations would have shocked universal conscience, but the laws of armed conflict would have had little to say about them. Why? Because both Tadic and his victims are citizens of the same state.

In reaching its judgment, the Appeals Chamber confronted a legal question as to which few signposts were available to guide it: by what legal regime should it judge the war crimes charges against Dusko Tadic? Although humanitarian law now regulates internal as well as interstate conflicts, much of the law of armed conflict still applies only to wars between states. Whether inhumane conduct is an international crime might depend on whether it occurred during an interstate or internal armed conflict.

The backdrop to the crimes with which Tadic was charged made this issue crucial—and a nightmarish tangle of disputed facts. By the time these crimes occurred, Bosnia had been recognized as an independent state. Tadic's alleged depredations were committed against other citizens of that state in the context of what seemed to be essentially a civil war. Yet the Bosnian Serbs opposing the Bosnian government were receiving support from Belgrade—a fact that might "internationalize" their rebellion.

In this setting, the tribunal had four options. The most conservative approach would be to maintain a rigid wall between the legal regimes governing international and internal armed conflicts, while narrowly construing the latter: some scholars doubted whether violations of the law governing noninternational armed conflict could give rise to criminal responsibility under international law.[2] Yet this approach would have produced unconscionable results. Suppose, for example, that a Serb from the Federal Republic of Yugoslavia joined a Bosnian Serb in raping a Bosnian Muslim. The Yugoslav Serb could be convicted of a war crime, while the Bosnian Serb might be acquitted of the same charge on virtually identical facts.

Alternatively, the tribunal could—as in the first option—maintain the traditional distinction between the laws governing international and internal armed conflicts, but construe the facts in a manner that would make the former legal regime applicable. In light of the circumstances prevailing during the Bosnian conflict, the tribunal could rule that the support received by Bosnian Serbs from Belgrade had the legal effect of internationalizing the entire conflict. This approach was advanced by the prosecutor, the UN Commission of Experts (a human rights body that preceded the tribunal) and several noted scholars. Under this approach, even crimes committed by Bosnian Serbs against Bosnian Muslims would be judged by the legal regime governing international armed conflicts.

The third—and perhaps most legally innovative—option was to hold that, at least in proceedings before the Hague Tribunal, rules widely believed to apply only to international armed conflicts apply with equal force to noninternational conflicts. The Trial Chamber did just that. It ruled, for example, that "Grave Breaches of the Geneva Conventions of 1949"—one of the two war crimes categories in the tribunal's statute—can occur in internal as well as international armed conflicts. Although it is widely accepted that "grave breaches" can occur only in international armed conflicts, the Trial Chamber did not believe that this general restriction had been imported into its statute.

The Appeals Chamber took a fourth course. It ruled, in effect, that significant distinctions between international and noninternational armed conflicts remain—but that the significance of the distinctions has radically diminished. The Appeals Chamber rejected the Trial Chamber's ruling that the "grave breaches" basis of the tribunal's jurisdiction applies equally in internal and international armed conflicts. But it also found that international law has evolved in a manner that now affords significant humanitarian protections in non-international as well as interstate armed conflicts. In its most important conclusion, the Appeals Chamber held that the "violations at issue here . . . entail individual criminal responsibility, regardless of whether they are committed in internal or international armed conflicts."[3]

The implications of this ruling sweep far beyond the Balkans. Having ruled that some breaches of the law governing internal conflicts are international crimes, the Appeals Chamber noted that "universal jurisdiction" is "nowadays acknowledged in the case of international crimes." Certain violations of humanitarian law committed in internal armed conflicts can, therefore, be punished by any state to which the perpetrator may travel. Thus serious crimes committed during civil wars in places like El Salvador and Guatemala, where the wall of impunity may be largely impregnable, can nonetheless be prosecuted by any state to which the perpetrators may travel. As for war crimes committed in Bosnia and Croatia, the Appeals Chamber helped assure that those responsible will face the specter of prosecution the world over—if not by the tribunal, then by any state.

In larger perspective, the Appeals Chamber's decision made clear that the Hague Tribunal has emerged as a genuinely independent body. Notably, the decision reversed key portions of the Trial Chamber's ruling on jurisdiction, demonstrating the Appeals Chamber's ability and willingness to provide meaningful review. In contrast, there was no appeal from judgments at Nuremberg. In a further demonstration of judicial independence, the Appeals Chamber declined to adopt some of the key positions advanced by the prosecution.

These hallmarks of independence are especially noteworthy in view of the Tribunal's creation by the quintessential political body—the UN Security Council. The Appeals Chamber declared itself competent to judge the Security Council's own authority in establishing the tribunal, and proceeded to do just that.

In his closing argument at Nuremberg, Chief American Prosecutor Robert Jackson memorably invoked the redemptive power of law. "Goaded," he said, by the immensity of Nazi evil, "we were moved to redress the blight on the record of our era." Fifty years later, the international community has once again acted to redress its failure to halt "ethnic cleansing" in the heart of Europe by establishing an international criminal tribunal. While the Hague Tribunal still faces formidable challenges, it has already given cause to hope that its accomplishments may emerge as "one of the most significant tributes that power has every paid to reason"—and, at last, to the rule of law.

Notes

1. Adapted from "War Crimes Tribunal Dismisses Jurisdictional Challenge," *Human Rights Brief* 3, no. 1 (Fall 1995). I am grateful to Rod Dixon, Robert K. Goldman and Alan Tieger for their comments on an earlier draft.

2. The International Criminal Tribunal for Rwanda was spared this dilemma. Its statute confers jurisdiction over serious violations of Common Article 3 of the Geneva Conventions of 1949, which explicitly applies to noninternational armed conflicts.

3. While making clear that certain acts constitute war crimes whether committed in internal or international armed conflicts, this ruling left open the possibility that the more elaborate legal regime governing interstate armed conflicts might be applicable if relevant facts were established.

   When, however, the Trial Chamber rendered its verdict in the *Tadic* case on May 7, 1997, it found that the prosecution had failed adequately to prove all of the requirements for applying the grave breaches provisions in respect of certain charges against Tadic. To prove that Tadic's treatment of Bosnian citizens constituted grave breaches, the prosecution had to establish that, although armed forces of the Federal Republic of Yugoslavia (FRY) had officially withdrawn from Bosnia before the date of the relevant charges, Bosnian Serb forces nonetheless acted as agents of the FRY in their conduct toward Bosnian citizens. Holding that the relevant legal standard in this respect was one of "effective control" of Bosnian Serb forces by the FRY, a majority of the Trial Chamber—with its presiding judge dissenting—found that the prosecution had not adequately proved effective control. The Trial Chamber did, however, convict Tadic of committing serious violations of humanitarian law applicable in noninternational as well as international armed conflicts. As of this writing, the Trial Chamber's ruling is pending appeal.

In the meantime, the Trial Chamber in another case has reached a different conclusion regarding application of the grave breaches provisions of the Geneva Conventions. The verdict in the *Celebici* case, rendered on November 16, 1998, found that the FRY's withdrawal of armed forces from Bosnia "constituted a deliberate attempt to mask the continued involvement of the FRY in the conflict while its Government remained in fact the controlling force behind the Bosnian Serbs" at the time the alleged crimes occurred. It concluded that the armed conflict in which the alleged acts occurred was, therefore, international.

Rape Under International Law

Patricia Viseur Sellers[1]

> In medieval times, opportunities to rape and loot were among the few
> advantages open to common foot soldiers, who were paid with great
> irregularity by their leaders. The Byzantine emperor Alexius is sup-
> posed to have extolled the beauty of Greek women in his appeals for
> recruits for the First Crusade. When the city of Constantinople was
> sacked in 1204, rape and plunder went hand in hand, as in the sack of
> almost every ancient city.... "To the victor belong the spoils" has ap-
> plied to women since Helen of Troy, but the sheer property worth of
> women was replaced in time by a far more subtle system of values.
> Down through the ages, triumph over women by rape became a way
> to measure victory, part of a soldier's proof of masculinity and success,
> a tangible reward for services rendered... an actual reward of war.
>
> Susan Brownmiller[2]

Introduction

War is a staggeringly public manifestation. Hills are charged, flags are
raised, and enemy cities are bombed. Amid these militarily directed acts
of destruction exists a less public underside of war—rape and other sexual
violence. The prevalence of rapes committed during modern warfare has
kept pace with, if not exceeded, the sexual violence of ancient conflicts.

A World War I metaphor, the "Belgian humiliation," alluded to the extraordinary number of Belgian women raped by the advancing army of
Kaiser Wilhelm II. Less than a generation later, World War II witnessed
the massive rapes of Soviet women as German forces invaded the eastern
front, only to have countless German women sexually assaulted by Soviet
troops marching victoriously into Berlin several years later. In the Pacific
theater, the Rape of Nanking refers to the pervasive sexual violence inflicted upon women during the surrender of the Chinese city to the Japanese. The wartime Japanese government instituted brothels and subjugated
nearly 200,000 Asian women into prostitution for the "comfort" of Japanese soldiers. Decades later, the partition of Pakistan wrought civil war and
resulted in the infliction of rape on thousands of Bangladeshi women and
girls. Today, war in the former Yugoslavia and the genocide of Rwanda
perpetuate the duality of armed conflict and rape.

Given the prevalence of rape in twentieth century conflict, it is critical to examine the evolution of the law on wartime sexual assault, culminating in the current jurisprudence of the International Criminal Tribunals for former Yugoslavia and Rwanda. These modern tribunals are not the first instances in which the international community has considered the issue of wartime rape. The nineteenth and twentieth centuries saw the prolific drafting of international legal instruments to regulate the conduct of war, and conventions and treaties clearly show that rape is well entrenched within international humanitarian law. Judicial opinions, however, reveal that rape lacks a developed jurisprudence. Rape has often been a "veiled" and reluctantly understood crime. The ad hoc international criminal tribunals and the increasing prospect of a permanent international criminal court could alter the imbalance between rape as an established crime, on the one hand, and the dearth of judicial pronouncements on the subject, on the other.

Rape Under International Humanitarian Law

The genesis of war, the rationale for war's persistence, adaptability and universality, are subjects for philosophers, historians, political scientists or sociologists. Lawyers have generally sought not to understand or outlaw war, but to regulate and codify the conduct of belligerents. For example, the Hague Conventions of 1899 and 1907 proscribed the use of certain weapons and methods of warfare. The Geneva Conventions of 1864, 1906 and 1929 restricted abuses committed by belligerents and aimed at individuals, particularly noncombatants.

From the point of view of women's concerns, even these inceptive treaties used surprisingly gender-neutral terms. The conventions rarely gender-differentiated the crime or the protected group. Nominally, conventions safeguarded the wounded, the shipwrecked and civilians—men and women alike—from the illegal excesses of war.

How have conventions protected women against rape? Early conventions acknowledged that rape violated the legal norms of war; however, the drafters generally shrouded sex crimes in Victorian-style nomenclature. Phrases such as "family honor and rights" were typically utilized when invoking prohibitions of rape and other sexual assaults. The wording is quaint, if not evasive, by today's standards; however, the violation, as drafted, was legally substantive and avoided vagueness.

The Lieber Code, issued in 1863 and formally entitled the Instructions for Government of Armies of the United States in the Field, refrained from the use of Victorian language. This military code, which governed the behavior of Union troops during the United States Civil War, explicitly forbade, under penalty of death, the "rape...of such inhabitants" by Union soldiers. In succeeding years, the Lieber Code, with its prohibition of rape, was indicative of customary law, the expected practice of all nations.

Victorian gentility aside, the diplomats' pledge to abide by the Hague Conventions was shattered as World War I engulfed Europe, and eventually the United States. Obedience to enlightened principles drafted to govern battle and occupation disintegrated as German forces marched—and raped—throughout Europe. The Germans conducted a campaign of terror in the first three months of World War I. It is unclear, however, whether the sexual "terror" was a previously organized and implemented scheme or the result of encouragement (and lack of discouragement), coupled with abundant opportunity due to the manner in which warfare was conducted at the time (that is, a maneuvering, marching army). Regardless of which is true, the frequency and publicity of the rapes highlighted the humiliation of the nations thus terrorized and raised the level of horror vis-à-vis the Germans. Additionally, the incidents of rape were used by the Allied propaganda machine to build support against the Germans.

After the Armistice, the Allies set up a War Crimes Commission to determine whether Kaiser Wilhelm II and his high-ranking commanders should be prosecuted. The commission recommended establishment of an international judicial body to adjudicate thirty-two recognized war crimes, including rape and forced prostitution. The Allied powers eventually were dissuaded from prosecution, owing in part to the refusal of the Netherlands to surrender Kaiser Wilhelm to an international tribunal. Nevertheless, the legal exercise demonstrated that rape contravened the laws of armed conflict and was subject to the jurisdiction of an international court.

In 1923, a diplomatic conference reviewed the applicable Geneva law for prisoners of war and resulted in the drafting of the 1929 Geneva Convention. The convention affirmed that prisoners are entitled to respect for their "honor." Interestingly, it was the German delegation to the conference that pressed for a provision to clarify the phrase and to recognize that women combatants indeed fell under enemy control as prisoners. The convention thus stated that as prisoners, "women shall be treated with all consideration due to their sex."

After World War II, the Allies' legal response to the crimes committed by the Nazi regime culminated in the establishment of the International Military Tribunals at Nuremberg and at Tokyo. The major war criminals of the European and Asian Axis stood trial for crimes against the peace, war crimes and crimes against humanity. Rape was not named as a war crime nor as a crime against humanity in the Nuremberg or the Tokyo Charter. However, the French and Russian prosecutors did submit evidence of sexual assaults committed during the German invasion of Russia and the occupation in France under the Vichy regime, as well as sexual violence inflicted upon concentration camp inmates. Most acts of sexual violence were prosecuted as "inhumane acts."

The prosecution of Japanese defendants in Tokyo afforded greater attention to rape, although the most egregious crime, involving the so-called "comfort women," was completely ignored by the prosecutor and the judges. Nevertheless, evidence was presented about the occupation of Nanking, Borneo, Manila, and other parts of China, where Japanese soldiers raped nurses, prisoners and a large number of the female inhabitants. The defendants were convicted for acts of rape committed by their subordinates under the doctrine of command responsibility. Rape was characterized as a violation of the laws and customs of war and a crime against humanity, a form of inhumane treatment, ill treatment and failure to respect family honor and rights.

The Nuremberg trials bequeathed very qualified jurisprudence on criminalizing sexual assault in wartime, noting merely that rape was justiciable as a crime against humanity or a war crime, thus confirming the recommended charges of the post-World War I War Crimes Commission. The Tokyo jurisprudence on rape offered an improvement over that of Nuremberg, since explicit allegations of rape were contained in the bills of particulars, and convictions undoubtedly gave great weight to evidence of sexual violence.

After the International Military Tribunals' verdicts, trials of lesser Axis war criminals were conducted by national military courts, such as the Chinese and the Dutch. The United States military prosecuted lesser criminals under Control Council Law No. 10, which enumerated rape as a crime against humanity, possibly originating from the principles in the Hague Conventions or the Lieber Code. Treating rape as a separate crime against humanity in this way set a drafting precedent; however, the U.S. prosecutors retreated from its use, although prosecutions of medical experiments involving fertility, reproduction and forced sterility were successfully adjudicated. In the Far East Theatre, in contrast, Chinese, Dutch, British, and U.S. prosecutors did pursue convictions based upon sexual violence.

The end of World War II sparked another drafting phase. Within six years of the unconditional surrenders of Germany and Japan, several major international humanitarian law instruments were completed. The United Nations led the reexamination of humanitarian law. The UN General Assembly directed the International Law Commission to codify the law of Nuremberg. The codification, entitled the Nuremberg Principles, discarded allusive sexual assault language, but failed to enumerate rape as a crime. This legal silence was an embarrassing omission.

The same spate of drafting also produced the four Geneva Conventions of 1949 that detailed the protection states owed to specific groups—noncombatants, humanitarian aid personnel, the shipwrecked, prisoners of war and the civilian population, respectively. Each of the four Geneva Conventions culminated in a list of identical grave breaches, or serious violations, consisting of willful killing, torture or inhuman treatment, including biological experiments, willfully causing great suffering or serious injury to body or health, and extensive destruction and appropriation of property not justified by military necessity and carried out unlawfully and wantonly.

During the drafting convention, the Commission of Government Experts, advisors to the delegates, urged that a principle concerning sexual violence be incorporated into the civilian convention, since "the decency and dignity of women calls for more precise definition... . Countless women of all ages, and even small girls, were the victims of the most abominable outrages... rape... and indecent assault. Thousands were placed in disorderly houses against their will, or obliged to submit to troops."

The fourth Geneva Convention, regarding civilians, embodied such a principle. Article 27 cited rape, enforced prostitution and indecent assault as prohibited acts that assailed the honor of women. However, failure to include rape as a grave breach placed in doubt whether soldiers could be held criminally liable for acts of rape under the convention. Forty years later, an aide-mémoire issued by the International Committee of the Red Cross officially recognized that rape could be prosecuted under the grave breaches provision of the Geneva Conventions of 1949. While an aide-mémoire lacks the precedential value of an enumerated breach or an official commentary, it does provide some indication of the possible scope of the referenced provisions.

The other three Geneva Conventions do not explicitly prohibit rape, enforced prostitution or forms of indecent assault; however, women who are among the wounded, shipwrecked or prisoners of war are to be granted "the consideration due to their sex." Likewise, Article 3, common to the four Geneva Conventions, imposes a minimum standard of behavior for belligerents during *internal* armed conflicts and, in veiled language, prohibits outrages upon personal dignity, in particular humiliating and degrading treatment.

The postwar Convention for the Suppression and Punishment of the Crime of Genocide directly addressed atrocities other than rape that affected women and were committed by the Nazis against European Jews. Owing more to the racist Nazi notion of superiority and racial purity than to respect for sexual integrity, rape of Jewish women during the Holocaust was overshadowed by other assaults on their sexual integrity. The Genocide Convention more concretely prohibits biological experiments to sterilize men and women or to prevent births, intentional acts of separation of the sexes, and the transfer of children, although other sexually violent conduct can be interpreted to satisfy its provisions.

The last twenty-five years have generated instruments that affirm rape as a serious, and therefore justiciable, violation of international humanitarian law. Prompted in part by the decolonization of Africa and portions of Asia, two Additional Protocols to the Geneva Conventions were drafted to supplement and extend the protection of the grave breaches provision to situations of internal armed conflict. Both prefatory paragraphs to the grave breach sections state that the protocols must be applied without adverse distinction based on sex.

Additional Protocol I, influenced by Common Article 3, recognizes as a fundamental guarantee that individuals be protected from outrages upon personal dignity, in particular humiliating and degrading treatment, enforced prostitution and any form of indecent assault. The Victorian phrasing previously favored by drafters gave way to forthright language within the text of a fundamental guarantees provision. Protocol I went on to provide for the special protection of women against rape, forced prostitution and any form of indecent assault. Protocol II similarly protects persons not taking part in hostilities from subjection to rape, enforced prostitution and any form of indecent assault.

The 1990s have seen the advance of several groundbreaking international humanitarian law instruments. Undoubtedly the most significant inheres from the ad hoc International Criminal Tribunals for the former Yugoslavia and Rwanda.

In 1992, a vicious armed conflict that engendered killings, detention of civilians, forced removals of population and massive rapes accompanied the dissolution of the former Republic of Yugoslavia. United Nations Security Council resolutions demanded a halt to atrocities and condemned the abominable objective of ethnic cleansing. Invoking Chapter VII of the United Nations Charter, the Security Council members voted to create an ad hoc tribunal to adjudicate serious violations of international humanitarian law. Within sixty days, the Security Council accepted a governing statute for the tribunal.

The international humanitarian law principles embodied in the conventions and treaties produced during the past century served as the statute's legal foundation. Crimes under the Yugoslavia statute incorporate verbatim the grave breaches of the Geneva Conventions of 1949 and portions of the Genocide Convention. Article 5 of the statute includes crimes against humanity, with the notable addition that rape is unequivocally enumerated as a separate crime. This is the first time that a functioning international criminal tribunal has granted rape equal legal status as a crime against humanity.

Equally significant is the Yugoslavia Tribunal's mandate to investigate, adjudicate and, upon a finding of guilt, punish perpetrators or their superiors for rape and other sexual assaults. The Office of the Prosecutor has assiduously pursued this mandate, and as of May 1998, approximately one-fifth of all counts brought in the indictments were sex-based crimes, charged as grave breaches, war crimes, crimes against humanity or acts of genocide. Sexual assaults committed against males are likewise the basis for certain indictments.

The need to regulate armed conflicts continued to surface in the 1990s. In April 1994, after an airplane carrying the presidents of Rwanda and Burundi crashed, Rwanda erupted into genocidal havoc.[3] The UN Security Council again resorted to Chapter VII and established the International Criminal Tribunal for Rwanda (ICTR), "for the sole purpose of prosecuting persons responsible for genocide and other serious violations of international law in the territory of Rwanda...." The crimes under the Rwandan statute give primacy to parts of the Genocide Convention. The crimes against humanity provision explicitly lists rape as a separate crime, reaffirming the status conveyed in the Yugoslavia statute. The Rwanda statute also incorporates the Protocol II and Common Article 3 proscriptions for internal conflicts. For purposes of the Rwanda Tribunal, four explicit sexual assaults are enumerated in the provisions of the ICTR statute. The Crimes against Humanity provision (Article 3) includes rape as a prosecutable offense, and the Violations of Common Article 3 provision (Article 4) includes, in addition to rape, "outrages upon personal dignity... enforced prostitution and any form of indecent assault." Additionally, the ICTR statute mandates international criminal liability for these offenses, even when they are committed during internal conflict. By virtue of the enumeration of four explicit sexual assaults, the Rwanda Tribunal could greatly impact the jurisprudence of international humanitarian law by providing case law on sexual violence as a specific sex-based crime.[4]

The International Law Commission's assignments will conclude in the 1990s. After nearly fifty years of committee meetings and special rapporteurs, the Commission adopted the Draft Code for the Peace and Security of Mankind throughout 1997 and 1998. Influenced by the statutes of the ad hoc tribunals and drafting precedent from World War II, the Commission, for the first time, explicitly incorporated rape, enforced prostitution and other forms of sexual abuse into the Crimes against Humanity article. The more epochal labor of the International Law Commission was the wording of a Draft Statute for an International Criminal Court. The Preparatory Committee sessions throughout 1997 and 1998 expressly accepted the inclusion of rape as a crime against humanity and a war crime. The permanent international criminal court will clearly be mandated to investigate and prosecute sexual violence that has attained the level of an international crime.

Conclusion

Women are raped in cruel war after cruel war. Rape has been subjected since the last century, either implicitly or explicitly, to substantive legal regulation, along with other perennial atrocities of armed conflict. The current outcry to make rape a war crime is redundant. Rape is already a war crime, a crime against humanity and the basis for prosecution under grave breaches and genocide provisions, whether committed in an international or internal armed conflict.

The neglect that rape has suffered has not been in the drafting of conventions, but in war's legal aftermath. Infrequent prosecution has rendered the crime all but invisible. Sexual violence, the private underbelly of war, has been shrouded in silence due to neglectful application of law; like other international crimes, its condemnation is only as strong as the jurisprudence it generates. The potential jurisprudence issuing from the ad hoc tribunals and the eventual establishment of a permanent international criminal court represent a chance that sexual violence will finally be fully exposed and punished.

The potential development of jurisprudence for rape as an offense under international criminal law relies in part on the recent and ever-increasing influence and involvement of woman in all areas of investigation, prosecution and judicial reasoning. The importance of gender-integrated investigation teams, as well as female lawyers and judges, is central to the continued discussion and development of this historically taboo subject.

Notes

1. The opinions expressed in this chapter are attributable to the author and do not officially reflect the views of the Office of the Prosecutor or of the United Nations.
2. Susan Brownmiller, *Against Our Will: Men, Women and Rape* (New York: Simon and Schuster, 1975), 35.
3. For a detailed description of these events, see Alison des Forges, "Documentary Horror: The Administration of the Rwandan Genocide," this volume.
4. Editor's note: In convicting Jean-Paul Akayesu of genocide in September 1998, the ICTR found mass rape to be an act of genocide.

WHY AN INTERNATIONAL TRIBUNAL?
Analysis and Alternatives to International Adjudication

War Crimes Trials:
Who Should Conduct Them—and How

Neil J. Kritz[1]

Emsud Bahonjic and Fidele Kayabugoyi never met. They came from very different backgrounds and cultures, and were separated by more than 3,500 miles. History will remember them, however, for the sad facts they share in common: both were brutally and sadistically killed because of their respective Bosnian Muslim and Rwandan Tutsi ethnicity—victims of genocide, "ethnic cleansing," and related mass crimes in their countries. How their respective societies and the world deal with the killers of these two men, and with the many other perpetrators of odious crimes in the former Yugoslavia and Rwanda, may have significant consequences for the long-term peace in their ravaged lands.

How can peace and reconciliation be achieved after atrocities such as these? What role, constructive or otherwise, might prosecution of war crimes play in putting these societies back together? Some would suggest that the best way to reconcile is to leave the past in the past. They argue that war crimes prosecutions will most likely be show trials unbefitting a sincere effort to establish peace and democracy, that a public review of wartime atrocities will inflame passions and hatreds rather than calming them, that shattered societies should focus their limited human and material resources on the urgent task of economic reconstruction—building a brighter tomorrow—rather than diverting those limited resources to dwell on the sins of yesterday.

If the goal in these countries, however, is something more than a tenuous, temporary pause in the violence, dealing in a clear and determined manner with war crimes and genocide is essential. To assume that individuals and groups who have been the victims of hideous atrocities will simply forget about them or expunge their feelings without some form of accounting, some semblance of justice, is to misunderstand human psychology and to leave in place the seeds of future conflict. What is true of individuals emerging from massive abuse and trauma is no less true of nations: mechanisms are needed to confront and reckon with that past, facilitating closure rather than repression. Otherwise, the past can be expected to haunt and infect the present and future. Victims may harbor deep resentments that, if not addressed through a process of justice, may ultimately be dealt with through one of vengeance. A public airing and condemnation of these crimes may be the best way to draw a line between times past and present, lest the public perceive the new order as simply more of the same. Dealing with the grievances and the grieving, accountability and forgiveness, and the rehabilitation of victims and perpetrators will be a painful and delicate process. It will take time—certainly longer than the time allotted for technical tasks like the separation and reduction of military forces. But doing nothing in response to war crimes and related atrocities adds to the injury of victims, perpetuates a culture of impunity that can only encourage future abuses, and contributes to the likelihood of vigilante justice and retribution.

In this context, war crimes prosecutions can serve several functions. They can provide victims with a sense of justice and catharsis—a sense that their grievances have been addressed and can more easily be put to rest, rather than smoldering in anticipation of the next round of conflict. In addition, they can establish a new dynamic in society, an understanding that aggressors and those who attempt to abuse the rights of others will henceforth be held accountable. Perhaps most important for purposes of long-term reconciliation, this approach makes the statement that specific individuals—not entire ethnic or religious or political groups—committed atrocities for which they need to be held accountable. In so doing, it rejects the dangerous culture of collective guilt and retribution that often produces further cycles of resentment and violence.

Were these not sufficiently compelling reasons to confront rather than ignore war crimes, one should also note that in places like Rwanda and Bosnia, the repatriation of massive numbers of refugees is integrally related to the question of justice and accountability. For more than two years after the genocide in Rwanda, well over one million Hutus remained in refugee camps in neighboring countries. The former military leaders, militia members and architects of the genocide—who controlled the camps and had good reason to fear the prospect of justice and accountability for the carnage of 1994—used these refugees as a human shield and fed them continuous propaganda that they would all be held maximally accountable by the new Rwandan government if they dared to return. At the end of 1996, most of the Hutu refugees finally left the camps in what was then Zaire and Tanzania and poured back home across the border to Rwanda. A major challenge facing the government is the need to reabsorb these large numbers of its citizens while reckoning with thousands of perpetrators of the genocide. In Bosnia, the converse is true: fully half the population was displaced during the war, and refugees are wary, if not incapable, of venturing back to their villages of origin while those who perpetrated crimes against humanity remain in control there.

International Prosecution of War Crimes

When war crimes trials are undertaken, are they better conducted by an international tribunal—like those in Nuremberg and Tokyo or those for the former Yugoslavia and Rwanda—or by the local courts of the country concerned? There are sound policy reasons for each approach.

An international tribunal is better positioned to convey a clear message that the international community will not tolerate such atrocities, hopefully deterring future carnage of this sort both in the country in question and worldwide. It is more likely to be staffed by experts able to apply and interpret evolving international standards in a sometimes murky field of the law. It can do more to advance the development and enforcement of international criminal norms. Relative to the often shattered judicial system of a country emerging from genocide or other mass atrocities, an international tribunal is more likely to have the necessary human and material resources at its disposal. It can more readily function—and be perceived as functioning—on the basis of independence and impartiality rather than retribution. Finally, where the majority of senior planners and perpetrators of these atrocities have left the territory where the crimes were committed or otherwise are out of the domestic judicial reach of their former victims (as is the case in both Rwanda and Bosnia), an international tribunal stands a greater chance than local courts of obtaining their physical custody and extradition.

The most important precedent for international treatment of war crimes is, of course, the post-World War II trials at Nuremberg. The prosecution of Nazi atrocities before the International Military Tribunal (IMT) and the subsequent Nuremberg tribunals established several key principles that continue to influence international conduct. Among these are the notions that the human rights of individuals and groups are a matter of international concern; that the international community's interest in preventing or punishing offenses against humanity committed within states qualifies any concept of national sovereignty; that not just states but individuals can be held accountable under international law for their role in genocide and other atrocities; and that "following orders" is no defense to such accountability.

In May 1993, responding to overwhelming evidence of "ethnic cleansing" and genocidal activity in the ongoing war in the former Yugoslavia, the United Nations Security Council voted to create the first international war crimes tribunal since those at Nuremberg and Tokyo. The Security Council established the "International Tribunal for the Prosecution of Persons Responsible for Serious Violations of International Humanitarian Law Committed in the Territory of the Former Yugoslavia since 1991" in the explicit belief that accountability would "contribute to the restoration and maintenance of peace."[2] The tribunal has its seat in the Hague. It is comprised of eleven judges from as many countries, divided into two trial chambers and an appellate chamber.[3]

The Yugoslavia Tribunal is in several ways an improvement on the

Nuremberg model. Its rules of procedure incorporate positive developments over the past fifty years with respect to the rights of criminal defendants under international law. Second, to the extent that Nuremberg was perceived as a prosecution of World War II's losing parties by the victors, the Yugoslavia Tribunal is nothing of the sort. As noted above, it is a truly international exercise, and the countries which supply its judges, prosecutors and staff are not parties to the conflict. In addition, it is committed to the investigation and prosecution of war crimes committed by persons from each side in the war.

Considering that almost fifty years passed between the Nuremberg and Yugoslavia tribunals, the next major institutional development occurred in rapid succession. In November 1994, "convinced that in the particular circumstances of Rwanda, the prosecution of persons responsible for serious violations of international humanitarian law would ... contribute to the process of national reconciliation and to the restoration and maintenance of peace,"[4] the Security Council voted to create an International Criminal Tribunal for Rwanda. Not surprisingly, the structure and mandate of the new tribunal closely tracked that of its counterpart for the former Yugoslavia. To maximize the efficient sharing of resources, avoid the potential for conflicting legal approaches, and minimize start-up time, the two tribunals share their chief prosecutor and their appellate chamber; their respective rules of evidence and procedure are virtually identical. A deputy prosecutor directs a small team of investigators and criminal attorneys in the Rwandan capital of Kigali. The actual trials take place at the tribunal's seat in Arusha, Tanzania, but segments are broadcast into Rwanda. For the tribunal to have its maximum effect, it is essential that its proceedings be accessible to the Rwandan population, at least by radio.

These two tribunals are playing a truly historic role, expanding the horizons for the international treatment of war crimes and establishing important precedents. Owing to its own perseverence and that of a few key supporters, the Yugoslavia Tribunal firmly held its ground in spite of an early and misguided willingness in some circles to sacrifice it to the peace process. In the year following the Dayton Accord, the tribunal made significant advances in the conduct of investigations (including access to and exhumation of certain mass graves in Srebrenica and elsewhere), the commencement of the first trials, and the public review of evidence and issuance of international arrest warrants in several cases. Having overcome many of the initial hurdles of organization, funding, staffing and the development of suitable procedural rules, both tribunals have moved forward in the development of increasingly honed and effective prosecution strategies. More important than the numbers of cases they have pursued are their important contributions to international law, including the recognition that certain rules of conduct that had previously applied only to wars between states are now enforceable in intrastate conflicts, and the determination that the systematic use of rape may constitute a war crime.

The tribunals have certainly not been without their problems and constraints. Two issues in particular warrant brief mention.

In his final report to the U.S. Secretary of the Army on the Nuremberg proceedings, chief prosecutor Telford Taylor noted that after the initial IMT trial, the need to organize new structures, administration and staffing for the twelve trials to follow delayed the war crimes program by almost a year. The delay had its cost. "If the trials . . . had started and been finished a year earlier," observed Taylor, "it might well have been possible to bring their lessons home to the public at large far more effectively."[5] These words ring at least as true half a century later. The building of a properly functioning new international judicial institution will necessarily take time under the best of circumstances. Even so, delays in establishment, funding, staffing and organization of the two international tribunals for the former Yugoslavia and Rwanda undercut the effort to bring their message home during the early phase of their development. As a result, it took a year and a half for the Yugoslavia Tribunal to issue its first indictment; in the Rwandan case, while the architects of genocide moved about in various countries with relative impunity and the Rwandan government undertook efforts to handle the challenge of accountability on its own, the international tribunal did not begin its first trial until two and a half years after the genocide. Such start-up delays plainly hampered the initial effectiveness of these institutions. This is an issue that will need to be addressed in future cases.

Global attitudes toward justice are shifting. In just the past fifty years, the need to establish mechanisms of accountability for mass abuses has arisen not only in the immediate post-World War II period, but in the transitions from tyranny or war in Greece, Argentina, Chile, Uganda, Ethiopia, South Africa and much of post-communist Europe, to name but a few.[6] These and several other cases have both drawn from and informed a growing international consensus. The emerging doctrine holds that, at least in the aftermath of widespread atrocities, justice is a necessary element of any stable peace. This is nothing less than a sea change in international thinking on this question.

But sea changes occur gradually, and there is not yet an accompanying doctrinal acceptance of the responsibilities that come with establishment of these international criminal tribunals. States and municipalities cannot expect their courts to enforce criminal law on their own without the enforcement power of the police; the international community must similarly recognize that it cannot create these international criminal tribunals without being willing to provide these institutions with assistance and muscle to enforce their orders and decisions. This problem has, of course, been most clearly manifest in the reluctance to assist in the apprehension of those indicted by the tribunals—an issue that undermines the credibility of international resolve.

One can hope that this situation will improve as the international approach to justice and accountability evolves, and, in the case of the Yugoslavia and Rwanda tribunals, as actions catch up with pledges. In the post-Dayton period, the Yugoslavia Tribunal has already garnered increased public and media support and has made some impressive gains, as noted above. Public pressure and a growing realization that the non-arrest of alleged war criminals impeded implementation of the peace process led to a more robust NATO posture. Between the spring of 1997 and the spring of 1998, international peacekeeping troops apprehended eight indictees and killed a ninth who resisted arrest. This tougher stance also facilitated several surrenders. After a somewhat rocky start, the Rwanda tribunal's increasing effectiveness, combined with such developments as the return to Rwanda of over one million refugees from then-Zaire and Tanzania (behind whom many leaders of the 1994 carnage had until then been able to hide), rendered the principal *genocidaires* more exposed and vulnerable. At a time when Dr. Karadzic and General Mladic remained beyond the reach of its Yugoslav counterpart, the Rwanda tribunal's detainees include the former prime minister—who has pleaded guilty to genocide charges—the former military chief and other senior architects and enforcers of the slaughter.

Temporary Tribunals or a Permanent Institution?

Many expected the momentum generated by Nuremberg to result in the prompt creation of a more permanent international court for the prosecution of war crimes and related atrocities. The 1948 Genocide Convention reflected this assumption, providing for trials "by such international penal tribunal as may have jurisdiction."[7] The immediate entry into the Cold War, however, froze any prospects for such a development for the next four decades.

The end of the Cold War, combined with the establishment of the two ad hoc tribunals, provided significant impetus for resurrecting the long-dormant discussion regarding creation of a permanent international criminal authority. In 1993, at the request of the UN General Assembly, the International Law Commission produced a detailed draft statute for such a court, which it further refined in 1994. Between 1996 and early 1998, a preparatory committee established by the General Assembly conducted several weeks of deliberations on the draft charter for the International Criminal Court, with delegations from nearly 100 countries participating. There were a number of important issues to be ironed out—e.g., the role of the Security Council as a gatekeeper for referral of cases to the court; possible jurisdiction over such crimes as terrorism, aggression, and drug-trafficking; the authority of the prosecutor to initiate investigations; and questions of extradition and of procedure. The preparatory committee examined how to define fair trial standards in a way that reflected the world's various legal systems. There was extensive debate over what the court's relationship should be with the United Nations and how it should be financed. Among the 100 countries participating in the discussion, however, there emerged a broad consensus that the new court would have jurisdiction over individuals for the core international crimes of genocide, war crimes and crimes against humanity. Establishment of this body would, of course, obviate the need for creation of further ad hoc tribunals and would significantly reduce the delays that have hampered the commencement of these tribunals. After various revisions and negotiations, a plenipotentiary conference took place in 1998 to draft and adopt a treaty establishing this permanent international criminal court.[8] Creation of the permanent court is a major step forward in the effort to ensure justice and accountability.

Some skeptics suggest that international legal norms and international tribunals are an ineffective waste of resources, the fantasy land of liberal academics unappreciative of political realities. The culture of respect for the rule of law that permeates many Western societies, it is argued, is hardly a universal phenomenon. In the real world, both individual villains and the rogue states that harbor them flaunt their noncompliance with the decisions of these international panels, and they are not going to change their conduct just because international law or an international court so directs them. These international courts have no independent enforcement power for their decisions, and the world community feels no obligation to provide such enforcement.

These skeptics would do well to reflect on the development of American legal culture. In 1831, for example, a half-century after the founding of the U.S. legal system, the state of Georgia asserted jurisdiction over the Cherokee Indian tribe in violation of a federal treaty. The U.S. Supreme Court overturned the state actions. Far from feeling obliged to uphold the decision of the highest court, President Andrew Jackson is reputed to have said, "[Chief Justice] John Marshall has made his decision, now let him enforce it." Earlier, in 1809, the governor of Pennsylvania actually sent out the state militia to resist enforcement of a federal court judgment. In 1793, the state of Georgia rejected the authority of the Supreme Court, assigned by the Constitution, to examine claims of state abuse of citizens of another state; the Georgia House of Representatives then declared that any federal marshall attempting to enter the state to execute any process of the Supreme Court in such cases would be "deemed guilty of felony, and shall suffer death without benefit of clergy, by being hanged."[9] These incidents and others like them might have led earlier skeptics to question the viability of the U.S. judicial system.

Building a loyal and consistent adherence to the rule of law is a long-term process. Today, after more than two hundred years, such occurences are all but inconceivable and forgotten in the United States. But these early American cases clearly have their contemporary international parallels, when NATO is reluctant to enforce the arrest orders of an international criminal tribunal because of threats of armed resistance from the local militia, or when President Daniel Arap Moi of Kenya declared in October 1995 that any staff of the International Criminal Tribunal for Rwanda who entered Kenya to pursue their investigations would be promptly arrested.[10] (The Kenyan authorities, like those in Georgia two centuries earlier, ultimately backed down.) Viewed against this background, the still relatively nascent international legal regime for prosecution for war crimes and crimes against humanity may seem more viable and realistic than that suggested at times by the frustrations and weaknesses of the present system. A sustained sense of principled determination and political will produced the American respect for the rule of law; such determination will hopefully now be applied to the international system as well.

The Domestic Component

Prosecution of war crimes before domestic courts can also serve some important purposes, distinct from those that underlie international trials. It can enhance the legitimacy and credibility of a fragile new government, demonstrating its determination to hold individuals accountable for their crimes. Because these trials tend to be high-profile proceedings that receive significant attention from the local population and foreign observers, they can provide an important focus for rebuilding the domestic judiciary and criminal justice system, establishing the courts as a credible forum for the redress of grievances in a nonviolent manner. Finally, as noted in 1994 by the UN Commission of Experts appointed to investigate the Rwandan genocide, domestic courts can be more sensitive to the nuances of local culture, and resulting decisions "could be of greater and more immediate symbolic force because verdicts would be rendered by courts familiar to the local community."[11]

In addition, the reality is that not all cases of war crimes will result in the creation of another international judicial entity. Atrocities committed by the Mengistu regime in Ethiopia, for example, are today being handled by a Special Prosecutor's Office established for this purpose by the new government. Various countries have provided technical and financial assistance to this process, but a separate international body was not deemed necessary.

Finally, even where an international tribunal has been established to prosecute war crimes, an additional factor motivating separate local efforts at justice is the sheer pressure of numbers. For reasons of both practicality and policy, the international tribunals for Rwanda and the former Yugoslavia can be expected to limit their prosecutions to a relatively small number of people. By way of comparison, the Nuremberg operation had vastly more substantial resources than its two contemporary progeny. At peak staffing in 1947, for example, the Nuremberg proceedings employed the services of nearly 900 Allied personnel and about an equal number of Germans. The authorities at Nuremberg had virtually complete control of the field of operations and sources of evidence, and the prosecution team had the benefit of paper trails not matched in the Yugoslav and Rwandan cases. Even with these advantages, the Nuremberg trials ultimately involved the prosecution of only some 200 defendants, grouped into thirteen cases and lasting four years. It is doubtful that the two current international tribunals *combined* will ultimately prosecute that many cases; even half the number would be a major success.

This means that, even if the international bodies achieve their maximum effectiveness, thousands of additional cases of war crimes and related atrocities will be left untouched. In the former Yugoslavia, the cases of thousands of war criminals—Bosnian Serbs, Croats and Muslims—and tens of thousands of their victims will not be addressed by the international tribunal, yet reconciliation requires that Bosnian society come to terms in some fashion with this legacy and these people. Seven cantonal prosecution offices in the Federation of Bosnia and Herzegovina are actively pursuing war crimes cases, primarily involving abuses perpetrated against Muslims. As of September 1997, some 350 cases, involving over 4,500 potential defendants, were in various stages of investigation or, in a few cases, prosecution. Bosnian Serb and Croat authorities each have their war crimes cases as well. My own discussions with Bosnian authorities from each of the three ethnic groups indicate that they collectively claim at least 25,000 war crimes cases and regard some 5,000 to 8,000 of these as appropriate for prosecution. Notwithstanding the adoption of the so-called "rules of the road" to regulate arrests by local authorities in these cases, this dimension of the problem of war crimes in Bosnia has received surprisingly little attention in the Western policy community, particularly considering its potential impact.[12] After the foreign troops are gone, after the international tribunals have completed their operations, local government, judiciary and society will still need to deal with this legacy and these people—whether by prosecution or otherwise.

The Rwandan challenge with respect to domestic trials has been further complicated by the dizzying numbers in that case, as discussed below. In both countries, implementation of their national war crimes program will be influenced by their perception of the degree to which the international community is serious and committed to supporting the work of the international tribunals. In each case, how they handle the question will have significant consequences for the viabililty of peace and the establishment of the rule of law.

The charters of the international tribunals for Yugoslavia and Rwanda recognize this domestic component and provide for shared concurrent jurisdiction with national courts over the crimes in question, although each international tribunal can assert its primacy over the domestic judicial process and require the national courts to defer to it whenever appropriate.[13] The draft statute for the permanent international criminal court also stressed this domestic component, declaring that the international body was to be "complementary to national criminal justice systems in cases where such trial procedures may not be available or may be ineffective."[14] This concept of "complementarity" was, in fact, one of the more nettlesome problems facing those designing this permanent institution. As this chapter suggests, achieving justice after war crimes requires a determination of the proper balance between domestic and international treatment of the problem. Although the best case will be the one in which a viable and independent domestic system of justice establishes accountability and thereby lays the groundwork for future adherence to the rule of law, this balance point shifts from case to case owing to a variety of factors. Criteria need to be developed to objectively evaluate the availability and effectiveness of domestic procedures in each case, and to decide where the international criminal court should intervene and where it would be wiser to let local institutions and society grapple on their own with the legacy of war crimes.

Managing the Numbers

Where prosecutions are undertaken, how widely should the net be cast? There is a growing consensus in international law that, at least for the most heinous violations of human rights and international humanitarian law, a sweeping amnesty is impermissible.[15] International law does not, however, demand the prosecution of every individual implicated in the atrocities. A symbolic or representative number of prosecutions of those most culpable may satisfy international obligations, especially where an overly extensive trial program will threaten the stability of the country. This approach has been adopted, for example, in Argentina, Malawi and in some of the countries of Central and Eastern Europe in dealing with the legacy of massive human rights abuses by their ousted regimes.

In several cases ranging from Nuremberg to Ethiopia, given the large number of potential defendants, an effort has been made to distinguish three categories of culpability and design different approaches for each. Roughly, these classifications break down into (1) the leaders, those who gave the orders to commit war crimes, and those who actually carried out the worst offenses (inevitably the smallest category numerically); (2) those who perpetrated serious abuses but not of a caliber or quantity that would place them in the first category; and (3) those whose offenses were minimal. The severity of treatment then follows accordingly. The 1995 Dayton Accord concluding the war in the former Yugoslavia more or less adopted this approach, as discussed below.

The Rwandan case demonstrates the need for pragmatism to temper an absolutist approach to prosecution. In one of the most horrific genocidal massacres in recent memory, up to one million Rwandan Tutsis and moderate Hutus were brutally slaughtered in just fourteen weeks in 1994. Rather than permitting large-scale revenge killings and other forms of vigilante justice, the new government determined that it was essential to put the country on a new footing, replacing a culture of impunity (which would produce further cycles of violence) with one of accountability. Insisting on the imperative of establishing the rule of law, throughout their first year in office, many senior members of the new government insisted that *every person* who participated in the atrocities should be prosecuted and punished. This approach, however, would put well over 100,000 Rwandans in the dock, a situation that would be wholly unmanageable and certainly destabilizing to the transition. By early 1998, although few formal charges had yet been filed, some 130,000 Rwandans were detained in prisons built to house a fraction of that number on allegations of involvement in the genocide. The U.S. legal system, with its half a million lawyers, or other legal systems similarly rich in human and material resources would be overwhelmed by the prospect of such a vast number of genocide cases, and would likely be incapable of processing them. To compound the problem, the criminal justice system of Rwanda was decimated during the genocide, with some ninety-five percent of the country's lawyers and judges either killed, in exile or in prison. Justice for war crimes in Rwanda thus required a creative approach that would take into account the staggeringly large number of potential cases and the overwhelmingly small number of available personnel to process them.

After extensive deliberation and input from a number of experts in various countries, the Rwandan government enacted legislation in 1996 that attempts to respond to this challenge. The law creates four levels of culpability for the genocide: (1) the planners and leaders of the genocide, those in positions of authority who fostered these crimes, and particularly notorious killers and sexual torturers—all subject to full prosecution and punishment; (2) others who killed; (3) those who committed other crimes against the person; and (4) those who committed offenses against property. Those in category (4) will not be subject to any criminal penalties. Persons in categories (2) and (3) who voluntarily provide a full confession of their crimes, information on accomplices or co-conspirators, and, importantly, an apology to the victims of their crimes will benefit from an expedited process and a significantly reduced schedule of penalties. It was hoped that participation in this confession program would shift a significant share of the burden for preparing cases away from prosecutors and investigators, rendering the number of cases remaining for prosecution slightly more manageable. The trial process got underway in 1997. By mid-1998, the Rwandan justice system had rendered judgments in over 300 cases, with more than 5,000 confessions under consideration. While this is still only 2 percent of the total caseload, it is an impressive beginning. Additional innovations and modifications will undoubtedly be examined as Rwandan society pursues the effort to achieve justice in a meaningful and manageable way.

Other Alternatives:
Toward a More Comprehensive Approach to Justice

Criminal trials are the most obvious way of reckoning with genocide and similar atrocities. From the perspectives of political stabilization or allocation of legal and financial resources, however, it will rarely be advisable to attempt to prosecute every participant in these mass abuses, which by their very nature can generally only be undertaken through the mobilization of a vast number of people. In the types of cases under consideration, prosecution—whether by international tribunals or domestic courts—has its limits. Depending on the particular conditions in a country, justice for these crimes may entail a variety of alternative or supplemental approaches. In Greece, hundreds of soldiers and officers were prosecuted for torture of former prisoners. But in Spain, both sides fully acknowledged their sins (no one has done so in Bosnia) and then granted each other a mutual amnesty. In South Africa, amnesty is currently being granted on a case-by-case basis to those who committed abuses, but only after the individual offender applies for that amnesty and provides a detailed confession of his or her crimes. In countries like Chile and El Salvador, "truth commissions" have produced a national historical accounting as a form of justice. In the Czech Republic, Lithuania and post-communist Germany, administrative purges have temporarily removed those affiliated with past abuses from positions in the public sector. An effort at justice may also involve official recognition and rehabilitation of victims. A simplistic dichotomy between international and domestic prosecution, or between prosecution of every participant, on the one hand, and total amnesty, on the other, should be avoided. More often than not, a wholistic and integrated concept of justice is required, which considers the appropriate mix of these various mechanisms most appropriate to the context and culture of the society in question.

As noted, the Dayton Accord distinguishes various categories of culpability and integrates various approaches to accountability. In the first category, the signatories commit themselves to provide full cooperation and assistance to the international tribunal as it prosecutes those who perpetrated the most heinous offenses. The agreement also prohibits any individuals indicted by the tribunal from holding public office. In the second tier of culpability, the accord characterizes as a confidence-building measure the obligation of the parties to immediately undertake "the prosecution, dismissal or transfer, as appropriate, of persons in military, paramilitary, and police forces, and other public servants, responsible for serious violations of the basic rights of persons belonging to ethnic or minority groups."[16] This recognizes a simple reality: even though it is not necessary or possible to prosecute everyone who committed abuses, how secure will a community member feel if the local police include the very criminals who last year tortured his son or gang-raped his wife? What confidence can returning refugees be expected to have in the new order if the current mayor personally helped torch their homes in the campaign of ethnic cleansing? At the third level, for the largest and least culpable category, it is reasonable to suggest that former adversaries let bygones be bygones and focus instead on building a better today and tomorrow. The Dayton Accord commits each of the parties to grant a full amnesty to all returning refugees and displaced persons charged with any crime related to the conflict—so long as it was not a "serious violation of international humanitarian law."[17] While the postwar period has exhibited some serious shortcomings in the implementation of these provisions, the basic conceptual framework they create is a sound one.

The Broader Impact

The way accountability for mass atrocities is handled may be relevant beyond the borders of the country in question; it may also have consequences for future, seemingly unrelated conflicts in other parts of the world. When asked whether he was concerned about the international community holding him accountable for his diabolical campaign of genocide, Adolph Hitler is reputed to have scoffed, "Who remembers the Armenians?" referring to the victims of a genocide only twenty-five years earlier for which no one had been brought to book. In pursuing their campaign of ethnic cleansing and genocide, Bosnian Serb leaders were asked the same question, and pointed to the absence of any trials for the atrocities committed in Cambodia and Vietnam in the 1970s. As poignantly noted by Jose Ayala Lasso, the former UN High Commissioner for Human Rights, "a person stands a better chance of being tried and judged for killing one human being than for killing 100,000."[18]

One of the many reasons advanced for creation of the Rwanda Tribunal was the need to demonstrate that the international community would not tolerate such atrocities, deterring future carnage not only in Rwanda but notably in Burundi, where renewed ethnic violence was beginning to escalate. If the international community had promptly established the Rwanda Tribunal and provided it with adequate personnel and resources—if the tribunal had been born as a robust entity with the wherewithal to pursue its mandate aggressively—it would almost certainly have given pause to those inclined toward extremist violence in neighboring Burundi. Unfortunately, the initial message of warning to Rwanda's southern twin was relatively anemic. Rwandans and Burundians each took note of the enormous delays in getting the tribunal even partially staffed, financed and operational, and Burundi sadly slipped deeper into violence and chaos, with the UN Secretary General eventually urging preparations for intervention by a multilateral military force. As noted above, the International Criminal Tribunal for Rwanda made dramatic progress in 1997–98, gaining custody of and prosecuting many key leaders of the 1994 genocide. As the tribunal exhibits a determination and ability to hold such malfeasants accountable, it will hopefully still be able to play a constructive role in the region.

Some analysts and diplomats will no doubt continue to suggest that justice for genocide and other mass abuses is a luxury that post-traumatic societies can ill afford; they will still argue that peace is best achieved by simply closing the door on past wrongs. But there were thousands and thousands like Emsud Bahonjic and Fidele Kayabugoyi, and they are survived by millions of relatives and friends who will tell you otherwise. The survivors will demand justice sooner or later; the challenge is to achieve that justice in a manner that best facilitates a durable peace.

Notes

1. The opinions expressed in this chapter are the author's and do not necessarily represent the views of the United States Institute of Peace or the U.S. government.
2. United Nations Security Council Resolution 827 (May 25, 1993), reprinted in 32 *International Legal Materials* 32 (1993): 1159.
3. In May 1998, following a request from the president of the tribunal, the Security Council authorized the addition of a third trial chamber to more expeditiously handle the growing caseload.
4. United Nations Security Council Resolution 955 (November 8, 1994), reprinted in *International Legal Materials* 33 (1994): 1600.
5. Telford Taylor, *Final Report to the Secretary of the Army on the Nuernberg War Crimes Trials under Control Council Law No. 10* (1949), 105.
6. For a more comprehensive review of the approaches and mechanisms adopted by more than thirty countries to deal with the aftermath of mass abuses, see Neil J. Kritz, ed., *Transitional Justice: How Emerging Democracies Reckon With Former Regimes* (3 volumes) (Washington, DC: United States Institute of Peace Press, 1995).

7. Convention on the Prevention and Punishment of the Crime of Genocide, Article VI, *United Nations Treaty Series* no. 1021, vol. 78 (1948), 277.

8. For details, see Part III and Epilogue, this volume.

9. Warren, "Legislative and Judicial Attacks on the Supreme Court of the United States—A History of the the Twenty-Fifth Section of the Judiciary Act" (pts. 1 & 2), *American Law Review* 47 (1913): 161, 166.

10. "Goldstone Presses Moi on Rwanda Tribunal Stance," *Reuters World Service*, October 5, 1995.

11. *Preliminary Report of the Independent Commission of Experts Established in Accordance with Security Council Resolution 935 (1994)*, September 29, 1994), 31.

12. On February 18, 1996, the parties to the Dayton Accord agreed to the "rules of the road," which prohibit local authorities from arresting or detaining anyone for serious violations of international humanitarian law unless (1) the person has already been indicted by the international tribunal, or (2) the tribunal has previously reviewed a domestic arrest warrant or indictment against the individual and found it to be consistent with international legal standards.

13. Statute of the International Criminal Tribunal for the Prosecution of Persons Responsible for Serious Violations of International Humanitarian Law Committed in the Territory of the Former Yugoslavia Since 1991, Art. 9, *International Legal Materials* 32 (1993): 1159; Statute of the International Criminal Tribunal for the Prosecution of Persons Responsible for Genocide and Other Serious Violations of International Humanitarian Law Committed in the Territory of Rwanda and Rwandan Citizens Responsible for Genocide and Other Such Violations Committed in the Territory of Neighbouring States, between 1 January 1994 and 31 December 1994, Article 8, *International Legal Materials* 33 (1994): 1600.

14. UN GAOR, 49th Session, Supplement 10, *Report of the International Law Commission on the work of its forty-sixth session, 49th Sess.* UN Doc. A/49/10 (1994), 44.

15. See, e.g., Diane F. Orentlicher, "Settling Accounts: The Duty to Prosecute Human Rights Violations of a Prior Regime," *Yale Law Journal* 100 (1991): 2537-2615.

16. Dayton Agreement, Annex 7, Article I, Paragraph 3(e), *International Legal Materials* 35 (1996): 89.

17. Dayton Agreement, Annex 7, Article VI. Recognizing the connection between justice issues and refugee repatriation, the Dayton Accord places much of this language in its section on refugees.

18. Third Annual Report of the International Tribunal for the Prosecution of Persons Responsible for Serious Violations of International Humanitarian Law Committed in the Territory of the Former Yugoslavia Since 1991, UN Doc. A/51/292, S/1996/665, August 16, 1996, 10.

Ethnicity and Conflict in Africa:
The Methods Behind the Madness

Bill Berkeley

"You is sharks, sartin; but if you gobern de shark in you, why den you
be angel; for all angel is not'ing mor dan de shark well goberned."
Herman Melville, Moby Dick

"For the liberation of a people more is needed than an economic
policy, more than industry: if a people is to become free, it needs
pride and willpower, defiance, hate, hate and once again hate."
Adolf Hitler, 1923

"I killed because I was forced to," says this man in a dirty white shirt,
his face knotted with anxiety, eyes averted. "I either had to do it or
I would die myself. Many were killed for refusing to kill."

His name is François-Xavier Sibomana, forty-seven years old and bald-
ing. He has thin wrists and knobby, calloused fingers. He is talking about
the murder of his brother-in-law, Isaac Kimonyo.

"I did not kill him singlehandedly," François explains. "We would con-
verge on a person. We killed a number of people—but jointly." In his
own village they killed nine people. He used a machete; others used
clubs. "I knew some of them personally," he concedes. "They were neighbors." But his own brother-in-law? "I believe he did not deserve to die.
He was an old man."

François rubs his hands on his worn grey cotton trousers, crudely re-
paired with black stitches at the crotch. He brushes the ground with his
feet, clad in blue canvas sneakers with no laces, no socks.

"We killed him in his house," he continues. "He was dragged from the
bedroom and killed in the sitting room. Emmanuel struck him first. He
was the leader of the militia. I could not do it myself. For me, I stood by
and watched. There was nothing I could do." Nothing he could do? "I
made no effort to stop the killers because we were led by the leader of the
militia. So nobody would dare to ask to spare the man."

François Sibomana is a "simple" peasant who has spent most of his life
cultivating sorghum and sweet potatoes on the steep mountain slopes of
Kibungo prefecture in eastern Rwanda. He says he had never killed before. He has a wife and eight children, though he doesn't know where
they are. He is now in captivity—an admitted member of the *Intera-*

hamwe militia, "those with a common purpose," the Hutu death squads that have stabbed, clubbed and hacked to death up to half a million Rwandans, mostly ethnic Tutsis and opposition Hutus, in the weeks just prior to our meeting.

"Everybody had to join," François tells me. "It was the thing to do." We are sitting in a vacant lot in a rubble-strewn, rebel-held town called Kabuga, on the outskirts of Kigali, the Rwandan capital. It is June 1994. Rwanda's genocide is still unfolding in the south. Hundreds of dazed survivors of the massacres, some of them wrapped in gauze that barely conceals their hideous machete wounds, loiter amid the wreckage of their lives in the looted and gutted ruins nearby.

From a crackling transistor radio behind me, I can hear Radio Rwanda, the state-owned broadcasting arm. "Defend your rights and rise up!" a voice on the radio is singing. There are drums and guitars in the background. The singer, a popular crooner named Simon Bikindi, is beseeching his fellow Hutus—the *Bene sebahinzi*, the sons of cultivators—to carry on the slaughter without delay. "Defend your rights and rise up against those who want to oppress you!" The drumming and strumming have an oddly intimate effect. Bikindi is singing in riddles, addressing *Mbira abumva*, "those who can understand." He is warning his listeners of the malign intentions of the *Bene sebatunzi*, the sons of the pastoralists—the Tutsis, also known as *Inyenzi*, cockroaches. "You have missed some of the enemies," he sings. "You must go back there and finish them off. The graves are not yet full!"

In the days just prior to this meeting, I have visited a plain brick church by a dirt road south of here that was filled waist-high with about 200 putrid, maggot-riddled, freshly slaughtered corpses. I have met a wide-eyed eleven-year-old girl named Umilisa, who laughed at me hysterically, irrepressibly, rather than tell me in her own words about the day two weeks earlier when she fled from her home as the militia arrived, then returned an hour later and discovered her mother and father, brothers and sisters, aunts and uncles in a heap of severed heads and arms and legs on the floor of her living room.

And here in Kabuga, just last evening, in an abandoned store less than a block from the lot in which François and I are speaking, I had met a middle-aged gentleman named Isadore, who survived with his wife and children but lost twenty immediate relatives in all. Isadore had looked at me with a quizzical expression and said, "I was very much surprised because, looking at my neighbors, I thought they were good friends. I was very much surprised that they were among the people who came to try to kill us."

How is such a horror possible? Why did ordinary men like François Sibomana—middle-aged, a father of eight—participate in a monstrous crime? What malignant blend of bigotry and fear, coercion or cowardice, history, politics, poverty and ignorance, envy, opportunism, unquestioning obedience, peer pressure perhaps—what brought out the shark in this man?

I look into François's eyes. He seems bewildered by my questions. All he says is this: "The message from the top was passed down to the local village chiefs, the *conseillers*. The *conseillers* had lists of Tutsis who should be killed. They simply organized their constituents."

He kicks a pebble and stares into the middle distance. "The leaders of the party and the leaders of the militia rounded up all the men in the village. We were told that we had a mission. We were given a list of people to kill. If we met someone on the list, they would be killed."

"Kill the Slave Through the Slave"

Most Americans are as bewildered as they are horrified by what looks like endemic violence in Africa. Rwanda, Burundi; Zaire, Liberia, Sudan, Somalia, even parts of newly freed South Africa—from afar Americans may wonder if all this carnage flows from some mysterious, exotic savagery in the African soul. Most American media coverage of Africa's wars leaves an impression of ancient, inscrutable "tribal" hatreds. It is precisely this impression which moves us to throw up our hands in despair that nothing can be done to stop them.

But these conflicts are not as senseless as they seem. They are not inevitable products of primordial, immutable hatreds. There is method in the madness.

Rwanda's genocide is but the clearest example of a pattern that runs through nearly all of Africa's ruinous civil conflicts, a pattern not of "age-old hatreds" but of calculated tyranny. The forces tearing these countries apart are the same forces that have ravaged other parts of the world throughout history: the forces of despotism, Machiavellian intrigue, "divide-and-rule."

In South Africa, where "black on black" violence has killed 20,000 and nearly derailed the vaunted transition to majority rule, the Afrikaner police who fueled the fighting called it the *kleur teen kleur beginsel*—the "color against color principle."

In Sudan, where northern Arabs through the decades have dominated the state and decimated southern Sudan by pitting one black African tribe against another, they say *"Aktul al-Abid bil abid"*—"Kill the slave through the slave."

In Rwanda, more than a year before the genocide, Leon Mugesera, provincial vice president of Rwanda's corrupt and embattled ruling party and a learned linguist-turned-"Hutu Power" propagandist, beseeched his fellow Hutus to embark on what would come to be called a "final solution" to the Tutsi problem.

"What are we waiting for?" he railed. "And what about those accomplices who are sending their children to the [Tutsi rebels]? Why are we waiting to get rid of these families? We have to take responsibility into our own hands and wipe out these hoodlums. . . . They belong in Ethiopia, and we are going to find them a short cut by throwing them into the Nyabarongo River. I must insist on this point. We have to act. Wipe them all out!"

It is a phenomenon that runs like poison through many of Africa's seemingly senseless wars: Big Men using little men, a handful of elites fanning the flames of ethnicity, manipulating the poor and the ignorant, cynically maneuvering for power and booty while thousands perish.

Call it "tribalism," call it racism, call it nationalism—the divisive power of ethnicity is one of the most complex and volatile issues of our time, and often the least understood. From the Balkans to Sri Lanka, from Afghanistan to the strife-torn republics of the former Soviet Union, proliferating ethnic and sectarian conflicts have killed hundreds of thousands, scattered millions from their homes, and all but extinguished hopes for a less fractious world order after the collapse of the Berlin Wall in 1989. Africa is merely the part of the world where such conflicts have been most destructive by far.

Yet what we think of today as a resurgence of "ethnic conflict" in the post-Cold War era was in fact a staple of the Cold War as well. Harold Isaacs, in his seminal 1975 work, *Idols of the Tribe*, estimated that ten million died in thirty-five "major bloodlettings" involving group identity around the world between 1945 and 1974.[1] "In politics," Isaacs wrote, "there is a constant flux in power relationships, and in the struggles of who is up and who is down the most effective basis for mobilizing support remains the bedrock of group identity."[2]

Inflamed ethnic passions are not the cause of political conflict, but its consequence. A common illusion of the post-Cold War era is that the superpower rivalry suppressed traditional rivalries that have since resurfaced with a vengeance. In fact, all too often the opposite has been the case. The superpowers did precious little to suppress ethnic conflicts and much to spawn them—not least by elevating, financing and arming despotic clients like Samuel Doe in Liberia, Mohammed Siad Barre in Somalia and Mobutu Sese Seko in Zaire, who would one day think nothing of exploiting ethnicity as a means of clinging to power. Buffeted by history's changing winds, bereft of their superpower backing, one by one the embattled creatures of the old world order have struggled to survive in the new by playing the ethnic card.

The responsibility of states and political leaders in fomenting communal conflict is the paramount human rights issue of the post-Cold War era.[3] Harnessing proxies, arming tribal militias, cultivating warlords, propagating hate and fear, preying on ignorance, manufacturing rumors, stacking the police and army with ethnic kinsmen, demonizing dissidents as traitors to the tribe, or faith, or *Volk*—these are the tactics of the crafty despot with his back against the wall.

The Law of the Jungle

No less than those of Bosnia or Nazi Germany, the story of Rwanda's descent into genocide is a story about evil. The setting is Africa. The characters are mostly African. The time is now, meaning post-Cold War, end of the century, end of the millennium. But the questions are timeless and universal: How do evil people operate? What accounts for their power? Why do people follow?

Africa today offers some especially revealing windows on these age-old problems. Some of its villains, the "Big Men" and their acolytes, are especially vulnerable now—and therefore especially dangerous—for reasons of history and circumstance much akin to those in other parts of the world that have likewise plunged into chaos with the end of the Cold War, including the Balkans, Afghanistan and parts of the former Soviet Union. In all of these places the divisive potential of ethnicity has been magnified in the twilight zone between tyranny and anarchy.

We tend to think of tyranny and anarchy as being at opposite ends of a linear spectrum, the one signifying the antithesis of the other. In fact, they often exist side by side on what would better be described as a circle: the one is a product of the other and vice versa. At times they may be indistinguishable, for the rules of the game are the same. These rules are defined by their central common denominator: the absence of legitimate law.

Anarchy—the law of the jungle—is a vacuum that brings out the worst in men and selects for the worst among them. The pursuit of power in this lawless environment is a life-and-death struggle. Those who excel are men (and sometimes women—the clique that plotted Rwanda's genocide revolved around Madame Agathe Habyarimana, Hutu Power's queen bee, the wife of the president, Juvenal Habyarimana, whose murder triggered the genocide) who distinguish themselves through nothing more exotic than boundless cunning and ruthlessness. The most successful of all become tyrants, and the anarchy in which they thrive is called tyranny.

Yet even the most rigidly institutionalized tyrannies—Rwanda was one, South Africa another—depend fundamentally on their ability to harness the forces of anarchy to their own ends, the forces of lawlessness and terror. They rely above all on the total absence of lawful accountability for the criminal abuse of power. When their power is threatened, tyrants great and petty may chose to unleash those same forces of lawlessness: murder, rape, arson, theft. For them, anarchy is an instrument of tyranny.

This is the Hobbesian world in which ethnicity becomes paramount, both as a source of legitimacy for those at the top who otherwise lack any basis for legitimacy, and as a source of protection for those at the bottom. Lesser men—men like François Sibomana—survive more often than not by going along with the group, suspending personal judgement in exchange for protection. They may appear to be acting on mindless, "primitive" impulse; in fact, they are making rational calculations of their own self-interest, not least survival. The depth of their preexisting prejudices may explain the potency of the symbols which their leaders choose to exploit, but it is the logic of their lawless environment that transforms those prejudices into terror.

In other parts of the world at other times in history, comparable circumstances, not least in Germany in the 1920s and 1930s, have yielded comparable horrors.[4] Hence the radical importance in Africa, as elsewhere, of an idea that from afar is easy to take for granted: the rule of law.

The "culture" driving Africa's conflicts is no more exotic than that of the Sicilian mafia, or of the Crips and Bloods in Los Angeles, with the same imperatives of blood and family that bind such gangs together. Africa's warring factions are best understood not as "tribes" but as criminal racketeering enterprises, their leaders calculating strategy after the time-honored logic of Don Vito Corleone.

It is the stakes in Africa that are different—multiplied exponentially in circumstances where the state itself is a gang and the law does not exist. It is as if men like Don Corleone, invariably abetted by a foreign power, seized control of not just "turf" on the margins of society, but of the state itself and all its organs: police and army, secret police, the courts, the central bank, the civil service, the press, TV and radio.[5]

Rwanda offers a clear example of the state as a racketeering enterprise. Juvenal Habyarimana was the Rwandan president whose death in a still unexplained plane crash on April 6, 1994, triggered the genocide. Habyarimana had governed Rwanda for twenty-three years after the model of his mentor, President Mobutu Sese Seko of Zaire. Amply funded and armed by *his* foreign friends, the French, Habyarimana ran lucrative rackets in everything from development aid to marijuana smuggling. He and his in-laws operated the country's sole black-market foreign exchange bureau in tandem with the central bank. Habyarimana also was implicated in the poaching of mountain gorillas, selling the skulls and feet of baby primates. Habyarimana's brother-in-law was the principal suspect in the murder of the American anthropologist Dian Fossey.

This was the criminal culture in which the genocide was hatched. Like gangsters and despots through the ages, Habyarimana apparently was consumed by the monster he created. Habyarimana's plane, most independent analysts believe, was shot down by his own allies, who feared he was edging close to reforms that would threaten their power. The genocide began within hours.

A widespread misconception of the post-Cold War era is that ethnic conflict is a by-product of "failed states." Rwanda represents the opposite: a state—albeit criminal—that was all too successful in mobilizing along rigidly hierarchical lines from the top down, from the head of state and his ruling clique of co-conspirators down to the last village mayor and prefect, making possible the slaughter of hundreds of thousands in barely three months, mostly with clubs and machetes.[6]

"I Believed the Government Was Telling the Truth"

Justice Richard Goldstone of South Africa, who until recently served as chief prosecutor of the International War Crimes Tribunal, told the journalist Lawrence Weschler that he envisioned the tribunal's central mission as nothing less than arresting the historic cycle of vengeance-inspired ethnic slaughter. He rejected the widely held assumption that such violence is inevitable:

> For the great majority of their histories, the Croats and Serbs and Muslims, and the Tutsis and Hutus, have lived in relative peace with one another—and they were all doing that relatively nicely once again until just recently. Such interethnic violence usually gets stoked by specific individuals intent on immediate political or material advantage, who then call forth the legacies of earlier and previously unaddressed grievances. But the guilt for the violence that results does not adhere to the entire group. Specific individuals bear the major share of the responsibility, and it is they, not the group as a whole, who need to be held to account, through a fair and meticulously detailed presentation and evaluation of evidence, precisely so that the next time around no one will be able to claim that all the Serbs did this, or all Croats or all Hutus—so that people are able to see how it is specific individuals who are continually endeavoring to manipulate them in that fashion. I really believe that this is the only way the cycle can be broken.[7]

Justice Goldstone's point is especially apt with regard to the devastating cycle of slaughter among Hutus and Tutsis in Rwanda and neighboring Burundi. Beginning in 1959, 20,000 Rwandan Tutsis were killed by

Hutu insurgents and several hundred thousand were driven into exile. Beginning in 1965, some 5,000-10,000 Burundian Hutus were killed by a Tutsi-dominated army. That turned out to be a premonitory sign of the awesome carnage of 1972, when upwards of 100,000 Burundian Hutus— some say 200,000—were killed. Then, in 1988, Burundi's army killed 20,000 Hutus, and another 3,000 in 1991. As many as 50,000 Burundians—Hutus and Tutsis—were butchered after a failed Tutsi-led coup in 1993, and another 50,000 have died in Burundi's continuing bloodshed since then. Finally, between 500,000 and 800,000 Rwandan Tutsis and moderate Hutus were killed in the 1994 genocide.

Tutsis killing Hutus, Hutus killing Tutsis—what is all too often overlooked in this exotic-sounding chaos is that both Rwanda and Burundi have for most of this century been dominated by radical tyrannies. Other factors clearly played a significant role in these catastrophes: acute economic and population pressures, external arms deliveries to all sides, chicanery and lack of political will to intervene by leading Western states, dereliction of duty by supposed international peacekeepers, and some very real, deep-seated ethnic prejudices and stereotypes of both ancient and recent vintage. But the common denominator in all this slaughter has been the total absence of legal accountability for a single perpetrator at any stage over the last four decades.[8] In the absence of individual accountability for a single general, tyrant, militia leader or gangster, and with no commonly agreed-upon set of historical facts based on a "fair and meticulously detailed presentation and evaluation of evidence," as Goldstone put it, Tutsis and Hutus alike have blamed each other as a group. And so each has been prepared to believe the worst about each other's intentions in times of chaos, making both Tutsis and Hutus especially vulnerable to the machinations of the propagandists, and especially amenable to the protection that those wearing the badge of ethnicity claim to afford.

Fear, not hatred, was the dominant theme of the Hutu propagandists in Rwanda, who relentlessly terrorized their listeners on two state-owned radio stations both before and throughout the genocide. These radio broadcasts fabricated tales of harrowing massacres attributed to Tutsi guerrillas and civilians. They warned Hutus that Tutsi-led rebels were bent on reimposing feudalism, wiping out all the Hutus and taking all their land.

My own interviews with admitted participants in the genocide, including François Sibomana, left little doubt this propaganda was extremely effective. "The government told us that the RPF [Rwandan Patriotic Front] is Tutsi and if it wins the war all the Hutus will be killed," said Emmanuel Kamuhanda, an eighteen-year-old *Interahamwe* militiaman who admitted killing fifteen neighbors from his home village. "As of now I don't believe this is true." And as he was killing? "At the time, I believed the government was telling the truth."

The importance of justice as a basis for establishing truth was underscored by defense counsel Luc de Temmerman at the opening session of the International Tribunal for Rwanda in Arusha, Tanzania, in September 1996. The Belgian lawyer, who represents Georges Rutaganda, the vice president of the *Interahamwe* militia, sought not merely to assert his client's innocence but to deny the crime itself. He claimed there was no slaughter of Rwanda's Tutsis. "It will come out clearly that it is not Hutus who are guilty," De Temmerman told the court. "There was no genocide. It was a situation of mass killings in a state of war where everyone was killing their enemies."

So trials in Rwanda are essential—but fraught with difficulty. With more than 120,000 prisoners awaiting trial by summer 1998, there were inevitable problems of funding and logistics, and the problems were compounded by the fact that Rwanda's existing judiciary, like most of the rest of the Rwandan state, was essentially dismantled, looted and abandoned in 1994. Amnesty International issued a report in April 1997 expressing "grave doubts" about the fairness of the first genocide trials in Rwandan courts. After observing the first trials in January and February 1997, Amnesty concluded that the trials had been "largely unfair," based on "an apparent assumption that defendants are guilty unless proven innocent." Most prosecutors and judges had received only six months of training, with no prior legal training whatsoever. Amnesty reported that judges had failed to investigate claims by some defendants that they had incriminated themselves under torture, and in at least two trials judges made no effort to prevent defendants from being jeered by spectators. Amnesty noted that there were only sixteen defense lawyers currently practicing in Rwanda, and that in the existing climate of hostility toward those accused of genocide many lawyers were reluctant to be involved in the trials.

There have been some improvements in Rwanda's domestic trials over the last year. A Belgian group, *Advocats Sans Frontiers* (Lawyers Without Borders) has established a program for providing defense counsel, mostly non-Rwandans, in many trials. This has helped to reduce the number of flagrant procedural failings. But the overwhelming shortage of human and material resources remains, and this has been compounded by the deteriorating security situation in western Rwanda. The ongoing Hutu-led insurgency in that region has created an environment fundamentally incompatible with due process. Among its chronic symptoms, for example, is a problem familiar to any prosecutor of organized crime: intimidation of witnesses. From 1996 to 1998, hundreds of Tutsis who survived the 1994 genocide were killed by veterans of the *Interahamwe* who operate in the region with the presumed protection of their fellow Hutus. The motive for these killings is not always clear, but witnesses believe one aim is to silence survivors who could testify in court about the genocide. These killings, in turn, have brought out the worst in the new Tutsi-led Rwandan army, which has killed thousands of Hutu civilians in counterinsurgency operations along the Zairian border over the last two years. So while the very fact of Rwanda's ongoing genocide trials represents an admirable step toward establishing the rule of law in Rwanda, objective factors beyond the control of judges and lawyers in the courtroom make real justice all but impossible for the foreseeable future.

The crisis that began along that border in November 1996, and which swept across the breadth of Zaire throughout 1997, vividly illustrated the pattern discussed above. The crisis began when escalating armed conflict forced close to a million Rwandan Hutu refugees to abandon the camps in Zaire; most returned to Rwanda, but a minority headed west into the vast reaches of Zaire. Meanwhile, the armed rebellion in Zaire led by Laurent Kabila, and backed by Rwanda and Uganda, arose almost overnight and swept across the country, finally toppling Mobutu Sese Seko from power in May 1997. Even as Kabila was struggling to establish his legitimacy and consolidate his control over Zaire, reports emerged that thousands of Rwandan Hutu refugees had been massacred by rebel soldiers. Many of these refugees undoubtedly were former Rwandan army troops or militiamen who participated in the genocide; many more— Human Rights Watch/Africa investigators put the figure at "tens of thousands"—were civilians, the weakest remnants of the Hutu exodus who were overtaken by the advancing rebel front, itself comprised, Human Rights Watch/Africa said, primarily of Kinyarwanda-speaking Tutsi soldiers from Rwanda. So the cycle of summary vengeance, hitherto confined to Rwanda and Burundi, has extended into Zaire.

These events underscored the durability of old patterns even as governments rise and fall in one country after another. Tyrannies may come and go, and sometimes those who wind up on top are better than their predecessors, but the rules of the game remain the same. There has been much talk of a "new generation of leaders" ushering in a more enlightened age in Central Africa. Men like Yoweri Museveni, the president of Uganda, and Paul Kagame, the Rwandan Tutsi general who is now the Big Man in that shattered nation, are clearly better men, or at least better-intentioned, than those whom they replaced. Yet the fact of these huge-scale massacres, on territory in which they are the powers to reckon with, underlines how difficult it is to rise above the old familiar logic. These men have gotten to where they are by excelling at the same old game, the game of lawless violence. They may seek to rise above it, or to change the rules as they go, but their ability to do so, even assuming their best intentions, is constrained by the standards of their adversaries. They must hold onto power in the same lawless jungle in which they achieved it. Laurent Kabila, for his part, set up one obstacle after another to block a United Nations team from investigating the massacres in eastern Zaire, evidently bowing to his Rwandan and Ugandan backers, who, as *The New York Times* put it, "have no interest in light being shed on these matters." That, too, is the old familiar pattern.

The events in Zaire/Congo beginning in November 1996 marked one last turn in the limelight for the venerable gangster-tyrant Mobutu of Zaire. One of the enduring myths of the Cold War era, often promoted by his American backers, was that Mobutu was the glue holding his otherwise fractious nation together. Nothing could be further from the truth. Mobutu over the years had proven himself one of the great tacticians of "divide-and-rule." Again and again over the three decades of his predatory rule, Mobutu unleashed the forces of anarchy—not least his infamously looting and pillaging national army—in order to disable and discredit his opponents. It was Mobutu's government that triggered the latest chaos in eastern Zaire by arming and coddling the Hutu militias, his long-time allies, and by issuing an arbitrary edict to expel—that is, ethnically cleanse—Zairian Tutsis from Zaire. It should not be forgotten that the armed insurgency that touched off the crisis in November 1996 began as a rebellion against ethnic cleansing.

Of course, the subsequent success of that armed rebellion that finally toppled Mobutu in mid-1997 highlighted the great risks of anarchy as strategy. It can only be used as a last resort. There is always the possibility that deliberately provoked chaos will backfire and consume the tyranny it was intended to preserve, as the Hutus in Rwanda also learned. But Mobutu would not have survived in power as long as he did if such tactics had not previously been successful.

Mobutu was, in fact, one of the last surviving five-star despots of the Cold War era. Ever since the collapse of the Berlin Wall in 1989, Zairians and foreigners alike had been predicting his imminent demise. That he endured as long as he did was a measure of his skillful playing of the ethnic card, his promotion of anarchy as strategy. In 1992 and 1993, at the height of pressures for democratization in Zaire, ethnic cleansing was Mobutu's tactic of choice in Zaire's mineral-rich southern province of Shaba. There Mobutu showed himself a peerless master of a delicate and risky maneuver: mobilizing well-founded hatred toward his own rapacious regime and deflecting it onto others, in that case the Luba of Kasai, the tribe of Zaire's most popular and tenacious opposition figure, Etienne Tshisekedi. The resulting chaos drove 100,000 people from their homes,

and sixty people a day died from measles, dysentery and respiratory in-
fections. The whole democratization movement was thrown into chaos,
and Mobutu hung on for four more years.

"Cooptation Rather Than Confrontation"

Rwanda is but one of several African countries that are struggling with
limited success to confront a murderous past and build the rule of law.
Ethiopia has begun to prosecute officials of Mengistu Haile Mariam's old
regime on charges that include genocide and crimes against humanity.
Uganda, on Rwanda's northern border, has tried through trials and a
Truth Commission to hold individuals accountable for the crimes of Idi
Amin and Milton Obote. And South Africa is currently engaged in both
a Truth Commission and a series of criminal trials aimed at assigning individual guilt, rather than collective guilt, for criminal political violence.

These undertakings represent a recognition by Africans themselves
that the failure of states to investigate and prosecute criminal political violence opens the way to chaos. Yet these same proceedings have also underscored the awesome difficulty of building the rule of law in conditions
of scarce resources, untrained personnel and continuing instability.

Ethiopia's ongoing war crimes trials represent the most dramatic and
far-reaching attempt by any African country to bring to book officials of
an ousted tyranny. More than seventy former Mengistu officials have been
charged in the systematic killing of an estimated 150,000 Ethiopians in
the so-called Red Terror, which followed Mengistu's seizure of power from
Emperor Haile Selassi in 1974. That figure does not count the estimated
100,000 who died in forced relocation programs or one million who died
in ensuing famines. The prosecution's case is based in large measure on
thousands of pages of detailed records seized from the files of the ousted
dergue, as Mengistu's regime was called. The dergue, it seems, was nearly
as compulsive as the Nazis in recording its crimes for posterity.

The government of President Meles Zenawi has emphasized that the
Ethiopian trials are intended to achieve not just justice for past crimes,
but also a clear break with centuries of lawless tyranny by building a
foundation for the rule of law. But it has taken nearly five years to bring
to trial the first twenty defendants, and more than 1,200 other Mengistu
regime officials languished in prison for five years without even being
charged. Charges were finally brought against these remaining 1,200 detainees in January 1997, but neither the prosecutor nor the court would
release the names of the defendants. (Mengistu himself is living in exile
in Zimbabwe.) Ethiopia's Special Prosecutor's Office has received millions of dollars in assistance from Western donors, but it is clearly overwhelmed by the scale of the challenge and barely competent; observers

have serious doubts about the quality of justice these trials will achieve. Meanwhile, President Zenawi's regime, which toppled Mengistu in 1991, has itself been accused of serious human rights violations, raising questions about whether it is using war crimes trials against a previous regime as a means of claiming legitimacy for itself which it may not deserve.

Then there is Uganda. Uganda offers a cautionary tale of particular interest to Rwanda's present leaders, in part because many of them grew up as refugees there. In the 1970s and early 1980s, Idi Amin, and the less notorious but no less wanton Milton Obote, plunged Uganda into a nightmare every bit as dark and sinister as the one that engulfed Rwanda in 1994. Perhaps a million Ugandans were killed in two decades of sheer terror.

Today Uganda is largely at peace, led by the newly elected regime of President Yoweri Museveni, who originally seized power in 1986 after a ruinous civil war. Uganda's relative tranquility is an extraordinary achievement, all the more so because of the murderous divisions now consuming nearly all of its surrounding neighbors. Yet the country remains sharply polarized along ethnic lines, in part because Ugandans ultimately shied away from holding individuals accountable for the crimes of the past.

President Museveni has brought peace to Uganda through a strategy known as "cooptation rather than confrontation." Hundreds of soldiers and their leaders from the myriad erstwhile fighting forces, police and intelligence units, private militias and bandit gangs, as well as numerous officials from previous regimes, have been lured out of the bush or exile with the promise of amnesty and integrated into Museveni's umbrella-like National Resistance Movement (NRM) and its army, the National Resistance Army (NRA).

Museveni's goal has been reconciliation, and the success he has achieved has been widely hailed as a beacon of hope in a turbulent region that includes such devastated neighbors as Sudan, Somalia, Rwanda and Burundi. Most Ugandans are living in peace. The economy is picking up. Roads have been repaved. Refugees have returned. Hospitals and schools have reopened. An independent press is flourishing, and other independent civic and political associations are emerging. A new constitution has been passed, and elections for president and parliament were held in 1997. People walk the streets at night without fear of soldiers or criminals. Ugandans are living with hope.

"Let's agree on the essential points," Museveni told me, "Regular elections, universal franchise, free press, separation of powers."

But for all this good news, Ugandans remain sharply polarized along ethnic and regional lines. After Museveni's guerrilla forces took power in

1986, in a continuation of the cycle of fighting that had consumed the country since independence from Britain in 1962, remnants of Milton Obote's defeated army went back into the bush in northern Uganda and waged yet another guerrilla campaign. Museveni's forces have been battling a succession of insurgencies in the north ever since, by turns crushing and coopting the insurgents and their presumed supporters. The fighting has not been on a scale comparable with what occurred under previous regimes, yet thousands of civilians have been displaced from their homes.

Uganda's continued polarization is worrisome not just because of the legacy of past ethnic conflict but because of the continued absence or weakness of the mediating institutions of law and civil society. Amin and Obote destroyed the rule of law in Uganda. Police, courts, the army—all were either politicized along ethnic lines or eviscerated. The law of the jungle obtained—the rule of the gun. For years state crimes went unpunished. And in the absence of individual accountability for these crimes, groups were blamed—and groups were relied upon to achieve justice.

President Museveni, to his credit, has made it a priority to reestablish the rule of law. He virtually scrapped the discredited police force he inherited in 1986 and has hired and trained a new one. He is rebuilding a cowed and withered judiciary with the help of Western aid—he told me there were only "three or four" high court justices left in the entire country when he came to power. He has also worked to diversify and professionalize the army. By all accounts (except in the north), the progress on these fronts has been remarkable. But there is still a long way to go, and abuses still occur.

Meanwhile, there remains the dicey problem of legal accountability for the many heinous crimes committed under past regimes. Uganda's attempts to confront its ugly past have been disappointing. One of Museveni's first acts when he came to power in 1986 was to establish a Human Rights Commission to document the country's history of abuses and, it was hoped, identify and prosecute the culprits. The aim was to clearly identify his regime as a "break from the past." Ten years later the commission's findings were finally published in a modest pamphlet that received scant attention. Meanwhile, almost no individuals have been successfully prosecuted.

There were logistical problems. As in Rwanda today, money and resources were limited. Evidence was poor. The continuing fragility and incompetence of the law undermined efforts to successfully prosecute even those individuals whom the Human Rights Commission recommended prosecuting. A few prominent individuals were arrested and tried, only to be acquitted for lack of sufficient evidence. These failures discredited the process and discouraged witnesses.

But the main problem was political. As in Rwanda, past regimes were closely identified with different regions and tribes; going after accused human rights abusers was perceived in those regions as persecuting their tribes. In some instances communities refused to cooperate with investigators, shielding criminals in their midst on grounds of ethnic solidarity. And there was concern that so many people had blood on their hands that settling accounts would be impossible. "Where will it end?" I was told.

The recurring insurgencies in the north also created problems. Many northern insurgents, ex-Obote fighters, were motivated by fear that they would be brought to account by a government dominated by southerners (Obote himself is living in mostly drunken exile in Zambia; Amin, a Moslem, is in Saudi Arabia). In 1987, a general amnesty was declared in hopes of luring northern rebels out of the bush. This was Museveni's strategy of "buying peace." He offered rebels a chance to be integrated into the national army. Many took it. "We thought that trying to punish everybody—it would be an endless process," Museveni told me.

The downside, of course, is that a great many people have never had to answer for their crimes. "A government has given an amnesty, but the people against whom these crimes have been committed didn't give that amnesty—the people have not forgiven them," said Joan Kakwenziri, a historian at Makerere University in Kampala who is a member of the Human Rights Commission. "Amnesty is really just a cover-up of the problem. It's like pushing dirt and dust under the rug. Eventually it begins to smell. It doesn't work."

"Buying peace" has deprived Ugandans of the kind of official records that could have emerged from systematic Nuremberg-style prosecutions. The country lacks a common version of its own history. People living in different regions of Uganda know little of what occurred in other regions, and they are vulnerable to the machinations of revisionist historians such as Amos Kjube, editor of The People newspaper, a mouthpiece for Milton Obote's old Uganda Peoples' Congress. In 1994, Kjube published a series of articles purporting to prove that in fact Museveni's forces—not those under Obote—were responsible for most of the 300,000 civilian deaths in the notorious Luwero triangle north of Kampala during the early 1980s. In fact, the NRA did kill many civilians in Luwero—accused collaborators, government agents and such. The NRA did engage in psychological warfare, deploying agents provocateurs to commit atrocities that would alienate communities from the government.

In the flurry of charges and countercharges, people are free to believe what they want to believe, or to believe what others want them to believe. And if all sides are to blame, no one is to blame. In the meantime, Museveni's government has had its own crimes to answer for in the

north. Observed Joan Kakwenziri: "I think they feel quite inadequate to
be the judges."

"Under Certain Circumstances Things Happen"

In South Africa, meanwhile, efforts to hold individuals accountable
for the crimes of apartheid hit a major snag in October 1996, when former Defense Minister Magnus Malan and other high officials of the old
South African regime were acquitted by a Durban judge on charges of
murder and conspiracy.

The Malan prosecution focused on South Africa's long-running "dirty
war" in Natal Province, now called Kwazulu-Natal, between Nelson
Mandela's African National Congress (ANC) and Mangosuthu Buthelezi's Inkatha. The trial opened a window on the "third force" conspiracy
that has fueled Natal's war for a decade. Interestingly, the charges grew
out of a years-long judicial inquiry led by Justice Richard Goldstone, who
went on to become the chief prosecutor of the International War Crimes
Tribunal. It was Goldstone who, in a landmark report published on
March 16, 1994, barely a month before South Africa's historic elections,
confirmed the existence of a "third force" conspiracy between Inkatha
and top-ranking South African police officials to "destabilize" South
Africa and thereby undermine the ANC.

Kwazulu-Natal offers an especially revealing example of "tribalism"
because the fighting there pits Zulu against Zulu. So the most obvious
and superficial explanation for conflict—ethnicity alone—falls away.
One must focus on all the other myriad elements in the equation: the
legacies of tyranny, the fusion of politics and crime, the engine of anarchy and above all the machinations of the Big Men, black and white,
who were seeking, through what came to be known as the "third force,"
to stem the advancing tide of democratic rule.

The six-month trial in the Durban Supreme Court was the most
prominent in a series of criminal prosecutions aimed at building the rule
of law in Kwazulu-Natal by at long last holding individuals accountable
for political violence. Malan and thirteen other retired white generals,
along with seven Zulu Inkatha partisans, including Buthelezi's right-hand
man, M.Z. Khumalo, were accused of complicity in a 1986 massacre of
thirteen Zulus—and of thereby setting in motion the vicious cycle of
"black-on-black" killings that have thus far claimed 20,000 lives. The
trial represented a bold attempt by Mandela's government to bring to
book those at the very top of apartheid's security forces who had deliberately fanned violence among blacks by covertly arming and training one
faction—Inkatha—in the time-honored tradition of "divide and rule."

But in October 1996, Malan and all of his co-accused were acquitted.

Justice Jan Hugo concluded that the 1986 massacre at issue in the trial had indeed been carried out by an Inkatha death squad created and trained by the South African army to fight the ANC. But the judge said the prosecution had failed to link the defendants to the massacre. Judge Hugo concluded that the testimony of two key state witnesses, both of them top security officers who were confessed accomplices in the 1986 massacre, could not be relied upon. He also said that a key document presented to the court and signed by nearly all of the top defendants, which explicitly proposed the training of Inkatha partisans in "offensive" military techniques, did not by itself constitute a conspiracy to murder.

The Malan verdict was not the last word on justice for apartheid's criminals. Prominent—albeit mid-level—security officials have already been convicted and others may still face trial. But the acquittal appears to represent the last chance for criminal prosecutions against those at the top—including Buthelezi himself—who are widely believed to have played a role in fomenting the violence in Kwazulu-Natal.

The acquittals were a major blow to the credibility of South Africa's criminal justice system—long associated in the minds of black South Africans with the arbitrary enforcement of apartheid's security laws. It was not lost on black South Africans that both the chief judge and the prosecutor were white holdovers from the old regime, compounding the sense of a time warp. South Africa's courts have not been purged, and prosecutors enjoy legal protections from political interference that were passed by the old white-led National Party in the waning days of the old order.

The evidence against Malan and his co-defendants was assembled by an independent team of investigators appointed by Mandela. But it was then handed over to a prosecutor appointed by the old white regime. Both Judge Hugo and the prosecutor, Kwazulu-Natal Attorney General Tim McNally, had a history of skepticism about state-sponsored hit squads. In the view of many trial observers, both the judge and the prosecutor, like white South Africans generally, seemed intuitively unable to grasp the malign intentions of the old apartheid security forces. They seemed unable to fathom the grubby world of covert operatives waging unconventional war during the years of what the securocrats called "total onslaught" against white rule. It was a world of murderers, psychopaths, gangsters and pimps—a far cry from the more recognizable picture painted by defense counsel of starched uniforms and military discipline. Judge Hugo, for example, said he found "no reason to doubt" the credibility of one defense witness who admittedly played a leading role in covert operations in support of the notorious Mozambican guerrilla force Renamo.

A central theme in the case against Malan was that the "dirty war" in Kwazulu-Natal was of a piece with South Africa's awesomely destructive covert wars in the 1980s against Mozambique and Angola. In those wars South Africa armed and trained proxy guerrilla armies, Renamo in Mozambique and Jonas Savimbi's Unita in Angola, in a campaign of "destabilization" that killed hundreds of thousands and brought both countries to utter ruin. Indeed, Judge Hugo accepted that Inkatha hit squads were trained at the same South African army base where Mozambican and Angolan rebel forces were trained. But the judge rejected on technical legal grounds what has long been obvious to most black South Africans: that the army deliberately stoked violence among blacks by backing a surrogate force, Inkatha, just as it had done in Mozambique and Angola.

Thus the Magnus Malan trial has resonated in South Africa much as the O.J. Simpson trial resonated in the United States, with blacks and all but a small minority of whites forming completely different judgments of guilt or innocence based on the same set of facts. The difference is that in South Africa blacks are the vast majority of the population—and the stakes involve not two but 20,000 unsolved murders.

The verdict highlights other acute problems South Africa faces in trying to build the rule of law. The court system is strapped for resources even as it is overwhelmed by rising violent crime. Prosecutors have been on strike for higher pay. Incompetent and coercive police practices that flourished under years of emergency rule, when confessions were the basis of most convictions, have stubbornly persisted. As with the courts, Mandela's government, afraid to be left with no experienced police officers, never carried out the purge of the police that many believed was called for. Some officers are still involved with both criminal and political gangs that apartheid spawned. They still block trials of their friends by destroying evidence and intimidating witnesses.

All this has ominous consequences for Kwazulu-Natal, because the cycle of violence there has long been propelled by the engine of anarchy—the all-but-complete absence of legitimate law, and thus of legal accountability for crimes including mass murder—which was the order of the day for blacks under apartheid. Here, too, anarchy was an instrument of tyranny. In the absence of lawful justice, people took the law into their own hands, and in turn people sought the protection of those strong enough to provide it—whether Inkatha, wearing the badge of Zulu nationalism, or the ANC, flying the banner of black liberation. The ANC, alas, compounded the problem with its own deliberate promotion of anarchy—they called it "ungovernability"—as an antidote to tyranny. These conditions brought out the worst in all sides. They selected for all manner of gangsters and warlords, who thrived in the resulting chaos. The concern now is that, with no credible system of justice, this long-running cycle will continue.

S'Kumbuzo Miya, political editor of the Zulu-language Catholic weekly *Umafrica*, who has covered Kwazulu-Natal's war for a decade and also covered the Malan trial, put it this way: "Here in Kwazulu-Natal it's difficult to have peace because of the collaboration of Inkatha and the army in the past. When such cases come into the limelight in the new South Africa and then the judiciary fails, people may think the best way to solve this thing is revenge. The previous police service failed to do any investigation. When police in the new South Africa tried to dig up these things, their attempt to get to the truth was frustrated by officials of the past. People lose hope and think the only solution is revenge. The killers have been identified but there is no conviction. What are people to think?"

President Mandela nevertheless moved quickly to express his acceptance of the verdict. "We must respect the institutions of government," he said, "and the judiciary is a very important arm of government." But relatives of victims of the massacre had another view. One victim's relative declared, "This is South African justice, it has always been like this. "

South Africa has a Truth and Reconciliation Commission, headed by former Archbishop Desmond Tutu, which is charged with documenting the truth about apartheid crimes and giving thousands of victims—many more than would get satisfaction through trials—the chance to tell their stories and receive some form of restitution. But the Truth and Reconciliation Commission's task is greatly complicated by the Malan acquittal, because it diminishes the threat of prosecution that might otherwise prompt confessions in return for amnesty. Barely a week after the Malan verdict, former Police Commissioner Johann van der Merwe startled the nation by admitting before the Truth and Reconciliation Commission that he issued the orders in two notorious atrocities in the mid-1980's. He said that he had acted under orders from a former justice minister as well as then President P.W. Botha. Van der Merwe's testimony was viewed as a breakthrough for the Truth and Reconciliation Commission, but thus far few top apartheid police and army officials have come forward to admit complicity in the much more destructive "third force" conspiracy. Malan, after his acquittal, called on his former compatriots not to cooperate with the Truth and Reconciliation Commission. Buthelezi has denounced the commission as a "national tragedy" and refused to cooperate.

Meanwhile, Kwazulu-Natal's dirty war festers on. At least 1,500 blacks have been murdered in politically related attacks since the election in 1994—148 in the three months prior to the Malan verdict. Buthelezi's Inkatha, essentially a syndicate of traditional chiefs and urban bosses who lorded over the old Kwazulu "homeland" under the delegation of repression known as "indirect rule," is struggling to preserve its feudal hegemony. Inkatha still dominates the province after highly problematical voting.

Backed by a shadowy network of right-wing white police and intelligence operatives, private security firms, ex-Rhodesians and mercenaries, Inkatha appears to be digging itself in for a protracted struggle to preserve itself in power. "It's the death throes of apartheid in this province," I was told. "It's apartheid kicking and screaming, refusing to die."

I had previously met one of the principal defendants in the trial, Tienie Groenewald, chief of the South African Defense Force's Military Intelligence, at the height of the state of emergency in the mid-1980s. We met in Pretoria in December 1994, before he knew, or even imagined, that he would be indicted. Pink-cheeked and avuncular in post-apartheid retirement, Groenewald frankly admitted that he was the man who hatched the "third force" conspiracy after meeting with Buthelezi in 1986. "Naturally," he confided, "under certain circumstances things happen which shouldn't happen. Under normal circumstances it wouldn't happen."

The legacy of white rule in Africa is central to its current conflicts for reasons common to the wars in the Balkan states and in the strife-torn republics of the former Soviet Union. As we have seen, they have to do with the legacy of a lawless state, and with the manipulative machinations of those who thrived in the resulting jungle.[9] Just as Slobodan Milosevic, by most accounts the principal villain in the Balkan conflicts, emerged from the old Yugoslav Communist Party, so Idi Amin got his start in the old British colonial army, the King's African Rifles. Juvenal Habyarimana of Rwanda, like his mentor, Mobutu of Zaire, found his calling in the Belgian colonial army. Samuel Doe was a product of the armed forces of Liberia, the enforcement arm of the Americo-Liberians. These were "loyal natives," collaborators in the dirty business of subjugating their own people. In the scramble to survive after the demise of their former masters, ethnicity was their lever of first resort.

Mangosuthu Buthelezi and his Inkatha confederates were "loyal natives." They derived their power from apartheid's "homelands" system. When that system began to crumble, they found themselves cornered. They struggled to survive in a covert alliance with right-wing whites—and by playing the ethnic card. Without Zulu "unity" under his leadership, Buthelezi warns his partisans, Zulus will be subjected to "genocide" and "ethnic cleansing" at the hands of the Xhosa-led ANC.

I spoke with Buthelezi in March 1996 in his office in Cape Town, where he is now home affairs minister in a government of national unity. The embattled chief was once lionized by the West as a "moderate" alternative to Nelson Mandela's ANC. His office is lined with framed portraits of Buthelezi with Ronald Reagan, Buthelezi with Margaret Thatcher, Buthelezi with Helmut Kohl, Buthelezi with the Pope.

That very morning, testimony had begun in the Malan trial. Buthelezi was essentially an unindicted co-conspirator: his name appeared twenty-seven times in the indictment, a catalogue of alleged covert collusion with apartheid's security forces. The alleged conspiracy was called "Operation Marion," derived from "marionette."

For the moment Buthelezi and his top confederates are off the hook. The Malan acquittal makes it less likely than ever that he will be indicted. Yet in my own interview with Buthelezi, he implicitly admitted to the central charge in the indictment: that he, a proud Zulu and avowed opponent of apartheid, had nonetheless entered into a military alliance with apartheid's murderous security forces. "It was only after they [the ANC] started killing my colleagues that I started to consult with the government," he told me. "They declared a war. They were necklacing people. They would kill anyone they would label a collaborator. We had no choice. I didn't have any means of protecting myself and my people."

Was Buthelezi in bed with the devil? "I'm not a person who gets in bed with anybody," Buthelezi snarled. Collaborator? Stooge? Puppet? "I'm not going to respond to the propaganda of my enemies. I'm not going to get into these insults!" And what of his repeated threats of further bloodshed if the "third force" prosecutions are not suspended? "It's not a threat! I've never threatened! It's just ordinary common sense! To say I'm inciting is just nonsense!"

In fact, it is just ordinary common sense, since violence has always been the currency of power in South Africa. The vaunted negotiations between the National Party and the ANC, which paved the way for the 1994 elections, were very much driven by the fear on all sides of escalating violence—and by the demonstrated capacity of all sides to engage in violence. The Truth and Reconciliation Commission was established in large part to accommodate the controversial guarantee of amnesty for political crimes, which was written into the transitional constitution under threat of violence.

Inkatha's election victories in rural Kwazulu-Natal occurred in a context of violent intimidation over many years, just as the ANC's election successes in urban townships were guaranteed by violent intimidation. The ANC's decision to include Inkatha in the government of national unity was likewise driven by fear of violence. The decision not to indict Buthelezi along with Malan and his co-defendants was widely assumed to have been made at least in part out of fear of violence. The danger is that Kwazulu-Natal's ongoing violence will be exported elsewhere in the country, as it was exported to the townships around Johannesburg after the ban on the ANC was lifted in 1990.

South Africa thus far has avoided the fate of its neighbors, in part because of the wisdom of its leaders, most notably Mandela, and because of the vigor of its independent civil society: human rights groups, church organizations, women's groups, street committees, a vigilant press. But it cannot long endure without the safeguard of a credible system of justice.

South Africa still has deep structural problems that will threaten stability for years to come. There remain gross disparities of wealth and poverty, acute housing shortages, unemployment that approaches fifty percent among blacks. Rising violent crime is heavily concentrated in the poorest townships and in the huge, squalid shantytowns and squatter settlements that have mushroomed around major cities since the lifting of influx control in the late 1980s. Yet there are overwhelming short-term constraints on redistribution of wealth. Any attempt to expand the capacity of the state to redress imbalances would require substantial tax hikes, but that would scare off much-needed investment, without which the only real long-term solution—economic growth—is impossible. So would nationalizing private industries or expropriating white properties. So the deep inequalities of apartheid, and the dangers they imply, will endure for the foreseeable future. The issue is not whether there will be social unrest, but whether the inevitable unrest will take place in a context of law or anarchy.

By the same token, when Mandela leaves the scene, political competition will be extremely fierce. The question is whether that competition will unfold in an environment purged of violence or rife with it. The pattern has always been that criminal interests tend to exploit political interests, and vice versa. Organized criminal interests, black and white, have long cited political motives—liberation from white domination, survival of the Zulu nation, preservation of the last outpost of white Christian civilization in darkest Africa—in order to legitimize their criminal ends. Political interests, in turn, have long relied on organized criminal gangs to do their dirty work. In the absence of legitimate law, this pattern is likely to continue. So persistent violent crime and festering political violence reinforce each other—and scare away investors, which in turn hobbles economic growth, which in turn breeds still higher unemployment and crime, which in turn feeds social and political unrest, which in turn creates opportunities for gangsters and demagogues. This is the cycle that South Africa is struggling to arrest.

Buthelezi's interests today would appear to be what they have always been: power—and immunity from any sort of accountability for past abuses of power. For the moment, Buthelezi and his top confederates are off the hook. The Malan acquittal makes it less likely than ever that Buthelezi will be indicted. The continuing bloodshed in Kwazulu-Natal is evidence that Buthelezi's forces still possess the capacity—and the will—to destabilize South Africa if their interests are disregarded. In the present environment of unproven charges and countercharges, in which each side blames the other and neither side acknowledges any legitimacy in the other side's version of events, one lesson is certain to have been learned by all: violence works.

"The Standards of Africa"

Meanwhile, back in Rwanda, François-Xavier Sibomana remains in custody four years after the genocide. The middle-aged father of eight, who in June 1994 had told me that he was "forced to kill" his brother-in-law, is being held in the huge Nsimda Prison in his native Kibungo Prefecture. He is one of 125,000 accused *genocidaires* languishing in densely crowded, stench-filled, disease-ridden jails across Rwanda.

When I tracked François down in March 1998, he looked fitter than he had four years earlier, dressed now in the standard prison-issue pink cotton tunic and shorts, with white rubber flip-flops. Like nearly all of the accused in custody now, François this time denied participating in the genocide. "I killed nobody," he told me. He said he has never been charged, never seen a lawyer, and knows of no plans for a trial. Had he not, after all, killed his brother-in-law? "It's not true," he replied. "That's not what happened. I did not tell you that."

By April 1998, a month after my reunion with François, at least 330 people had been tried on genocide charges in Rwanda's domestic courts, and 116 had been sentenced to death. Another 110 had been convicted and sentenced to life in prison, with most of the rest sentenced to lesser prison terms. Twenty had been acquitted. On April 24, 1998, the Rwandan government executed the first 22 condemned killers in public ceremonies across the country. The most notorious of those executed was Froduard Karamira, a notorious radio propagandist. Two of the others were local government officials in François' Kibungo Prefecture. Deogratius Bizimmana and Egide Gatanaza were convicted and sentenced to death after a four-hour trial in January 1997. They had no lawyer and no witnesses were called in their defense.

Back in June 1994, the night before my original conversation with François in Kabuga, two middle-aged Tutsi men, well-educated career civil servants, sat on benches in the looted remains of a corner store, amid the pervasive smells of excrement and half-healed machete wounds. They were trying to explain to me how it was possible, how tens of thousands of their fellow countrymen could have been lured into participating in genocide.

Isadore Munyakazi, who had lost twenty relatives and had told me how "surprised" he was to discover his neighbors, his "good friends," he thought, among the the marauding pack of machete-wielding men who came to kill his family, began by stressing subjective factors peculiar to Rwanda. "Illiteracy is part of it," he said. "Politicians say, 'if you don't do this, it will go back to the fifties. You will be like a slave.' Illiterate people will believe it. They believe what they hear on the radio. They believe what their leaders say. They cannot discover the truth for themselves because of the low level of their education. There is ninety percent illiteracy in some of these areas."

Isadore's friend, Bonaventure Niyibizi, shook his head. Bonaventure, like Isadore, had managed to survive with his wife and three children, but his mother, who was seventy, was killed, along with his sister and her five children, his wife's sister and *her* three children, his wife's four uncle's and all of their children—as many as fifty murdered relatives in all. "Really," he sighed, "I cannot understand it myself."

"It's true," Isadore conceded. "We cannot understand it ourselves. We are still at a primitive level where people think they have to resolve a misunderstanding with a machete."

Bonaventure interrupted his friend. "Remember the rule of law. It did not exist. People in the country have not learned about the rule of law. There has been no justice in Rwanda. For all the killings and massacres over the years, there has been no justice."

I asked how Rwanda could overcome this disaster.

"There is only one way," Bonaventure replied. "That is to find the people who have been responsible for this and to bring them to trial according to the law."

Isadore agreed, and he quickly enumerated those he would bring to trial, beginning with Colonel Théoneste Bagasora, the notorious defense chief who is widely viewed as the mastermind behind the genocide. I asked Isadore if he would bring his neighbors to trial—the ones he thought were his "good friends." "To me, they are just instruments," Isadore replied. "If you will bring these people to justice, you'll take everybody. It will be an endless process. But if the people at the top are punished according to the law, and the population knows that, that is the only way."

Bonaventure disagreed. "People who have murdered have to be punished. The level of responsibility is not the same, but you cannot say this person who took a machete and killed this baby—he must be responsible for his acts. Ignorance is no defense."

It was an exchange about an existential problem of justice; it could have taken place in Nuremberg in 1945. Instead, it took place in Africa—two African men, angry, grieving, bewildered, in 1994.

The worst genocide in recorded African history was perpetrated not by Africans but by the Belgians, in what came to be known as the Belgian

Congo, now Mobutu's Zaire. It was Europe's richest colony in Africa, Conrad's "Heart of Darkness." Between 1885 and 1912, King Leopold's private army, comprised primarily of African conscripts led by European officers, killed between five and ten million native inhabitants.

Hitler killed six million Jews. Stalin killed twenty million Soviets. Japanese imperial troops machine-gunned, bayonetted, raped and beheaded some 300,000 Chinese civilians in just six weeks in the infamous Rape of Nanking in 1937–1938. Mao, in turn, by some accounts killed forty million Chinese in the Cultural Revolution.

The forces driving Africans to savagery are no more peculiar to Africa—and no less evil—than the forces that drove the tribes of Bach and Tolstoy to savagery. And no less than in the heart of Europe in the last half of the twentieth century, the end of savagery in Africa will depend on the same essential elements: accountable government and the rule of law. This is not a policy prescription from afar; it is what Africans themselves across a broad spectrum are daily risking their lives and livelihoods for. It may sound obvious. In fact it is new and as yet untested. Until the end of the Cold War, the United States—like the Soviets, like the French, like the British—gave nary a nod to the rule of law in Africa. We threw in our lot with the bad guys. The little men didn't exist. We sometimes rationalized our choice of clients with patronizing references to the "standards of Africa." But those were the Big Man's standards: the standards of gangsters and tyrants the world over throughout history. We neglected a basic lesson taught by all of Africa's wars: injustice causes conflict. Racial hatred is a consequence of injustice as well as its cause. That includes injustice in its most basic sense: the absence of legitimate law. The "civilized world" should hold Africans up to the standard to which we hold ourselves. It is the standard of ordinary Africans all across the continent who yearn for nothing more exotic than the rule of law.

Notes

1. They included two million Hindus and Muslims in India at the time of partition; one million Nigerians in the Biafra war; 500,000 south Sudanese in Sudan's first civil war; unknown hundreds of thousands in the Congo and Chad; one million Ugandans under Idi Amin and Milton Obote; Indians killing 100,000 Nagas and Mizos in Assam in their effort to separate from India; Indonesians killing 100,000 Chinese in Indonesia; Chinese killing 35,000 Khambas in Tibet; Tutsi killing 100,000 Hutus in Burundi; Hutus killing 20,000 Tutsis in Rwanda; Burmese killing 100,000 Karens, Shans and Kachins in Burma; 100,000 Kurds in Iraq; 10,000 Berbers in Algeria and Morocco; Turks and Greeks in Cyprus; Catholics and Protestants in Northern Ireland; Israelis and Arabs.

2. Harold R. Isaacs, *Idols of the Tribe: Group Identity and Political Change* (Cambridge, MA: Harvard University Press, 1975), ix.

3. See Human Rights Watch, *Playing the "Communal Card": Communal Violence and Human Rights* (New York: April 1995). The report begins: "The current epidemic of communal violence—violence involving groups that define themselves by their differences of religion, ethnicity, language or race—is today's paramount human rights problem."

4. Daniel Jonah Goldhagen, in his controversial book, *Hitler's Willing Executioners: Ordinary Germans and the Holocaust* (New York: Alfred A. Knopf, 1996), argues that an especially virulent strain of "eliminationist antisemitism" in Germany provides the most important explanation for the Holocaust. "The German perpetrators of the Holocaust," he writes, "were motivated to kill Jews principally by their belief that the extermination was necessary and just." In support of this argument he cites the more recent slaughters in Bosnia, Rwanda and Burundi. "Who doubts that the Tutsis who slaughtered Hutus in Burundi or the Hutus who slaughtered Tutsis in Rwanda...that the Serbs who have killed Croats or Bosnian Moslems, did so out of conviction in the justice of their actions? Why do we not believe the same for the German perpetrators?" Ibid., 14. If indeed no one doubts this about Rwanda, Burundi and Bosnia, it may be because few outsiders are familiar with the complex circumstances in those countries which brought latent fears and animosities to the surface. For Hutus, Tutsis and Serbs, no less than for Germans, these circumstances included an environment of acute lawlessness and insecurity, dominated by fundamentally criminal regimes bent on mobilizing their subjects through a combination of terror and massive propaganda.

5. The gangland model of tyranny is increasingly being used to explain the proliferation of organized crime—and ethnic conflict—in the former Soviet Union. Numerous commentators, notably Stephen Handelman in his book, *Comrade Criminal: Russia's New Mafia* (New Haven, CT: Yale University Press, 1995), have noted the extent to which the old Soviet Communist Party was modeled after organized crime and colluded with criminal syndicates from its very inception. Lenin, Stalin and the other Bolshevik founding fathers, Handelman writes, admired the conspiratorial mores of the criminal underworld, a world they came to know well in the tsar's prisons. Much of Bolshevik Party structure and its code of conduct were modeled on these criminal gangs, and in its early years the party obtained a large part of its financing from criminal activity such as bank robberies.

Jack F. Matlock, a former U.S. ambassador to the Soviet Union and, in the early 1980s, to Czechoslovakia, tells the story of an enterprising Czech publisher who once tried to publish a Czech translation of Mario Puzo's *The Godfather*. It would show, he believed, the moral decadence of Western society. But he was blocked from publishing by the ideological section of the

Communist Party Central Committee. They accused the publisher of subversive intent for daring to publish a book which was obviously a veiled description of the modus operandi of the Czech Communist Party. See Jack F. Matlock, "Russia: The Power of the Mob," *New York Review of Books,* July 13, 1995.

6. Three excellent books have thus far been published on the crisis in Rwanda and Burundi: Rene Lemarchand, *Burundi: Ethnocide as Discourse and Practice,* (Cambridge, UK: Cambridge University Press, 1994). Gerhard Prunier, *The Rwanda Crisis: History of a Genocide* (New York: Columbia University Press, 1995), and Fergal Keane, *Season of Blood* (New York: Viking, 1996). See also *Africa Rights, Death, Despair and Defiance* (London: 1994), and the many authoritative reports on Rwanda and Burundi published by Human Rights Watch/Africa.

7. Quoted in Lawrence Weschler, "Inventing Peace," *New Yorker,* Nov. 20, 1995, 64.

8. Belated exceptions to this rule include a series of recent prosecutions in Burundi. *The New York Times* reported in August 1997 that six people convicted for having taken part in ethnic massacres in Burundi's four-year-old civil war were hanged on July 31. The executions of three Hutu, two Tutsi and one Twa were the first since the Tutsi-controlled government of Pierre Buyoya began trials in 1996 of people accused of war crimes. At least 126 people had been sentenced to death as of August 1997. Coming on the eve of peace talks with ethnic Hutu rebel groups, the Times reported, the executions appeared calculated to send a message that President Buyoya was determined to hold people on both sides of the conflict accountable for atrocities. However, it was not clear how high up the defendants were in the chain of command.

The most notorious among the executed men was a Hutu schoolteacher who was convicted of burning seventy schoolchildren alive in October 1993 and early 1994 after Tutsi military officers killed the country's first elected president, Melchior Ndadate, a Hutu, setting off the current civil war. The 1993 coup prompted a cycle of ethnic bloodshed across the country, as Hutu militants slaughtered thousands of Tutsi civilians and Tutsi soldiers took reprisals against thousands of Hutu villagers. Since then, an estimated 150,000 have died at the hands of Hutu rebels and government soldiers.

Earlier in 1997, President Buyoya asked the United Nations to set up a war crimes tribunal to look into the massacres like the court investigating the 1994 genocide in Rwanda. But in July the UN rejected the idea, citing Burundi's own dismal human rights record and the squalid conditions in the regroupment camps.

9. A March 1995 report by Human Rights Watch, for example, regarding "General Patterns of Conflict in the Former Soviet Republics," includes an analysis of ongoing civil conflict in the former Soviet republic of Georgia,

in which several thousand civilians have so far been killed and hundreds of thousands made homeless. The report addresses what it calls "the turn from ethnicity as a cultural fact in Abkhazia during the Soviet era to ethnicity as a reason for war." A central factor, the report says, was "the collapse of virtually all modern state structures and authority into anarchy, gangsterism and lawlessness that have characterized Georgia in recent years."

This social breakdown was rooted in large part in the dictatorial rule of the late Georgian leader Zviad Gamsakhurdia, and the "systematic abuses of human rights during his tenure as head of state." The result was "the rise of independent armed groups, some with political pretensions and some simply armed bands. . . . In the vacuum left by the collapse of state controls, other loyalties were able to come to the foreground: loyalty to a militia leader, for example, or loyalty to one's ethnic group. Ethnic sentiment was then mobilized and whipped up even further by the militias and other paramilitary groups, who pursued ethnic agendas of the worst chauvinist sort to serve their own private ends."

Justice in the Wake of Genocide: Rwanda

Madeline H. Morris

During three months in 1994, genocide was committed in the central African republic of Rwanda. In the three years since those events, efforts have been made at both the national and international levels to bring to justice the perpetrators of the brutal crimes committed. The following will briefly describe the context of the genocide, examine the approaches to justice that have been employed in Rwanda, and consider the obstacles to justice that have been encountered despite—or in some instances because of—the approaches taken.

The Context of Genocide

In the weeks from April 6 to July 17, 1994, between half a million and a million Rwandans were butchered by their neighbors. The murdered included men, women and children. The killings, accomplished largely through hacking to death with machetes and other rudimentary instruments, were accompanied by acts of torture and rape.

The great majority of the killers were members of the Hutu ethnic group, which constituted approximately eighty-five percent of the population. The majority of the victims were Tutsi, the group that constituted approximately fourteen percent of the population. Hutu moderates—those identified as favoring the sharing of political power—were slaughtered as well.

Substantial evidence indicates that the mass killings were preplanned and orchestrated by high officials of the then government of Rwanda in a desperate attempt to avoid a broadened sharing of power. During the Rwandan colonial period, Belgium governed the Rwandan populace through a privileged class of Tutsi. In 1959, shortly before Rwanda gained independence from Belgium, persecution of Tutsi began, including widespread massacres, and for the next several years drove many Tutsi from their homes. A large proportion of the Tutsi population fled Rwanda during this period, resettling as refugees in surrounding countries. In the following decades, the government of Rwanda prevented their return. Thirty years later, on October 1, 1990, a rebel group—the Rwandan Patriotic Front (RPF)—comprised largely of Tutsi refugees in Uganda began a military campaign, invading Rwanda from Uganda. Their goal was to enforce the right of the refugees to return to Rwanda, and to do so on acceptable political terms. Halting political negotiations and intermittent fighting ensued for nearly three years until, on August 4, 1993, the Arusha Peace Accords were signed by the government of Rwanda and the RPF. The accords provided for political power-sharing and for the repatriation of refugees.

Regime hardliners, displeased with this turn of events, took steps to obstruct implementation of the Arusha Accords. Then, on April 6, 1994, the airplane carrying Rwandan President Juvénal Habyarimana and President Ntaryamira of neighboring Burundi was shot out of the sky as the presidents returned from a meeting in Tanzania. Theories abound on who downed the plane, but no dispositive proof of responsibility has been established.

Within hours of the plane crash, the killings in Rwanda began. Roadblocks were thrown up to prevent escape, leaders viewed as moderate or "pro-Tutsi" were singled out to be killed first, and then the campaign of exterminating all Tutsi began. The events unfolded in what was unmistakably a preplanned and organized manner.[1]

The killings continued, day and night, for the next fifteen weeks. The international community did virtually nothing to intervene. Indeed, the United Nations Assistance Mission for Rwanda (UNAMIR), which had 2,500 troops in Rwanda on April 6, within weeks pulled out all but a token force of 450 and gave the remaining troops no mandate to intervene to stop the killing of civilians.

The Rwandan Patriotic Army (RPA), the army of the RPF, began a final offensive on April 7 to take over the country militarily. As the RPA forces progressed through the country in the following three months, RPA soldiers incarcerated those whom they identified as perpetrators of the ongoing genocide. As RPA troops entered a village, they often found that much of the Tutsi population had been massacred. Soldiers, untrained in law or police work, would simply identify those who appeared to be the genocidaires, incarcerate them in a local facility and move on with the military operation. There was no systematic collection of evidence; most prisoners were not formally charged; and, for many, no file at all was prepared.

On July 17, over three months after the killings had begun, the RPA achieved military victory and formed the core of what would become the new government of Rwanda. By that time Rwanda's prisons, designed to hold a maximum of 15,000 prisoners, were crowded well beyond capacity.

Justice in the Wake of Genocide

Rwanda was largely destroyed in the spring of 1994. A substantial part of the population had been massacred (half a million to a million people, out of a population of seven to eight million), and another two million had fled the country. A large proportion of the remaining population was displaced within Rwanda. Those who remained were gravely traumatized, and many were seriously injured or maimed. Crops, in a country that survives largely on subsistence farming, had been left untended. The buildings and physical infrastructure had been very substantially damaged. The treasury as well as the physical assets of the country had been plundered or destroyed.

Along with the overall destruction of Rwanda in the spring of 1994 came the devastation of Rwanda's judicial structures. The great majority of judicial and law enforcement personnel had been killed or had fled the country. Moreover, the basic resources needed to run a legal system—books, vehicles, even paper—were essentially unavailable. It was in this context that Rwanda confronted the question of how to pursue justice in the wake of genocide.

The International Criminal Tribunal for Rwanda

In September 1994, sixteen months after the establishment of the International Criminal Tribunal for the former Yugoslavia (ICTY), the new government of Rwanda requested that the United Nations establish an International Criminal Tribunal for Rwanda (ICTR) to adjudicate genocide, war crimes and crimes against humanity that had been committed in the country. As negotiations over the terms for establishment of an ICTR proceeded, however, Rwanda objected to a number of provisions.

First, Rwanda took exception to the time period over which the ICTR would have jurisdiction. According to the ICTR Statute then being drafted, only crimes committed between January 1 and December 31, 1994, would come within the jurisdiction of the ICTR. Manzi Bakuramutsa, then Rwandan representative to the UN, argued that such limited temporal jurisdiction would prevent the ICTR from fully capturing within its prosecutorial scope the criminal activities that culminated in the genocide of 1994. Those activities, he observed, began with planning and sporadic massacres—"pilot projects for extermination" as Mr. Bakuramutsa called them—dating back to 1990.

In evaluating this objection, one must understand not only the ICTR's temporal jurisdiction, but also its subject-matter jurisdiction—that is, not only the time period to be covered but also the exact definition of the crimes to be covered by the ICTR. While the ICTR was to have jurisdiction over actual killings, rapes and other acts constituting genocide, war crimes and crimes against humanity only if those acts were committed in 1994, it is likely that, under the terms of the ICTR Statute, the planning, preparation, or aiding and abetting of those 1994 acts can also form the basis for criminal liability through complicity, even if that preparation occurred prior to 1994. A final determination on whether that form of accomplice liability will be recognized by the ICTR must await a judicial ruling. If such aiding and abetting, prior to 1994, of crimes completed in 1994 is determined to come within the temporal jurisdiction of the ICTR, then not as much was lost by the limitation of the ICTR's temporal jurisdiction as one might at first have imagined.

However, there are certain crimes that the temporal limitation will indeed exclude. For example, killings and other crimes committed in massacres prior to 1994 would be excluded. In addition, significant acts of incitement would not be covered. It appears that incitement to commit genocide is punishable under the ICTR Statute even without proof that the incitement actually led to subsequent acts of genocide. Unlike planning or aiding and abetting, which form the basis for criminal liability only when they can be linked to a completed crime, incitement to genocide probably will be interpreted as constituting a crime in itself. Here, once again, the temporal jurisdiction limit of the ICTR is significant: incitements to genocide that occurred prior to 1994 (and they did) would be excluded from the prosecutorial scope of the international tribunal.

The Rwandans also objected that the proposed ICTR Statute provided for so little personnel, both judicial and prosecutorial, that the ICTR could not possibly be expected to fulfill the monumental task before it. Not only was the total number of judges very small (six trial judges and five appellate judges), but the appellate judges were to be shared with the ICTY. Moreover, the ICTR and ICTY were to share one chief prosecutor.

One can perhaps concur with the rationale behind maintaining a shared appellate chamber for the two international tribunals: the importance of developing a coherent body of international criminal law may weigh against having separate appellate courts potentially rendering conflicting statements of international law (with no final authority or "Supreme Court" to resolve those conflicts). But that rationale does not explain why a larger *total* number of judges could not be provided.

Nor is it clear exactly what benefit was to be gained by the two tribunals sharing one chief prosecutor. The explanation offered, that having one prosecutor would ensure consistency in prosecutorial approach, is less than compelling (indeed, exploration of a range of prosecutorial approaches might be most valuable in the nascent enterprise of international prosecution). Those who viewed the ICTY and ICTR as important precedents and perhaps forerunners of a permanent international criminal court would presumably have favored establishment of a single prosecutorial authority. One advantage, at least in the short term, of having only one prosecutor was that a protracted selection process such as that which preceded selection of the ICTY prosecutor was avoided in the case of the ICTR.

Another major objection raised by the Rwandans concerned the death penalty. The ICTR statute provided for imprisonment as the most severe sentence, precluding imposition of capital punishment by the ICTR. The Rwandan Penal Code, by contrast, does provide for the death penalty. Since the ICTR was expected to try the leaders and organizers of the genocide, the specter of disparate sentencing was raised: the leaders of the genocide, tried before the international tribunal, would escape the death penalty while lower-level perpetrators, tried in Rwandan national courts, might be executed. As Mr. Bakuramutsa noted with considerable understatement: "That situation is not conducive to national reconciliation in Rwanda."[2]

These, then, were some of Rwanda's objections to the statute that would establish the ICTR.[3] By strange coincidence, Rwanda held a seat on the UN Security Council while the ICTR was being established. Ironically, because of its objections to the ICTR Statute as it was finally drafted, Rwanda cast the sole vote opposing adoption of the Security Council resolution establishing the ICTR. Nevertheless, the ICTR was established and, notwithstanding its vote against the ICTR Statute, Rwanda expressed its intention to support the tribunal and cooperate with its work.

But the ICTR is not expected by any means to address the bulk of Rwanda's staggering volume of genocide-related criminal cases. By early 1998, Rwanda's prison population had grown to over 120,000, virtually all awaiting prosecution for genocide-related crimes. The caseload of the ICTR is expected to be in the hundreds at most.

National Justice

Rwanda is thus faced with the enormous problem of how to handle the other 100,000-plus criminal cases arising from the Rwandan genocide. Specialized legislation to facilitate handling of the genocide-related caseload was designed and drafted over the course of several months in 1995–96. On September 1, 1996, after prolonged debate over the legislation's controversial provisions, the "Organic Law on the Organization of the Prosecutions for Offenses Constituting the Crime of Genocide or Crimes Against Humanity Committed since October 1, 1990" came into force as the law that would govern Rwanda's national prosecutions for the genocide.

The specialized criminal justice program laid out in that law is, in essence, quite simple. Suspects will be classified in four categories, according to their degree of culpability in the Rwandan genocide. The most culpable category, Category One, will include leaders and organizers of the genocide and perpetrators of particularly heinous murders or sexual torture. All others who committed homicides will come under Category Two. Category Three will include perpetrators of grave assaults against the person not resulting in death. Those who committed property crimes in connection with the genocide will fall into Category Four.

This specialized criminal justice program relies heavily on a system of plea agreements. All perpetrators other than those in Category One (who are subject to the death penalty) are entitled to a reduced sentence as part of a guilty plea agreement. Specifically, a preset, fixed reduction in the penalty that would otherwise be imposed for their crimes is available to all non-Category One perpetrators in return for an accurate and complete confession, a plea of guilty to the crimes committed and an apology to the victims. A greater penalty reduction is made available to perpetrators who confess and plead guilty prior to prosecution than to perpetrators who come forward only after prosecution has begun.

The sentences provided under the specialized legislation are as follows. Category Two perpetrators receive a sentence of seven to eleven years' imprisonment if they plead guilty prior to prosecution, a sentence of twelve to fifteen years' imprisonment if they plead guilty after prosecution has begun, or a sentence of life imprisonment if convicted at trial. (Thus the death penalty is excluded even for those Category Two perpetrators convicted at trial. This exclusion of the death penalty constitutes a reduction from the severity of sentence that could ordinarily be imposed under the Rwandan penal code, which imposes capital punishment for murder. This reduction reflects a policy decision regarding the undesirability, for the society generally and for national reconciliation and security, of undertaking the execution of literally thousands of perpetrators.) Category Three perpetrators receive a penalty of one-third the prison sentence normally applicable to their crimes if they plead guilty before prosecution, a sentence of half the term of years normally applicable if they plead guilty after prosecution has begun, and the sentence ordinarily applicable if convicted at trial. All Category Four defendants convicted of criminal offenses receive suspended sentences.

A substantial reduction in sentence is thus provided where a Category Two or Three defendant submits a guilty plea before prosecution. This leniency is extended in order to encourage perpetrators to come forward before prosecution. A perpetrator who pleads guilty prior to the start of prosecution eliminates the need for the prosecutor to conduct a full-scale investigation and prepare a complete dossier for the case in question. For that reason, perpetrators are given an incentive, in the form of a relatively lenient sentence, to come forward prior to prosecution. Similarly, the penalties to be imposed pursuant to a guilty plea submitted after prosecution has begun but before conviction at trial are less severe than the penalties to be imposed pursuant to a conviction at trial, in order to maintain incentives even after the initiation of prosecution for perpetrators to plead guilty.

While uncommon (and largely unacknowledged) in inquisitorial criminal justice systems such as those of Rwanda and continental Europe, plea agreement systems are pervasive in adversarial systems such as that of the United States. A plea agreement is essentially an agreement between a criminal defendant and the government that "settles" the criminal case without a trial. The specialized plea agreement system in Rwanda is being relied upon to do much to relieve the extraordinary burden posed by the enormous criminal caseload arising from the genocide.

The Rwandan specialized criminal justice program, as noted earlier, requires that the defendant, as part of the plea agreement package, make an accurate and complete confession of crimes committed, including disclosure of any accomplices. This confession requirement is important to establish a truthful historical record of the Rwandan genocide, to allow meaningful verification of the accuracy of the confession, and to assist in prosecutors' continuing investigations and prosecutions of genocide-related crimes.

The additional requirement that a perpetrator participating in the confession and guilty plea program make an apology to the victims of his or her crimes is intended to contribute to the process of national healing and reconciliation. While it is true that defendants may have an ulterior motive for making these apologies (to obtain the reduced sentences offered), the apologies will nevertheless represent at least some statement of recognition of wrongdoing which may, in the aggregate, contribute to national reconciliation.

The specialized Rwandan criminal justice program represents a complex compromise reflecting a multitude of difficult choices. While full and regular criminal prosecution of every suspected perpetrator of genocide and related crimes might in many respects be the most desirable course of action, the resources demanded by such an approach would quickly overwhelm national capacities. Therefore, a decision has been made in the Rwandan context to establish a program to accomplish the crucial purposes of criminal justice, while also respecting resource limitations and the need to support rebuilding of other aspects of Rwandan society.

An approach such as that adopted in Rwanda offers the benefit of expediency in handling an enormous volume of cases and may make some contribution to national healing and reconciliation. At the same time, however, there is reason for concern about the potential for miscarriage of justice under such a system. Factually innocent suspects may choose to plead guilty for fear of a worse outcome at trial or to avoid extensive delays before trial. These concerns are exacerbated by the fact that no provision has been made to date for any form of defense counsel for many of the indigent defendants in Rwanda. On the other side of the equation, survivors and others rightly ask why perpetrators of these horrific crimes should receive leniency, especially when an "ordinary criminal" who committed a murder in Rwanda tomorrow would not receive that same leniency.

The question to ask in designing legal responses to the complex situations surrounding crimes of mass violence is: What action will do the most good and the least harm under the circumstances? Full trial of 100,000 defendants—more than one percent of the national population—would be infeasible in even the wealthiest nation, and is emphatically not an option under the circumstances in Rwanda. The alternative at the other extreme, releasing prisoners *en masse* under an explicit or implicit grant of amnesty, would perpetuate a culture of impunity, be unacceptable to the survivor population, and constitute a heightened security risk both to the regime and to the individuals released. As implementation of the Rwandan specialized criminal justice system unfolds, evaluations of that system should be made in light of the relevant circumstances and the realistically available options.

The Trials of Concurrent Jurisdiction

The administration of justice in post-genocide Rwanda is rendered uniquely complex by the fact that concurrent jurisdiction for the genocide-related crimes is actively exercised by two different entities: the government of Rwanda and the ICTR. This concurrent exercise of jurisdiction has exposed difficult issues that are likely to recur in future contexts in which similar structures of actively shared jurisdiction are created.[4]

Concurrent jurisdiction raises complex questions regarding cooperation in investigations and the sharing of evidence. Obvious advantages in efficiency and effectiveness are to be gained by close national and international cooperation in these areas. But difficulties concerning confidentiality of evidence, witness protection, due process standards and the need to avoid any appearance of partiality of the international tribunal[5] raise delicate questions that have yet to be systematically addressed. Discussion of these matters has been ongoing between the ICTR and the government of Rwanda. But the issues, for the most part, remain largely open.

An area that has been of particular concern in the exercise of concurrent jurisdiction is the distribution of defendants between the national and international fora. The question of the appropriate distribution of defendants has been the cause of uncertainty and, at times, tension between national governments and the ICTR. On more than one occasion, the ICTR and the government of Rwanda have sought to obtain custody of the same suspect. In one instance, not only the ICTR and the Rwandan government but also the Belgian government were attempting to gain custody of the same suspects who were being held in Cameroon.

It is worth noting that, while many speculated that these conflicts over custody were really illusory because no country would be willing to transfer a suspect to Rwanda for domestic prosecution, that speculation has proven false. At least one defendant has already been transferred to Rwanda (by Ethiopia), and other countries have expressed a willingness in principle to do the same.

The tensions between the government of Rwanda and the ICTR over distribution of defendants have resulted, in part, from lack of communication, and also from a more fundamental conflict of interests, or at least of agendas. When the ICTR was established, the Rwandan government had not yet decided upon an approach to national prosecutions. The approach ultimately adopted relies heavily on plea agreements, as discussed above. That plea agreement program turned out to be somewhat incompatible with the operation of an international tribunal that believes its mandate is to prosecute the top-level leaders of the genocide.

The reasons for this incompatibility are easy to understand. The leniency in sentencing that goes with plea agreements can easily create a perception that impunity has prevailed—unless at least the leaders are fully prosecuted and punished. If, however, the leaders are brought before an international tribunal, where they receive more favorable treatment than they would have in the national courts, this leaves a gap in the national justice picture. The advantages enjoyed by defendants before the international tribunal include escaping the death penalty (which may be imposed by Rwandan courts, but not by the ICTR), imprisonment under better conditions than those in Rwandan prisons, and guarantees of various due process safeguards, such as appointed defense counsel. If the leaders are away receiving "international justice," which is perceived as lenient, while the followers are at home getting "bargains" in the national justice system, then no one is being punished fully and severely, relative to national standards, for the horrors perpetrated. A perception may thus be created, especially among the survivor population, that the plea agreement program is no more than a program of impunity. Thus, one can readily see why trying at least some Category One defendants would be important to Rwanda's justice system.

This problem became apparent over time. When the ICTR had been in place for many months, and ICTR personnel thought the tribunal was finally showing results and deserved to be congratulated, it was instead reaping the wrath of Rwandans each time it pursued a leader to be prosecuted. ICTR personnel and supporters found this wrath especially difficult to accept, as Rwanda had not managed actually to begin *any* trials,

of leaders or otherwise. In reply, the Rwandans noted that the ICTR had
been no swifter, having so far also tried no one. This friction was caused,
at least in part, by the fact that the parties had failed to communicate regarding policies to govern the distribution of defendants as the national
justice program evolved. But the friction also reflects what may be a more
fundamental conflict between a national and an international jurisdiction, each of which aspires to prosecute leaders.

On the authority of the UN Security Council resolution that brought
the ICTR into being, the ICTR enjoys primacy of jurisdiction. This
means that, where the ICTR and a national body each have a legal basis
for jurisdiction over a given case, the ICTR is entitled—but not obliged—
to exercise jurisdiction to the exclusion of the national body (a defendant
cannot be tried by both, except in very limited, exceptional circumstances). But the criteria to be employed in deciding whether to exercise
jurisdiction in any particular case have yet to be articulated by the ICTR.
Certainly, no articulation of principles for the distribution of defendants
has been reflected in any agreement or memorandum of understanding between the ICTR and the government of Rwanda. Conflicts over exercise
of jurisdiction to date have been resolved on an ad hoc basis.[6]

A more satisfactory basis for consistent decision-making regarding the
distribution of defendants will have to rest upon a careful analysis of the
purposes of international criminal tribunals and of their concurrent jurisdiction with national courts. Oddly, though perhaps not surprisingly,
this analytic process still remains to be completed.

Identifying the appropriate criteria for distribution of defendants between national and international fora is tricky within any one context.
The issues are further complicated when one recognizes the need to articulate underlying principles and guidelines that will serve *across* contexts—in Bosnia or in Croatia as well as in Rwanda and, very likely, in
future instances as well.

In anticipation of such future instances, a statute for a permanent international criminal court is currently under consideration by the United
Nations. That draft statute to some extent averts potential conflicts over
defendants by giving deference to national-level prosecutions under most
circumstances. But those deferral provisions would not apply in genocide
prosecutions or in cases where the international criminal court's jurisdiction had been invoked by the Security Council, as can occur under the
draft statute. In such instances, the same difficulties regarding distribution of defendants as have arisen in Rwanda would be likely to recur.

Nor does the draft statute for a permanent international criminal court
directly address whether an international court's role is especially tied to
trying leadership-level defendants. Article 35 (c) of the draft provides that

the court might decide "that a case before it is inadmissible on the ground that the crime in question... is not of such gravity as to justify further action by the Court."[7] One might imagine that such a provision, if adopted, would form the basis for an admissibility challenge by a defendant (such as Dusko Tadic, the first defendant to be tried in the Hague) who was not in a leadership position in the overall criminal enterprise. Such a challenge would be based on the proposition that "gravity" includes the notion of leadership or other special responsibility. The claim, in other words, would be that it is not the role of an international court to try "small fry" (as Antonio Cassesse, former president of the ad hoc international criminal tribunals for Rwanda and former Yugoslavia, has implied).

Whether the role of an international criminal tribunal is specially tied to the prosecution of leaders depends, obviously, on what the purpose of an international criminal tribunal is. Some have suggested that a primary role or purpose of such a tribunal is to supplement or substitute for national courts where national justice systems are overwhelmed or incapacitated. This function of an international criminal tribunal carries no implications for the best distribution of defendants other than that the international tribunal should do that which best assists or complements national efforts. Others have suggested that an international criminal tribunal should exercise jurisdiction only when there is "little prospect of fair trial under national criminal jurisdiction." Once again, this conception of the purpose of an international criminal court suggests no general principle regarding the distribution of defendants on the basis of leadership.

Clearly, the rationale for a regime of "stratified concurrent jurisdiction," in which the international tribunal prosecutes (or strives to prosecute) the upper strata, the leaders, leaving the rest of the defendants to national governments, cannot rest on a view of international tribunals as supplements or substitutes for reluctant, ineffective or incapacitated national courts. Having an international tribunal try a few top-level defendants while leaving the staggering bulk of the caseload to national courts would not necessarily be a sensible strategy if the goal were to provide a stand-in or supplement for an incapacitated or unwilling national judicial system. (In the Rwandan context, for instance, application of the stratified concurrent jurisdiction model results in the ICTR trying a tiny fraction of the defendants while leaving 100,000-plus cases to Rwandan national courts.) Rather, massive assistance to the national system or, taking the opposite tack, provision of an international court designed to handle the bulk of the cases would be a more appropriate strategy if the goal were to respond to incapacity or recalcitrance in a national system.

A different rationale sometimes offered to support a regime of stratified concurrent jurisdiction is based on the need for deterrence. The ar-

gument here is that ensuring strong deterrents against leading and organizing mass crimes is of surpassing importance because, without leaders, the mass crimes would not occur. Be that as it may,[8] this argument
actually is not relevant to the question of the *distribution* of defendants
between national and international fora. Few would deny that it is important for deterrent (and other) purposes to prosecute the leaders of
crimes of mass violence. But the issue under consideration is the forum
in which those leaders should be tried. Presumably, deterrence can be accomplished through trial and punishment in either national or international fora. So the deterrence argument tells us little about which forum
should exercise jurisdiction over the leaders.

Some may argue that, while in theory deterrence can be accomplished
through trial at the national or the international level, in practice leaders typically will have fled their countries before they can be prosecuted
by national authorities. Moreover, those "leaders-in-exile" often will
have the resources and influence to find refuge in countries that will
shield them from the reach of their own national prosecutorial authorities. In such cases where national judicial authorities cannot obtain extradition of suspects, an *international* criminal tribunal may well have
more success in gaining custody of prospective defendants. Therefore,
the argument concludes, if effective deterrence is to be achieved at the
leadership level, it will have to rest on the realistic threat of prosecution
before an international tribunal.

Again, while this may at first appear to be a strong argument for stratified concurrent jurisdiction, closer inspection reveals flaws in its logic. *If*
it is possible for an international tribunal but not a national tribunal to
gain custody of a particular suspect who should be prosecuted, then it
makes sense for the international tribunal to prosecute that suspect. But
that proposition is, in fact, not at all related to whether the suspect in
question was a leader. The proposition could apply equally to any suspect,
leader or otherwise. Thus, potential problems in obtaining custody, and
the fact that those problems may arise disproportionately where leaders
are involved, does not constitute a sound argument for a regime of stratified concurrent jurisdiction. It is true that, if the custody issue tends to
arise disproportionately where leaders are involved, then this may result
in an international tribunal trying a disproportionate number of leaders.
But that would be a result of the politics of custody, *not* an argument for
an international tribunal *seeking* to prosecute leadership-level defendants
pursuant to a stratified concurrent jurisdiction model.

Putting the same point somewhat differently, the issue of which jurisdiction is more likely to be successful in obtaining custody is separate and
not logically related to the question: If the country holding a suspect

were equally willing to transfer that suspect to the custody of the national or the international forum, which forum then should exercise jurisdiction? Instances in which this was the operative question—where a third-party state has been willing to transfer a particular suspect to the international or the national jurisdiction—have already arisen in the Rwandan context. Notwithstanding the ability of the national courts to gain custody, the argument still was made in such cases that the ICTR should exercise jurisdiction if the suspect was a major leader. Obviously, in those cases, the view that the ICTR should try the leaders was not based on relative likelihood of gaining custody. The custody factor thus does not appear to provide a satisfactory explanation of the stratified concurrent jurisdiction model in theory or in practice.

The rationales for stratified concurrent jurisdiction considered thus far have failed to withstand careful scrutiny. The final rationale to be considered as a possible basis for stratified concurrent jurisdiction is an essentially moral and philosophical proposition: that crimes of a certain magnitude and of a certain nature should be condemned by an international entity, a "voice of humanity."

Even accepting the premise that an essential purpose of an international criminal tribunal is to condemn certain crimes on behalf of all humanity, we must still ask why it is the leaders in those crimes—the architects and not the executors—who should be prosecuted before an international court. Does it manifest greater evil to organize the murder of thousands at a distance than to torture or kill while looking into the eyes of a pleading victim? No self-evident moral truth that "organizing is worse" can be relied upon to support the pervasive assumption that the role of an international tribunal is to prosecute the leaders.

One might, however, make a related but somewhat different argument for stratified concurrent jurisdiction based on the international nature of the responsibility of leadership. The reasoning would be that those who lead others and hold the power to create a holocaust have a particular duty, in the nature of a fiduciary duty, that extends beyond national boundaries. A breach of that duty of leadership is a distinctive type of crime, a crime against the world community. Thus, one might reason, an international court's role is to try the leaders, because the nature of the leaders' transgressions is global.

But a regime of stratified concurrent jurisdiction is not satisfactorily supported even by this conception of international responsibility. All crimes of genocide and crimes against humanity, whether committed by leaders or by followers, are international crimes. As such, *all* of those crimes are, by definition, of distinctly international concern.

It may be true that, while the international community has an interest in denouncing international crime committed by persons at all levels, it has an added interest, based on special international responsibility, where the perpetrator is a leader. But this added interest is not of sufficient significance or force to make it the *sine qua non* of an international tribunal's proper exercise of jurisdiction. The benefits of trying the leaders before an international tribunal are not sufficiently compelling to define the proper distribution of defendants between national and international fora.[9] Rather, those benefits may better be viewed as constituting one consideration among others to be taken into account in balancing the benefits of national and international exercise of jurisdiction.

Given the lack of a compelling categorical argument supporting stratified concurrent jurisdiction, it is questionable whether a thoroughgoing regime of stratified concurrent jurisdiction rests on a secure foundation in principle. This issue would be far less pressing if stratified concurrent jurisdiction did not have nefarious practical consequences. Unfortunately, however, as currently practiced, such a jurisdictional model creates a number of anomalous consequences and potential obstacles to justice.

First, stratified concurrent jurisdiction tends in practice to render injustices, because trial before an international tribunal will tend, systematically, to be more favorable to defendants than trial before national courts (leaving aside sham courts established to whitewash defendants). As illustrated in the Rwandan case, defendants reap several advantages from trial in an international rather than a national forum. First, an international court will not have a death penalty, while many national courts (such as Rwanda's) do. Second, the prisons used for sentences imposed by an international court may afford better conditions of incarceration than the national prisons in question. Third, an international tribunal would be expected to guarantee defendants the utmost in due process, while national courts (especially those struggling with post-holocaust resources and an overwhelming caseload) may not. Finally, defendants in national courts will have more reason than defendants tried before an international tribunal to fear bias, in the form of victors' justice or of personal partiality.

Thus there are very substantial advantages, possibly making the difference between life and death, to prosecution in an international rather than a national forum. Anomalously, under the stratified concurrent jurisdiction model, all of those advantages accrue to the *leaders*, those who were at the helm of the holocaust. This surely is an unintended and an unjust outcome. Yet such "anomalies of inversion," in which the most responsible defendants receive the least harsh treatment, are not coincidental; they are a predictable, structural problem that will recur under the stratified concurrent jurisdiction model, in which the international tribunal tries the leaders and the national courts try the rest.

Anomalies of inversion are not the only obstacles to justice that may be posed by this jurisdiction model. Stratified concurrent jurisdiction may also tend to undermine the use of plea agreements, which may be a particularly important tool in the prosecution of mass-scale crimes, as exemplified in the Rwandan case.

Not only is it unclear, therefore, that stratified concurrent jurisdiction rests on a sound principled basis; in practice, it also engenders significant anomalies of inversion and other obstacles to the administration of justice. For these reasons, it is far from clear that the stratified concurrent jurisdiction approach should take pride of place among possible models for the distribution of defendants. Rather, the arguably added value of prosecuting leadership-level perpetrators before an international tribunal may be one factor, to be weighed among others, relevant to the distribution of defendants.

Along with issues involving distribution of defendants, the dilemmas that arise more generally from the concurrent exercise of national and international jurisdiction over crimes of mass violence are starkly posed in the context of Rwanda. But Rwanda is unlikely to remain unique in this respect. The same problems predictably will arise in future contexts where concurrent jurisdiction is actively exercised. The broad range of issues concerning the interaction of national and international jurisdictions forms the basis for ongoing debates on "complementarity" between national criminal jurisdictions and a permanent international criminal court.

A threshold requirement for greater coherence in the interaction of national and international jurisdictions is a clear articulation, in each case in which an international tribunal is to be convened, of the needs which that particular tribunal is intended to meet. The needs that are likely to be present to a greater or lesser degree, singly or in combination, include: responding to an overwhelmed national justice system; substituting for a national system in which the fact or appearance of bias would substantially undermine the process of justice (whether because of a lack of will to prosecute or because of a will to prosecute "with a vengeance"); substituting for a national justice system where the national system would be unable to obtain custody of suspects; and/or expressing, through the exercise of international jurisdiction, a universal condemnation of some special feature of the crimes in question, such as the special international responsibility of certain perpetrators. Thus the purposes of an international tribunal will not be identical across contexts.

Two important benefits can be gained by articulating, in each context, the particular needs to be met by convening that international tribunal.

First, such an articulation will permit confirmation of whether an international tribunal will best serve the goals sought in that particular context. For instance, if the purpose is to respond to a situation in which the national system is overwhelmed, we can analyze whether it is best to provide an international tribunal or provide assistance to the national system, or some combination of the two. Second, referring to clearly articulated purposes for convening an international tribunal will allow the operation of that particular tribunal—and especially its interaction with national jurisdictions—to be appropriately tailored to those goals. For example, if the purpose is to substitute for national courts when they cannot obtain custody, then, arguably, that international tribunal should defer to the national justice system if it *can* gain custody in a particular case. By contrast, if the purpose is to express universal condemnation of certain crimes, then that international tribunal may wish to exercise jurisdiction even if the national court *could* gain custody. In such an instance, a very careful analysis would be required of how the international interest in "universal condemnation" should be weighed against the national (and international) interest in successful operation of the national justice system should the two conflict. In sum, it will be essential to the fruitful operation of an international court that its purposes are clearly articulated *in each instance* and that its operations are appropriately tailored to those purposes in each case.

The Future in Rwanda and Beyond

In Rwanda, the performance of the national justice system and that of the ICTR remains to be seen. Some years after the massacres, and still at the beginning of trials in both jurisdictions, it is clear that the best form of justice that the ICTR or the national courts will be able to render will be justice delayed. The slow progress of justice in Rwanda points to the need for protocols for prompt international assistance to national justice systems; for permanent bodies, such as an international criminal court, that can be readily called into service when warranted; and for clear articulation of the purposes of each international tribunal, in order that both national and international jurisdictions may be as effective as possible in responding to crimes of mass violence.

Notes

1. For a detailed description of these events, see African Rights, *Rwanda: Death, Despair and Defiance* (London, revised edition 1995), 177–98.
2. UN Doc. S/PV.3453 (1994), 16.
3. The Rwandan delegation to the Security Council also voiced certain other objections to the ICTR Statute. These can be found at UN S/PV.3453 (1994).

4. Concurrent jurisdiction also exists in the context of the ICTY. As domestic prosecutions proceed in the former Yugoslavia, we may see these issues reiterated in that very different context.

5. In addition to the issue of impartiality generally, there is also the question of impartiality regarding claims against members of the current Rwandan regime. The jurisdiction of the ICTR includes any crimes against humanity committed in Rwanda in 1994. The impartiality of the tribunal must therefore include objective assessment of allegations that crimes against humanity were committed by members of the RPA during the 1994 war. The former ICTR prosecutor has stated that, if any such allegations were substantiated, the ICTR would investigate, but that, to date, no evidence has been presented to support such allegations. See speech by Richard Goldstone, then ICTR prosecutor, at "Justice in Cataclysm" conference, July 21, 1996, Brussels, Belgium. Were the government and the ICTR to be closely allied in prosecutorial pursuits, the objectivity of the ICTR in evaluating claims against RPA members could be called into question.

6. For example, discussion ensued between the ICTR prosecutor and the government of Rwanda in the spring of 1996 regarding the disposition of twelve suspects who had been arrested in Cameroon. In those discussions, the ICTR prosecutor insisted upon the ICTR pursuing prosecution of three of those individuals, citing their leadership positions as a critical criterion making it essential that the ICTR exercise its primacy of jurisdiction in those cases. Some high officials of the Rwandan government understood those discussions also to have included a commitment by the ICTR prosecutor to the effect that, in the future, the ICTR would not pursue prosecution of suspects whom the government of Rwanda had already begun pursuing. The ICTR Prosecutor, however, did not understand those discussions to have included any such commitment.

   After the discussions on the Cameroon arrestees, Froduard Karamira became the object of a brief tug of war between the ICTR and the government of Rwanda. Karamira was believed to have been among the leaders of the Rwandan genocide. He was in the course of being deported from India to Rwanda, at the request of the government of Rwanda, when he attempted to leave the airport during a transit stopover in Addis Ababa, Ethiopia. At that point, the ICTR requested that the government of Ethiopia detain Karamira on behalf of the ICTR. As it happened, several days later, a number of Rwandan cabinet ministers and the ICTR prosecutor were in Geneva for a round table of countries donating funds for the rebuilding of Rwanda. At the request of the Rwandan minister of justice, she and the ICTR prosecutor (and several other parties) met to discuss the Karamira matter. The minister of justice pointed out the importance to the Rwandan justice system that Karamira be tried in Rwanda, and also pointed to the extensive efforts that Rwanda had already invested in gaining custody of Karamira. The

ICTR prosecutor stated that he had not been aware that Karamira had been detained at the instance of the Rwandan government. In light of that information, he stated, he would reconsider his request to the Ethiopian government. Several hours after that meeting, the ICTR prosecutor informed the Ethiopian government that he was withdrawing his request for the detention of Karamira until the earlier request of the Rwandan government had been acted upon. Karamira was subsequently deported to Rwanda from Ethiopia. He was executed in April 1998 after trial and sentencing in Rwandan national courts.

7. Editor's note: This clause was included as Article 17(1)(d) in the statute for a permanent international criminal court adopted in Rome in June 1998, after completion of this chapter.

8. The proposition that the most effective deterrent effect can be achieved by deterring potential *leaders* of mass crimes is, in fact, a debatable one. Perhaps leaders tend to be more zealous, more driven, less reticent and, hence, less deterrable than others. If so, then focusing deterrence efforts on the leaders may not be the most effective strategy.

9. This is not to overlook the possibility that there might be political or policy reasons for focusing international prosecutorial efforts on leaders in some contexts. The point, rather, is that there does not appear to be a compelling argument for an overarching or axiomatic policy of stratified concurrent jurisdiction.

Only a War Crimes Tribunal:
Triumph of the "International Community,"
Pain of the Survivors

Julie Mertus

I used to believe that the world was full of many colors,
now I know it's just black.
I used to believe that all people are kind,
now I know only some of them are.
I used to believe that my friends would be with me all of my life,
now I know that none of them would give any part of their body for me.
I used to believe that I could trust people,
now I know that I should be careful.
I used to believe that I would have a good life with my neighbors,
but now I know it is easy for them to kill in war.
I used to believe that no one could force me away from my homeland,
but now I know this isn't a dream.
I couldn't believe that my generation could be worse than the
*   older generation,*
but now I know they are.
I used to believe in everything,
but now I believe in nothing.

I used to believe in happiness,
but now I cannot even believe my eyes.
I used to believe that I would live by my wishes,
but now I know I will live by other people's wishes.
What I couldn't believe, I now believe.

> "Group Poem," one line each told by
> Adisa, Nasir, Hajra, Muriz, Mirsada, Remzija,
> Melisa, Senid, Aziz, Uzeir, Mevlida, Sahza,
> ages 13 to about 54, refugees from Sarajevo,
> Jajce and Donji Vakuf in Islamabad, Pakistan,
> August 1994.[1]

From the Voices of Survivors to the War Crimes Tribunal

The problem with the war crimes tribunals for the former Yugoslavia
and Rwanda is that they are war crimes tribunals. The stuff of law—the

elements of the crimes, the rules of procedure, the dance of witness, lawyer, judge—can do only so much. And the closer one is to the crime, the less likely "so much" will be enough.

Aristotle said that the pursuit of justice should bring pleasure. Tribunal justice may bring pleasure to lawyers drafting pleonastic legal documents in the Hague, diplomats declaring success at stabilizing conflict, and local politicians staking their claims to power amid the smoldering embers of destroyed communities. But little satisfaction will come to survivors. Genocide, mass murder, rape, torture and other crimes may be tried, and a small percentage of the perpetrators may be convicted. International principles will triumph or fail; respect for international law will expand or diminish. The new governments arising out of conflict will be legitimized or delegitimized. Still, regardless of the outcome, the voices of survivors will remain largely unheard and unaddressed.

For survivors, storytelling is not a luxury. War has served to strip them of control over their lives and erase all sense of a volitional past and future. As Elaine Scarry observes in *The Body in Pain*, the discourses of torture, rape, murder and other forms of violence teach their targets that they are nothing but objects.[2] The process of telling and of observing one's story being heard allows survivors to become subjects again, to retrieve and resurrect their individual and group identities. From voice comes hope.

The Bosnian Muslim refugees who sat in a circle on the floor in their refugee camp in Pakistan and, line by line, contributed to the poem of lost beliefs reprinted above reclaimed a small corner of their identities. When first asked to contribute to the poem, many had difficulty answering—not because they did not have ideas, but because, in the words of one participant, "no one has asked us what we think in such a long time." They had been treated as mere objects, first by their tormentors, then by refugee camp handlers, government spokespeople, asylum officers, visiting journalists. They had been denied their complex selves and stamped with unitary identities: enemy, victim, refugee, the "ethnically cleansed," asylum seeker, spectacle.

And now war crimes tribunals? The survivors now bear the stamp of potential witness; they become the conduit through which investigators and prosecutors can make their case. Despite their good intentions, investigators and prosecutors—the agents of law—must focus on piecing together facts to prove the crime. Even if they avoid putting the personal suffering of survivors on trial, they cannot return survivors' rightful claim to subjecthood. By opening and closing to let in only enough information to prove the issue at hand, law is inherently counternarrative. Victims can testify about the hand that beat them, confirm the size of the room, the color of the door, the width of the wooden table on which bodies were broken. But they cannot talk about how their child's face looked when the paramilitary troops dragged them away, they cannot remember what they ate for dinner on the last day the entire family was alive and together, they cannot cry about their dog who was left behind or reminisce about long walks through their old town square. No one will see the stories, poems, pictures, jokes, coffees, gossip, walks around the refugee camp yard—no one will know the little things that helped them survive.[3]

A war crimes tribunal is, after all, a war crimes tribunal.

A Paradigm of Functions and Interests

The refugee woman who listened to the asylum officer calmly inform her that her application was rejected because she was only threatened with rape, but not actually raped or tortured in a concentration camp; the newlywed doctors who escaped Bosnia by paying an aid convoy 4,000 German marks each and somehow made it across borders to Germany, where they disappeared into the ranks of the shadow labor force; the teenage girl who carries in her rucksack the poetry of her dead soldier boyfriend; the four-year-old boy who wants to become a plane so he can fly his family back home; the elderly couple who lived in their basement for four months before a sympathetic enemy neighbor found them and arranged their safe passage out: a tribunal can fulfill many functions, but it cannot serve the needs of these and other survivors. As in other criminal cases, evenhanded investigations and fair prosecutions before the tribunal can potentially fulfill the following narrow set of functions: *naming* crimes; *blaming* individual perpetrators; *punishing* the guilty and *deterring* potential perpetrators; *delivering reparations* to survivors; *reforming* lawless societies; and *recording* what happened for history.

The problem is not that the war crimes tribunals will utterly fail to address these functions. It is rather that their success in doing so will be measured differently depending on one's particular interest. To be sure, everyone has some interest in "justice" being served. But this thing called justice often depends on the observer's position, in all senses of the word—meaning one's relative proximity to the crimes, the conflict, the region and the issues; assessment of the origins of conflict, the accountability of various actors for crimes and their continuation, and need to remember or desire to forget; role and responsibility as an international, regional, national, community or family leader; and social status—that is, position inside or outside international, regional, national and community power structures, and the worth ascribed to one's existence depending on that position. When measured according to these attributes, most survivors, close to the crime, are far from achieving their vision of justice.

This chapter places in context those whose interests will not be heard: those closest to the crime, those who need to remember, out-siders to power—the survivors.

The discussion below illuminates some of the intersections between the *functions* outlined above and *position*. It considers the interests served by each function for three main groups of actors: (1) the "international community"—international and regional institutions and organizations, states and individual actors outside Rwanda and the former Yugoslavia; (2) local power brokers, including the states, territories and communities arising out of the conflicts and their opposition; and (3) individual sur-vivors, including both those who stayed in the area in conflict and those who fled to safer ground (but excluding those who previously held or presently hold positions of power). Within each of these groups, interests can vary further according to the nuances of position—proximity, atti-tude, job and social status.

In general, as explained below, the tribunals are most likely to address (if not satisfy) the interests of the international community, and least likely to even hear the interests of survivors. The tribunals should thus be understood as necessary, although not sufficient, responses to the aftermath of conflict and the need for healing.

Naming Crimes

The naming of crimes can serve important, although vastly different, interests for the three groups of actors listed above. For the international community, the naming provides a historical opportunity to establish, re-fine and/or enforce the boundaries of international law. For example, by naming the crime of genocide, the tribunals have become the first inter-national criminal courts to define the meaning and application of the Genocide Convention, a post-World War II treaty. By naming the crime of rape as a "crime against humanity," they have become the first interna-tional criminal courts to refine when and how rape in war can be prose-cuted as such (although rape in conflict had been prosecuted previously as torture, inhumane treatment, a crime against personal dignity and other national or international criminal offenses[4]). By naming superior officers' actions as criminal, the tribunals are defining the limits of command re-sponsibility; by naming foot soldiers' actions as criminal, the tribunals are setting the limits of the defense of "superior orders." Within the inter-national community, those who have made it their profession to promote the existence and enforcement of international law—an ever-growing cadre of lawyers, scholars, judges, activists and diplomats—are most in-terested in the potential of the war crimes tribunals to fulfill this function.

The naming of crimes, even without the trials themselves, also pro-vides the international community with a stage from which to express its moral condemnation. International leaders can thus reaffirm by words, if not by deeds, a vision of a just world in which evil cannot go unaddressed. The very naming can serve the international community's interest in saving face and explaining its own failure to take early, decisive action to stop the slaughter, or even later steps to minimize the carnage once it had begun. At least we are doing something now, the powerful countries behind the tribunals can declare. Those who experienced moral conflict about their country's or institution's equivocal response to the bloodshed may find solace in these words.

Local power brokers have their own interest in saving face and explaining their present and past actions to their own constituents and the international community at large. Those presently in government are interested in using the naming of crimes to absolve current leaders of responsibility; those outside government seek to use the naming of crimes to discredit and undermine the present leadership. Depending on one's attitude toward the accused and the current leadership, then, the naming of crimes can either legitimize or delegitimize the new governments or states arising out of conflict. While local leaders care little for international law and institutions, they do have an interest in (re)establishing their own legitimacy and authority.

The naming of crimes carries an entirely different meaning for survivors. Individual survivors are searching for a way to become whole again. Some want to forget what is too painful to remember. For them, the war crimes tribunals are shows to avoid. But most survivors want a public remembrance. They need to hear their stories told aloud and to see others hearing their stories. For them, the naming of crimes may suffice as public acknowledgment of what happened. Without such acknowledgment, survivors feel invisible, erased, forgotten.

The language of the tribunals can provide victims with a way to speak about the unspeakable. "Language and culture encode ways of seeing the world that facilitate common understanding of experience."[5] Without a language to express themselves, many survivors play out their feelings through the "hidden transcripts" of anger, aggression and disguised discourses of dignity, such as gossip, rumor and the creation of autonomous, private spaces for assertion of dignity.[6] The legitimized, distant words of law open a door to remembrance for some, providing words with which to talk about personal suffering. The naming may help survivors redefine themselves "as a collective self engaged in common struggle."[7]

Most survivors, however, do not see themselves reflected in the work of the tribunals. Their individual situations do not find a way into legal cases, either because there are too many crimes to try, or because their experiences, although horrible and morally reprehensible, do not consti-

WAR CRIMES

tute crimes under international law. There is no crime of destruction of souls, deprivation of childhood, erasure of dreams.

There are crimes of murder, torture and inhumane treatment, but there is no crime of being forced to watch helplessly while one's loved one suffers—the injury many survivors swear is most severe. Even when the tribunals do name his or her crime, the survivor may barely recognize it, as the process and language of law transmutes individual experiences into a categorically neat something else. Law does not permit a single witness to tell his or her own coherent narrative; it chops the stories into digestible parts, selects a handful of these parts, and sorts and refines them to create a new narrative—the legal antinarrative. Women who have survived rape and sexual assault, for example, describe the harm suffered in words far different from the sterile language and performance of law, no matter how the crime of rape is configured. So, too, the Convention on Torture and the legal steps necessary to prove abuses under its provisions tell a different story than the one concentration camp victims would choose to reveal. The law at times limits examination of such witnesses, in order to protect them and ensure that their suffering is not put on trial. Yet some witnesses long for the opportunity to finish their story, to name the crimes for themselves. To do so, they must look beyond the legal system.

Blaming Individual Perpetrators

The function of blaming individual perpetrators serves varied interests that may directly conflict. While the international community seeks stability (defined narrowly as the continuation of the present government and the absence of war), local power brokers and survivors may have something very different in mind.

In order to maintain its own credibility, the international community needs to secure peace and maintain stability in the former Yugoslavia and Rwanda. The blaming of individual perpetrators, the international community hopes, will help the people of Rwanda and the former Yugoslavia find some way to go forward and to forget. Without individualized guilt, the injustice of the past may go on forever, as a cycle of vengeance perpetuates itself; the new emerging states will never have the chance to make the transition to democracy, which requires, at the very least, the absence of conflict.[8]

The naming of individuals also serves to pave the way for normalization of international economic and political relations. When individual perpetrators have been named and the accused are not among those in power, members of the international community can feel license to resume business as usual. This interest is particularly acute among leaders and states with a strong economic interest in resuming or beginning relations with successor leaders and/or successor states. For example, Germany has strong and growing economic interests in Croatia, Bosnia and Serbia: Croatia because of trade and investments, and Croatia, Bosnia and Serbia because of a desire to return refugees and undocumented arrivals from the former Yugoslavia. Germany's interest in ensuring the absence of war in the Balkans may be colored by these economic interests.

Like the international power brokers, many local leaders have an interest in securing peace and maintaining stability, to prevent interference in seemingly more important matters such as reconstructing communities, building governments and amassing new power and wealth. Conversely, some local power brokers have an interest in undermining peace, recementing the dividing line between foes and friends, and preparing for the next phase of war. Depending on their ultimate goals, local power brokers may view the blaming of individuals as a component of forgetting and moving on, or of remembering and fighting onward.

The blaming process also enables local leaders to claim and assert their authority over the violators. This step can be stabilizing or destabilizing, according to whether the blamed are inside or outside the present government and the degree to which the blaming conflicts with popular will.[9] When the accused are identified with the old power structure, blaming can underscore the discontinuity between old and new regimes and promote confidence in the new leadership.[10] When the accused are inside the present government or blaming conflicts strongly with popular will, those on the outside can seize the opportunity for destabilization, promoting their own conflicting agendas instead.

Although they may long to feel secure, many survivors have long since ceased to believe in their own governments, and perhaps in any governments. The stability of the newly emerging state is not at the top of their wish list. When the war crimes tribunals make their indictments public, some refugee camps erupt in celebration—not because their leaders have won a victory, but because one of their tormentors is getting what he deserves. For them, the individualization of guilt meets their desire for revenge. The problem, as noted above, is that the tribunals will never be able to spread their nets wide enough to catch every criminal, to quiet every call for vengeance. The desire for revenge thus remains strong, threatening to perpetuate the cycle of conflict.

For survivors belonging to groups that have been accused of crimes, blaming serves another distinct purpose: helping them save face among neighbors and before the international community. It is not me, the individualized indictments allow them to say, it is someone else. In this manner, the tribunals will help the enormous population of bystanders regain its own sense of identity and worth.[11] As with survivors, bystanders can regain subjecthood and identity by telling their stories. Their stories are thus important even if they are not true.[12] However, like survivors, bystanders cannot rely on the tribunals alone for the telling. Since the list of potential defendants is short, bystanders need to rely on other tellings if they are persuasively to argue, "It was not me."

Punishing the Guilty

The function of punishment could potentially serve the parties' divergent interests. Given the circumstances and nature of the tribunal and life on the ground in emerging societies, however, it is unlikely that punishment will entirely serve anyone's interests.

In addition to demonstrating the existence and force of international law, the international community hopes that the tribunals will deter potential perpetrators worldwide (that is, general deterrence). Whether application of international law to conflict has any deterrent effect is open to debate.[13] While formal states may respect international law in order to retain the respect and cooperation of other states and of international bodies, paramilitary troops and rebel regimes rarely care much about popular opinion—particularly not in the heat of battle. Nevertheless, the consistent and fair application of international law in conflict situations, accompanied by credible threats of international investigations, trials and punishments, could provide some deterrent effect. As the tribunals now stand, as ad hoc bodies with no authority to punish crimes anywhere except Rwanda and the former Yugoslavia, their ability to deter crimes in war elsewhere is limited.

Local power brokers are more interested in specific deterrence—that is, preventing perpetrators from repeating their acts. Those in power hope that punishment will displace threats of personal revenge, build confidence among the citizenry and legitimize local efforts to try crimes. At the same time, they do not want punishment to become too complete, lest it interfere with the objective of "national reconstruction" and "national pacification" (and, for some, even result in their own arrest).[14] Thus they are willing to support the trials superficially, as long as international busybodies do not dig too deeply. Responsive to their concerns and wary of the potential of punishment to destabilize emerging governments, the international community has been reluctant to support prosecutions of some of the "biggest fish" responsible for the conflicts. Hence the deterrent effect of the tribunals within the countries themselves is circumscribed.

Survivors have little interest in deterrence. Instead, they see the punishment function of the tribunals as a means to achieve revenge and retribution, to force expiation of guilt. Although many survivors do not advocate group blame or seek revenge against an entire group called the "enemy," many confess a desire for vengeance against the particular individual(s) who harmed family members and other members of their communities.[15] That the punishment they demand may destabilize their homeland is of little concern.

Apart from mere vengeance, which may seem an illegitimate interest, punishment can lend significance to the victims' suffering, aiding the process of reclaiming an entitlement to subjecthood. Punishment itself serves as important public recognition of the crime. Yet the tribunals can try relatively few cases, and can thus result in few instances of punishment. They can never try the many instances in which harm has no name as a crime—the harm of lost time and dreams shattered, the suffering that comes of endless waiting, the humiliation of asking for someone else's help. The limited reach of the tribunals will leave survivors still longing for revenge and meaning.

Delivering Reparations to Survivors

Very little effort has been made to use the war crimes tribunals as a means of delivering reparations to survivors. As criminal courts of limited jurisdiction, the tribunals may not have the authority to issue what are normally seen as civil remedies. Should they have the power and will to do so, reparations would, like punishment, demonstrate the existence and force of international law. Moreover, reparations in the form of economic penalties against responsible individuals and governments—to then be turned over in the form of compensation to survivors—might be at least as effective a deterrent as criminal punishments (perhaps even more effective, as it may be easier to enforce economic measures against commanding officers and governments that supported war criminals).

Nor have local power brokers emphasized the issue of reparations. Yet as long as they are not held responsible for actually paying reparations themselves, emerging leaders would have much to gain from them. Reparations, like punishment, would displace threats of revenge. Monetary reparations could also improve the welfare of survivors, thus taking pressure off local governments to provide for their needs. Reparations for some would benefit the entire community, freeing up resources for use in other aspects of rebuilding. A family receiving reparations would no longer seek state assistance for minimal needs, and might be able to use reparations to rebuild its own home and contribute to general community reconstruction.

Survivors in Rwanda and the former Yugoslavia would have a great interest in reparations. Although nothing can compensate for the loss of loved ones, dreams destroyed and days lost, reparations would dignify survivors with a partial remedy for their suffering. Practically speaking, reparations could mean an improvement in living conditions and general

welfare. Above all, however, reparations would constitute a public acknowledgment of guilt by the violator. A violator's admission of guilt,
more even than actual punishment of the violator, can mark a turning
point in the survivors' search for meaning and closure.

After over fifty years, the Japanese government admitted in 1993 to
enslaving Korean, Chinese and Philippine women as prostitutes during
World War II (the so-called "comfort women"). The remaining survivors
refused Japan's offer of a lump sum in compensation for their suffering,
instead pressing for individual compensation. Individual compensation is
important, the survivors and their advocates argued, because it signals
recognition of guilt for each individual act. To date, survivors in Rwanda
and the former Yugoslavia have not demanded similar compensation, although they may in the future. Should they do so, the war crimes tribunals, courts with narrowly limited criminal jurisdiction, would not be
sufficient to meet their demand.

Reforming Lawlessness

War crimes tribunals have been widely trumpeted as an important
component in reestablishing the rule of law. The international community, local power brokers and survivors have an interest in (re)establish-
ing the principle that something called law exists, above power and force.
The international community is most interested in (re)establishing the
force of international law in a lawless world; local power brokers want to
(re)establish the force of law in their own lawless societies. Survivors, for
their part, acutely skeptical of anything called law, do not much care
what is (re)established where, as long as they do not have to live through
another conflict (unless, some will concede, it is a conflict of their own
choosing—a "just" war).

The adjudication of crimes in the Hague and Arusha based on principles of international law may make small steps toward reforming global
lawlessness. Although their ad hoc nature undercuts their call for universal lawfulness, the tribunals' very existence helps (re)establish the rule
of international law. It sends a message to the world that some international norms exist, beyond brute force.

Still, justice before the tribunals will not necessarily trickle down to
local legal systems. In other words, just because, internationally, the
world seems to be getting its act together on justice, this does not mean
the courts and other institutions in Rwanda and the former Yugoslavia
are willing and/or able to follow suit. As of this writing, few trials have
been held in Rwanda, and the country did not pass legislation to en-
able genocide prosecutions until August 1996. And although local indictments and trials for war crimes have occurred in many of the new

states of the former Yugoslavia,[16] observers doubt the ability of many local courts to hold fair trials.

Survivors continue to pay bribes to local authorities for their daily needs; local syndicates continue to control the markets for many goods; illegal trade in weapons continues to flow across borders; the media continues to be dominated by one-sided propaganda; and free speech belongs to the brave few who risk community (and, in some cases, state-condoned) harassment. While calling for justice against war criminals, many governments act intransigently or, some survivors believe, in conspiracy with the principal war criminals, failing to arrest them and even harboring them within their own borders. In such a world, survivors are discovering that the principle of lawfulness exists somewhere "out there," far from their lives. The war crimes tribunals may be a necessary, but not a sufficient, step in reforming lawlessness.

Recording for History

The recording function of a tribunal is important for the international community and local power brokers; for survivors, it is imperative. The record that will emerge from the trials, however, will possess the form and substance that best serves the interests of the international elite.

If all goes well with the tribunals, the international community hopes to use it to demonstrate the efficiency and force of international institutions. Beyond mere verdicts, the tribunals will showcase what international law has been able to accomplish. (If all goes poorly, however, the record could become international law's Achilles heel.) A positive record could be used to warn potential perpetrators of the existence of international laws, as well as for global education on the limits of evil and the triumph of international humanitarian and human rights principles.

Those in government locally will use the record to prove the legitimacy of their rule and the illegitimacy of their predecessors. Local history will underscore the extent to which the new governments cooperated with the tribunals and advanced justice. (Those outside government may try to use the record for the opposite reason—to prove the illegitimacy of the present regime.) The record could become the backbone of a call for national healing and a warning to potential perpetrators. School textbooks could be rewritten to educate future generations about the evils of the past and prepare them for a better future. Of course, there is no guarantee that local histories will ring of reconciliation—they could just as well warn young people of the enemy "other" and emphasize the need to fortify the collective identity against future attack.

Survivors have the greatest need for a record, but it is the kind of record a war crimes tribunal cannot provide. First, the few survivors who will be called before the tribunals may be too afraid to testify, as they will not be provided with adequate protection once they leave the Hague or Arusha. Survivors of all crimes—and in particular survivors of rape and sexual abuse—have a pressing need for protection of their identity. In some cases, the entire family of the survivor must be assured long-term protection (including relocation and change of identity) if the survivor is to be safe to speak. So far, the tribunals have fallen short of respecting these needs.[17]

Antonio Cassese, former president of the tribunal for former Yugoslavia, has acknowledged that, before they enter the jurisdiction of the tribunals and after they leave the witness box at the Hague, many witnesses require substantial long-term protection, including, in some cases, a change of identity and relocation to a third country. Such programs, in his view, can be provided only by states willing to cooperate and receive these people, but not by a war crimes tribunal acting on its own.[18] Above all, witnesses need a full and public account of what happened—an account in which they see their own memories reflected. They need an account that exposes truths—that is, what survivors believe to be true. These truths have taken on a life of their own. They are so thick with history, power and fear that the actual truth no longer matters. Allowing competing truths to float in the same space, unjudged and unquestioned, can be a revolutionary act. These truths may always exist. But their very telling can narrow the gap between truths, creating a common bridge toward something else—toward an existence beyond these truths. Since legal institutions attempt to discover a single truth, they are incapable of fulfilling the need to hear and acknowledge competing truths.

Survivors need to feel a part of whatever record is created. Only then will they believe that others hear and acknowledge their suffering. Only then can they begin to remember or start to forget. The record may be used to educate future generations, but its greatest utility comes in the telling itself. By pressing the words of survivors into the language of law, no court can fulfill this task.

To fill this void, local organizations, such as IZI: Refugees for Refugees, in Slovenia, and MOST ("Bridge"), in Belgrade, have been providing forums in which survivors can tell their stories. In Belgrade, the antiwar, antimilitarist organization Women in Black held "I remember" writing workshops with women refugees. Sitting at a makeshift table in a former workers' shack, now home to three dozen refugee families, fifty-year-old Saja Atic wrote her first (and last) poem:

> I remember my neighbor, Hodzic Taiba. We used
> to sit for hours in front of the house and talk talk
> talk. . . . Who would ever know all that we talked

about. And we laughed. Still now I wear the blue
scarf that Taiba gave to me. Before she escaped with
her daughter to Munich, she gave this blue scarf as
a gift to me. She had blue eyes like the scarf.
"When I return we shall go together to have
hamburgers at Asim Place. And we shall keep all the stories
so that we have something to laugh about. Take care."
Taiba, my best neighbor. Same as my sister. Even
more. That is why I am silent now and I keep all
the beautiful stories for us. So when she comes back
we shall have something to laugh about.[19]

For the refugee memory project "The Suitcase," Eleonora Birsl, a
twenty-three-year-old refugee from Sarajevo (living in Harpstedt, Germany), wrote ten pages in cramped black ink:

What is left behind me?
Nineteen years of wonderful living,
my mother in tears,
my big white house,
unforgettable friendships.
Sarajevo,
sleepy in the mist,
startled.
My statistics text book opened midway,
the essay on morals half accomplished,
one love story, half begun . . .
Half of me left, half of me stayed.
Now,
two halves of one soul and one body,
unknown to
each other.
My things all over the room,
a date I never went to,
my youth,
stayed behind.[20]

These and hundreds of thousands of other survivors' voices from the
former Yugoslavia and Rwanda will not be heard by the war crimes tribunals. The war crimes tribunals are, after all, war crimes tribunals.

The tribunals may serve several important functions and address many
parties' interests. They will stop short, however, of addressing the con-

cerns of survivors. The tribunals cannot be "fixed" to address what is missing; instead, additional avenues must be found to address the concerns of survivors. Public truth commissions in which witnesses and survivors speak, memory projects that collect and publish without judging the accounts of survivors, popular education campaigns that encourage survivors to test their voices—such efforts are needed to supplement the work of the tribunals. To channel all resources in the direction of the tribunals alone disserves the people of Rwanda and the former Yugoslavia.

Notes

1. Reprinted from Julie Mertus et al., *The Suitcase: Refugees' Voices from Bosnia and Croatia* (Berkeley, CA: University of California Press, 1996).
2. Elaine Scarry, *The Body in Pain: The Making and Unmaking of the World* (New York: Oxford University Press, 1985).
3. Such survivors' testimonies are collected in Mertus et al., *The Suitcase*.
4. Deborah Blatt, "Recognizing Rape as a Method of Torture," *NYU Review of Law and Social Change* 19 (1992): 821.
5. J. Senehi, "Language, Culture and Conflict: Storytelling as a Matter of Life and Death," *Mind and Human Interaction* 7, no. 3 (1996):150–164. See also K. Narayan, *Storytellers, Saints and Scoundrels: Folk Narrative in Hindu Religions and Teachings* (Philadelphia: University of Pennsylvania Press, 1989).
6. J.C. Scott, *Domination and the Arts of Resistance: Hidden Transcripts* (New Haven, CT: Yale University Press, 1990).
7. G. Gugelberger and M. Kearney, "Voices for the Voiceless: Testimonial Literature in Latin America," *Latin American Perspective* 18:3–14 (1991).
8. J. Tobin, "Accountability and the Transition to Democracy," *American University Journal of International Law and Policy* 5, no. 4 (1990): 1033–1063.
9. See Lawrence Weschler, *A Miracle, a Universe: Settling Accounts with Torturers* (New York: Pantheon Books, 1990).
10. Jose Zalaquett, "Confronting Human Rights Violations Committed by Former Governments: Principles Applicable and Political Constraints," in Aspen Institute, *State Crimes: Punishment or Pardon* (Queenstown, MD: The Aspen Institute, 1988).
11. E. Staub, *The Roots of Evil: The Origins of Genocide and Other Group Violence* (New York: Cambridge University Press, 1989).
12. Salman Rushdie, *Haroun and the Sea of Stories* (New York: Viking Penguin, 1990).
13. Diane Orentlicher, "Settling Accounts: The Duty to Prosecute Human Rights Violations of a Prior Regime," *Yale Law Journal* 100 (1991): 2537–2615.
14. Zalaquett, "Confronting Human Rights Violations Committed by Former Governments."
15. Mertus et al., *The Suitcase*.

16. Human Rights Watch/Helsinki, *Civil and Political Rights in Croatia* (October 1995).

17. Elenor Richter-Lyonette, "The Real Evidence to Protect," *Tribunal* no. 5 (September-October 1996): 6.

18. Antonio Cassese, address at Harvard Law School, October 17, 1996.

19. Composed in 1994 and published in Women in Black, *I remember* (Belgrade: 1994) and in Mertus, et al., *The Suitcase*.

20. Composed in 1995 and published in Mertus et al., *The Suitcase*.

When Prosecution Is Not Possible: Alternative Means of Seeking Accountability for War Crimes

Timothy Phillips and Mary Albon

Without determining accountability for politically motivated atrocities, a society that is emerging from a period of violent repression or civil conflict will remain in thrall to the past. Seeking justice through the institutions of the law is the best means of determining responsibility for acts of genocide, war crimes and other politically motivated violations of human rights. Criminal prosecutions of crimes of this magnitude not only punish the individuals who committed them, demonstrating that impunity does not exist, but also help to restore dignity to their victims. They can provide a cathartic experience not only for individual victims, but also for society as a whole. By holding individuals responsible for their misdeeds, criminal trials may also deter the commission of abuses in the future. Moreover, if conducted in strict accordance with legal due process, criminal prosecutions of war crimes can help to strengthen the rule of law and establish the truth about the past through accepted legal means.

But practical realities, particularly during an unstable transition from war to peace, may hinder the pursuit of justice. For example, the perpetrators of human rights abuses or their allies may remain in positions of power, making effective prosecution impossible. In such a situation, principles must be balanced with reality. Nevertheless, determining responsibility for the crimes may still be possible, even if punishing the perpetrators is not.

This chapter explores alternative means of seeking accountability for politically motivated human rights violations and rehabilitating their victims that may help societies which have been brutalized by genocide or other atrocities to come to terms with their experience and move forward. The task is to find ways to condemn criminal acts and the political and social structures that encouraged them without returning these societies to violence. However, this should not be understood as implying that criminal prosecutions should be replaced by another mechanism. Rather, whereas some of the approaches discussed here (particularly truth commissions) may be especially beneficial if a country is not able to conduct criminal trials, they can also be implemented in tandem with criminal prosecutions and thus enhance the catharsis and healing process. Moreover, all of these approaches to dealing with past crimes, including prosecutions, should be part of a broader process of institutional reform that will help prevent future abuses from occurring.

Limitations on Criminal Prosecutions

There are numerous factors that can make criminal prosecutions of war crimes and acts of genocide ineffective or extremely difficult, if not impossible, to carry out.

The scale of the crimes may be overwhelming. In Rwanda, within the short span of three months in the spring of 1994, well over 500,000 people, mainly members of the Tutsi minority, were brutally massacred, and countless thousands more were raped or wounded, by majority Hutus. Upwards of 100,000 individuals have subsequently been imprisoned, accused of participating in the genocide, but no more than a handful are ever likely to come to trial. The Rwandan courts simply do not have the human or financial means to prosecute so many people.

This is not an uncommon scenario in the case of war crimes. Moreover, since intellectuals and professionals are often among the first targets of genocide, the ranks of the judiciary and the legal profession may end up decimated and in disarray. Alternatively, the courts may have been in alliance with the forces of repression, and thus cannot be trusted to serve as impartial arbiters of justice in the prosecution of alleged war criminals.

Under these various limitations, the choice may be made to prosecute selectively, condemning paradigmatic behavior in an effort to demonstrate that impunity does not exist and to deter the commission of similar violations in the future.

Yet even selective prosecution of war crimes may be difficult or even impossible to carry out in accordance with the rule of law and the principles of legal due process. There may be evidentiary problems: the passage of time may make it difficult to locate witnesses, or witnesses may refuse to testify out of fear of retribution. Evidence linking specific individuals to crimes may have disappeared. Access to the scene of a massacre or the site of a mass grave may be blocked, or the site may have been altered. Alleged perpetrators and/or the leaders who incited them to action may have gone into hiding or fled abroad. The higher in the hierarchy of leadership one looks, the more difficult it may become to determine who was actually responsible for criminal actions. In many cases, orders may have been destroyed, or they may have been given orally and not documented. In other cases, minions may have acted in anticipation of what they thought their superiors would want, but without their request or command. For these reasons it may be particularly hard to pin convictions on the top officials who bear both criminal and moral responsibility for crimes that were committed under their leadership.

It also may be difficult to guarantee a fair trial, operating on the presumption of the defendant's innocence, when the public is clamoring for justice—or revenge. Justice is malleable, and criminal prosecutions of war crimes can easily become politicized. Especially after one side has lost power, there is the risk of "victors' justice": prosecutions may be politically motivated, and may devolve into a search for vengeance rather than justice. This can exacerbate existing divisions within a country, and perhaps even lead to a new outbreak of violence.

The situation grows more complicated when the perpetrators of gross violations of human rights or their allies remain in positions of influence. This circumstance alone may make it impossible to prosecute alleged war criminals.

Alternatives to Criminal Prosecutions

Alternative means of dealing with past crimes that aim to move away from confrontation and toward reconciliation include amnesties, screening and disqualification measures, official acknowledgment of past crimes and investigative commissions, often called "truth commissions." Each of these methods has been introduced in countries emerging from repression or violent civil conflict, with varying effects. Each option has its limitations, and may not be appropriate in all instances. In the case of amnesties, critics argue that they are never an appropriate means of dealing with the past, but only serve to push the old tensions beneath the surface, and that it will only be a matter of time before they re-erupt, with potentially devastating consequences. Disqualification measures have been criticized for the ease with which they can be used as political weapons and tools of revenge rather than reconciliation. Official acknowledgment of the past, if not broadly publicized or not carried out in conjunction with institutional changes that will lessen the likelihood of new abuses in the future, will have little or no positive impact. Truth commissions also have their critics, but if a commission is established with great care in such a way that the broad public considers it to be a trustworthy, neutral body and its findings to be well documented, it may offer a given country one of the brightest hopes for coming to terms with a violent past and fostering national reconciliation.

Amnesties: The Decision to Forget

When perpetrators of human rights abuses retain significant military and/or political power at the end of a civil conflict or after a repressive regime has fallen, the new government may be too weak to prosecute those who committed atrocities. Under pressure from the elites of the previous regime (often including the military or secret police), the new government may institute an amnesty for human rights abuses or political crimes on the grounds that it will allow society to start over with a clean slate.

Amnesties have been enacted in many countries victimized by human rights abuses. Uruguay is one case in point. In 1984, after years of military dictatorship, Uruguay negotiated a return to democracy. The Uruguayan people expected that the military would be prosecuted for their crimes, which included illegal imprisonment and torture as well as "disappearances," but the document that codified the political transition did not address the military's responsibility for human rights violations committed under the previous government. As a result, when attempts were made to prosecute, the military pressured the new government to enact an amnesty law, which it did in 1986. Enormous popular indignation erupted over the amnesty, and the families of the victims launched a petition campaign for a plebiscite on the law. In spite of tremendous institutional opposition, the petition campaign was successful. However, by a narrow margin, the people of Uruguay voted to uphold the amnesty law, and as a result, there were no further investigations into human rights abuses and all trials then under way were canceled. The main argument given for upholding the law was that it was necessary for national reconciliation and to preserve the peace.

Although it did not prevent the introduction of an amnesty for human rights violators, Uruguay's referendum campaign brought attention and sympathy to the victims and greater regard for human rights—no one, not even the defenders of the amnesty law, denied that the crimes had been committed. This heightened awareness may pose some sort of obstacle to future authoritarian temptation.

In Spain, by contrast, the idea of an amnesty received broad support from all political parties and groups during the transition from dictatorship to democracy, and, by many accounts, it proved to be a very successful means of achieving national reconciliation. During the bloody Spanish civil war and the more than 40 years of the repressive Franco regime, both sides committed great violence in Spain. To allow the country to move forward and strengthen its fledgling forces of democracy, in 1977 the Spanish parliament passed a general amnesty law for all politically based crimes committed during the civil war and the Franco era. The law pardoned both individuals who had opposed the dictatorship and the civil servants and police who had been in charge of repression under Franco. In addition, all police files from the Franco period were sealed indefinitely.

In the view of the international human rights community, amnesty laws give the perpetrators license to repeat their crimes. Instead of establishing reconciliation, amnesties may deeply divide society and pervert the rule of law. Through "official forgetting," amnesties can make second-class citizens of the victims by eliminating their legal recourse. If there is the appearance of impunity for past crimes, people may not trust in the rule of law, and some may return to vigilante justice. Yet in the case of Spain, the amnesty contributed to national reconciliation. Social consensus on the decision to seal off the past and the strong commitment to democracy of the post-Franco government likely helped to prevent a resurgence of violent political conflict. The worst atrocities had been committed decades earlier, and the passage of time may have blunted the Spaniards' desire to stir up painful memories. Instead, they chose to forge ahead together toward democracy.

Screening and Disqualification Measures

Another alternative to criminal prosecutions is the introduction of laws and administrative measures designed to bar former elites, security agents and their collaborators from holding influential public positions. Often called "lustration," from the Latin word meaning purification, screening and disqualification measures of this sort have been introduced in many of the formerly communist countries of Eastern Europe, several former Soviet republics, as well as in Bosnia via the Dayton peace agreement, which prohibits individuals indicted by the International War Crimes Tribunal from holding or running for public office. Advocates of these policies usually present them as necessary to hasten the transition from war to peace or from repression to democracy. Their expressed aims are to seek justice for the victims by removing their oppressors from positions of influence, and to express the moral disgust of society toward the abuses committed under the old regime.

Yet screening and disqualification measures, which tend to be implemented by administrative rather than judicial means, are vulnerable to accusations of abuse. The legal objections to lustration laws that have been enacted or proposed in the formerly communist countries are legion. These measures have been criticized for running counter to efforts to institute and uphold the rule of law by circumventing legal due process (e.g., not giving the accused access to their state security files or other evidence used against them, or even refusing to inform them of the allegations against them), accepting the principles of collective guilt and guilt by association, and utilizing the often unreliable files of the communist security apparatus as primary evidence.

Moreover, the stated rationales for disqualification measures may not match the actual motivations for these policies. Lustration, at least in principle, should not be retributive, but should instead help to support the transition to peace and democracy. But a search for justice can easily turn into a campaign for revenge: lustration can be used as a means to settle accounts, disguised in legal form. It can also be manipulated in the pursuit of personal advantage; in the political realm in particular, the past can be used as a weapon against rival parties or personalities in the competition for office and influence.

Disqualification measures pose political dangers as well. Many opponents of lustration are concerned that the manipulation of society through fear—in much the same fashion as under communism and other repressive systems—will continue to control and divide society, and they contend that democracy cannot be established by resorting to police-state methods. Particularly during a period of vast political, social and economic upheaval, such as the former Soviet bloc is now experiencing, there is also the risk that by ostracizing a group from society, whether by legal, administrative or even informal means, these people may turn against democracy. This is an even greater threat when human rights violators are the object of disqualification measures. In their case, if the new government is strong enough to enforce lustration measures, it should be strong enough to carry out criminal prosecutions of human rights abusers—and should do so.

Official Acknowledgment

Particularly when there are obstacles to criminal prosecution of war crimes, acts of genocide and other politically motivated atrocities, official acknowledgment of the truth about the past can achieve a sense of justice for the victims, restoring their dignity by recognizing their fates, and can help smooth the way for national reconciliation. Telling the truth about the past responds to the psychological need of people to try to make sense of what their society and they themselves endured. And even without criminal punishment, truth-telling may help deter future violations of human rights and acts of genocide.

In countries where there are no independent media and atrocities have been committed in only certain regions, the broad public may not know about, or may not believe in, their occurrence. This appears to have been the case in Serbia during the Bosnian conflict. In other cases of genocide, such as in Cambodia and Rwanda, the massacres and atrocities were so widespread that no one could not know what was going on. Yet general knowledge of the crimes is not sufficient, in their aftermath, to allow society to put the past behind it and move forward into a peaceful future; what is necessary is some form of official recognition or sanctioning of the truth.

Official acknowledgment of genocide, war crimes and other politically motivated human rights violations can be achieved in a variety of ways. Heads of state may make public announcements about the past, or even apologize, on behalf of the state, to the victims. For example, over the years, a number of postwar German leaders have made such statements about the Holocaust. Or the government may offer monetary or other forms of restitution to the victims or their families as another means of officially acknowledging past wrongs and returning dignity to the victims. Even if the perpetrators are not punished, the government has recognized the wrong done to the victims. Or the government may authorize an independent commission to investigate the abuses of the past, the findings of which will then be officially recognized as the truth. This latter option is discussed in greater detail in the following sections.

Truth Commissions

Particularly when criminal prosecutions of alleged war criminals and perpetrators of genocide are not feasible, officially sanctioned, independent commissions of inquiry that uncover and evaluate the motivations for past atrocities can offer another way to address society's need to know the truth without jeopardizing a fragile peace. These so-called "truth commissions" can have the same kind of cathartic effect that criminal prosecutions offer by presenting and officially acknowledging the truth about the past, making an official moral condemnation of the abuses that occurred, and contributing to the construction (or reconstruction) of civil society and the institutional mechanisms of democracy that protect human rights and can prevent new abuses from being committed in the future. In a growing number of examples from all over the world, the findings of many of these commissions have had a tremendous moral impact that has contributed to national reconciliation.

Truth commissions are usually established at a point of political transition to emphasize the break with the past, to foster national reconciliation and/or to strengthen the political legitimacy of the new government. Of course, as with all approaches to dealing with past abuses, there is a risk that truth commissions will be manipulated politically. Critics also argue that truth commissions aggravate divisions within a country, reopening old wounds and perhaps spurring a return to violence; however, the experience of truth commissions to date has generally not borne out this prediction.[1]

A truth commission can determine what happened to individual victims, analyze the mechanisms and institutions that enabled the abuses to occur, or undertake both tasks, investigating the fate of individuals and of the nation as a whole. In contrast to criminal prosecutions, which focus on specific individuals and their alleged crimes, truth commissions look at the broad pattern of abuses.

In the 1980s and 1990s, truth commissions of various types have operated in over a dozen countries, including Argentina, Chile, El Salvador, Germany, Ethiopia and South Africa. Not all have been deemed successful. While there is no single model that will guarantee that a commission charged with investigating genocide, war crimes or other past abuses will have a positive influence on national reconciliation, there are certain features that lend a greater likelihood of success. How a truth commission is perceived by society—which in turn depends on its mandate, how it is structured and administered, as well as how its findings are publicized—affects its impact. These issues and other critical aspects of truth commissions will be examined in greater detail following brief discussions of the operation and impact of truth commissions in Chile, El Salvador and South Africa.

Chile: The National Commission for Truth and Reconciliation

In Chile, during the authoritarian military dictatorship of General Augusto Pinochet, who controlled the country from 1973 until 1989, 3,000 Chileans were killed or disappeared, and tens of thousands were imprisoned or exiled. Even after the democratic election of President Patricio Aylwin in 1989, General Pinochet retained control of the military and remained a powerful political force. Before President Aylwin's election, General Pinochet had instituted an amnesty for all human rights violations committed between 1973 and 1978, which significantly restricted the possibility of pursuing criminal prosecutions against the perpetrators.

President Aylwin had three moral objectives during the transition from dictatorship to democracy: (1) to publicly establish as soon as possible an official truth about the past that could be commonly accepted; (2) to begin to rebuild institutional mechanisms in order to prevent repetition of the abuses in the future; and (3) to use truth-telling as a starting point for healing society. Soon after assuming office in March 1990, he established an eight-member National Commission for Truth and Reconciliation charged with investigating the fates of those who had been killed or had disappeared at the hands of both the Pinochet regime and the opposition,[2] and how the military dictatorship had maintained its hold over Chilean society.

The membership of the National Commission for Truth and Reconciliation was broadly drawn, even including people with links to the military so that it could not be accused of bias. The commissioners were supported by a staff of sixty and provided with sufficient financial resources to carry out their investigations thoroughly during the commission's nine-month term.

The commission had no power to subpoena witnesses or to pass judgment. It based its work on the findings of previous investigations by independent human rights organizations, the church and others, and on the voluntary testimony of victims and past collaborators with the secret police. The commission did not name the perpetrators of human rights abuses because this would have violated their right to due process, but it did send any evidence of crimes to the courts.

The findings of the National Commission for Truth and Reconciliation were compiled in a two-volume, 1,800-page report. When President Aylwin presented the report to the Chilean public, he also offered a formal apology on behalf of the state to the victims and their families, and called on the military to take responsibility for its role in the violence.

The report presented an analysis of the political and doctrinal content of Chile's military dictatorship. It documented the acts of violence committed by both sides, and the details of the fates of each victim of the crimes covered by the commission's mandate. According to this official truth, torture and disappearances had a systematic, institutional character, and there had been no internal war that justified the excesses of the Pinochet regime.

The report had a tremendous moral impact in Chile. It was widely disseminated within the country, given away for free. Families of the victims and human rights groups publicly acknowledged it as the truth. However, the Right rejected the report's conclusion that there had been no internal war in Chile, and in the weeks immediately following the report's release, several retributive assassinations were carried out. Although these developments significantly muted public discussion of the commission's findings, they did not prevent the Aylwin government from acting on the report's recommendations. The government's most important step was to establish the National Corporation for Reparation and Reconciliation, which was charged with implementing the report's recommendations, which included locating the remains of the disappeared, resolving those cases that the commission had not closed, archiving the commission's files and instituting reparations for the families of victims, including awarding pensions and providing health care, scholarships and other forms of social support.

Chile's National Commission for Truth and Reconciliation helped bring about national reconciliation when punishment of the violators was not possible. The commission's efforts served as a starting point for the moral revitalization of Chilean society and helped rebuild the institutions of democracy and reestablish the rule of law without jeopardizing the transition process.

El Salvador: The Commission on the Truth

The April 1991 United Nations-brokered peace accords that ended El Salvador's twelve-year-long civil war included in their terms the establishment of a truth commission charged with investigating serious acts of violence that had been committed by both the leftist guerrillas of the Farabundo Martí National Liberation Front (FMLN) and the rightist government. Unlike the Chilean commission and all prior truth commissions, the Commission on the Truth for El Salvador was not to be a domestic body directed and staffed by Salvadorans. The civil war had radically polarized Salvadoran society, making the formation of a truly neutral and universally respected truth commission comprised solely of Salvadorans all but impossible. Thus the United Nations, which oversaw the implementation of the peace accords and had peacekeeping forces on the ground in El Salvador throughout the transition, not only funded the truth commission, but also appointed three internationally prominent individuals as commissioners and hired the commission's international staff. Special care was taken to ensure that none of the staff had previously worked on Salvadoran human rights issues so as to avoid putting into question the commission's neutrality.

The UN sponsorship of the Commission on the Truth for El Salvador not only helped to ensure its impartiality,[3] but also demonstrated the strong support of the international community for the commission's work, and, by focusing international attention on El Salvador, increased the pressure on the new government to adhere to the commission's recommendations. Moreover, the lack of any Salvadoran participation in the commission's investigation, combined with the presence of UN troops, gave the commission much greater latitude to confront even the most powerful sectors of society without fear of reprisal. Nevertheless, many Salvadorans believed that, while international participation in the commission was critical, excluding Salvadoran citizens from both its panel and its staff prevented them from having a say in the commission's final report and thus from having a stake in its findings.

The Commission on the Truth for El Salvador was given six months (later extended to eight) in which to conduct its investigations and produce a report of its findings. It was left to the commissioners to determine the parameters of their investigation; they chose to investigate in depth a number of representative cases that would illustrate the kind of violence that had occurred during the civil war.[4] Their aim was to determine as fully as possible what had happened in these cases, who had perpetrated the crimes, and who had been the victims.

Because of the fragility of the peace and the extreme divisions within Salvadoran society, the truth commission conducted its investigations quietly, with only a bare minimum of information about its work made known to the public prior to the release of its report. The rationale was not to keep the commission's existence or its work a secret—on the contrary, the public was well aware of both—but to protect the safety of the witnesses as well as of the accused, and to minimize public pressure on the commissioners and their staff.

When the truth commission's report was released, many were surprised by its unflinching dedication to portraying the full truth, including naming perpetrators of abuses, and by the extent of its other recommendations for reform. While clearly emphasizing that the commission was not a court of law and that its conclusions were not legal judgments but only statements of opinion, the commissioners asserted that, in cases where there was an overwhelming preponderance of evidence implicating specific individuals, it would have been morally wrong to refrain from naming them despite the lack of legal due process. They underscored their conviction that to do so would have granted impunity, which contradicted the commission's mandate, and would have prevented the country from fully confronting its past and from erecting the necessary safeguards to prevent abuses in the future. The commission's report, *From Madness to Hope,* named more than forty individuals, including the minister of defense, the president of the Supreme Court and numerous military officers, as responsible for planning or carrying out political executions and directing mass killings of civilians, or for obstructing investigations into specific actions. The report recommended dismissing these individuals from their positions, prohibiting them from holding any public post for ten years, and barring them for life from serving in either the military or the security forces.

The decision to name names was a controversial one, both within El Salvador and within the international human rights community. Members of the military called the commission's investigations a witch hunt, and claimed that its recommendations were vengeful. International human rights organizations objected to the lack of due process and the inability of the accused to defend themselves.

Although the Salvadoran government was obliged under the peace accords to implement the commission's recommendations, it was slow to purge the individuals named in the report, and several ran for office in the 1994 elections.[5] And within days of the report's release, the Salvadoran legislature passed a general amnesty for abuses committed during the civil war, virtually ensuring that neither the individuals named in the report nor other violators would ever stand trial.

South Africa: The Truth and Reconciliation Commission

South Africa's racist apartheid regime left behind a bitter legacy of vast social and economic inequalities as well as a culture of violence stemming from years of state-sponsored repression and abuses. Perhaps the central challenge facing the government of President Nelson Mandela is finding ways to bring about national reconciliation that will unite South Africans to work together toward a shared future.

In 1995, in its attempt to deal with the human rights abuses committed during the apartheid era, the South African parliament established a Truth and Reconciliation Commission based on the experiences of previous commissions, including those of Chile and El Salvador. According to Dullah Omar, South African minister of justice and one of the commission's chief architects, the Truth and Reconciliation Commission offers South Africa the best means of establishing accountability, the rule of law and respect for human rights, and demonstrates a clear break with the country's repressive past. In his words, the commission's objective is to "promote reconciliation in the spirit of understanding which transcends the divisions of the past."[6]

The Truth and Reconciliation Commission, which began its work in December 1995, provides a mechanism and a process for dealing with gross human rights violations committed during the apartheid period. The commission's presidentially appointed membership comprises seventeen highly esteemed South African men and women who represent a broad spectrum of society; its chairman is Desmond Tutu, former Anglican archbishop of South Africa and winner of the Nobel Peace Prize. The commission is expected to conclude its investigations and issue a report of its findings and recommendations to the public within two and a half years; the final report is due in the fall of 1998.[7] The commission's mandate was twice extended in order to accommodate the volume of testimonies and amnesty applications it received. In addition to the final report, the commission is compiling a database and other archival materials (including videotapes of its hearings) that will be available to the public. Like the report of the Commission on the Truth for El Salvador, the Truth and Reconciliation Commission's final report will name perpetrators of abuses.

The Truth and Reconciliation Commission is not a court of law and does not conduct trials or mete out punishment. Its hearings do not replace criminal trials for alleged human rights abusers, and it forwards any evidence of crimes it discovers on to the courts. The commission has three subcommittees: the Committee on Human Rights Violations investigates gross abuses, identifies victims and recommends ways to prevent further violations and to restore dignity to the victims; the Committee on Amnesty holds hearings for individuals who committed politically motivated, gross violations of human rights who have come forward voluntarily to confess and request clemency; and the Committee on Reparation and Rehabilitation provides victims and their families with an opportunity to tell their stories, and considers steps to take to restore their dignity and provide them with appropriate reparation. The commission seeks to understand both the perspectives of the victims and their families, and the perspectives and motives of the perpetrators. It also seeks insights into the systemic nature of abuses, and thus, in addition to holding hearings on the fates of individuals, the commission also holds hearings that focus on specific incidents that are illustrative of wider patterns of human rights violations. It has also asked political parties, businesses, the media and other organizations to make submissions to help establish the broad political context in which violations occurred.

The Truth and Reconciliation Commission's mandate differs from that of previous truth commissions in one significant way: it has the authority to grant amnesty to individuals who voluntarily admit to and accept responsibility for committing politically motivated crimes. The provision for amnesty applies to individuals on all sides in the conflict; according to the commission's June 1996 interim report,

> While most people would draw a moral distinction between violence used to maintain an unjust system and violence to oppose that system, the law governing the Commission recognizes no such distinction. A person is judged solely on whether that individual has suffered a gross violation of his/her human rights or not. The political affiliation of the perpetrator or the victim/survivor is of no relevance. The Amnesty Committee is by law not required to make any finding about the morality of a perpetrator as a criterion for granting or withholding amnesty.[8]

South Africa chose this approach to amnesty for politically motivated crimes because it takes into account the victims of abuses, their families and their communities, and because it establishes individual accountability for past crimes. Whereas a general amnesty would have sent a message of impunity and may have led to retributive acts of violence, granting clemency on a case-by-case basis addresses the need to restore the dignity of victims and strengthens South Africa's fledgling institutions of democracy as well as its commitment to the rule of law and to upholding the principles of human rights.

The Truth and Reconciliation Commission has not been universally embraced. Among right-wing whites, the commission's investigations are seen as a witch hunt. On the opposite end of the spectrum, some relatives of victims believe that the amnesty provision has deprived them of their right to seek justice through criminal or even civil prosecution of the perpetrators. In 1996, the families of several anti-apartheid activists who had been murdered went to court to attempt to halt the commission's work, but they were unsuccessful.

The commission is making every effort to carry out its mandate as even-handedly and transparently as possible. The cases it hears involve victims and perpetrators from all sides, and its investigative unit evaluates and substantiates the details of every case, as well as every request for amnesty. Despite accusations that the commission is biased toward the African National Congress (ANC), ANC leaders who testified before the commission were not allowed to claim the defense that in their case the ends justified the means because their struggle was just, and a controversial blanket amnesty granted to 37 leading members of the ANC was retracted.

Over 8,000 applications for amnesty have been filed with the Truth and Reconciliation Commission. The applicants include more than 300 members of the African National Congress, including many members of President Mandela's cabinet and Deputy President Thabo Mbeki, Mandela's likely successor. (However, many rank-and-file ANC members who were involved in violent actions have not applied for amnesty, and virtually no one from the Inkatha Freedom Party has applied.) Although only two former high-level officials of the National Party and only a few former military officers have applied for amnesty, a number of former police officers have come forward to confess to some of the most notorious human rights crimes of the apartheid era, including the brutal political murders of prominent anti-apartheid activists like Steve Biko. Moreover, the requirement that applicants for amnesty must make full disclosure, including naming those who gave them their orders, has begun to directly implicate members of the top leadership of the old regime.

As a result, the amnesty procedure, in South Africa's approach to it, is bringing to light details of the truth about the past that matter most to the victims and their families: whether a missing person was killed, who the killer is, where the body is buried. Without the amnesty procedure, the details of many politically motivated crimes of the apartheid era would likely never be known. This public acknowledgment of the truth grants dignity to the victims and their families, validating their memory and their loss. Their stories have become a part of the official record, imbued with a larger historical meaning.

But the amnesty procedure also prevents people from remaining ignorant of the abuses that were committed under apartheid. No one in South Africa can avoid hearing about the findings of the Truth and Reconciliation Commission: commission hearings are open to the public, and they are covered extensively in the media, including on the nightly TV news and in a weekly program that has become the third most watched television program in the country.[9] The confessions of perpetrators of some of the most brutal crimes committed during the apartheid era, particularly those of former police officers and other agents of the apartheid state, leave no room for denial. Moreover, these confessions mark one of the first steps toward establishing accountability for the abuses of the past, and fostering respect for human rights and the rule of law in the new South Africa.

In October 1997, the Truth and Reconciliation Commission announced a series of proposed reparation and rehabilitation policies for victims from the apartheid era that it would recommend to the government in its final report.[10] These measures, the commission emphasized, are needed to counterbalance the amnesty process, for without substantial reparations, the true beneficiaries of the Truth and Reconciliation Commission might appear to be those who committed atrocities rather than their victims. The commission recommended that the South African government spend approximately $650 million over six years to provide annual grants to victims or their surviving families, as well as to fund community rehabilitation programs devoted to health care, mental health care, education and housing. The aim of these measures is to empower both individuals and communities to take control of their lives. An estimated 22,000 individuals, including some whites who were victims of black guerrilla attacks, will qualify for the payments; the total amount represents about 0.25 of the national budget.[11] The commission also recommended a series of legal, administrative and institutional measures that would help to prevent future abuses, as well as a series of symbolic efforts, such as establishing a national day of remembrance and reconciliation, erecting memorials and renaming streets and community facilities in memory of specific individuals or events. Individuals should also be able to receive assistance in obtaining death certificates for family members who were victims of apartheid, clearing their names from criminal records, having the bodies of relatives exhumed and reburied or receiving a tombstone for them.

The Truth and Reconciliation Commission appears to be helping South Africa to put the past behind it and to unite its citizens to work together toward a common future. According to Justice Minister Omar, through the work of the Truth and Reconciliation Commission, "[t]he new democratic state will be able to say to victims and victim communities that it is sorry for what happened in the past, that what happened in the past should never be allowed to happen again, and that together we need to build a new order based on respect for human life and human dignity. On the basis thereof South Africa and the victims will be able to forgive but not to forget."[12]

Coming to Terms with History
According to José Zalaquett, one of the commissioners of Chile's Na-

tional Commission for Truth and Reconciliation, the overarching aim during the transition from civil war to peace, or from a criminal regime to democracy, should be to seek "all the truth, and as much justice as possible."[13] If past crimes are not addressed, they will continue to fester beneath society's surface, waiting for an opportunity to erupt. Of greatest importance is conveying the message to society that there should be no impunity for perpetrators of genocide, war crimes or other gross violations of human rights. This can be achieved by legal means such as criminal prosecutions, or by other methods, several of which have been discussed here. The challenge is to find a way that allows the victims— and society as a whole—to heal the wounds of the past and create conditions to prevent these crimes from being repeated.

While criminal prosecutions offer the best way to deal with past crimes, seeking justice through the courts is not always possible. If justice cannot be achieved, the next best alternative is to seek the truth about the past and make it widely known. Neither individuals nor nations can free themselves of the past unless they first understand it and come to terms with it. Without national truth-telling and a shared understanding of the past, memory becomes the guide to the past, and different groups may interpret the past in different ways. Victims of abuses may feel alienated and defeated, or they may harbor a desire for revenge. Perpetrators may consider themselves free to further terrorize society since they have not been made accountable for their past actions. Such different memories and interpretations can feed future conflicts.

Yet knowledge about the past is not sufficient in and of itself to put an end to such poisonous influences; *official acknowledgment* of past abuses is also necessary to help restore dignity to the victims and to help heal society's wounds. Acknowledgment is more than merely remembering: it is a way of remembering that conveys respect for the victims, and condemns those who wronged them. Official truth-telling helps make a clear break with the past, and shows that the new government is trying to earn the respect of its citizens and to strengthen its democratic institutions and commitment to protecting human rights. Truth-telling restores dignity not only to the individual, but also to the nation. However, the truth should not be used as a weapon, for policies whose true aim is revenge will only continue to divide society and prevent old wounds from healing.

As discussed in this chapter, truth commissions, if carefully crafted, can serve as an effective means of officially acknowledging the cruelties of the past in a way that releases society from their consequences rather than binding it to them. With a clear mandate sanctioned by the state and accepted by the public, adequate resources and sufficient time for investigation and evaluation, an independent commission of inquiry can provide a country emerging from civil strife or repression with a means of coming to terms with its past. While there is no single model for an effective truth commission, since each country's history, culture and circumstances are different, it is possible to learn from and build on the prior experiences of others while taking into consideration specific political realities. Based on the recent experiences of commissions of inquiry into past abuses in some dozen countries, including the three discussed here, a number of recommendations can be made:

There must be consensus in society that a truth commission is needed. Without adequate public support, the commission will have difficulty conducting its investigations, and its findings will be discounted or ignored.

The commission must be established as an independent, impartial body. Its mandate can come from the president or national legislature, or from an international body like the United Nations.[14] This kind of official imprimatur also reinforces the state's respect for the victims.

The commission should have a very clear mandate, stating its broad aims, what it will investigate, how it will conduct its inquiries, and how its findings will be reported and publicized. The commission's existence and mandate should be made widely known at the outset, which will encourage cooperation with its investigations.

In order to maintain its independence and to endow its work and its findings with credibility, the commission's membership must be selected with great care. Commissioners should be nationally respected figures who as a group represent a political balance and will be accepted as an impartial moral authority.

The commission should be given a specific period of time in which its mandate is in effect. Open-ended tenure can undermine the urgency of the commission's work, and the public may lose faith that it will ever report on its findings. However, the commission's term of operation should not be so short that it has insufficient time to organize its work, collect information and conduct investigations, or issue a final report. Based on past experiences, truth commissions can operate effectively within a prescribed period of six months to two years.

The commission should be allocated sufficient human and financial resources to be effective.

Although it is not a court of law, the commission should have the power to subpoena witnesses and guarantee their rights and safety. It should also protect the rights of alleged violators by adhering to legal due process.

The commission's investigations should be conducted professionally and systematically, and with a maximum degree of transparency. At a minimum, its findings should be made public in a published final report that is widely publicized and disseminated. During the course of the commission's investigations, public hearings, which may also be broadcast on radio or television, are often an appropriate and effective means of informing the public; however, when society is highly polarized and could easily slip back into violence, hearings should not be open to the public, but a final report must still be issued and broadly distributed.

The commission should not only document the past, but also submit evidence of crimes to the courts for criminal prosecutions. The commission's existence, even when practical realities preclude criminal trials of human rights violators, should not exclude the possibility of eventual prosecution.

The commission should consider making recommendations about how best to protect human rights in the future, as well as suggestions for providing compensation and rehabilitation to the victims of past crimes.

A caveat is necessary, however: truth commissions are not a magic salve that can be applied to any deeply divided society to heal the brutal, festering wounds of its past. For example, it is unlikely that a truth commission could contribute to reconciliation among Bosnia's three ethnic communities; indeed, it might jeopardize the fragile peace brought about by the Dayton Accord. Because the level of distrust among Bosnian Serbs, Croats and Muslims remains high, no commission, including one established by an international body like the Organization for Security and Cooperation in Europe or the United Nations, would be perceived as neutral at this stage in the peace process.[15] Particularly when there is no clear winner, the cessation of hostilities alone is not likely to produce the kind of social consensus that is needed to give a truth commission popular legitimacy. Nevertheless, in order to ensure a lasting peace, at some point the roots of the violence, its extent and impact, its victims and perpetrators must be officially acknowledged. A case can be made that the suppression of the full history of the atrocities committed in Yugoslavia during World War II, rather than so-called "ancient ethnic hatreds," was at the root of the bloodshed in the 1990s; nationalist provocateurs were able to play upon the living memories of World War II to fan the flames of hatred and violence. Similarly, without an official acknowledgment of the truth about the atrocities that have been committed in Bosnia in this decade, peace is not likely to endure. However, until Bosnia has a democratic government that is broadly accepted as legitimate by all three of its communities, the findings of an officially sponsored truth commission would not be perceived as credible.

If there is a conclusion to be drawn, it is that neither individuals nor societies can be free of the past without first coming to terms with it. Toward this end, official truth-telling can help to reestablish a common reality that can serve as a basis for national reconciliation, renewed social cohesiveness and the moral rejuvenation of society. This renovation process includes changing the guiding principles of certain political and social institutions as well as changing people's mindsets, and it encourages the development of popular trust in the public institutions of democracy. Rebuilding—or in some cases, building for the first time—a healthy civil society in which individuals are guaranteed the freedom of independent association and the free exchange of ideas can also support this process. An independent civil society fosters social solidarity and the defense of society by its members, and encourages further exploration of the truth about the past—all of which may help to guard against a repetition of abuses in the future. Journalists, historians, artists and writers, as well as religious groups and nongovernmental organizations, have the potential to play central, positive roles in the process of exploring old wounds, honoring grief and coming to terms with past wrongs.

While truth commissions and other forms of official acknowledgment may have a greater impact if a country is not able to conduct criminal trials, by no means should they replace criminal prosecutions. National reconciliation cannot be achieved at the expense of morality or human rights standards: perpetrators of genocide, war crimes and other gross violations of human rights must be made accountable for their actions, and to the extent possible, they must be punished within the framework of the law. But truth commissions can conduct their work in parallel to criminal prosecutions. Whereas prosecutions focus on individual accountability for past abuses, truth commissions center their efforts around the victims, giving voice to their suffering, and look for broad patterns within society and an overall truth about the past.

Moreover, both criminal prosecutions and truth commissions should be part of a broader process of institutional reform that will help prevent future abuses from occurring. After a country has emerged from a period of civil war or violent repression, it is critical for the new government to establish and adhere to standards of justice, accountability and the rule of law when dealing with past crimes, whether in the courts or in commissions. If these steps are not taken with respect to the past, there is no guarantee that these protections will be enforced in the future.

Notes

1. For an excellent examination of truth commissions and their impact, see Priscilla Hayner, "Fifteen Truth Commissions—1974 to 1994: A Comparative Study," *Human Rights Quarterly* 16 (1994): 598–655.
2. Of the 3,400 cases brought to the commission, 2,920 were deemed to fall within its mandate. Of these cases, the state security forces were found responsible for 2,025, and the armed opposition was determined responsible for ninety. Of the remaining cases, 164 had fallen victim to shootouts and

other violent political confrontations, and 641 were unresolved. It is also important to note that international human rights organizations criticized the commission's mandate for not including in its investigations victims of torture and other abuses who did not die from their mistreatment. See Hayner, "Fifteen Truth Commissions—1974 to 1994," p. 621.

3. This rationale was broadly accepted within El Salvador until the release of its report, when certain sectors of Salvadoran society criticized the commission on the grounds that it represented foreign meddling in El Salvador's domestic affairs. Other criticisms of international sponsorship and staffing of truth commissions include the staff's lack of knowledge about the country's history and culture, which can limit the effectiveness of their efforts; and that international sponsorship does not strengthen indigenous democratic institutions or civil society. For a more detailed discussion of the issue, as well as the pros and cons of international sponsorship, see Hayner, pp. 642–644.

4. Oddly, the commission did not include the activities of the notorious death squads, which had killed thousands of Salvadorans during the war, among the targets of its investigations. The commission was criticized by many Salvadorans and by the international human rights community for this grave omission. See Hayner, pp. 628–629.

5. See Hayner, p. 649, note 117.

6. Abdulah M. Omar, South African minister of justice, remarks at an international conference in Belfast on "Reconciliation and Community: The Future of Peace in Northern Ireland" sponsored by the Project on Justice in Times of Transition, INCORE and the University of Ulster, June 8, 1995.

7. Editor's note: The Truth and Reconciliation Commission submitted its final report in October 1998. It is available on the Commission's home page (see note 8).

8. *Truth and Reconciliation Commission Interim Report*, June 1996. Available on the Truth and Reconciliation Commission home page: http://www.truth.org.za.

9. Ibid.

10. See "Introductory Notes to the Presentation of the Truth and Reconciliation Commission's Proposed Reparation and Rehabilitation Policies" by Hlengiwe Mkhize, chairperson of the Reparation and Rehabilitation Committee, issued on October 23, 1997, to the Truth and Reconciliation Commission's electronic mailing list (accessible on the commission's website: http://www.truth.org.za).

11. See Suzanne Daley, "South Africa Panel Recommends Aid for Apartheid-Era Victims," *The New York Times*, October 24, 1997.

12. Abdulah M. Omar, South African minister of justice, remarks at an international conference in Belfast on "Reconciliation and Community: The Future of Peace in Northern Ireland" sponsored by the Project on Justice in Times of Transition, INCORE and the University of Ulster, June 8, 1995.

13. José Zalaquett, remarks at an international conference on "Democracy and Decommunization: Disqualification Measures in Eastern and Central Europe and the Former Soviet Union" sponsored by the Project on Justice in Times of Transition of the Foundation for a Civil Society with the cooperation of the European Commission for Democracy through Law of the Council of Europe, Venice, Italy, November 14–15, 1993.

14. In some countries, nongovernmental organizations or churches have sponsored similar commissions of inquiry into past abuses, but because they have lacked the state's formal support, their findings are not considered "official" history. For an in-depth exploration of one of the most extensive efforts of this sort, the documentation of abuses in Brazil sponsored by the Catholic Archbishop of São Paulo and the World Council of Churches, see Lawrence Weschler, A Miracle, a Universe: Settling Accounts with Torturers (New York: Penguin Books, 1990).

15. Nevertheless, a proposal to establish a Commission for the Development of Trust in Bosnia has been put forward and has received support from political leaders in the three ethnic communities. The proposal was presented and debated at a November 1996 conference in London which was attended by Bosnian Serb, Croat and Muslim community and political leaders. It was supported by the president of the Republika Srpska Parliament and the president of the House of Representatives of the Muslim-Croat Federation Parliament, among others. The proposal called for a commission that would include representatives of all three communities, and would investigate the unresolved legacy of human rights violations, genocide and missing persons, as well as the root causes of the war. (See conference report, "Workshop on Reconciliation for Bosnia," cosponsored by the Project on Justice in Times of Transition and the British Association for Central and Eastern Europe, November 13–16, 1996, London.) The proposal was also endorsed by political and community leaders from the three ethnic groups at an August 1997 follow-on workshop in Bosnia sponsored by the Project on Justice in Times of Transition.

Suing for Genocide in the United States: The Case of Jane Doe v. Radovan Karadzic

Beth Stephens and Jennifer Green

As the atrocities in Bosnia-Herzegovina mounted in 1992 and early 1993, many survivors of rapes and other gross human rights abuses despaired of an international response that would hold accountable those responsible for their ordeals. The international community was unable to halt the ongoing violations, much less devise a means to provide redress to the injured, punish the perpetrators and deter future atrocities. Upon learning that Bosnian Serb leader Radovan Karadzic planned to come to the United States, a group of survivors and activists turned to a legal process that had achieved success in the United States since 1980: civil litigation in U.S. courts for violations of international law. In February 1993, they filed a class action lawsuit against Karadzic,[1] serving him while he was in New York.[2] Their right to file such a lawsuit was upheld by the U.S. Court of Appeals in October 1995.

The *Karadzic* litigation is based upon a line of U.S. cases upholding the right of victims of gross violations of international law to sue in U.S. courts whenever the perpetrator can be found within the United States. The first such case, *Filártiga v. Peña-Irala*,[3] was filed by the family of a young man tortured to death by a police officer in Paraguay. The Filártiga family filed a civil lawsuit against the torturer—who had settled in New York to escape legal action in Paraguay—on the basis of a little-known 200-year-old U.S. statute, the Alien Tort Claims Act, which authorizes suits in U.S. federal courts for violations of international law.[4] In a landmark decision, the U.S. appellate court held that the law applied to the Filártigas' claim, using language that referred directly to the need to deter and punish international human rights violations:

> In the twentieth century the international community has come to recognize the common danger posed by the flagrant disregard of basic human rights and particularly the right to be free of torture.... Spurred first by the Great War, and then the Second, civilized nations have banded together to prescribe acceptable norms of international behavior.... Among the rights universally proclaimed by all nations ... is the right to be free of physical torture. Indeed, for purposes of civil liability, the torturer has become—like the pirate and slave trader before him—*hostis humani generis*, an enemy of all mankind. Our holding today ... is a small but impor-

tant step in the fulfillment of the ageless dream to free all people from brutal violence.[5]

Since the *Filártiga* decision, about two dozen cases have been filed in the United States, alleging human rights abuses in countries such as Argentina, the Philippines, Guatemala, Ethiopia, Haiti, Rwanda and East Timor.

The lawsuit against Karadzic was filed by two "Jane Does"—women who wish to preserve their anonymity—on behalf of women and men killed, raped and otherwise tortured by his forces. The individual plaintiffs were two of the thousands of women who have been abused by Bosnian Serb forces. They filed the class action as representatives of the entire class of victims of the Bosnian Serbs' gross human rights abuses.[6]

The multimillion-dollar civil lawsuit charges Karadzic with legal responsibility for the massive killings, rapes, forced pregnancies and other brutalities inflicted by his forces. As the so-called "president" and head of the armed forces of the Bosnian Serbs, Karadzic was legally responsible for the actions of his forces under international law, which holds commanders responsible for crimes committed by their troops if they knew or should have known of the violations and failed to prevent or punish them.

The case alleges genocide, crimes against humanity, violations of the laws of war and other human rights violations, based on the two U.S. statutes that authorize civil suits in U.S. federal court for human rights abuses committed in other countries.[7] The lawsuit seeks money damages, not imprisonment, because U.S. law does not permit private citizens to file criminal charges or put the defendant in jail.

The *Karadzic* lawsuits were held up for nearly three years because of a motion to dismiss filed by Karadzic and an erroneous decision by the trial judge, who granted the motion and dismissed the cases. The judge made two key mistakes. First, he held that international law, as incorporated into the Alien Tort Claims Act, applies only to "official" conduct—that is, conduct performed under the authorization of a government. Second, he held that only governments that have received diplomatic recognition from other countries are bound by international law. He concluded that Karadzic and his forces were not bound by international law because they did not act on behalf of a government that had been recognized diplomatically by other governments.

In October 1995, an appeals court reversed the trial court's dismissal and reinstated the lawsuit. The appellate court ruled correctly that, as the head of a de facto regime charged with genocide and war crimes as well as other international human rights violations, Karadzic and his forces are bound by international law. The court made several important rulings about international law:

- ▸ The prohibition against genocide applies to private persons, as well as to governments and people acting on their behalf, and includes sexual violence.
- ▸ The prohibitions against war crimes apply to nongovernmental actors such as armed insurgents.
- ▸ International human rights law binds people acting on behalf of de facto governments as well as those acting on behalf of legally recognized governments.

In other words, Karadzic and his forces are not immune from liability under international law while they employ brutal human rights violations as a weapon in their battle to seize power.

These rulings are a tremendously important recognition of the fact that international law, in some circumstances, does govern "private" behavior. In particular, the Genocide Convention contains specific language binding private parties, as well as official actors, to obey its prohibitions. Similarly, the most basic rules of humanitarian law govern the conduct of all sides to internal conflicts, as well as international warfare. The decision thus closes what threatened to be a devastating loophole in international law: the trial court's narrow ruling would have enabled insurgent movements to commit human rights violations with impunity until the international community recognized them as governments, at which point they could claim immunity from civil lawsuits under the doctrine of sovereign immunity.

The Second Circuit *Karadzic* decision recognizes the importance of holding insurgencies and de facto governments responsible for the abuses committed by their forces. The court noted that from the perspective of victims of human rights abuses, it is the abuse of power by a governing entity that transforms what would otherwise be a private crime into an international law violation, not the diplomatic niceties of formal recognition:

> [It] is likely that the state action concept, where applicable for some violations like "official" torture, requires merely the semblance of official authority. The inquiry, after all, is whether a person purporting to wield official power has exceeded internationally recognized standards of civilized conduct, not whether statehood in all its formal aspects exists.[8]

The *Karadzic* decision, an important statement about international law by an influential U.S. court, will contribute to greater accountability for human rights abuses committed by unrecognized regimes and insurgencies.

In addition, the appellate court noted that the plaintiffs are entitled to prove that Karadzic acted with the assistance of the government of Yugoslavia, a recognized government. Such actions would meet even the trial court's overly narrow view of international law violations. The case could thus play an important role in establishing the links between the Bosnian Serbs and Belgrade—links that much of the international diplomatic community long seemed eager to bury.

Finally, the court rejected Karadzic's challenge to the U.S. court's right to assert jurisdiction over him while he was in New York attending sessions of the United Nations. Under the terms of the 1947 Headquarters Agreement between the United States and the United Nations, visitors and "invitees" to the United Nations clearly are not immune from suit while in the United States.[9]

Karadzic unsuccessfully asked the U.S. Supreme Court to reconsider the Second Circuit's ruling. The Supreme Court declined to do so, leaving the appellate decision intact. The effect of the decision was to reinstate the lawsuit before the trial court. After a year of pretrial proceedings, Karadzic informed the court that he did not intend to continue his defense in the trial court proceedings.[10] This probably means that he will default, permitting the judge to enter a default judgment against him. Such a judgment will be fully enforceable against Karadzic: since the U.S. court has jurisdiction over him,[11] U.S. law requires Karadzic to either defend the action or suffer the consequences of a judgment against him.

In July 1997, plaintiffs asked the court to authorize the case to proceed as a class action, with a group of named plaintiffs representing the thousands of victims of Karadzic's forces.[12] A class action would allow all victims and survivors an opportunity to present their claims to the court.

As the case proceeds either to a default judgment or a trial, the judicial process will provide an opportunity to present in public the case against Karadzic, through the submission of written affidavits from experts and survivors (some of whom may be able to submit their statements anonymously) and possibly through public testimony. The goal would be to make a public record of the atrocities, drawing attention to the proceeding both in the United States and internationally.

The *Karadzic* cases were filed in the context of an international movement to force recognition of women's rights as human rights, and to include protections against violence against women within the international human rights framework. Women have suffered rapes and other abuses by soldiers on all sides of all wars, including this one—as well as during peacetime. For too long, the international community has failed to punish or even condemn the violent abuse of women. Forceful action in this case, where one side to the conflict has employed tactics so brutal and systematic as to shock most of the world, may help draw attention to the less-publicized brutality suffered by women in other wars and in their daily lives. One result of the international effort to expose, condemn and punish violence against women in Bosnia-Herzegovina and elsewhere has been the growing acknowledgment that rape is included within existing prohibitions against torture, war crimes, crimes against humanity and genocide.[13]

While not a substitute for collective international criminal mechanisms such as war crimes tribunals or a permanent international criminal court, civil litigation in the domestic courts of the United States or elsewhere provides the survivors of gross human rights abuses an opportunity to take action without waiting for glacially slow diplomatic processes to reach a consensus on legal action. The litigation is controlled by the plaintiffs and their attorneys, not by governments or state officials. The survivors need not wait for the International Criminal Tribunal for the former Yugoslavia to act, and need not depend upon the political or diplomatic will of governments or other negotiators. The processes in fact are complementary, and developments in each contribute to the other.

In filing this civil lawsuit against one of the men responsible for the most egregious human rights violations in Bosnia-Herzegovina, the survivors were asserting their right to pursue justice in whatever forum is open to them. They asked the court to find the defendant responsible for these crimes and award damages to the victims. Such a judgment would aid their emotional and physical recovery and also help deter future violations. The evidence presented in this case and the likely judgment against Karadzic may exert further pressure on the international community to arrest, try and punish Karadzic for his crimes.

A lawsuit such as this sends a message to war criminals and human rights violators everywhere: even if they have impunity within their own country or obtain immunity from other politicians, they are not free to travel the world without running the risk that those injured by their abuses will seek to hold them accountable. Further, this lawsuit may result in a money judgment that might result in compensation to the victims of war crimes.

Civil litigation in domestic courts can play an important role in the struggle to protect human rights through its impact on the individual plaintiffs and on the human rights movements in their home countries, in the United States and internationally. The lawsuits force gross human rights abusers to answer for their crimes—abusers who had escaped responsibility for their actions because of the weakness of other enforcement mechanisms. Multimillion-dollar judgments have been awarded to victims of gross human rights violations. Although collection is difficult in most cases, it is not impossible. For example, a judgment may become enforceable in a defendant's home country due to a changing political climate.

More than money, however, the plaintiffs in these cases take tremendous personal satisfaction from filing a lawsuit, forcing the defendant to answer in court or to abandon the United States, and creating an official record of the human rights abuses inflicted on them or their families. Judgments may also result in other kinds of restrictions on the defendants: Hector Gramajo, the former minister of defense of Guatemala, lost his U.S. visa after a group of indigenous Guatemalans, joined by U.S. nun Dianna Ortiz, won a $47 million judgment against him for gross human rights violations.

These cases also contribute to the human rights movement in the United States and worldwide, enabling activists to pressure governments to take stronger positions on human rights issues. In the United States, the litigation helps to push human rights issues to the front burner at times when our own government may choose to ignore such abuses. Through this litigation, survivors, activists and human rights lawyers are able to act as private prosecutors, pursuing wrongdoers without awaiting governmental action. This is particularly appropriate when governments around the world are complicit in the human rights abuses, providing active or tacit support or protection to the offending parties.

Human rights lawsuits also help develop and strengthen new international human rights norms, as those norms evolve over time. As new norms emerge and gain acceptance, they can be the basis for further civil litigation. The ability to strengthen and then incorporate emerging norms is of particular importance in areas that have been slow to attain international recognition, such as violence against women, long viewed as a private problem rather than a human rights violation. Thus, the development of the civil remedy as a global option could provide women an important forum for challenging human rights violations.

Notes

1. *Doe v. Karadzic*, 866 F. Supp. 734 (S.D.N.Y. 1994), rev'd sub nom. *Kadic v. Karadzic*, 70 F.3d 232 (2d Cir. 1995), cert. denied 116 S.Ct. 2524 (1996).
2. The lawsuit was filed by the Center for Constitutional Rights in conjunction with the International Women's Human Rights Clinic at the City University of New York Law School and the International League for Human Rights. The Lowenstein International Human Rights Clinic at Yale Law

School and a private New York law firm, Howard, Darby and Levin, have since joined the legal team.

3. *Filártiga v. Peña-Irala*, 630 F.2d 876 (2d Cir. 1980).

4. Alien Tort Claims Act, 28 U.S.C. § 1350 (1988).

5. *Filártiga*, 630 F.2d at 890.

6. A similar lawsuit was filed in March 1993 by an individual Bosnian woman and two organizations of survivors of human rights abuses. *Kadic v. Karadzic*, 866 F. Supp. 734 (S.D.N.Y. 1994), rev'd, 70 F.3d 232 (2d Cir. 1995), cert. denied 116 S.Ct. 2524 (1996). The *Doe* and *Kadic* cases have been handled jointly by the trial and appellate courts.

7. The case is brought under both the Alien Tort Claims Act, 28 U.S.C. § 1350, and the Torture Victim Protection Act (TVPA), 28 U.S.C. § 1350 (note), which was passed by Congress in 1992. The TVPA provides causes of action for torture or summary execution. For detailed information about litigation under these statutes and a full description of prior cases, see Beth Stephen and Michael Ratner, *International Human Rights Litigation in U.S. Courts* (Irvington-on-Hudson: Transnational Publications, 1996); see also *An Activist's Guide: Bringing International Human Rights Claims in U.S. Courts* (New York: Center for Constitutional Rights, 1996).

8. *Karadzic*, 70 F.3d at 245.

9. The Headquarters Agreement does guarantee immunity to a wide range of representatives of governments and nongovernmental organizations, and bars service of process within the UN headquarters district without the consent of the UN secretary general.

10. Karadzic announced this decision after a magistrate ordered that he appear in New York for his deposition. The magistrate found that the fact that Karadzic might be arrested if he came to New York (because of the indictment pending before the International Criminal Tribunal in the Hague) does not excuse him from his obligation to appear in the civil case, because Karadzic's status as a fugitive from justice should not afford him an advantage in this litigation. "Any other result would place this Court in the inappropriate role of assisting defendant in his efforts to evade apprehension on these charges." *Doe v. Karadzic*, No. 93-878, 1997 WL 45515 (S.D.N.Y. Feb. 4, 1997).

11. In an earlier ruling, the trial court found that Karadzic had been properly served in the Doe case, an issue left open by the Second Circuit decision.

12. Class certification was granted in December 1997.

13. This argument was developed in detail in an *amicus curiae* brief filed on January 17, 1995, in the Second Circuit on behalf of women's groups from around the world.

PART III

NUREMBERG AND BEYOND

Introduction

The most recent step in the progression leading from Nuremberg through the international tribunals for Rwanda and former Yugoslavia is the attempt to institute a more permanent legal institution to deal with violations of international humanitarian law—a permanent international criminal court. The current ad hoc tribunals have shown that it is possible for lawyers and judges from many different countries and legal systems to work together toward the common goal of prosecuting international criminals. What remains is for UN members to agree to the principles and mechanisms of a permanent court and to accept its jurisdiction, even over their own nationals.

The discussions leading up to the the court's establishment have made it clear that the process will not be easy; agreeing to a court in principle is very different from accepting its authority in fact. Who will have the power to bring defendants to court and on what charges; how such decisions will be made; whether countries will be able to block suits against their own nationals—all these are crucial issues if the court is to have more than merely symbolic significance. Yet however they are decided, the very fact that such a permanent court seems likely to become a reality in the near future is a startling advance in international cooperation, a direct legacy of Nuremberg that, once established, can be further developed and built upon.

The chapters in this section summarize and synthesize the Nuremberg legacy, following its evolution up to this point and ultimately pointing the way toward a future that is hopeful, if not yet clearly defined. Journalist Tina Rosenberg provides an overview of the evolution of international criminal adjudication from a political and historical perspective, concluding with a discussion of the current push toward an international court, the controversies it involves and particularly the not always constructive role played by the United States. M. Cherif Bassiouni, one of those most responsible for both the ad hoc tribunals and the proposed permanent international court, provides a similar overview from a more legal perspective, analyzing Nuremberg's overall legal as well as ethical legacy and enumerating the developments it catalyzed. Finally, Donna Axel, formerly of the Women's Caucus for Gender Justice in the International Criminal Court, describes the process leading up to the 1998 conference in Rome that produced a statute for a permanent international court. The Epilogue following the section describes the outcome of the Rome Conference in greater detail.

Tipping the Scales of Justice

Tina Rosenberg[1]

Fifty years ago, U.S. Supreme Court Justice Robert H. Jackson inaugurated what is now recognized as the watershed in international law, the International Military Tribunal at Nuremberg. Jackson, chief prosecutor for the United States, ended the first paragraph of his opening statement thus: "That four great nations, flushed with victory and stung with injury, stay the hand of vengeance and voluntarily submit their captive enemies to the judgment of the law is one of the most significant tributes that Power has ever paid to Reason." Over the next eight months, films of the liberation of Auschwitz and other concentration camps exposed to a stunned world the full extent of German atrocities, while nineteen Nazi leaders were convicted and three acquitted in the first international trials for war crimes, crimes against peace and crimes against humanity.

Paradoxically, Nuremberg's weaknesses, not its strengths, have proven most enduring. Even Nuremberg's most vociferous supporters admit that the prosecutions had only the shakiest foundations in existing law; prosecutors at the International Military Tribunal and in later U.S. tribunals in Nuremberg and international tribunals in Tokyo improvised as they went along. But Nuremberg's principles have now been codified and accepted by most nations of the world and form the basis for much of current international and human rights law. Nuremberg's great strength, by contrast—that genocidal leaders were tried and punished by an international court—is only now being echoed, and only faintly. International law has blossomed, but enforcement of that law—the tribute power pays to reason—continues to count Nuremberg as its zenith.

From today's perspective, it is hard to remember the touchingly high expectations the world held for international law after Nuremberg. The United Nations was born, and with it a host of new conventions and declarations protecting human rights. Diplomats spoke of outlawing war. Drafts of a code of international crimes all nations could agree on circulated in the United Nations.

Two years after Nuremberg, the UN International Law Commission recommended the establishment of a permanent international criminal court to try those who violated the code. Then the Cold War began. Votes in the United Nations were postponed and debate prolonged. The code of international crimes faded away because the United States and the Soviet Union could not agree on a definition of the crime of aggression. As for a court, neither country had much interest in exposing its own citizens to trial by an international court that included the strong presence of its enemy. Since 1954, the issue of a permanent court has been in hibernation—until today. Serious work on the matter began in 1992 and now sits just short of the ultimate step: a diplomatic conference to hammer out the final details, which will take place in June 1998.[2] Although many important questions still need to be worked out, the conference is likely to produce a treaty ready for ratification by the end of that year, and a working international criminal court shortly after.

Proponents show none of the post-Nuremberg romanticism. They know a permanent international court will arrive slowly—since it is now based in a treaty that will have to be ratified. (Although twenty nations ratified a treaty outlawing genocide in the first two years after it was signed, it took forty years for the U.S. Senate to give it the required two-thirds majority—and even then it passed with a clause requiring the Senate to approve any trial of an American.)

The Paradox of International Law

More important, the court will suffer from the classic paradox of international law: with no serious police, and courts that depend on voluntary compliance, international law is as powerful as any national legal system with no police or courts would be. It has usually given the world one of two extremes: victors' justice or no justice at all. An admirable body of treaties, laws, and covenants exists, but they have almost always depended on raw power for their enforcement.

It is likely that any version of a court that nations will accept will be weak enough to allow them to comply only when they want to. The final version may allow countries to pick and choose the crimes for which they accept the court's jurisdiction—except genocide, which will be mandatory. And if Peru, say, refuses to surrender the general accused of wiping out an Andean village, there will be no SWAT team of international police poised to arrest him. Probably the most the court could do would be to issue an international arrest warrant, ensuring that the general could not set foot outside Peru. If the Security Council mustered the resolve, it could slap travel or other sanctions on Peru until it handed over the fugitive.

Although the situations that most require the court would be precisely where it is least effective, one can imagine other times when justice would be both imperative and achievable. Nations might be willing to surrender accused criminals in a variety of circumstances. The accused might be foreigners. Cameroon, Kenya and Zambia, for example, have turned over Rwandan genocide leaders found on their territory to the already existing International Criminal Tribunal for Rwanda. They would not likely have done so if it had been Rwanda alone asking for their extradition. They might be citizens governments feel too weak to put on trial. A court with jurisdiction over drug trafficking could be a boon for Colombia, which seems able—and lately willing—to capture its cocaine barons but unable to give them serious prison sentences, and is certainly unwilling to make the politically charged gesture of extraditing them. Cambodia's leaders have invited the international community to prosecute Khmer Rouge leaders, a feat beyond the ability of Cambodia's feeble courts. The need for this trial is obvious to anyone who watched the television broadcast of Pol Pot's bizarre show trial by the Khmer Rouge, an event that seemed overwhelmingly trivial. It is terrible to think that Armageddon for a man who killed a quarter of his countrymen came in the form of a metal shed in the jungle with a few dozen young people shouting "crush, crush, crush" with their fists in the air. The trial's numerous flaws—and by extension, the elements needed for real justice—turned the concept of justice from an intellectual idea into something many viewers could viscerally feel.

New democratic governments fearful that prosecuting powerful former officials could imperil democracy—Corazon Aquino in the Philippines, for example—might find the muscle to at least put them on a plane to transfer them to international authorities, and, indeed, might be grateful for a way to make the democracy-strengthening point that human rights violations carry a cost.

Nations might also be willing to surrender citizens for crimes that do not implicate government officials: if terrorism were one of the crimes in the court's jurisdiction, it is easy to picture Algeria turning over accused antigovernment fundamentalists. Or nations might choose to turn over individuals in custody to avoid retaliation: when Germany prosecuted two fundamentalists accused of hijacking a TWA plane in Lebanon, their group took two German citizens hostage. Leaders might choose to surrender even powerful colleagues accused of serious, government-backed crimes in order to score points internationally and rid themselves of competition.

The last few years have offered numerous examples of situations when a court might have been useful. Libya refused to extradite the two suspects in the Lockerbie Pan Am bombing to the United States or the United Kingdom, but claimed it would have turned them over to an international court. Unfortunately, there was no way of calling Libya's bluff. After the attack on UN peacekeeping troops in Somalia on the orders of General Mohammed Farah Aidid, the UN Security Council responded with a resolution authorizing the secretary general to arrest, try and punish those responsible—but the United Nations had no appropriate court. An international court would have been a better forum for the trial of Panamanian dictator Manuel Noriega than prosecution in U.S. courts, which was, of course, victors' justice. In short, even hardheaded realists will be able to find uses for a permanent international criminal court.

Why this is important will be discussed later. Why this is necessary, however, bears mentioning here: only such a court can begin to solve the problem at the root of its own limited effectiveness. A court, even one too weak to impose the law on powerful criminals, is the only possible next step in a chain of events that has steadily, although with maddeningly glacial speed, progressed toward a system possessing that strength. To see why, we must look at how attempts at international justice have reached this point.

Inventing the Law

The world's first attempt to create an international criminal court came with the end of World War I. Britain's prime minister, David Lloyd George, was the strongest advocate of trying Kaiser Wilhelm II and other German officials for war crimes before a tribunal of Allied powers. But U.S. President Woodrow Wilson believed that trials would endanger two things he valued more: the fragile Weimar Republic and the proposed League of Nations. In a compromise, the 1919 Treaty of Versailles provided for the Kaiser's trial, not for war crimes, but for "a supreme offense against international morality and the sanctity of treaties." These charges had so little basis in international law that the Dutch, who had custody of the Kaiser, refused to turn him over, and he died in the Netherlands in 1941, untried.

The Versailles Treaty also called for an international tribunal to try lower-ranking officials and presented a list to the German government of 854 citizens. Germany made a counteroffer to have the German Supreme Court try them, which the United States, fearful for German democracy, accepted. The trials, which began in Leipzig in 1921, were a farce; of 901 cases, 888 were dismissed or ended in acquittal.

The Allies had more interest in trying Turkish officials for the mass slaughter of a million Armenians. Just before the war, a group of military officers calling themselves the Ittihad took power in Turkey and allied themselves with Germany. Over the next four years, they drove their Armenian population into resettlement camps, raped the women, rounded up the men for forced labor and then expelled the survivors into the desert, where they died of starvation and exposure. After the war, a Turkish military court convicted two officials, hanging one. But no international trials were ever held—genocide was not yet considered an international crime—and the 1923 Treaty of Lausanne granted amnesty to the killers as part of the price of the division of the Ottoman Empire.

Then came Nuremberg. It was not a foregone conclusion that the Allied powers would grant Nazi leaders fair trials. Within the U.S. government, Secretary of the Treasury Henry Morgenthau pushed for summary execution, which was also the preference of Winston Churchill and Anthony Eden. And existing international law was not auspicious. Of the three categories of crimes prosecuted at Nuremberg, only war crimes and international aggression were established crimes under international law. But the war crimes category did not cover atrocities committed against German citizens (which, of course, German Jews were) or anything that happened before the invasion of Poland in 1939, which marked the start of World War II. Outsiders had no legal basis for sticking their noses into matters between governments and their own citizens. And under Third Reich law, the Holocaust was perfectly legal. There was no law, therefore, under which its perpetrators could be prosecuted. International prohibitions on crimes against humanity had not yet been written.

So Nuremberg invented them. This was ex post facto justice—and the law frowns on prosecuting people for acts that were not crimes when committed. There were other flaws. The tribunal used the concept of collective guilt to indict whole organizations such as the SS—members who had enlisted and stayed after knowing of its deeds were *presumed* guilty of the organization's crimes. Martin Bormann was tried in absentia. Julius Streicher, publisher of the Nazi newspaper *Der Stürmer*, was hanged purely for the expression of Nazi views.

Nuremberg was also, famously, victors' justice. No Allies were tried for the bombings of Dresden or Hiroshima. But the Nuremberg trials were not show trials with predetermined outcomes, a usual feature of victors' justice. In the International Military Tribunal, the defense's case took longer to present than the prosecution's, and three defendants and half the indicted organizations were acquitted. Subsequent U.S. military tribunals in Nuremberg brought cases against 182 defendants, including members of the roaming death squads (the *Einsatzgruppen*), doctors who had experimented on concentration camp inmates, and Nazi judges and industrialists. In 1946, an international military tribunal at Tokyo began trials of twenty-five wartime leaders (with the notable exception of Emperor Hirohito), sentencing sixteen to life imprisonment and seven to death.

If the Nuremberg tribunals stretched existing law, it was to prosecute men who had stretched existing ideas of state criminality. It was a series of abnormal trials in an abnormal period for abnormal crimes. As Hannah Arendt argued, bureaucratic mass murder is a twentieth-century hallmark of progress, and legal structures did not exist to cope with it. The law had to evolve if it were not to condone such practices.

It is hard to exaggerate Nuremberg's impact on human rights and international law. Nuremberg gave rise to the 1949 Geneva Conventions.

These contained two important advances over earlier war-crimes conventions, which had laid out the laws of war but no mechanisms to enforce them. For the first time, countries ratifying the treaty had the *obligation* to punish those who committed "grave breaches" of the conventions—including torture, killing, hostage-taking and unlawful deportation. Unlike at Nuremberg, nations were obligated to punish their own citizens, even when victorious in war. In addition, these crimes had no statute of limitation and came with universal jurisdiction, which meant that any country party to the conventions could put those who violated them on trial. In theory, if the Spanish government had discovered Lieutenant William Calley vacationing in Barcelona and the United States had refused to put him on trial, Spain would have been within its legal rights to have held him and brought him to justice for the My Lai massacre in Vietnam.

In 1950, the United Nations adopted a list of seven principles from the trials' charter and judgments known as the Nuremberg Principles, which have since been adopted by almost every major nation. To give just one example of their impact, soldiers who commit atrocious crimes can no longer win acquittal by arguing that they were only following orders.

Nuremberg's single most important contribution, however, was to give legitimacy to the concept that the world had something to say about how governments treat their own citizens. It dissolved the shield of sovereignty that tyrants had used to escape judgment. While before Nuremberg, punishing sovereign officials guilty of crimes against humanity was nobody's business, after the International Military Tribunal and the 1949 Geneva Conventions, it was everybody's business.

Regional Courts

The next step was the establishment of regional courts. When the European Court of Human Rights was formed in 1950, few governments paid attention. It has now evolved into a serious guardian of human rights for citizens of the thirty nations that have ratified the European Convention for the Protection of Human Rights and Freedoms. In 1994, rules were changed to allow citizens to petition the court directly once they have tried and failed to get their own domestic courts to solve a problem. The court cannot try individuals; it can only hold governments responsible for abuse. The whole process can take up to eight years, but in most cases governments have complied with the court's rulings, even changing domestic laws. This is in part due to pressure from strong European organizations, and in part because most European countries are predisposed to pay attention to such niceties. When the colonels came to power in Greece in 1967, Greece stopped complying.

The Organization of American States set up a court modeled on Europe's. In 1988, the Inter-American Court of Human Rights, based in San José, Costa Rica, issued its first decisions, two judgments holding the Honduran government responsible for the forced disappearances of citizens. The court meets only part-time, and its lack of enforcement mechanisms has proven a more serious problem in Latin America than in Europe. Honduras, for example, never paid the ordered reparations to the victims' families.

But the court is still useful. It has prodded national courts to get serious. Thanks to the threat of a court judgment, for example, Guatemala in 1993 took the unprecedented step of trying and sentencing two former Civil Patrol officials to twenty years' imprisonment each for killing two human rights workers in the village of Chunimá. The court's writs of protection for witnesses have saved lives, and its rulings have convinced several Latin countries to change repressive laws. Argentina, for example, agreeing to a friendly settlement before the court, repealed one of the region's most draconian laws limiting free speech, which prohibited "offending in any way the person, dignity, or honor of a public official"—whether or not a statement was true.

One regional court, however, stands out for effectiveness: the European Court of Justice. "It's one of the wonders of the modern world," says Anne-Marie Slaughter, who teaches international law at Harvard Law School. "It gets its judgments enforced." This court works differently from others: national courts use it as a sort of a special expert tribunal. A citizen in Lisbon, for example, might challenge a tariff, arguing it violates the Treaty of Rome. The Portuguese courts will send the question to the European Court. If the European Court turns its thumbs down, the Portuguese courts then rule that the tariff must go. "It works because it gets hooked up to domestic legal systems," says Slaughter. "Once the West German government tried to overrule a court decision, and there was a huge outcry that the government was interfering with the independence of the German judiciary."

The only court with world jurisdiction is the International Court of Justice in the Hague, born with the United Nations fifty years ago, although a similar court was set up under the 1919 Versailles Treaty to settle disputes between nations. The rate of compliance with its decisions is good only in those cases in which both countries have voluntarily agreed to go to the court to settle a dispute—over a border, for example. In more political cases, nations have often told the court to go to hell. The United States had always supported the court and its precursor and had complied with its decisions. But in 1986, the Reagan administration refused to comply with its ruling in favor of Nicaragua, which had sued the United States for arming and supplying the contras and mining its harbors. The Bush administration even held an aid package for post-Sandinista Nicaragua hostage until Nicaragua agreed to withdraw its claim for reparations in 1991. In 1993, after Bosnia sued Yugoslavia, the court ordered Yugoslavia to take all measures to prevent the crime of genocide. Suffice it to say, Yugoslavia has yet to comply.

The limited success of these courts can be viewed two ways—first, as a cautionary tale of power's dominance over law. But there is a more optimistic lesson: international pressure counts. Even with no enforcement mechanisms and the most political type of judgments—it is not people but government policies that are on trial—these courts win compliance in many cases.

Negligent Bystanders

In 1993, the UN Security Council established the first international criminal tribunal since Nuremberg: the International Criminal Tribunal for the former Yugoslavia. It was expanded the next year to cover Rwanda. There were many excellent reasons for establishing the Yugoslavia tribunal—to break the endless cycle of retribution that has kept the Balkans violent for millennia, for starters—but it probably owes its birth to a bad reason: the international community, a tower of weakness and indecision on the war, wanted a painless way of showing it was doing something. The Yugoslavia tribunal is not victors' justice, but negligent bystanders' justice.

On November 7, 1994, the Yugoslavia tribunal indicted Dragan Nikolic, a commander of the Bosnian Serb Susica camp, charging him with willful killing, torture and inhumane treatment of prisoners. As of this writing, the tribunal has publicly indicted seventy-eight others, including Bosnian Serb leader Radovan Karadzic, for genocide, crimes against humanity and war crimes. Three of those indicted are Muslims, eighteen are Croats, and fifty-eight are Serbs. The tribunal has also issued sealed indictments against other suspects who remain unknown. The Rwanda tribunal has indicted thirty-five people on genocide and other charges, all of them Hutus.

As for the others, there will be no trials in absentia. For those who are not surrendered or captured, the prosecutor may present evidence to a panel of three judges, who may then issue a superindictment: an arrest warrant that, if ignored by Serbia, will become an international arrest warrant, good forever. The civilian and military leaders of the Bosnian Serbs during the war, Karadzic and General Ratko Mladic, and several other men have these kinds of warrants outstanding. And since this is a UN production, all member states are obligated to turn over these wanted men.

The tribunals, which were never designed to be serious, have now become feared powers. The Hague tribunal was built with only one courtroom, but in the spring of 1998 added a second and is building a third. In the same year, it employed more than 400 people and had a budget of more than $64 million. The UN was slow to fund and staff the Rwanda tribunal, and its first year of operation in Arusha, Tanzania, was marked by problems of nepotism and corruption. But the tribunal's chief prosecutor and chief registrar were replaced, and its administration has improved. It now has a budget similar to its Hague cousin and a slightly larger staff.

The tribunals' biggest moral advantage—that they are not victors' justice—is also their biggest practical problem. The Rwanda tribunal has well over half of its thirty-five indictees in custody. One serious problem is that several of the wanted men are in jail in Rwanda, being tried in highly problematic and unfair national trials. In the case of former Yugoslavia, the Muslims are the only ones who have cooperated fully in turning over the indicted to the Hague. Croatia and the Bosnian Croats have turned over most of their fugitives, but only after heavy pressure from the United States, which withheld needed international loans. The Serbs originally did not recognize the tribunal at all, and would not even provide documents to defend Serb indictees. But after Milorad Dodik, a more moderate Serb who opposes Radovan Karadzic and his gang, was elected prime minister of the Serb Republic in early 1998, that entity began to work with the tribunal to a limited extent. The government there is still not willing to suffer the political backlash that could come from arresting fugitives, however. The official line is that Karadzic and other wanted men should turn themselves in.

The most egregious defiance of the tribunal's directives, of course, belongs to the NATO soldiers enforcing the peace accords in Bosnia. Even though the peace accords pledge full compliance with the tribunal, NATO is still treating the world to the ridiculous spectacle of thousands of heavily armed soldiers tiptoeing around indicted war criminals such as Karadzic and Mladic. NATO soldiers have apprehended several suspects and shot one who shot back while resisting arrest. Some other UN troops have also made arrests. And NATO is doing more and more to enforce the peace accords, including taking over illegally seized television transmitters that broadcast hate propaganda and accompanying refugees returning to their homes. But NATO leaders have so far not been willing to take the risks involved in arresting men like Karadzic. Any normal policeman who behaved this way with a criminal suspect would be arrested as an accessory to the crime.

Not surprisingly, the twenty-six men in custody in the Hague include few big fish. The first to be convicted was a camp guard at the notorious Omarska camp, a Bosnian Serb named Dusan Tadic. He was given a twenty-five year sentence for crimes against humanity and war crimes. Another man pled guilty to war crimes and received a five-year sentence. The highest ranking men in custody in May 1998 were a general who commanded the Bosnian Croat army, the Bosnian Serb former mayor of the city of Vukovar, who is accused of killing hundreds of people evacuated from a hospital, and a Bosnian Serb accused of complicity in genocide for his role in running the Omarska and Keraterm concentration camps.

It is probably too soon to see any consequences of the Rwanda tribunal, but despite the lack of enforcement, the Yugoslavia tribunal has already had a positive effect. It kept Karadzic and other extreme hardliners from representing the Bosnian Serbs at peace negotiations, probably making a deal easier to reach. Because of his indictment, Karadzic was not allowed to run for office. Although he has defied the peace accords by continuing to run half of Bosnia with no formal portfolio, without the tribunal he would likely be the president of the Serb Republic now. The tribunal may even be responsible for the peace accords, as the Bosnian Muslims would not have joined peace negotiations without the tribunal's promise of justice. The tribunal's newest indictments are all sealed, a useful move that is disturbing the sleep of many in Bosnia who do not deserve a good night's rest. But there is no doubt that, as long as NATO soldiers continue to make a mockery of the tribunal's arrest warrants, there is little reason for most people to take its message of an end to impunity seriously.

Despite its foundations in hypocrisy and its serious limitations, the ad hoc criminal tribunals for former Yugoslavia and Rwanda represent another step forward for the enforcement of international law. It may take years, but it is likely that eventually the tribunals will hold even victorious leaders accountable for war crimes, crimes against humanity and genocide. They have also established rape and other sexual violence as international crimes. The next logical step is to remove the need to create such courts when events demand—which the United Nations will certainly tire of doing soon. In 1995, the United Nations devoted a huge effort to structuring forums for dealing with Iraqi war crimes, a project that eventually fizzled due to opposition from Gulf states. "If we had a permanent court, I know exactly what I'd be doing," said one official working on the issue. "I'd be delegating like hell to that court. But since we don't have it, we have to keep creating new processes." In the spring of 1998, the United States introduced a resolution in the Security Council to establish an international court to try the Khmer Rouge leaders responsible for genocide and other international crimes.

After languishing for forty years, the idea of a permanent international criminal court was revived in 1989, when Trinidad and Tobago, afraid that Colombian cocaine traffickers would begin to move their operations to the Caribbean, proposed such a court to fight drug trafficking. Mikhail

Gorbachev also praised the idea—again, to prosecute drug offenses. None of this would have mattered without the fall of communism, which made the United States the single most influential voice in designing the court and defining the crimes it would cover, and which removed the powerful bloc of nations bent on embarrassing U.S. citizens.

The Might/Right Dilemma

Many aspects of the international criminal court seem set. At least at first, it would be located at the International Court of Justice in the Hague, but judges would remain in their own countries until needed. (No one yet has the slightest idea how much the court would cost.) The court would complement, not replace, domestic legal systems. This means that states could try accused criminals at home rather than surrender them. But if the court determined that the domestic trial was a whitewash simply designed to keep it at bay, then it could go ahead and prosecute.

It is likely that the court would try people accused of genocide, crimes against humanity and serious violations of the laws of war. Every state ratifying the underlying treaty would be obligated to accept the court's jurisdiction over genocide. Some countries are pushing a version under which ratifiers would have to accept its jurisdiction over all the crimes in the court's brief. Other nations prefer a system under which countries would only be obligated to surrender people accused of the crimes they choose to accept. Still others, notably the United States, also seem to be urging a plan that would require states to consent before their own citizens could be prosecuted, so Iraq, for example, would have to agree to the prosecution of Saddam Hussein. Ironically, although it was drug trafficking that gave the court its second chance, that crime will probably not be in its mandate.

If a state that had accepted jurisdiction refused to surrender an indicted person, the court, like the Yugoslavia and Rwanda tribunals, would likely be able to issue a superindictment that would keep the defendant confined to his home country. It might also be able to ask the UN Security Council to apply sanctions to a recalcitrant nation, such as travel bans or exclusion from international events ranging from conferences to multilateral loans.

The bizarre arrangement of asking the states of potential defendants which laws they will accept and which defendants they will allow to be prosecuted is the product of the old might/right dilemma: the more sweeping the court's powers, the fewer governments will support it. The court is guaranteed to win widespread adherence only if it promises each nation that it would prosecute only everyone else's citizens.

However, after a few successful prosecutions, nations may suddenly take notice. The history of international law shows that most nations do respond to political and diplomatic pressure; not every country is Serbia. The desire for international legitimacy compels governments to sign treaties all the time that place constraints on their own behavior. Governments will be able to comply with the court's ruling with the face-saving excuse that it is individuals, not nations, that are targeted.

The single biggest obstacle to the court has been the U.S. government. The United States was not particularly interested in having a court to try drug traffickers. Officials worried that it would interfere with domestic drug prosecutions and warned that the detailed investigation necessary for a successful drug prosecution was too ambitious for an international court. In reality, the United States had little interest in any kind of court; nightmares loomed of Colin Powell being dragged into court to answer for civilian casualties during the bombing of Panama. "The tactic the United States has used throughout has been to delay," says Michael Scharf, who handled the court in the State Department Legal Advisor's office from 1989 to 1993 and now teaches law at the New England School of Law in Boston. "The United States was responsible for the issue being placed in the United Nations' International Law Commission rather than the General Assembly. The ILC had done a wonderful job of making no progress on a number of issues. It was a dumping ground."

In the fall of 1993, the administration—pushed largely by U.S. Ambassador to the United Nations Madeleine Albright—switched from open hostility to an attempt to shape the court to its liking. One important factor, according to Scharf and current administration officials, was the establishment of the Yugoslavia tribunal—a project the United States strongly supported. In less than a month, U.S. and other negotiators solved most of the same political, legal, and practical problems that Washington had claimed were blocking a permanent court.

U.S. objections to the permanent court also softened because the United Nations met the United States more than halfway. To everyone's surprise, the International Law Commission came up with detailed drafts for a court. The earliest drafts had contemplated giving the court exclusive jurisdiction (meaning it took precedence over national courts) over a large group of crimes, some of which—economic aggression and colonial domination, for example—left the U.S. government sweating.

But later drafts were far weaker—the court now only complements domestic courts. Nations can choose the international offenses for which they accept the court's jurisdiction. And the more controversial proposed crimes are gone; there is no possibility that the chairman of Chiquita Bananas will be tried for economic imperialism.

The United States got involved because it had no choice. "It's happening," said one Clinton administration official. "You can shape it to the best degree possible. Or you can stonewall and end up with a court where countries lodge complaints about American soldiers on their soil."

However, although the United States has found its voice, it is not a constructive one. It has voted for endless delay. And as the court went into a June 1998 diplomatic conference that would produce the final plan, the United States was raising objection after objection, ones that could cripple the court.

One of Washington's moves was to propose giving the five permanent members of the Security Council control over most of the court's docket. The would require the Security Council to give its approval before the prosecutor could look at situations that the Security Council was debating—which is most of the world's conflict zones. In effect, that would mean Russia could veto any prosecutions having to do with Chechnya, and China could veto anything concerning Tibet. The Security Council's members could protect themselves and their friends. "No other government in the world has its military so broadly extended globally," said a U.S. government official. "The Pentagon is concerned that our personnel [would be] subject to politically motivated lawsuits from any number of regions."

Many smaller nations, and even Britain, which is a permanent member of the Security Council, object, fearing that a court controlled by the Security Council would have very little legitimacy. It would inject a political vote—one completely tipped in favor of the powerful—into a supposedly impartial judicial process. It would give other nations an excuse to defy the court. It would make the court an instrument large nations could use against smaller ones. If the Security Council can define what is a crime, then crimes will become the things small nations with poor friends do: hacking your neighbor to death with machetes will qualify; aerial bombing will not. But it should. If Henry Kissinger had had to worry about prosecution, some dead Cambodians might be alive today, and the Khmer Rouge might never have come to power.

Those who object to the U.S. position also point out that a serious and independent court would not prosecute frivolous complaints, and that the United States has an effective system of military justice. The international court will not be allowed to prosecute if the defendant is being seriously prosecuted at home. Opponents of Security Council control have proposed a compromise that would require the Security Council—which means the unanimous vote of the permanent five—to veto the prosecutor's involvement in a region, rather than to approve it. This would mean that it would take all five permanent members to block prosecutions over Tibet or Chechnya, not just one.

While still opposing that compromise, the U.S. government has come up with other roadblocks, all of them designed to soothe Pentagon fears that American soldiers will be prosecuted. It is unclear which of them will be the official American negotiating position at the June conference. The worst possibility is that the United States will continue to advocate allowing countries to veto prosecutions of their own citizens. That would make the court an absurdity. If Saddam Hussein were to be indicted for his genocide against the Kurds, and arrested in Paris while receiving medical treatment, he could not be prosecuted unless his government— essentially, unless he—agreed. Since Senator Jesse Helms has announced that there is no possibility he will allow the U.S. Senate to ratify America's signature on a treaty creating the court, there is little reason for other nations to make accommodations to suit Washington. It is possible that nations wanting a strong court will simply ignore the United States and design one capable of dispensing justice. Perhaps some time in the future, Washington will come around to ratifying it.

What the U.S. opposition to a strong court overlooks is that a court capable of bringing U.S. nationals to trial—in other words, the strongest possible court—is the one most firmly in the U.S. interest. As the Pentagon notes, in today's global village, the sheriff wears a U.S. uniform. Anything that will deter war, war crimes or crimes against humanity will probably end up saving American lives and dollars. It will further the goals that the United States professes.

The Scales of Justice

The most likely version of an international criminal court will not be a strong deterrent, at least not at first; but at present, none exists at all. "Who, after all, is today speaking about the destruction of the Armenians?" asked Adolf Hitler in a 1936 speech. Then and now, genocide goes unpunished. Criminal leaders can operate snug in the notion that their domestic power protects them and, in an emergency, golden exile in the Riviera or Panama City awaits.

It would be no small inconvenience for a leader to be branded a war criminal by an international court and confined to his own territory. He would know he is doomed to live out his days at the mercy of political rivals in his own Asunción or Addis Ababa, and that eventually international sanctions might erode the goodwill of even his best friends. A court seen as serious and impartial enough to prosecute even powerful U.S. officials who violate international law will be a constant annoyance to abusive leaders—law students in their own countries will study it, human rights groups will cite it, foreign leaders will invoke it. It places a permanent thumb on the side of the scales that until now has borne only air.

The court could also help to break the cycle of violence that will continue so long as people feel justice has not been done. Ethnic conflict is especially prone to such cycles; the war in Yugoslavia really began when Slobodan Milosevic gave a speech in 1989 commemorating the 600th anniversary of the Serbs' defeat at Kosovo Polje. But people who see murderers and torturers tried and punished will be less likely to perpetuate a cycle of vengeance.

The history of international courts shows that while we are unlikely ever to make the world safe from future Hitlers, deterring more common atrocities is a possible and worthwhile goal. Power will always be able to dominate law. We cannot erase this equation, but we can rig it by creating fair and just legal institutions that are more powerful than the criminals. The strongest possible international criminal court is imperative if we are to begin to alter the balance.

Notes

1. This chapter is a revised and updated version of an article that first appeared in the *World Policy Journal* XII, no. 3 (Fall 1995): 55–64.
2. For discussion of that conference, see Epilogue, this volume.

The Nuremberg Legacy:
Historical Assessment Fifty Years Later[1]

M. Cherif Bassiouni

*The wrongs which we seek to condemn and punish have been so calcu-
lated, so malignant and so devastating, that civilization cannot tolerate
their being ignored, because it cannot survive their being repeated.*

Robert H. Jackson
Opening Speech for the Prosecution
Nuremberg, November 21, 1945

Introduction

On August 8, 1945, the London Charter was signed, clearing the way
for the prosecution of the major war criminals of the European theater of
operations before the International Military Tribunal (IMT) sitting at
Nuremberg.[2] The following year, the Allies established the International
Military Tribunal for the Far East (IMTFE) in Tokyo, a counterpart tribunal for the major war criminals of the Asia-Pacific theater of operations. The two, however, are legally distinguishable. The IMT was
established by a treaty, originally signed by the four major allies and acceded to by nineteen European states. The IMTFE, however, was established by the military order of General Douglas MacArthur pursuant to
his authority as Supreme Allied Commander for the Pacific.

Many in the world community expected the post-World War II trials
of major war criminals, particularly those of the IMT, to be the precur-
sors of a permanent international criminal court, a hope entertained
since the end of World War I. The IMT proceedings gave way to "subsequent proceedings" under Control Council Order No. 10 (CCL 10).
Under CCL 10, the four major allies conducted prosecutions in their respective zones of occupation.[3] Australia, China, France, the Netherlands, New Zealand, the Philippines and the United States established
military tribunals that prosecuted over 5,596 individuals. The Soviet
Union also prosecuted an unknown number of Japanese prisoners of war.

Various European countries that had been occupied by Axis powers
also carried out domestic prosecutions. However, these trials mainly concerned their respective nationals who had collaborated with the occupying forces. The United States also prosecuted Japanese officers for war
crimes by virtue of the military authority of General MacArthur. Among

them was the case of General Yamashita in the Philippines, which was a blot on justice, as it imposed a standard of military command responsibility through failure to act that was never subsequently applied.[4]

Since World War II, only a handful of countries have prosecuted war criminals under their domestic laws. They are: Germany (over 60,000, with a seventy percent conviction rate); Israel (the main case was that of Adolf Eichmann); Italy (one case in 1996 in which the defendant was convicted, but later released under the military code's statute of limitations); France,[5] whose laws on the subject developed in the aftermath of World War II (3 prosecutions of French collaborators, two convicted, one trial pending); and Canada, whose special law on this subject was passed in 1987 (one case, which resulted in acquittal). Australia, which has national legislation modeled on Canada's, attempted three prosecutions, but all were dismissed before trial. The United Kingdom passed a similar, though less strict, version of the Canadian law (one case pending). The United States has enacted legislation giving federal courts jurisdiction to denaturalize and deport persons who have concealed or willfully misrepresented their participation or involvement in criminal organizations and war crimes during World War II.[6]

In order to ensure prosecution, the United Nations sponsored a convention in 1968 on the Nonapplicability of Statutes of Limitations to War Crimes and Crimes Against Humanity.[7] To date, however, less than one-third of the member states have ratified it. The Council of Europe followed suit with a similar convention. The UN General Assembly also adopted two resolutions, in 1971[8] and 1973,[9] on the duty to extradite or prosecute persons accused of war crimes and crimes against humanity. These resolutions, however, have had little practical effect on the customs and practices of states.[10] Many other international instruments on substantive international criminal law, as discussed below, were developed between 1945 and 1994.

The process that commenced at Nuremberg continues to evolve. The latest and most important post-Nuremberg development has been the establishment of the International Criminal Tribunal for the former Yugoslavia (ICTY) and the International Criminal Tribunal for Rwanda (ICTR). However, almost fifty years after Nuremberg and nearly seventy-five years after the Versailles Treaty that ended World War I, no permanent international criminal court has yet been established, though there is movement in that direction. Some modest progress has also been made by the United Nations International Law Commission on codifying certain international crimes. But these modest results have disappointed the hopes of many and made more credible the claims of those who saw the Nuremberg and Tokyo trials as victors' justice. Subsequent legal developments can cure historic defects, eliminating the weaknesses of the past and enhancing the prospects for future improvements. Without these developments, however, the original infirmities that attended the early processes will tend to be confirmed.

There is also the danger that singularly unique legal events that are not repeated when similar circumstances warrant it may fall into *desuètude* or disuse—a legal concept known to many of the major legal systems of the world.[11] Indeed, the revival of a law after long disuse raises questions as to the legality of its application. But although the law and legal institutions of Nuremberg have not been duplicated since 1945, except by the ICTY and ICTR, the "Nuremberg legacy" remains significant and well-remembered. Consequently, it cannot be argued that it has been forgotten, despite the fact that it has not been replicated and has been relied upon only infrequently in national criminal proceedings outside Germany.

The historic impact and legacy of institutions are subject to wide-ranging individual and collective perceptions. Indeed, many factors bear upon human perceptions, including differing values, purposes, goals and personal experiences. But any *a posteriori* impact assessment of the legacy of historic institutions raises methodological questions. Among them are: what are the methods of legal analysis employed; what is the measure or standard by which to judge what took place; what were the expectations of accomplishment when the institutions were established, and what are the expectations at the time of the assessment; and if they are different, how can we compare them.

Furthermore, in making *a posteriori* historical legal assessments, it is difficult to fully appreciate all the contextual factors that existed at the time of the occurrence. Even if it were possible to attempt this with some degree of intellectual objectivity, it is nonetheless fraught with subjectivity. Those not part of the previous experience cannot completely grasp what was done earlier, under different circumstances and subject to exigencies that look otherwise after almost fifty years. In addition, there are always facts that occur at a given time that do not become publicly known or are never recorded, and therefore cannot be known and assessed at a later date.[12] Purely intellectual analysis cannot, therefore, objectively evaluate all the facts and circumstances of a time past. That is why so much of history is revisionist.

Lastly, it must be understood that institutions, like historic events, are shaped by people and affected by all the factors that bear on human motivations and interactions. Occasionally great individuals do emerge, dominating events and controlling the behavior of actors. Most commonly, however, personal and personality factors ultimately influence decisions and outcomes.

What is now called the "Nuremberg legacy" is made up of all this and more. But the starting point is the IMT, with which the word "Nuremberg" has become associated. The assessment that follows therefore deals with the IMT as the origin of subsequent developments. It is based on three interrelated levels of inquiry. They are:

1. The institutional legacy: the IMT and its processes.
2. The legal legacy: substantive legal developments—the law of the IMT and subsequent developments.
3. The moral-ethical legacy: The power of a principle that corresponds to basic human values and expectations and its influence on legal developments.

The Institutional Legacy: The IMT and its Processes

One remarkable accomplishment of the International Military Tribunal at Nuremberg was that, for all practical purposes, it was the first international criminal tribunal ever to be established. This is even more remarkable because the victors who established the IMT had an alternative: summary execution of those among the defeated whom the victors deemed to have violated the laws and customs of war.[13] The victors could have been totally arbitrary. They could have, even in so doing, been fair by some legal standards, without electing to establish a necessarily cumbersome, costly and to some extent unpredictable international legal institution. Its judicial decisions could not have been guaranteed even though it was carefully designed not to produce unexpected results.[14]

The British justified their position in favor of summary execution and against trials by arguing that the Germans would effectively challenge the trials and the legal process. They also argued that the Germans would use the forum to propagandize their claims and justify their positions in an attempt to rally national and even a portion of international public opinion to the proposition that the trials were a farce. Finally, the British argued that trials would make martyrs of some of the accused. The United States replied that such trials would establish an important historical record and develop what would hopefully become lasting international legal standards. Moreover, trials would deter future leaders from similar conduct and open a new chapter of rule-of-law government for Germany's postwar era. Contrary to the British, the United States argued that trials would avoid making martyrs of the Nazis. Even if the defense tried to use the trials as a forum for propaganda, the United States argued, the facts were so overwhelming that the risk of sympathy for the accused was not very great.

Fortunately for history, the United States position, championed by Justice Robert Jackson, prevailed. After months of discussions, the four major Allies signed the London Charter of August 8, 1945, to which the IMT Statute was attached.[15] The tribunal's very establishment is what constitutes the legal precedent for subsequent efforts to set up the ad hoc tribunal for the former Yugoslavia and eventually a permanent international criminal court. What gives credence to Nuremberg is that the IMT proceedings strove to be an "ordinary" international criminal court, as opposed to an "extraordinary" or "exceptional" tribunal of victors over the defeated conducted in sham proceedings; the accused were, for the most part, persons whose leadership responsibility for many atrocities before and during the war was notorious;[16] the facts were so overwhelming as to the type and quantum of victimization and so tragic in their perpetration that they overshadowed legal considerations; and the trial procedures were as fair as they could have been under the circumstances and by contemporary standards of ordinary criminal justice in most countries.

These and other factors contributed to overcoming several legal considerations that, under normal circumstances in ordinary domestic criminal proceedings, would have largely reduced the legitimacy of the exercise. These legal considerations included the facts that (1) the tribunal's status was ad hoc; (2) some of the applicable law was formulated to fit the facts and some provisions were in part ex post facto; (3) the makers of the law were also the judges and prosecutors; (4) the accused came only from the ranks of the defeated, and no one from the victors' side who committed similar violations of the laws and customs of war was prosecuted; (5) the accused were arbitrarily chosen by those who would eventually prosecute them; (6) the judges came only from the victors' side; (7) the victors, and among them some judges, selected the substantive law and procedure that applied; (8) the entire process was in the hands of the victors; (9) the defense of the accused depended upon the benevolence of the prosecution and the judges, who were essentially from the prosecution side; and (10) the penalties were not determined by preexisting law, but by the judges. Many critics raised these legally valid questions.[17]

Despite the legally questionable nature and effect of these considerations, world public perception then and now is that the entire process was substantially fair and the outcome substantially just. Besides the facts and the personalities of the accused, what appears to enhance the credibility of Nuremberg and outweigh the criticisms noted above are that: (1) the IMT was established by virtue of a treaty signed by the four Allied states and acceded to by nineteen others; (2) the charter included substantive law and rules of procedures that had the appearance of legal

validity and substantive fairness; (3) the tribunal functioned fairly; and
(4) the proceedings were conducted with judicial decorum and procedural dignity. That is the perceived validity of the precedent, irrespective
of what legal critics may argue.

With time, the criticisms, whether justifiable or not, have scarcely diminished the perception of the validity of the Nuremberg legacy. On the
contrary, these weaknesses have been forgotten and the symbolic and
precedential value of the IMT has been strengthened over the years.
Thus, with the establishment of the ICTY and the ICTR and the continued work of the United Nations to establish a permanent international criminal tribunal, the institutional Nuremberg legacy looms large
in the expectations of the world community.

Since World War II, practitioners of realpolitik have pursued political
settlements at the cost of impunity, allowing many serious crimes to go
unpunished. This situation has reinforced the general public's perception
of the Nuremberg institutional legacy and the need to establish a permanent system of international justice. A question, however, arises: Is it the
actual validity of the institutional precedent that created its positive
legacy, or is it the needs and aspirations of the world community in search
of a precedent to idealize as valid that created this perception of legal validity? This question cannot be answered in purely legal terms, for it is the
cumulative effect of all the considerations examined in this assessment
and others that produced this contemporary outcome. In any event, what
matters now is the perception and its impact on future development.

The Legal Legacy

Two sets of considerations arise in this context. First are those arising
out of the substantive law applied by the IMT at its proceedings. Second
are those legal developments arising as a consequence of that application. The first considerations include, among others, (1) the legal validity and sufficiency of the specific crimes charged; and (2) the legal
validity of the principles of responsibility applied.

The second set of considerations include, among others: (1) the flow
of substantive legal developments that derived from or are ascribed to
the "Nuremberg" precedent; and (2) the stimulation of efforts to codify
international criminal law and establish a permanent international
criminal court.

Article 6 of its charter contained the substantive charges of the IMT,
namely "crimes against peace," "war crimes" and "crimes against humanity." These charges raised issues concerning the principles of legality in
criminal law, which are in some ways part of the general principles of law.
The Latin maxims *nullum crimen sine lege previae* and *nulla poena sine lege*

(no crime without previous law and no penalty without law) reflect these principles and are among the most serious issues raised about the substantive law applied by the IMT. The charter also raised ex post facto questions concerning certain historically valid defenses. The traditional defense of "obedience to superior orders" was disallowed in Article 8. However, the subsequent judgment qualified this rejection by establishing that, if a person who obeyed an order, even if unlawful, had no "moral choice," he or she could be exonerated from criminal responsibility. That is the same as the defense of coercion familiar to all legal systems.

Article 7 of the charter also eliminated the "act of state" defense, under which heads of state and other actors can claim their conduct was inherent to national sovereignty and thus cannot be questioned by others. Ex post facto problems could also be found in certain new offenses set out in the charter. Article 9 introduced the new concept of group criminality, and Article 10 provided for individual criminal responsibility based on group or collective responsibility for membership in "criminal organizations." Except for common law systems, most legal systems consider criminal responsibility to be individual. Legal entities, because they are legal abstractions, are excluded from this definition. Thus only persons may be charged with crimes, and they may not be charged as a result of some notion of collective responsibility, or for being part of an organization, even if it is deemed criminal, unless their own personal conduct violates the law.

The problem with the charge of "crimes against peace" was the absence of a specific convention declaring aggression a justiciable international crime for which individual criminal responsibility could be ascribed. Reliance on several previous treaties, such as the 1928 Treaty on the Renunciation of War, which did not criminalize the resort to war by states, was certainly not adequate to satisfy even a less than rigorous interpretation of the principles of legality. Indeed, there is nothing in international legal instruments prior to the London Charter to suggest that the conduct of those accused of "crimes against peace" was an international crime for which individual criminal penalties could be imposed. This is true despite the Allies' unsuccessful efforts to prosecute Kaiser Wilhelm II at the end of World War I via Article 227 of the Treaty of Versailles. Thus, prosecutions of "crimes against peace" were a form of ex post facto legal application of hitherto questionable legal norms.

With respect to the charges of "war crimes," the customary and conventional international law regulating armed conflicts had developed sufficient legal norms to avoid any ex post facto problems. The Treaty of Versailles also provided a limited legal precedent. Articles 228 and 229 of the Versailles Treaty had provided for the prosecution of war criminals, though its precedential value was limited, since there were no international prosecutions and few persons were ultimately prosecuted before the German Supreme Court at Leipzig.[18] However, the Allies who applied these norms to the Germans did not act similarly with respect to their own violators. The German army had established a section in the *Wehrmacht* to document war crimes by the Allies, but none of the documented cases were pursued. Thus a double standard quite clearly applied. Furthermore, the Allies did not allow the Germans on trial to argue that they had acted no differently than their enemies. This, too, was one-sided.

The ex post facto problem also arose in part with respect to "crimes against humanity." As a solution, the drafters of the London Charter linked this category of crimes to the charges of "crimes against peace" and "war crimes." Thus the definition of "crimes against humanity" included only those crimes committed in relation to the initiation and waging of the war, while similar crimes committed before the outbreak of war in 1939 were not deemed within the purview of applicable law. This link between "crimes against humanity" and the initiation and waging of aggressive war, or "war crimes," was eliminated in 1950 by the United Nations International Law Convention. Since then, the link has been deemed unnecessary, and the charge "crimes against humanity" is applicable in times of war and of peace. This was a significant change in the law.[19]

The essential argument against the legal validity of the charge of "crimes against humanity" rests on the fact that the charge violates "principles of legality"; therefore, the issue cannot be ignored. But several legally significant qualifying factors substantially mitigate the criticism. The "principles of legality," namely that there can be no crime that is not established by law, no penalty without law and no criminal law with ex post facto effect, were embodied in the German Criminal Code of 1871. But in 1935 the Nazi regime removed those principles from the German Criminal Code. The change allowed criminal law to be applied by analogy, meaning it could be interpreted in many new ways and applied ex post facto. The Nazi leadership made this change in the law to facilitate perpetration of their crimes by giving them the color of legal legitimacy. They could not, however, equitably argue at Nuremberg that the very principle they had overturned in 1935 should apply in 1945, when it happened to suit them.

There is probably no more apt statement on the legal nature and consequences of the International Military Tribunal at Nuremberg than Robert H. Jackson's in his Report to the President of the United States dated October 7, 1946, in which he stated, "Many mistakes have been made and many inadequacies must be confessed. But I am consoled by the fact that in proceedings of this novelty, errors and missteps may also be instructive to the future."

What is particularly significant with respect to the legal legacy is what followed the IMT proceedings. These developments are essentially:

(1) the establishment under international law of the Nuremberg principles;[20]
(2) the fact that these principles would become the starting point of codification and would ultimately become well established international criminal law;[21] and
(3) that the Nuremberg Tribunal would lead to the establishment of a permanent international criminal tribunal.

An objective assessment of post-Nuremberg legal developments can be appropriately based on the identification of international legal instruments attributable to Nuremberg. They include the following, some of which are more directly linked to that precedent than others:

- the 1946 General Assembly Resolution embodying the Nuremberg Principles;[22]
- the 1950 International Law Commission report embodying the Nuremberg Principles;
- the 1948 Genocide Convention;[23]
- in some respects, the 1949 Geneva Conventions;[24]
- the two draft statutes for the establishment of an international criminal court produced by a special committee of the UN General Assembly in 1951[25] and in 1953;[26]
- the 1968 Convention on the Non-Applicability of Statutory Limitations to War Crimes and Crimes Against Humanity;[27]
- the General Assembly resolutions on the duty to prosecute or extradite persons accused of war crimes and crimes against humanity of 1971 and 1973;
- the 1974 UN General Assembly Consensus Resolution defining aggression;[28]
- the 1996 Code of Crimes Against the Peace and Security of Mankind;[29] and
- the 1994 draft statute for an international criminal court and the work of the United Nation's 1996 Preparatory Committee on the establishment of an international criminal court.[30]

These international legal developments must, however, be appraised individually.

First, aggression, which reflects the charge of "crimes against peace" in Article 6 (a) of the IMT's statute, has not been embodied in an international convention that clearly states that aggression is an international crime for which individual responsibility exists and for which a penalty shall be imposed. Aggression is so far only embodied in a UN General Assembly resolution adopted by consensus. Furthermore, it is difficult to argue that the custom and practice of states evidences compliance with this resolution, considering the number of cases in which its prohibition has been violated. Nevertheless, it can be argued that general principles of law clearly prohibit aggression. However, the question is not whether treaties, some custom and general principles prohibit aggression, but whether the prohibition is in the nature of a prescriptive penal norm. That conclusion is, unfortunately, highly questionable. Thus, the legacy of Article 6 (a) has yet to have a realistic effect.

Second, "war crimes" have been significantly elaborated in the four Geneva Conventions of August 12, 1949, and the two Additional Protocols of 1977. Several other conventions on the regulation of armed conflicts have also emerged since 1945.[31] To the extent that one can trace the influence of Nuremberg on the elaboration of these international instruments, the legal legacy is a positive one.

Third, with respect to "crimes against humanity," no specific convention has been developed. The Genocide Convention of 1948 does cover a substantial portion of the conduct that was deemed within the meaning of "crimes against humanity." It fails, however, to include social and political groups within its scope. Also, it fails to include mass killings and mass degradation of human rights when they are not accompanied by the intent to destroy the protected group "in whole or in part." As a result, a number of mass killings whose numbers have reached extraordinary proportions, as did those in Bangladesh and Cambodia, are not necessarily included within the meaning of genocide because most of the victims do not belong to a different ethnic or religious group. This gap leaves many large-scale victimizations that have occurred in various countries outside the protective coverage of the convention. The fact that these and similar violations of international humanitarian law are included in the meaning of "crimes against humanity" is evidence of the need for a specialized convention on this category of crimes.

Fourth, as for the establishment of a permanent international criminal tribunal, the IMT's legacy was visible in the 1951 and 1953 United Nations drafts and subsequently in the 1993–94 reports of the International Law Commission (ILC). The United Nations has been considering these questions since 1995, as will be discussed below.

Fifth, concerning the codification of international crimes, the 1954 Draft Code of Offenses Against the Peace and Security of Mankind has been replaced by the 1996 Draft Code of Crimes Against the Peace and

Security of Mankind, which has been approved by the UN General Assembly. Considering both the slow progress and the lack of specificity with which the Draft Code of Crimes is presently drafted, it is difficult to predict wide acceptance by United Nations member states. Since it is limited to five crimes—namely aggression, war crimes, genocide, crimes against humanity and attacks upon United Nations personnel—it cannot be considered a codification of international criminal law, which includes twenty-five crimes.[32]

Sixth, Nuremberg focused on individual criminal responsibility for conduct that was the product of state policy and for which collective responsibility and state responsibility could have been assessed. Those who established the IMT were careful to avoid the notions of state and collective responsibility, except with respect to criminal organizations such as the SS, SD and SA. The simple reason is that these governments did not want to establish a principle that could one day be applied to them. The notion of collective criminal responsibility for membership in a criminal organization now seems to have become more than an extension of the common law's expanded concept of criminal conspiracy. Indeed, contemporary non-common law legislation on organized crime in many countries criminalizes individual conduct based on membership in a criminal organization or enterprise.

Finally, in addition to the specific instruments mentioned above, there were also instruments reflecting the moral-ethical values and intellectual ferment deriving from Nuremberg. To a large extent, one may include the various human rights instruments that have developed since World War II in this category.

For the reasons suggested earlier, it is difficult to assess and appraise the impact of the moral, ethical, intellectual and social consciousness dimensions of Nuremberg's legal legacy on the development of law and legal institutions in the fields of international humanitarian and international human rights law. Nevertheless, it seems a logical conclusion to attribute to this legacy some influence or impact on the development of law and legal institutions in these fields.

The Moral-Ethical Legacy

There is an intangible Nuremberg legacy that has permeated social values since 1945, shaping the social consciousness of subsequent generations. It is difficult to measure or evaluate the impact of such subjective factors on the individual and collective values and attitudes that have developed since then. However, one can readily perceive a certain moral-ethical impact on individual and social values and the social consciousness that reflects these values. These considerations are evidenced, in part, by the attitudes and values concerning peace and arms control, whose contemporary thrust is no longer the attempt to formulate legal norms prohibiting aggression or criminalizing crimes against peace, but instead to develop norms that insure a right to peace. The rise of the peace movement throughout the world, which has largely influenced contemporary developments in disarmament, may be considered an outgrowth, or at least a reflection of, Nuremberg, even though it is not directly related to Nuremberg as such. But it is Nuremberg, as a symbol of what occurred during World War II, that is present in the minds of those who seek to prevent a recurrence of such events.

Granted, it is not easy, nor at times desirable or useful, to distinguish between moral and ethical values and between moral-ethical and legal values. The reason is that all are factors on the same continuum: moral-ethical considerations shape social consciousness and social consciousness impacts on the development of law and legal institutions. However, and perhaps more important, the impact of moral-ethical factors on social consciousness may indeed be more significant in terms of the prevention of harmful conduct than the presumed general deterrence of the law, though they are interrelated. These social values and the social consciousness they generate produce more significant deterrence than the law, specifically when law is unenforced. The recurrent fact of international crimes is evidence of this unfortunate reality.

When we assess the impact of the past on the future, we must consider the new and commonly shared values of the world community. We must also consider in that assessment the heightening of social consciousness based on moral-ethical and social values, taken in their global context, along with the development of law and legal institutions that they engender.

There is a paradox, however, in that the Allies in establishing the IMT sought to demonstrate that "might does not make right." Yet, if it were not for their might, there could not have been a right, or at least there could not have been a trial. In that respect, the French philosopher Blaise Pascal reminds us that:

> Justice without force is important. Force without justice is tyrannical. Justice without force is infringed because there is always the mean. One must, therefore, combine justice and force, and, therefore make strong what is right and make right what is wrong.[33]

Establishing a Permanent International Criminal Court
The question of an international criminal court did not come up be-

fore the UN General Assembly until 1989, at a special session of the General Assembly on the subject of drugs. At that session, Trinidad and Tobago[34] suggested consideration of the establishment of a specialized international criminal court for drug-related offenses.[35]

On the basis of this 1989 special session, the ILC was asked in 1990 to report on international criminal jurisdiction, but not to prepare a draft statute. In 1991, the ILC prepared a report that was well received by the General Assembly's Sixth Committee and was asked to continue its work on the topic. In 1993 the ILC, to its credit, went beyond preparing a report; instead, it prepared a Draft Statute for an International Criminal Tribunal. The text was in many ways similar to the Draft Statute for the Creation of an International Criminal Jurisdiction to Implement the Apartheid Convention.[36] Though the 1993 draft statute was also well received by the Sixth Committee, the ILC amended its text to reflect certain governmental political considerations. The revised text was submitted to the Sixth Committee in 1994, at the General Assembly's forty-ninth session, and is the basis of current efforts.

In December 1994, the General Assembly adopted Resolution 49/53, which created an Ad Hoc Committee on the Establishment of an International Criminal Court. This committee, open to all United Nations member states, met twice in 1995 and thoroughly discussed the issues surrounding an international criminal court on the basis of the 1994 ILC Draft Statute. By then, a new political climate had developed; in December 1995, the General Assembly adopted Resolution 50/46 setting up a Preparatory Committee on the Establishment of an International Criminal Court, open to all member states, which would meet twice in 1996 and prepare "consolidated texts" for a draft international criminal court statute. Unlike the ad hoc committee, which essentially discussed issues, the preparatory committee had a mandate to draft a text. But states opposing an international criminal court or preferring to postpone it until some future date managed to delay drafting during the committee's first session.

The preparatory committee concluded its first session by adopting a summary report, which became part of a final report published as a United Nations document in October 1996. The preparatory committee continued its work in 1997, and a plenipotentiary conference was held in Italy in 1998.

Conclusion

The Nuremberg legacy has best been reflected in the intellectual ferment that developed in the wake of the events of World War II. Indeed, this intellectual ferment is tangible in books and articles, both scientific and fictional, movies and documentaries, speeches and debates in all media forms, as well as various other forms of human communication such as group discussion and public speeches; in educational materials, classroom instruction, legal doctrine and jurisprudence; and in the utterances and actions of governmental, intergovernmental, nongovernmental and international bodies. All these manifestations fall into the category of intellectual ferment, and it is precisely because of the moral-ethical component of the Nuremberg legacy that this process has developed.

It is beyond the scope of this chapter to attempt to develop a theory on how to quantify or appraise the significance or impact of Nuremberg on social consciousness and the development of law and legal institutions. Nevertheless, the point needs to be made that a corollary relationship exists, both objectively and subjectively, between all the interconnected and interacting factors mentioned above. Further, it is a valid assumption that the intellectual ferment that has persisted since that period has strengthened individual and collective values in many societies, and that in turn has contributed to a heightening of social consciousness, resulting in the development of law and legal institutions. Thus, to a large extent, the legal legacy of Nuremberg may be viewed as a direct outgrowth of the cumulative effect of these factors, which in some way can be traced to the moral-ethical legacy of Nuremberg. Regrettably, however, nothing said above has lessened the human tragedies of the post-Nuremberg world, even as the resulting human toll exceeds that of World War II. The contemporary examples of the wars in Cambodia, the former Yugoslavia and Rwanda, and the atrocities attendant to them, bear out this point. Thus deterrence, the ultimate goal of Nuremberg, has yet to be achieved in a world more divided today than it was fifty years ago.

The sense of justice, however philosophers and social and behavioral scientists may argue about it, is, in this author's opinion, an irreducible aspect of our social needs. It is also part of the fundamental value systems of most societies throughout the history of the varied civilizations that have existed since *homo sapiens* organized itself into social settings. What human experience indicates is that the value of justice, its content and application vary between individuals and from one social group to another. They can also be seen to change over time within the same individual and the same group. Yet at the risk of greatly oversimplifying this complex question, it is nonetheless correct to say that contemporary social values in almost every society include the aspiration toward international justice. A better world would be a system of equal and fair justice that would strengthen world order and provide deterrence and retribution on a nonselective basis for the decision-makers and major perpetrators who commit serious international crimes. But the need, no matter how much shared throughout the world community, is effectively thwarted by decision-makers whose cynicism and callousness are only too visible to those with eyes to see. Instead of promoting, they subvert and surely impede it, however pious their pronouncements may be.

As one who has carefully studied the evolution of international criminal law, and more recently has been a close and direct observer of one of the tragic events mentioned above, I must regrettably conclude that, so long as we are unable or unwilling to establish a permanent institution of international criminal justice free from political controls and capable of enforcing its judgments no matter where or against whom, we are condemned to repeat the mistakes of the past and suffer their consequences.[37]

The Nuremberg promise of justice is yet to be fulfilled. However, without its legacy we would not know how much we have progressed, nor how much progress is still needed to achieve international criminal justice.

World public opinion is far ahead of the cautious position of many governments on the establishment of an effective and fair system of international criminal justice. In fact, the gap is wide, and governments cannot ignore it if they wish to retain their credibility about establishing such a system of justice that would operate under the rule of law, free of the manipulations of realpolitik that give the pursuit of political settlements priority over justice.

The dedicated idealism of many scholars, researchers, public officials and concerned citizens throughout the world continues to demand an independent, fair and effective system of international criminal justice. This idealism is driven by our hope that it can overcome the opposition of political cynicism and the reticence that for so long led to inaction. Impunity must no longer be the reward of those who commit the most egregious international crimes and serious violations of human rights. The quantum of human harm produced since World War II by conflicts of a noninternational character, by purely internal conflicts and victimization by tyrannical regimes far exceeds the combined outcomes of World War I and World War II. Yet the overwhelming majority of perpetrators have escaped with impunity. World public opinion, however, rejects the cynicism and complacency of governments that manipulate the processes of justice to attain political ends.

An international system of criminal justice might not stop future conflicts and horrors, but it could have a deterrent effect. If so, it could save lives and prevent human depredations. If nothing else, however, it would symbolize certain shared values of the world community. And finally, it would vindicate the victims of international crimes, serving as a reminder to us and to future generations of the plight of the victims and the misdeeds of the perpetrators. To paraphrase the philosopher George

Santayana, if we do not record and learn the bitter lessons of the past, we are condemned to repeat our mistakes.[38]

Notes

1. This chapter is a modified English translation of "Das "Vermächtnis von Nürnberg:" eine historische Bewertung fünfzig Jahre danach," in Gerd Hankel and Gerhard Study, eds., *Strafgerichte gegen Menschheitsverbrechen* (Hamburg: Hamburger Edition, 1995).

2. Prosecution and Punishment of Major War Criminals of the European Axis (London Agreement), London, August 8, 1945, reprinted in Charles I. Bevans, ed., *Treaties and Other International Agreements of the United States of America* 3, 1238 (1970); Annex to Prosecution and Punishment of Major War Criminals of the European Axis (London Agreement), London, August 8, 1945, reprinted in Bevans, 1239 [hereinafter London Charter]. The Four Major Powers originally signed the London Agreement and nineteen other countries eventually acceded to it. For a history of international investigatory bodies and international prosecutions, see M. Cherif Bassiouni, "From Versailles to Rwanda in 75 Years: The Need to Establish a Permanent International Criminal Court," *Harvard Human Rights Journal* 10 (1997): 1.

3. The United States conducted its proceedings in the same Nuremberg courthouse where the IMT conducted its trials, giving rise to some confusion between IMT proceedings and what were then called the "American" trials.

4. In re Yamashita, 327 U.S. 1 (1945) (containing strong dissents by Justice Rutledge and Justice Murphy). See generally Richard Lael, *The Yamashita Precedent: War Crimes and Command Responsibility* (Wilmington, Del.: Scholarly Resources, 1982); A. Frank Reel, *The Case of General Yamashita* (Chicago: University of Chicago Press, 1949). Frank Reel defended General Yamashita before the Military Commission that tried him in the Philippines.

5. The case of Paul Touvier is a recent example. Touvier was convicted and sentenced to life in prison on April 19, 1994. See Ted Morgan, "The Hidden Henchman," *The New York Times*, May 22, 1994; Leila Sadat Wexler, "The Interpretation of the Nuremberg Principles by the French Court of Cassation: From Touvier to Barbie and Back Again," *Columbia Journal of Transnational Law* 32 (1994): 290.

6. 8 U.S.C.S. § 1451 (1994).

7. Germany had a twenty-five year statute of limitations on murder. This meant that, after 1969, no war crimes or crimes against humanity could be prosecuted.

8. G.A. Res. 2840 (XXVI), 26 UN GAOR Supp. (No. 29), p. 88, UN Doc. A/8429 (1971) (hereinafter GA Resolution 2840).

9. Principles of International Co-operation in the Detention, Arrest, Extradition and Punishment of Persons Guilty of War Crimes and Crimes Against

Humanity, G.A. Res. 3074 (XXXVII), 28 UN GAOR Supp. (No. 30), p. 78, UN Doc. A/9030, December 3, 1973 (hereinafter GA Resolution 3074).

10. Nowhere in the international legal literature on extradition is there any reported national case which relies upon or cites any of these resolutions.

11. Professor Antonio Cassese, former president of the ICTY, has said that the "concepts that emerged from Nuremberg—one of the highest points in our march towards legal civilization and an awareness of human dignity—are in danger of being silted up." Antonio Cassese, *Violence and Law in the Modern Age* (Princeton, New Jersey: Princeton University Press, 1988), 147–48.

12. For a personalized account of many behind the scenes decisions, see Telford Taylor, *The Anatomy of the Nuremberg Trials* (New York: Alfred A. Knopf, 1992).

13. In September 1944, Winston Churchill proposed that the Nazi leaders should be summarily executed. Franklin Roosevelt agreed. But by 1945, the United States had changed its position. See Bradley F. Smith, *The Road to Nuremberg* (New York: Basic Books, 1981), 46-47. The British persisted in their position, as evidenced in the aide-mémoire from the United Kingdom to the United States of April 23, 1945, reprinted in Robert H. Jackson, *Report of Robert H. Jackson, United States Representative to the International Conference on Military Trials* (Washington, DC: U.S. Government Printing Office, 1949), 11–12. The British aide-mémoire stated that it was "conceded" that the Nazi leaders "must suffer death," their summary execution without trial was the "preferable course." Ibid., 18. But see Henry L. Stimson, "The Nuremberg Trial: Landmark in Law," *Foreign Affairs* 25 (1947): 180, acknowledging the great triumph of the rule of law and stating that the accused were given "what they had denied their own opponents—the protection of the law."

14. During the debates on the charter in London, Professor André Gros of France repeatedly argued that no international law existed on the question of "crimes against peace." To which Sir David Maxwell Fyfe of Great Britain peremptorily concluded: "We declare what international law is.... there won't be any discussion on whether it is international law or not." See Jackson, Report, 97–99. The position of the USSR, expressed by General Nikitchenko, was based on a thesis that all the crimes derived from Hitlerite aggression. (ibid.). The British and Soviet positions fitted the U.S. view that all the crimes derived from a conspiracy and policy to commit aggression and that this was the basis for the prosecutions, a basis from which the other crimes flowed.

15. However, it should be added that it was premised on the certainty of guilty verdicts for the accused, with no risk that the very principles upon which guilt was to be established would be applied to the Allies. Thus the Allies opted for the legal process in the certainty that the law they established would prevail, the accused would be found guilty, and their own leaders and commanders would face no legal consequences.

16. Nevertheless, the selection of the twenty-four accused was arbitrary. No industrialist was prosecuted, even though many had used slave labor and could have been charged with crimes against humanity. Others were prosecuted only because they symbolically represented certain organizations or ideas. Some industrialists were, however, tried in the subsequent U.S. proceedings.

17. See Hans Laternser, "Looking Back at the Nuremberg Trials with Special Consideration of the Processes Against Military Leaders," *Whittier Law Review* 9 (1985): 557; A. Von Knieriem, *The Nuremberg Trials* (E.D. Schmitt, trans., Chicago: H. Regnery Co., 1959); Hans-Heinrich Jescheck, *Die Verantwortlichkeit der Staatsorgane seit Nürnberg* (1952); Hans Ehard, "The Nuremberg Trial against Major War Criminals and International Law," *American Journal of International Law* 43 (1949): 223; Gordon Ireland, "Ex Post Facto From Rome to Tokyo," *Temple Law Quarterly* 21 (1948): 22; Bernard D. Meltzer, "A Note on Some Aspects of the Nuremberg Debate," *University of Chicago Law Review* 14 (1947): 455. For interesting accounts by four of the defense counsels at the trials, see Carl Haensell, "The Nuremberg Trial Revisited," *DePaul Law Review* 13 (1964): 248; Herbert Kraus, "The Nuremberg Trial of the Major War Criminals: Reflections after Seventeen Years," *DePaul Law Review* 13 (1964): 233; Otto Kranzbuhler, "Nuremberg Eighteen Years Afterwards," *DePaul Law Review* 14 (1965): 333; Otto Pannenbecker, "The Nuremberg War-Crimes Tribunal," *DePaul Law Review* 14 (1965): 348.

18. The German Supreme Court had determined to try forty-five individuals out of a list of 895 cases, but only sixteen were tried.

19. At Nuremberg, only two defendants were convicted of crimes against humanity alone—Streicher and Von Schirach—but fourteen other defendants were convicted of war crimes and crimes against humanity. See, e.g., M. Cherif Bassiouni, *Crimes Against Humanity in International Criminal Law* (Dordrecht: Kluwer Academic Publishers, 1992).

20. Principles of the Nuremberg Tribunal, 1950 Report of the ILC, (Principles of International Law Recognized in the Tribunal), July 29, 1950, UN Doc. A/1316 (1950), reprinted in *American Journal of International Law* 4 (Supp.) (1950): 126 (hereinafter 1950 ILC Report).

21. For a history of the International Law Commission's efforts on codification, see M. Cherif Bassiouni, "The History of the Draft Code of Crimes Against the Peace and Security of Mankind," in "Commentaries on the International Law Commission's 1991 Draft Code of Crimes Against the Peace and Security of Mankind," *Nouvelles Etudes Penales* 11 (1993).

22. Affirmation of the Principles of International Law Recognized by the Charter of the Nuremberg Tribunal, December 11, 1946, UN General Assembly Resolution 95(I), UN Doc. A/64/Add.1 (1946) (hereinafter Nuremberg principles).

23. Convention on the Prevention and Suppression of the Crime of Genocide, December 9, 1948, reprinted in *American Journal of International Law* 45 (1951): 7 (Supp.) (hereinafter 1948 Genocide Convention).

24. See Geneva Convention for the Amelioration of the Condition of the Wounded and Sick in Armed Forces in the Field (August 12, 1949), *United Nations Treaty Series* 75: 31; Geneva Convention for the Amelioration of the Condition of the Wounded, Sick and Shipwrecked Members of the Armed Forces at Sea (August 12, 1949), *United Nations Treaty Series* 75: 85; Geneva Convention Relative to the Treatment of Prisoners of War (August 12, 1949), *United Nations Treaty Series* 75: 155; Geneva Convention Relative to the Protection of Civilian Persons in Time of War (August 12, 1949), *United Nations Treaty Series* 75: 287 (hereinafter 1949 Geneva Conventions).

25. Draft Statute for an International Criminal Court (Annex to the Report of the Committee on International Criminal Jurisdiction, August 31, 1951), 7 UN GAOR Supp. 11, UN Doc. A/2136 (1952), p. 23.

26. Revised Draft Statute for an International Court (Annex to the Report on International Criminal Jurisdiction, August 20, 1953), 9 UN GAOR Supp. 12, UN Doc. A/2645 at 21 (1954).

27. Convention on the Non-Applicability of Statutory Limitations to War Crimes and Crimes Against Humanity, opened for signatures, 26 November 1968, 754 UNT.S. 73 (entered into force 11 November 1970).

28. Definition of Aggression (United Nations General Assembly Resolution), adopted 14 December 1974, UN G.A. Res. 3314 (XXIX), 29 UNGAOR Supp. (No. 31), p. 142, UN Doc. A/9631 (1974) (hereinafter Definition of Aggression).

29. Draft Code of Crimes Against the Peace and Security of Mankind: Titles and texts of articles on the Draft Code of Crimes Against Peace and Security if Mankind adopted by the International Law Commission at its 48th Session (1996), UN GAOR International Law Commission 48th Sess., UN Doc. A/CN.4/L.532 (1996). See also Draft Code of Offenses Against the Peace and Security of Mankind, July 19, 1954, 9 UN GAOR Supp. (No. 9), p. 11, UN Doc. A/26/93 (1954).

30. See Report of the International Law Commission, 46th Sess., May 2-July 22, 1994, UN GAOR, 49th Sess., UN Doc. A/49/10 (1994); Report of the Preparatory Committee on the Establishment of an International Criminal Court (Proceedings of the Preparatory Committee during March-April and August 1996), UN GAOR, 51st Sess., Supp. No. 22, UN Doc. A/51/22 (1996); and Report of the Preparatory Committee on the Establishment of an International Criminal Court (comp. of proposals), UN GAOR, 51st Sess., Supp. No. 22A, UN Doc. A/51/22 (1996).

31. See, e.g., Convention for the Protection of Cultural Property in the Event of Armed Conflict (May 14, 1954), *United Nations Treaty Series* 249: 240.

32. They include aggression; genocide; crimes against humanity; war crimes; crimes against United Nations and associate personnel; unlawful possession or use or emplacement of weapons; theft of nuclear materials; mercenarism; apartheid; slavery and slave-related practices; torture and other forms of cruel, inhuman or degrading treatment or punishment; unlawful human experimentation; piracy; aircraft hijacking and unlawful acts against international air safety; unlawful acts against the safety of maritime navigation and the safety of platforms on the high seas; threat and use of force against internationally protected persons; taking of civilian hostages; unlawful use of the mail; unlawful traffic in drugs and related drug offenses; destruction and/or theft of national treasures; unlawful acts against certain internationally protected elements of the environment; international traffic in obscene materials; falsification and counterfeiting; unlawful interference with international submarine cables; and bribery of foreign public officials.

33. Blaise Pascal, *Pensées: The Provincial Letters*, trans. W.F. Trotter (1941).

34. This was due to the efforts of then Prime Minister Arthur Robinson, whose efforts of many years in support of an international criminal court deserve recognition.

35. An earlier convention on terrorism had been elaborated by the League of Nations in 1937, with a protocol establishing an international criminal court. That convention, however, was ratified only by India and never entered into effect. Vespasian Pella played an important role in bringing about that convention, and he is still remembered for this important contribution.

36. UN Doc E/CN.4/1426, January 19, 1980. That draft statute was prepared for the UN by this writer.

37. We are nevertheless one step closer, in that a diplomatic conference for the establishment of a permanent international criminal court was convened in Rome from June 15 to July 17, 1998. (Editor's note: see Epilogue, this volume.)

38. M. Cherif Bassiouni, "Searching for Peace and Achieving Justice: The Need for Accountability." *Law and Contemporary Problems* 59: 4 (1996): 9.

Toward a Permanent
International Criminal Court

Donna K. Axel[1]

Many people think that the International Court of Justice, known as the World Court, has the power to try perpetrators of international human rights and humanitarian law (the law of war) as individuals. But it does not. The International Court of Justice has jurisdiction only over complaints by states, and only in limited respects. Because there is no world criminal court of human rights at present, the United Nations Security Council created the ad hoc tribunals for the former Yugoslavia and Rwanda to provide a mechanism of accountability for these recent and terrible examples of genocide and gross violations of human rights and humanitarian law. These tribunals illustrate the importance of a permanent international justice mechanism, as well as the problems of carrying out justice on an ad hoc basis.

The attention paid to these tribunals bolstered a longstanding proposal to create a permanent international criminal court (ICC), which was revived in 1989 by Trinidad and Tobago. This international criminal court will be different from any other existing court. Unlike the tribunals created following World War II, a permanent international criminal court will not be limited to a specific situation or conflict. The ICC will also differ from the International Court of Justice based in the Hague in that the permanent court will try individuals. This means that the permanent court could enforce international human rights and humanitarian law against individual perpetrators wherever violations occur, because they have committed crimes that are universally condemned, without all the delays inherent in creating a court from scratch.

This chapter examines the recent progress toward establishing an international criminal court in the wake of increasing public demand for the amelioration of crises using nonmilitary alternatives. The first section provides a brief overview of the United Nations system relevant to understanding the historical development and current status of the ICC, discussed in the second and third sections. The final section emphasizes the significance of a permanent international criminal court against the backdrop of increasing internal armed conflicts with worldwide repercussions.

Background: The United Nations

The United Nations came into being with the signing of the UN Charter in San Francisco in 1945. At that time, fifty-one nations belonged to the organization. Today, 185 member states and observers send more than 3,000 representatives to participate in the annual sessions of the General Assembly. Observers include, for example, Switzerland, the Holy See and the International Committee of the Red Cross (ICRC). Without obtaining official permanent observer status, thousands of representatives of nongovernmental organizations (NGOs) are present during the General Assembly. Delegates representing member states and observers participate by making statements, also called "interventions," before the General Assembly and in various formal and informal discussion groups. NGOs provide documents to delegates and, under special circumstances, make statements, in order to influence the direction of international law.

The General Assembly is broken down into six committees, of which the Sixth Committee is particularly relevant to the formation of the ICC. This committee is the Legal Committee that reviewed the work of the Preparatory Committee (PrepCom) charged with drafting a statute to establish a permanent international criminal court. All countries of the world were invited to send representatives, largely drawn from the Sixth Committee, to participate in the preparatory meetings on the establishment of the ICC.

With respect to the ICC, the Sixth Committee's legal discussion format is taking on the significance of a legislative process, where delegates have begun to negotiate new treaties. The results of Sixth Committee meetings are considered by the General Assembly, the main deliberative organ of the United Nations, where each member state is represented by a single vote. The General Assembly, meeting annually in regular session from mid-September to mid-December, adopts resolutions submitted by the Sixth Committee, making recommendations that reflect the international community's concerns and carry the weight of customary law. Because it would be unprecedented for the General Assembly not to adopt the resolutions submitted by the Sixth Committee, Sixth Committee delegates have, in essence, been creating "soft law"—policy that influences customary law.

The History of the International Criminal Court Establishment Process

In the 1950s, the General Assembly mandated the International Law Commission (ILC) to codify the Nuremberg Principles and prepare a draft statute to create a permanent international criminal court. This commission, which continues to function, consists of thirty-four legal experts elected every five years. No woman has ever served on the ILC. The ILC shelved the task of drafting a statue for an international court primarily because of the polarizing politics of the Cold War, which allowed for no possibility of agreement. But in 1989, Trinidad and Tobago reintroduced the issue of establishment of an ICC because of the desperate situation of drug trafficking—a crime that most states today do not want included under the jurisdiction of the ICC. Nevertheless, in 1989 the General Assembly requested that the ILC prepare a draft statute for a permanent international criminal court.

That same year, the Berlin Wall fell, ending the Cold War and unleashing forces that would ultimately tear apart Yugoslavia. The atrocities occurring in the former Yugoslavia incensed the public, and by 1993 the UN Security Council had established the first ad hoc war crimes tribunal since the Nuremberg and Tokyo tribunals. But, in light of ongoing atrocities throughout the world, many states' delegates and individuals asked why the UN had created an ad hoc court to adjudicate issues only in Europe. The UN Security Council, acting before accusations of racism could escalate and in order to prevent further deaths from equally serious atrocities, created the ad hoc tribunal for Rwanda in 1994. In November 1994, also acting in response to pressure by NGOs, scholars and some delegations, and the increased media attention to the ongoing atrocities in Rwanda and Bosnia-Herzegovina, the ILC presented its final version of the draft statute to the Sixth Committee of the forty-ninth session of the General Assembly. It recommended that a conference of plenipotentiaries be called to draw up a treaty that would enact the statute establishing the court, but did not specify when this conference should be held. In response, the General Assembly established an Ad Hoc Committee to review this draft statute and directed this committee to meet from April 3 to April 13 and from August 14 to August 25, 1995.

At the meetings of the Ad Hoc Committee, most countries favored the establishment of the ICC, with several influential states remaining undecided or opposed. Countries such as China, France, the United Kingdom and the United States did not support the creation of the ICC, believing the time was not ripe for the international community to bring individuals to justice on the basis of international law. Notwithstanding their influence, in December 1995 the General Assembly created a Preparatory Committee and directed it to meet for two three-week sessions in 1996. The PrepCom's task was to assess and review the International Law Commission's draft, with a view to preparing a consolidated text of a treaty to create a permanent international criminal court to present at a diplomatic treaty conference.

During the PrepCom meetings, which took place from March 25 to April 12 and from August 12 to August 30, 1996, delegates discussed how to remedy some of the deficiencies of the ILC draft statute. The issues before the PrepCom included: the relationship of the ICC to the UN; the extent of Security Council control; the crimes and their definitions to be included under the jurisdiction of the court; penalties; general principles of criminal law; compensation for victims; access to the court by individuals as compared with states; the necessity for an independent prosecutor and mechanisms for triggering investigation by the prosecutor; the ICC's relationship to national courts; how to combine the procedures of various legal systems; and qualifications for judges, as well as the requirements of geographical diversity and gender balance.

By April 5, 1996, despite the tediousness of reviewing and compiling texts in preparation for a diplomatic conference, a sufficient number of states had committed themselves to a time-bound framework for completing a text as early as possible. Unofficial reports claimed that these states would press the autumn General Assembly session to decide on the time and place for the diplomatic conference, which Italy offered to host in June 1998.

During PrepCom II (from August 12 to August 30, 1996), a group of states emerged that called themselves the "Like-Minded." These states strongly supported the convening of an early diplomatic conference. At that time, the Like-Minded group included Argentina, Austria, Australia, Canada, Chile, Costa Rica, the Czech Republic, Denmark, Egypt, Finland, Germany, Ghana, Greece, Hungary, Italy, Lesotho, Malawi, New Zealand, Norway, Poland, Portugal, Samoa, Slovenia, South Africa, Sweden, the Netherlands, Trinidad and Tobago, and Venezuela.

Because of the Like-Minded's efforts to persuade their fellow delegates, the PrepCom concluded in its final report that it "considers that it is realistic to regard the holding of a diplomatic conference ... in 1998 as feasible."[2] The PrepCom also concluded that it would need nine more weeks in order to complete a text by April 1998, and resolved to encourage the widest possible participation of states in the process to ensure the legitimacy of that text. The PrepCom recommended that the General Assembly direct it to meet three or four times before the diplomatic conference.

The goals of PrepComs I and II were embodied in the Report of the Preparatory Committee on the Establishment of an International Criminal Court and reviewed by the Sixth Committee of the General Assembly from October 31 to November 1, 1996. The Sixth Committee debated some of the key issues and concerns, and renewed the PrepCom's mandate to complete a draft statute for a treaty conference in 1998.

From November 1 to November 14, 1996, in connection with the general debate of PrepComs I and II, Sixth Committee delegates debated the draft text of the Resolution on the Establishment of an International Criminal Court during informal and closed meetings. This resolution defined the parameters of the PrepCom's work and recommended dates for the PrepCom's future meetings and the date for the treaty conference. These meetings were closed even to accredited nongovernmental organizations. Some states preferred these meetings be kept confidential and requested that delegates not disclose the content of discussions even afterwards. In the end, the delegates agreed on the PrepCom's future workplan and the 1998 date for the diplomatic treaty conference.

The unwavering support of the Like-Minded was one of the key reasons the Sixth Committee adopted a resolution actually specifying 1998 as the year the conference would be held and acknowledging Italy's offer to host it in June of that year. In December 1996, the General Assembly adopted the resolution and directed the PrepCom to meet for three two-week sessions (February 11–21, August 4–15 and December 1–12, 1997) and then three weeks from March 16 to April 3, 1998.

By mid-1997, more states had joined the Like-Minded, to the point where they were "like minded" on some, but no longer all, issues relating to the court. During the August 1997 meetings, members of the group met informally to consider how to respond to other countries that might wish to join, particularly Security Council member states with very different interests, and concluded that it would henceforth be closed to new members. With the date of the treaty conference unofficially slated for June 15 through the end of July 1998, and the Like-Minded's initial goal achieved, this expanded group would now serve as a bloc working to ensure that the international criminal court would be free of Security Council domination and would not end up as just another UN failure.

Status of the ICC:
Issues before the 1997–1998 Preparatory Committee and Results of the Treaty Conference

Despite the progress of the 1996 PrepCom meetings and the Sixth Committee's draft resolution pledging to strive to hold a conference in 1998, a great deal of work remained for the Preparatory Committee at the end of 1997. Before the diplomatic treaty conference, the PrepCom strove to reach consensus on most of the issues involved in creating a new court, in order to leave only a limited number of disputes (reflected by bracketed language in the draft statute) for higher-level representatives to resolve at the actual diplomatic conference. In order for this consensus—necessary if the court is to function effectively and earn the respect of the international community—to be reached, a majority of countries must support the ICC. The ICC establishment process would easily be delayed if the delegates to the 1997 PrepCom could not reach consensus on substantive and procedural issues, or if the negotiation process fails to include a broad sector of society.

The court's legitimacy, however, can only be assured through the participation of delegates from the developing world and the inclusion of women's concerns in the negotiations. The ad hoc tribunals for Rwanda and former Yugoslavia have established the significant impact of war and violence on women and children and the importance of formally including their concerns in any international legal fora. They have also highlighted the differing treatment of women in different regions. Where female victims appearing as witnesses before the Yugoslavia tribunal, for example, were first interviewed privately by mixed teams of women and men, women victims in the same situation in Rwanda were interviewed in groups by male interlocutors, often from the same ethnic group as the accused war criminals. NGOs grouped themselves into caucuses, including a women's caucus, a children's rights caucus, and a victims' rights caucus, in order to ensure that these concerns were addressed in the ICC statute.

States appeared to fall into two categories: those supporting the creation of the ICC before the end of the millennium and those supporting the creation of the ICC in principle, but not in reality. The latter states made their position on the ICC strategically ambiguous by raising seemingly legitimate concerns. For example, states would claim to support the court but not specify an establishment date. While this may have been a real concern for some states that believe creating an effective court may take more time, it was also a delaying tactic. In their attempts to mask their intentions to the public, states opposed to the ICC tried to undermine the establishment process by supporting issues which would either weaken the court or delay a diplomatic conference.

Underlying an apparent agreement to see a permanent ICC come into being were the fundamental issues affecting its potential to do justice and function effectively as a mechanism of accountability: How will states relinquish some of their power to an independent judiciary? Will states permit a prosecutor to receive information from any source and investigate any matter ex officio? Other key issues included creating an efficient and judicious trigger mechanism to activate the ICC's prosecutorial role; determining when the ICC will supersede national courts; defining the relationship between the court and the UN; ensuring a diverse panel of judges; setting the scope of jurisdiction over certain crimes; and elaborating the state's role and liability as defendant.

Most states expressed support for an ICC that is independent, treaty-based (as opposed to one created by Security Council resolution, like the ad hoc tribunals) and closely linked to the UN, since a treaty could provide the court with the basis for independence and authority. States could then choose whether to become parties to the treaty. However, whether or not the treaty would permit states to limit their obligations through "reservations" was an issue to be reviewed. State representatives also recognized that a cooperative arrangement between the ICC and the UN would ensure the court's universality and moral authority, as well as its administrative and financial viability. Similarly, this close association would enhance the ICC's legitimacy and ensure proper performance of all its functions.

Government representatives were not in agreement as to the specific form of the UN–ICC relationship. Some states recognized the need for the ICC to interact with the UN—for example, where there are UN peacekeeping operations in progress, UN interests are at stake, and administrative matters need to be addressed. However, reliance upon UN personnel and administrative oversight is not necessarily the best arrangement for these international criminal tribunals, in light of the court's need for independence.

States generally supported the election of judges representing the principal legal systems of the world in order to ensure an equitable ICC. Accordingly, states commented during the 1996 PrepCom meetings that judges should be elected "on the basis of equitable geographical representation..." and that "there was a need for balance and diversity in [the court's] composition."[3] While it was also noted that the court's composition should ensure gender balance, the view was expressed that "there should be no quota system for female judges, nor quotas of any kind, since the sole criteria should be the high qualification and experience of the candidate." Despite the ideal of diversity, specified by some parties, states have not yet determined the mechanism to establish an equitably diverse court. Moreover, it was the 1996 commentary on the draft text, not the later draft going into the treaty conference, that specified the need to ensure geographical and gender balance. Therefore, there was a danger that this need could have been ignored by the high-level country representatives.

Due to heavy lobbying by women's groups, as well as recognition by some governments of the importance of including women and gender experts in the court system, the final treaty then did in fact include the provision that

> states parties shall, in the selection of judges, take into account the need, within the membership of the court, for: (i) the representation of the principal legal systems of the world; (ii) equitable geographical representation; and (iii) a fair representation of female and male judges.[4]

The treaty further states that

> states parties shall also take into account the need to include judges

with legal expertise on specific issues, including, but not limited to, violence against women or children.[5]

Many states recognize that a diverse and equitable court cannot be achieved without maintaining the same sort of diversity throughout the process of establishing the ICC. Despite some states' and NGOs' attempts to include more participants from developing states and experts on women's issues, the absence of such participants in PrepComs I and II threatened to limit the universal acceptance of this proposed court. Financial limitations and the perception that the ICC is being created by the richest countries in order to prosecute less powerful nations and their citizens are two key reasons that many developing nations were not significantly represented during the early Preparatory Committee meetings.

Many states and NGOs from developing nations, as well as NGOs representing women's concerns, did not participate in the ICC PrepCom until February 1997 (PrepCom III) because these negotiations had been considered merely theoretical in nature. Not until December 1996, when the General Assembly adopted the resolution providing for a treaty conference in 1998, did the states begin drafting an actual treaty. Prior to December 1996, NGOs that had been closely monitoring the progress of the negotiations made a strategic decision not to reach out to other NGOs or the media, fearing that spotlighting the issue could cause government decision-makers to back off from negotiations before any substantive progress had been made. These NGOs believed that maintaining a low profile would better help the negotiations move from their purely theoretical focus to the practical focus leading to an actual treaty conference.

The absence of gender experts and of representatives from developing states during the first stages of the ICC negotiations meant that these government and NGO representatives had to lobby to alter a draft text already reviewed by the delegates in 1996. In fact, the International Law Commission's draft text and the delegates' proposals of alternatives to this text are already embodied in Volume I of the Report of the Preparatory Committee on the Establishment of an International Criminal Court.[6] But because some PrepCom delegates recognize that the court will gain respect and legitimacy only if the statute incorporates a gender perspective and considers the views of representatives of developing states, they have been willing, if not compelled, to listen to the voices of these segments of society.

There has been general agreement that the jurisdiction of the court should be limited to the most serious crimes of concern to the international community as a whole, including genocide, war crimes and crimes against humanity. It is argued that this limitation exists to avoid trivializing the role and functions of the court and interfering with the jurisdiction of national courts. Although this was discussed at the February 1997 Prep-Com, the December 1997 PrepCom revisited the definition of war crimes.

During the treaty conference the delegates determined that other crimes could be included at a later stage under the court's jurisdiction in addition to the core crimes. In particular, some states' interventions stressed the importance of including crimes such as aggression and drug trafficking, but there were difficulties surrounding their immediate inclusion. To keep from stalling the process as a result of these difficulties, states chose to incorporate a provision in the statute permitting the inclusion of other serious crimes at a later date.

Prior to the February 1997 PrepCom, many states appeared to agree that, because there is no generally accepted definition of aggression for the purpose of determining individual criminal liability, any attempt to elaborate such a definition could substantially delay the creation of the court. However, during PrepCom III, Germany proposed a definition of aggression that was favorably received. The conflict here is that the Security Council has responsibility under the UN Charter to define and determine acts of aggression, but many delegates prefer to keep the court independent of Security Council control. If this charge is included under the jurisdiction of the court, will the ICC and the prosecutor depend upon the Security Council to determine when potential acts of aggression should be investigated? How will the Security Council's role interfere with the court's independence? Should the ICC prosecutor be permitted to investigate situations already under Security Council review? The final statute states that the crime of aggression will be included under the court's jurisdiction once the states can come to a consensus on its definition and on how the court will exercise jurisdiction over it.

The main reasons drug trafficking is not included under the jurisdiction of the court include the danger that the court would be flooded with cases and would lack the necessary resources to conduct the lengthy and complex investigations required to prosecute these crimes. Also, many states do not want to jeopardize the millions of dollars they confiscate in the course of handling such cases themselves. Moreover, because these crimes often involve highly sensitive information and confidential strategies to obtain such information, any international prosecution would likely reveal the clandestine strategies of undercover police forces.

Complementarity—achieving a proper balance between the ICC and national authorities, including national courts—was crucial to creating a text that was acceptable to a large number of states. Most states agreed that the court's jurisdiction should prevail in cases where national courts cannot or will not function effectively. They generally also agreed that the ICC was not intended to supersede the existing jurisdiction of national courts. Here, governments are concerned about the ICC's potential to limit their own sovereign authority and to undermine their own court's decisions, or even to be used against their own leaders. Thus far, states have been slow to relinquish their power, a symptom of a fundamental fear that almost stalled the establishment of the ICC and that hinders its independence.

There were a number of critical issues before the government representatives that speak to whether the international criminal court will be a truly independent court. The first question was whether states automatically consent to the ICC's jurisdiction when they become parties to the statute. Some states argued that the court should require states to "opt in" on a case-by-case basis, essentially asking for consent before establishing jurisdiction. Some states did not oppose the permanent court's jurisdiction over all core crimes because of their serious nature and their status as customary law. Other states supported inherent jurisdiction only for genocide, since many states are already a party to the genocide convention. However, requiring the "opt in" mechanism, whereby states can and must consent to being investigated, undermines the already universally binding nature of the most serious crimes, as established by the legacy of Nuremberg and Tokyo. This is another legal rationale for politically motivated behavior, allowing states to control who can be a defendant before the ICC. In the final statute, the ICC requires the consent of either the state of the accused or the state on whose territory the offense was committed before investigation can begin. In this way, the statute disregards the custodial state and the state whose nationals were victims for purposes of consent to an investigation of a suspected criminal or a crime committed elsewhere.

Prior to the treaty conference, all states agreed that the court had to be independent in order to exercise its power judiciously, but states had not agreed how cases would be brought to the court's attention in order to initiate investigation by the prosecutor. Governments that wanted a court only if they could control who may be investigated stalled progress at the Preparatory Committee meetings and undermined the potential for the court to be free from Security Council control. Some states supported a completely independent prosecutor's office that could initiate investigations ex officio (on its own authority), on the basis of information obtained from any source, including citizens' groups and individuals. States looked to the prosecutors of the two ad hoc tribunals as a successful model of this type of independence. However, some states opposed an independent prosecutor because they feared he or she would act out of political motivations, which would undermine the court's credibility.

The "anti-independent prosecutor" cloak most likely hides states' desire to preserve their power. States arguing in this way suggest that only states with a direct interest in a case should be entitled to lodge complaints. Interested states, as identified above, include the state where the crime was committed and the state of nationality of the suspect. This restriction is a fundamental limitation of the concept of universal jurisdiction in international law and of the rights and obligations of parties to prosecute violators of these laws. Besides, does not every state become an interested party once a national government fails to prosecute an international crime?

Prior to the treaty conference, another concern was that the ICC's independence would be sacrificed if the Security Council alone was authorized to initiate investigations by the prosecutor. The five permanent members (China, France, the Russian Federation, the United Kingdom and the United States) of the fifteen-member Security Council could insist that the council retain a veto power over which cases are brought to trial. Through its veto power, the Security Council's permanent members could keep their own citizens out of the court, or stop prosecutions and investigations in cases that went against their own interests. The ICC's independence and impartiality, and also its ability to conduct fair investigations, are essential to ensure the court's international respect. Although the Security Council's role is not clearly defined, it is limited in some respects. The final treaty permits the Security Council to prevent investigations only by unanimous vote. This means that the prosecutor may commence investigations until blocked by the Security Council. The problematic aspect here is that the Security Council can renew its veto annually—a process which is certain to ensure the disappearance of evidence and witnesses. States must be cautious not to grant more authority to it than already elaborated under the UN Charter.

Government representatives began discussing these topics seriously in early 1997, and they began to consider other issues, such as how the ICC will bring together common law and civil law traditions of procedure and evidence. The representatives attempted to resolve these critical issues before the treaty conference. Then, at the conference, still higher-level representatives ironed out the remaining political questions, and a treaty was opened for ratification. Once 60 countries have ratified the treaty, the court will have jurisdiction over violators of international humanitarian and human rights law.

Conclusion

What are the likely effects of the permanent establishment of an international criminal court? First, the structure of the permanent court itself may eliminate the biases and inefficiencies inherent in the ad hoc tribunals created by the Security Council for Rwanda and former Yugoslavia. Second, since civil strife within countries often triggers serious repercussions throughout the world, such as forced migrations and the spread of violence across borders, a permanent independent judicial body may settle such disputes and reduce their concurrent effects. In addition, threat of prosecution by the international criminal court could deter future genocide campaigns and individuals intending to commit crimes against humanity. Finally, as Cherif Bassiouni points out, the ICC would establish a historical record of serious international crimes and the world's response to those crimes.

The international criminal tribunals for the former Yugoslavia and Rwanda were created in response to the atrocities that occurred in those regions. Because of their ad hoc nature, these tribunals did not deter violators of international human rights and humanitarian law. However, experience with these tribunals indicates that a permanent court would avoid the delays inherent in ad hoc tribunals and reduce the geopolitical selectivity reflected in the choices involved in creating the ad hoc courts. The establishment of a permanent court holds out the promise of deterring atrocities through effective international accountability.

For many, the creation of a new permanent international criminal court seems idealistic, given the current political and financial problems faced by the ad hoc tribunals for the former Yugoslavia and Rwanda. Others recognize that negotiations at the United Nations have advanced to a degree not anticipated even by some of the most optimistic UN observers. Because the Preparatory Committee meetings achieved enough consensus on the issues of independence and effectiveness of the court, including the views and interests of a broad sector of society, the treaty establishing a permanent international criminal court marks a new level of multilateral cooperation and interdependency for the twenty-first century. Even if it takes longer to breathe life into the ICC statute, the codification of government consensus on many difficult issues is an unprecedented advance in the development of international law.

Notes

1. The author would like to thank Professor Rhonda Copelon and Brian Axel for their encouragement and assistance in preparing this chapter.
2. Report of the Preparatory Committee on the Establishment of an International Criminal Court, U.N. GAOR, 51st Sess., Supp. No. 22, at 11, U.N. Doc. A/51/22, (March–April and August 1996).
3. Ibid.
4. Rome Statute of the International Criminal Court, A/CONF.183/9, July 17, 1998, Article 36(8)(a).
5. Ibid., Article 36(8)(b).
6. Report of the Preparatory Committee, see note 2.

Epilogue

The UN diplomatic conference to hammer out the statute of an international criminal court took place from June 15 to July 17, 1998 in Rome, Italy. Delegates from 160 countries were present; they were joined by representatives of over 600 non-governmental organizations—as diverse as the Lawyer's Committee for Human Rights, the Women's Caucus for Gender Justice in the International Criminal Court, and the American Bar Association—who mounted an unprecedented lobbying campaign on behalf of a strong court. After five weeks of intense debate, 120 countries voted for the final draft of the court's statute. Seven voted against, including the United States, and 21 abstained.

The United States, which had been the motor behind both Nuremberg and the ad hoc courts and whose support is always crucial to such international undertakings, played an unexpectedly obstructive role at the conference, lobbying for the weakest possible court. Concerned with the safety of U.S. soldiers and influenced by strong Congressional resistance to anything resembling a sacrifice of sovereignty to an international body, the U.S. delegation resisted an independent court with broad jurisdiction. It was not entirely alone in its position; other countries, too, lobbied for a statute that would shield them and their own nationals as far as possible from the courts' purview. Fearing the court's possible significance for military and peacekeeping operations, representatives of armed forces—including the U.S. Pentagon—took an active behind-the-scenes part in establishing many countries' positions at the conference. The document ultimately adopted at Rome was clearly a compromise, creating a court with a significant degree of independence but also with important restrictions that could severely limit its ability to carry out its functions. At least for now, should the international criminal court come into existence, it may be weaker than either the Nuremberg Tribunal or the ad hoc tribunals for Rwanda and former Yugoslavia. Still, the very fact of its creation—pending ratification by 60 states—is a milestone in the development of human rights law in the twentieth century.

Of the numerous points of contention at the conference, the most significant involved the court's jurisdiction. What, precisely, are the crimes it will be able to prosecute, and under what circumstances? Most important, who will decide when to initiate a prosecution? In many respects, the thresholds that must be met before the prosecutor can bring a case before the court, or even investigate it, were set quite high; while this allays fears of a court running rampant with frivolous or politically-motivated prosecutions, it will also make it more difficult to prosecute real crimes.

In terms of its subject matter jurisdiction, the court will be able to prosecute genocide, crimes against humanity, war crimes, and aggression. All were defined at Rome except aggression, which is to be defined at a review conference scheduled to be held seven years after ratification. The inclusion of the crime of aggression in the statute is noteworthy, since it has been a controversial subject; aggression is a difficult crime to pin on individuals, as opposed to states, and even at Nuremberg, the charge of "crimes against peace" was eclipsed by crimes against humanity and war crimes.[1] The major concern at the Rome conference in this regard, however, was reconciling the court's independence in determining when a violation has occurred with the Security Council's authority, under the UN charter, to decide when aggression has taken place.

The court's statute defines crimes against humanity (which may be committed in peace or in war) broadly to include even such often neglected crimes as sexual slavery and other types of violence against women, which have gained prominence at the tribunals for Yugoslavia and Rwanda. But it is not enough for these acts to be one-time occurrences; to be prosecuted, they must be part of a widespread or systematic attack knowingly directed against a civilian population—a high threshold. For war crimes, the statute's language is somewhat less limiting; the court has jurisdiction over them "in particular [emphasis added] when committed as a part of a plan or policy…" Here proponents of a more powerful court could claim victory, since the clause leaves open the possibility of prosecuting isolated incidents of brutality in wartime, which is the guise in which war crimes quite often appear. In both cases, however, the limiting language—more restrictive than current international law— aims at ensuring that the court will concentrate on only the most serious crimes and addresses governments' fears for their military personnel.

Another NGO victory, despite some governments' protests, was the inclusion in the court's mandate of war crimes committed in internal conflicts, which comprise the majority of conflicts today. The applicability of the law of armed conflict to civil wars has been a controversial issue at the tribunal for former Yugoslavia,[2] and the inclusion of internal conflicts here reflects the development of recent thinking in international law. On the other hand, however, governments are permitted to use "all legitimate means" to "maintain or re-establish law and order" or "defend the unity and territorial integrity of the State," providing a loophole for countries dealing with insurgencies or other internal situations of conflict and making it more difficult to prosecute crimes committed in such situations. Several other provisions also restrict the court's reach in non-international cases.

Women's groups succeeded in having rape, enforced pregnancy, forced prostitution and other types of sexual violence enumerated as war crimes and crimes against humanity, despite opposition from the Vatican and others who feared this would serve as legal encouragement for abortion. Meanwhile, however, states' objections led to the omission of crimes such as use of biological or nuclear weapons and the slave trade from the court's jurisdiction, while the apparently politically-motivated inclusion, on the list of war crimes, of transfer of population to occupied territories led Israel, despite its historically-determined interest in prosecuting crimes against humanity, to vote against the statute.

The idea that superior orders are no defense is thought to be one of Nuremberg's most important legacies (though Nuremberg did allow the argument of superior orders in mitigation of punishment).[3] The statute agreed upon in Rome qualifies this concept to some extent: it will permit a defense of superior orders in some cases, if the orders were not "manifestly unlawful" or if the accused did not know that the order was unlawful. This does not apply to genocide and crimes against humanity, which are defined as manifestly unlawful per se, but it will apply to war crimes.

The most serious debates, as had been apparent even before the conference opened, concerned trigger mechanisms—the modalities for initiation and prosecution of cases. A majority of delegates rejected the option supported by the United States and some others that would have required a unanimous decision of the UN Security Council before the prosecutor could initiate investigations. This arrangement would have allowed individual countries to veto prosecutions and thus highly politicized the court. Instead, although cases may also be referred by the Security Council and state parties, the prosecutor is empowered to initiate investigations on his or her own. However, in an important compromise provision, the five permanent members of the Security Council may, by unanimous agreement, block a prosecution for a year at a time.

Although this part of the statute gives the prosecutor much of the independence many human rights organizations had advocated, a host of hurdles must still be overcome before the court can actually take up a case. Most important and most controversial, it may only do so if the state in which the crime occurred or the state of the accused's nationality has ratified the statute or agreed to the court's jurisdiction (except in cases that have been referred by the Security Council, in which case its jurisdiction is universal). Interestingly, this clause was seen as problematic by both supporters of a strong court and advocates of a more limited one. The latter, especially the United States, argued with some justification that it could permit prosecution of nationals of countries that have not ratified the treaty, although under international law, states that have not signed a treaty are not bound by it. For example, if an American were to commit a crime on the territory of a state, and that country is either a party to the treaty or agrees to the suspect's prosecution, he or she could be handed over to the tribunal despite the United States' non-ratification.

Human rights organizations, meanwhile, argued that this jurisdictional provision represents a dangerous limitation on the court's authority. It ignores the wishes of both the state with custody of the suspect and the country of nationality of the victims; even if a suspect were to be arrested in a third country that has ratified the treaty and wishes to transfer him or her to the court, this would only be possible with the agreement of the country of the accused's nationality or the country where the crime occurred. This makes it unlikely that suspects accused of crimes in their own countries in a situation that is still ongoing would be subject to prosecution; Saddam Hussein could not be brought to justice for his treatment of the Kurds, barring a massive change of system in Iraq.

As a further preliminary hurdle, the prosecutor must receive the permission of a three-judge pretrial panel before beginning an investigation into a case. Further, he or she can take up the case only if national courts with jurisdiction are "unwilling or unable genuinely" to investigate and prosecute. The court must notify state parties of an impending investigation, and a country may then block prosecution if it shows that it is investigating or prosecuting the case in good faith. In general, the court will most likely be able to take a case out of a domestic court's hands only if the country is clearly not interested in honest prosecution, or if its judicial system has broken down. That is, the prosecutor could not easily overrule a working justice system's decision not to prosecute a suspect if it has undertaken a legitimate investigation. Finally, subjects and state parties have the right to challenge the court's jurisdiction or a case's admissibility.

In a further concession to the fears of some countries, delegates included an "opt-out" provision specifically for war crimes. It permits a state to ratify the statute but to shield its nationals from war crimes prosecutions for a one-time seven year period from the date of ratification.

The court's other provisions are less controversial; among other things, they include some strong guarantees of fair trials, allow the court to award reparations to victims, and exclude the death penalty. Women's groups contributed to the inclusion in the final document of provisions requiring judicial expertise on issues concerning violence against women and children and ensuring fair representation of women in the court.

The United States and a handful of other countries continued to oppose the statute despite the various concessions to their concerns. Some U.S. commentators argued that, in reality, only a strong United States military response could prevent human rights violations, and that a court would discourage such military response by threatening to prosecute soldiers involved in peacekeeping or other activities. But the fact that the American politicians most opposed to the court are also frequently those least likely to support sending American troops overseas to protect non-Americans weakens this argument, as does the United States' unwillingness, in situations such as Bosnia and Rwanda, to take firm steps to deal with human rights violations. In fact, this reluctance was the very reason for the creation of the ad hoc tribunals to begin with.

Human rights organizations, meanwhile, worried that the various hurdles to be cleared before the court can even begin to investigate will prevent many cases from coming before it. Yet given the multiplicity of interests involved and the difficulty of convincing countries to sacrifice their sovereignty to a collective body, this may have been necessary for the time being, at least until the court has had a chance to prove itself. It has, after all, been more than fifty years in the making, and the very fact that it has come this far is astonishing. As the ad hoc tribunals for former Yugoslavia and Rwanda have shown, effective international legal cooperation takes time, but it is possible. At the same time, the political will of the international community—including the United States—is necessary to make such courts work. It remains to be seen whether the international criminal court, assuming it becomes reality, will overcome the doubts and fears of its detractors and succeed in developing into an effective and respected mechanism for punishing the worst international criminals.

Notes

1. See Edward M. Wise, *The Significance of Nuremberg*, this volume.
2. See Diane Orentlicher, *Internationalizing Civil Wars*, this volume.
3. For a critical discussion, see Jörg Friedrichs, *Nuremberg and the Germans*, this volume.

Appendix

The International Criminal Tribunal
for former Yugoslavia

The Court
The International Criminal Tribunal for the Former Yugoslavia (ICTY) is located in the Hague, the Netherlands. The tribunal was created by UN Security Council Resolution 827 in May 1993, and is funded by the UN General Assembly (which provided the court with over $64 million in 1998) as well as by donations from individual countries. The tribunal began with one courtroom, but had added two more by December 1998, by which time its staff had grown to over 600. Unlike the International Court of Justice, also located in the Hague, which hears civil disputes between nations, the ICTY prosecutes individuals.

Facts

JURISDICTION: The tribunal may prosecute four types of offenses: grave breaches of the 1949 Geneva Conventions, violations of the laws or customs of war (there has been some controversy over whether this applies to internal as well as international conflict), genocide, and crimes against humanity (which must be committed in connection with international or internal armed conflict). In practice, here and at the Rwanda tribunal, the same act may be charged as more than one type of offense. The tribunal's territorial jurisdiction is limited to the former Socialist Federal Republic of Yugoslavia. The time period is from January 1, 1991, until the time peace is restored and maintained; that is, jurisdiction is ongoing, unlike the Rwanda tribunal's temporally limited jurisdiction.

The tribunal has primacy over national courts, and may request that national courts discontinue proceedings in deference to the tribunal. A double jeopardy clause prevents anyone from being tried before a national court for the same offense that has been tried by the tribunal. However, the tribunal may try someone for a crime heard by a national court if it was classified as an ordinary crime or if the tribunal determines that the national court proceedings were not impartial or were not diligently pursued.

RULES OF PROCEDURE: These are a blend of civil and common law rules. There is no jury; as in civil law systems, the judges both find facts and determine guilt. Guilt must be proved beyond a reasonable doubt. No trials may be held in absentia.

Rule 61 permits evidence and an indictment to be entered in open court when an indicted suspect cannot be apprehended; this serves a primarily documentary function, but judges may issue an international arrest warrant after hearing the evidence, making the suspect an international fugitive. Five Rule 61 procedures have been held against eight indictees, including Radovan Karadzic.

SENTENCING: Maximum sentence is life imprisonment. Sentences will be served in one of eleven countries that have agreed to house tribunal prisoners. No death penalty may be imposed.

Pardons and commutation are possible if permitted by the state in which the criminal is imprisoned. The tribunal president determines whether pardon or commutation is appropriate.

INDICTMENTS: As of December 1998, fifty-six people were under public indictment by the prosecution (a number of the original indictments had been withdrawn for various reasons, and five of the accused had died), and an unknown number of secret indictments had also been issued. Twenty-six people were in custody. One indictee was captured and one killed by NATO forces in summer 1997, two more were taken into custody by Dutch commandos in December 1997, and still another was captured in January 1998. In October 1997, ten Bosnian Croat suspects surrendered voluntarily to the tribunal, and in February 1998, three Bosnian Serbs did the same. In December 1998, SFOR troops detained Radislav Krstic, a Bosnian Serb army commander.

Defendants and Trials

TADIC CASE: The trial of Dusan (Dusko or Dule) Tadic ran from May to November 1996. Tadic, a Bosnian Serb, was a former café owner, karate instructor, and policeman in Kozarac, Bosnia. He was originally charged with crimes against humanity and war crimes under the Geneva Conventions relating to a rape, several murders, assaults, and torture incidents committed in May, June, and July 1992. (The rape charge was dropped on the eve of trial, and other charges were dropped when a witness admitted to having lied.) Tadic was not charged with genocide, the most serious crime over which the tribunal has jurisdiction, nor was he charged with command responsibility. He denied all charges. In May 1997, he was convicted of five counts of violations of the laws and customs of war and six counts of crimes against humanity. He was acquitted of violations of the grave breaches provision of the Geneva Conventions of 1949, because two of the three judges found that the Bosnian conflict was not international in nature (U.S. judge Gabrielle Kirk McDonald disagreed in a strongly-worded dissent). Tadic was sentenced to twenty years' imprisonment in July 1997 and is appealing the ruling.

CELEBICI CASE: This case, the first joint trial, began in March 1997, and a judgment was handed down in October 1998. Zdravko Mucic (a Bosnian Croat), Esad Landzo, Zejnil Delalic and Hazim Delic (Bosnian Muslims) were charged with violations of international humanitarian law in connection with the operation of a camp at Celebici where the victims were largely Bosnian Serbs. All were charged with direct partic-ipation in the crimes, and three were charged with command responsi-bility for acts of their subordinates. Delic became the first person to be convicted of rape before the Hague Tribunal; Music was convicted on the basis of command responsibility in the first elucidation of this concept by an international court since Nuremberg. Delalic was acquitted of all charges against him. Unlike the Tadic court, the court in this case deter-mined that the conflict in Bosnia had in fact been an international armed conflict, based on the participation of the Federal Republic of Yu-goslavia in the hostilities.

ERDEMOVIC CASE: Drazen Erdemovic, an ethnic Croat, confessed to participating in an execution squad and killing unarmed men in Sre-brenica. He was charged with crimes against humanity. Because of his guilty plea, there was no trial. Erdemovic claimed that he had to kill or would have been killed. He was sentenced to ten years in prison in No-vember 1996; on appeal, the appeals chamber of the tribunal remanded the case for a new trial, arguing that Erdemovic's original guilty plea was "not informed." In March 1998, after Erdemovic submitted an amended guilty plea, a new trial chamber sentenced him to five years in prison.

FURUNDZIJA CASE: In December 1998, Anto Furundzija, a local com-mander of a special military police unit of the Croatian Defense Coun-cil, was found guilty of war crimes—specifically torture and outrages upon personal dignity, including rape—and sentenced to concurrent eight and ten year sentences.

BLASKIC CASE: The trial of Tihomir Blaskic began in June 1997. Blas-kic, a Bosnian Croat general and the highest level officer to go on trial so far at the Hague, is charged with command responsibility for attacks on communities in the Lasva Valley during the civil war between Bosn-ian Croats and Muslims. Blaskic surrendered voluntarily to the Tribunal.

Other cases in progress as of December 1998 were those of Zoran Kupreskic and others, Zlatko Aleksovski, and Goran Jelisic.

Prosecution

The first chief prosecutor of both the ICTY and the ICTR was Richard Goldstone of South Africa, who left in 1996 to become a justice on the South African Supreme Court. The current chief prosecutor is Louise Arbour of Canada, a former law professor and judge. The deputy prosecutor is Graham Blewitt of Australia.

Judges

The tribunal began with two rotating three-judge trial chambers and one five-judge appeals chamber; in October 1998, an additional three-judge chamber was added, for a total of 14 judges. The appeals chamber is shared with the tribunal for Rwanda. The judges are nominated by their countries and elected to four-year terms by the UN General Assembly. The current judges are:

Antonio Cassese of Italy (the tribunal's first president); Claude Jorda of France, a judge of the Court of Appeal in Paris; Richard May of the United Kingdom; Gabrielle Kirk McDonald of the United States (current president of the tribunal); Florence Ndepele Mwachande Mumba of Zambia; Rafael Nieto-Navia of Colombia; Fouad Riad of Egypt, professor of law, arbitrator and international legal consultant; Almiro Rodrigues of Portugal; Mohamed Shahabuddeen of Guyana, a former attorney general of Guyana who served as judge on the International Court of Justice; Tieya Wang of the People's Republic of China; Lal Chand Vohrah of Malaysia, a judge of the Malaysian High Court; David Anthony Hunt of Australia; Mohamed Bennouna of Morocco; and Patrick Lipton Robinson of Jamaica.

The International Criminal Tribunal
for Rwanda

The Court

The International Criminal Tribunal for Rwanda is located in Arusha, Tanzania. The Office of the Prosecutor is in Kigali, Rwanda. The tribunal was created by U.N. Security Council Resolution 955 in November 1994 and is funded by the General Assembly. Its budget for 1998 was over $50 million, and in the same year it had a staff of over 500. The tribunal added a second courtroom in September 1997.

Facts

JURISDICTION: The tribunal can prosecute individuals for genocide, crimes against humanity, and violations of Common Article 3 and Additional Protocol II of the Geneva Conventions (involving war crimes). In contrast to the Yugoslavia tribunal, crimes against humanity do not have to show a nexus to armed conflict. For war crimes, the court has specific jurisdiction over violations committed in internal armed conflicts, as provided for in Common Article 3 of the Geneva Conventions of 1949 (unlike the Yugoslavia tribunal, where there has been controversy over whether the court's authority under the laws of war extends to internal or only to international conflict). Territorial jurisdiction includes Rwandan territory as well as that of neighboring states, if violations were committed there by Rwandan citizens. The time period is limited to the period of the civil war, from January 1 to December 31, 1994.

CUSTODY: The ICTR has set up the United Nations Detention Facility in the complex of the Arusha prison.

INDICTMENTS: Thirty-five people have been indicted; as of December 1998, 31 people were in custody—26 indictees and five suspects. Countries that have transferred or extradited suspects to Arusha include Zambia, Belgium, Switzerland, Kenya and Cameroon. In July 1997, Kenya arrested seven suspects, two of whom were under indictment, and transferred them to Arusha. In December 1997, a Texas judge refused to extradite a suspect held in the U.S. to Arusha, but the decision was reversed on appeal.

Defendants and Trials

AKAYESU: The trial of Jean-Paul Akayesu began in January 1997 and ended in spring 1998. Akayesu, the mayor of Taba Commune from April 1993 until June 1994, was charged with ordering and overseeing killings and torturing people who aided Tutsis. He was convicted of nine counts of genocide and crimes against humanity, including rape. In a groundbreaking decision, the court specifically found that rape and sexual violence may constitute acts of genocide.

KAYISHEMA/RUZINDANA: Their joint trial began in April 1997. Clément Kayishema was the prefect, or governor, of Kibuye prefecture from July 1992 until July 1994. He is accused of responsibility for the massacres of thousands of people and is charged with a total of 25 counts of genocide, conspiracy to commit genocide, crimes against humanity, and violations of Common Article 3 and Additional Protocol II of the Geneva Conventions. Obed Ruzindana, a former businessman, is alleged to have taken part in a massacre in the district of Kibuye and in the killings of men, women and children who had taken refuge in a hospital. He is charged with genocide, conspiracy to commit genocide, complicity in genocide, crimes against humanity, and violations of Common Article 3 and Additional Protocol II of the Geneva Conventions.

RUTAGANDA: The trial of Georges Anderson Rutaganda, a member of the ruling party and vice president of the Interahamwe, began in March 1997. He is accused, among other things, of ordering and directing killings, and is charged with eight counts of genocide, crimes against humanity and violations of Common Article 3 of the Geneva Conventions.

BAGOSORA: Théoneste Bagosora, whose case has not yet gone to trial, was director of the cabinet of the Ministry of Defense in Rwanda from June 1992 until July 1994. Following the death of President Juvenal Habyarimana, he assumed de facto control of military and political affairs in Rwanda and is alleged to have masterminded the massacres of Rwandan civilians, as well as the murders of ten Belgian soldiers from the UNAMIR contingent. Bagosora was transferred to the tribunal from Cameroon in early 1997 and is charged with genocide, crimes against humanity, and violations of Common Article 3 and Additional Protocol II of the Geneva Conventions.

KAMBANDA: In a startling development, Jean Kambanda, prime minister of Rwanda during the genocide, pleaded guilty in May 1998 to the

crime of genocide and other charges and was sentenced to life imprisonment.

Prosecution

Louise Arbour is the chief prosecutor for both the ICTR and the
ICTY. The deputy prosecutor for Rwanda is Bernard Muna of Cameroon.

Judges

The tribunal began with two three-judge trial chambers and one five-
judge appeals chamber, which it shares with the tribunal for former Yugoslavia. A third trial chamber, consisting of three new judges, is being
added. The current trial judges are:

Laity Kama of Senegal (president of the tribunal); Yakov A. Ostrovsky
of the Russian Federation (vice president of the tribunal); Lennart As-
pegren of Sweden; Tafazzal H. Khan of Bangladesh; Navanethem Pillay
of South Africa; and William H. Sekule of Tanzania.

Documents

The following are excerpts from some of the main documents cited in the texts:

CHARTER OF THE INTERNATIONAL MILITARY TRIBUNAL AT NUREMBERG

ARTICLE 6. The Tribunal establishment by the Agreement referred to in Article 1 hereof for the trial and punishment of the major war criminals of the European Axis countries shall have the power to try and punish persons who, acting in the interests of the European Axis countries, whether as individuals or as members of organizations, committed any of the following crimes.

The following acts, or any of them, are crimes coming within the jurisdiction of the Tribunal for which there shall be individual responsibility:

(a) CRIMES AGAINST PEACE: namely, planning, preparation, initiation, or waging of wars of aggression, or a war in violation of international treaties, agreements or assurances, or participation in a common plan or conspiracy for the accomplishment of any of the foregoing;

(b) WAR CRIMES: namely, violations of the laws or customs of war. Such violations shall include, but not be limited to, murder, ill-treatment or deportation to slave labor or for any purpose of civilian population of or in occupied territory, murder or ill-treatment of prisoners of war or persons on the seas, killing of hostages, plunder of public or private property, wanton destruction of cities, towns, or villages, or devastation not justified by military necessity;

(c) CRIMES AGAINST HUMANITY: namely, murder, extermination, enslavement, deportation, and other inhumane acts committed against any civilian population, before or during the war; or persecution on political, racial or religious grounds in execution of or in connection with any crime within the jurisdiction of the Tribunal, whether or not in violation of domestic law of the country where perpetrated.

Leaders, organizers, instigators and accomplices participating in the formulation or execution of a common plan or conspiracy to commit any of the foregoing crimes are responsible for all acts performed by any persons in execution of such plan.

ARTICLE 7. The official position of the defendants, whether as Heads of

State or responsible officials in Government Departments, shall not be considered as freeing them from responsibility or mitigating punishment.

ARTICLE 8. The fact that the Defendant acted pursuant to order of his government or of a superior shall not free him from responsibility, but may be considered in mitigation of punishment if the Tribunal determine that justice so requires.

~

THE NUREMBERG PRINCIPLES

The principles were adopted by the International Law Commission of the United Nations, 1950.

Under General Assembly Resolution 177 (II), Paragraph (a), the International Law Commission was directed to "formulate the principles of international law recognized in the Charter of Nuremberg Tribunal and in the judgement of the Tribunal."

The Nuremberg Charter set forth the following acts punishable as crimes under international law:

Principle I
Any person who commits an act which constitutes a crime under international law is responsible therefore and liable to punishment.

Principle II
The fact that international law does not impose a penalty for an act which constitutes a crime under international law does not relieve the person who committed the act from responsibility under international law.

Principle III
The fact that a person who committed an act which constitutes a crime under international law acted as Head of State or responsible Government official does not relieve him from responsibility under international law.

Principle IV
The fact that a person acted pursuant to order of his Government or of a superior does not relieve him from responsibility under international law, provided a moral choice was in fact possible to him.

Principle V

Any person charged with a crime under international law has a right to a fair trial on the facts and law.

Principle VI

The crimes hereinafter set out are punishable as crimes under international law:

(a) CRIMES AGAINST PEACE:
  (i) Planning, preparation, initiation or waging of a war of aggression or a war in violation of international treaties, agreements or assurances;
  (ii) Participation in a common plan or conspiracy for the accomplishment of any of the acts mentioned under (i).

(b) WAR CRIMES:
Violations of the laws or customs of war which include, but are not limited to, murder, ill treatment or deportation to slave-labour of for any other purpose of civilian population of or in occupied territory, murder or ill-treatment of prisoners of war, of persons on the seas, killing of hostages, plunder of public or private property, wanton destruction of cities, towns, or villages, or devastation not justified by military necessity.

(c) CRIMES AGAINST HUMANITY:
Murder, extermination, enslavement, deportation and other inhuman acts done against any civilian population, or persecutions on political, racial or religious grounds, when such acts are done or such persecutions are carried on in execution of or in connection with any crime against peace or any war crime."

Principle VII

Complicity in the commission of a crime against peace, a war crime, or a crime against humanity as set forth in Principle VI is a crime under international law.

~

DEFINITION OF GENOCIDE IN THE GENOCIDE CONVENTION OF 1948

ARTICLE 1. The Contracting Parties confirm that genocide, whether committed in time of peace or in time of war, is a crime under international law which they undertake to prevent and to punish.

ARTICLE 2. In the present Convention, genocide means any of the following acts committed with intent to destroy, in whole or in part, a national, ethnical, racial or religious group, as such:
   (a) Killing members of the group;
   (b) Causing serious bodily or mental harm to members of the group;
   (c) Deliberately inflicting on the group conditions of life calculated to bring about its physical destruction in whole or in part;
   (d) Imposing measures intended to prevent births within the group;
   (e) Forcibly transferring children of the group to another group.

ARTICLE 3. The following acts shall be punishable:
   (a) Genocide;
   (b) Conspiracy to commit genocide;
   (c) Direct and public incitement to commit genocide;
   (d) Attempt to commit genocide;
   (e) Complicity in genocide.

ARTICLE 4. Persons committing genocide or any of the other acts enumerated in Article 3 shall be punished, whether they are constitutionally responsible rulers, public officials or private individuals.

~

COMMON ARTICLE 3 OF THE GENEVA CONVENTIONS OF 1949

ARTICLE 3

In the case of armed conflict not of an international character occurring in the territory of one of the High Contracting Parties, each party to the conflict shall be bound to apply, as a minimum, the following provisions:

1. Persons taking no active part in the hostilities, including members of armed forces who have laid down their arms and those placed hors de combat by sickness, wounds, detention, or any other cause, shall in all circumstances be treated humanely, without any adverse distinction founded on race, colour, religion or faith, sex, birth or wealth, or any other similar criteria. To this end the following acts are and shall re-

main prohibited at any time and in any place whatsoever with respect to the above-mentioned persons:

(a) Violence to life and person, in particular murder of all kinds, mutilation, cruel treatment and torture;

(b) Taking of hostages;

(c) Outrages upon personal dignity, in particular, humiliating and degrading treatment;

(d) The passing of sentences and the carrying out of executions without previous judgment pronounced by a regularly constituted court affording all the judicial guarantees which are recognized as indispensable by civilized peoples.

2. The wounded and sick shall be collected and cared for. An impartial humanitarian body, such as the International Committee of the Red Cross, may offer its services to the Parties to the conflict. The Parties to the conflict should further endeavour to bring into force, by means of special agreements, all or part of the other provisions of the present Convention.

The application of the preceding provisions shall not affect the legal status of the Parties to the conflict.

~

ARTICLES OF THE STATUTE OF THE INTERNATIONAL CRIMINAL COURT FOR FORMER YUGOSLAVIA SPECIFYING THE ACTS WITHIN THE COURT'S JURISDICTION

ARTICLE 2
Grave breaches of the Geneva Conventions of 1949

The International Tribunal shall have the power to prosecute persons committing or ordering to be committed grave breaches of the Geneva Conventions of 12 August 1949, namely the following acts against persons or property protected under the provisions of the relevant Geneva Convention:

(a) wilful killing;

(b) torture or inhuman treatment, including biological experiments;

(c) wilfully causing great suffering or serious injury to body or health;

(d) extensive destruction and appropriation of property, not justified by military necessity and carried out unlawfully and wantonly;

(e) compelling a prisoner of war or a civilian to serve in the forces of a hostile power;

(f) wilfully depriving a prisoner of war or a civilian of the rights of fair and regular trial;

(g) unlawful deportation or transfer or unlawful confinement of a civilian;

(h) taking civilians as hostages.

ARTICLE 3
Violations of the laws or customs of war

The International Tribunal shall have the power to prosecute persons violating the laws or customs of war. Such violations shall include, but not be limited to:

(a) employment of poisonous weapons or other weapons calculated to cause unnecessary suffering;

(b) wanton destruction of cities, towns or villages, or devastation not justified by military necessity;

(c) attack, or bombardment, by whatever means, of undefended towns, villages, dwellings, or buildings;

(d) seizure of, destruction or wilful damage done to institutions dedicated to religion, charity and education, the arts and sciences, historic monuments and works of art and science;

(e) plunder of public or private property.

ARTICLE 4
Genocide

1. The International Tribunal shall have the power to prosecute persons committing genocide as defined in paragraph 2 of this article or of committing any of the other acts enumerated in paragraph 3 of this article.

2. Genocide means any of the following acts committed with intent to destroy, in whole or in part, a national, ethnical, racial or religious group, as such:

   (a) killing members of the group;

   (b) causing serious bodily or mental harm to members of the group;

   (c) deliberately inflicting on the group conditions of life calculated to bring about its physical destruction in whole or in part;

   (d) imposing measures intended to prevent births within the group;

   (e) forcibly transferring children of the group to another group.

3. The following acts shall be punishable:

   (a) genocide;

   (b) conspiracy to commit genocide;

(c) direct and public incitement to commit genocide;
(d) attempt to commit genocide;
(e) complicity in genocide.

ARTICLE 5
Crimes against humanity

The International Tribunal shall have the power to prosecute persons responsible for the following crimes when committed in armed conflict, whether international or internal in character, and directed against any civilian population:

(a) murder;
(b) extermination;
(c) enslavement;
(d) deportation;
(e) imprisonment;
(f) torture;
(g) rape;
(h) persecutions on political, racial and religious grounds;
(i) other inhumane acts.

~

ARTICLES OF THE STATUTE OF THE INTERNATIONAL CRIMINAL COURT FOR RWANDA SPECIFYING THE ACTS WITHIN THE COURT'S JURISDICTION

ARTICLE 2
Genocide

1. The International Tribunal for Rwanda shall have the power to prosecute persons committing genocide as defined in paragraph 2 of this article or of committing any of the other acts enumerated in paragraph 3 of this article.
2. Genocide means any of the following acts committed with intent to destroy, in whole or in part, a national, ethnical, racial or religious group, as such:
   (a) Killing members of the group;
   (b) Causing serious bodily or mental harm to members of the group;
   (c) Deliberately inflicting on the group conditions of life calculated to bring about its physical destruction in whole or in part;
   (d) Imposing measures intended to prevent births within the group;

(e) Forcibly transferring children of the group to another group.
3. The following acts shall be punishable:
  (a) Genocide;
  (b) Conspiracy to commit genocide;
  (c) Direct and public incitement to commit genocide;
  (d) Attempt to commit genocide;
  (e) Complicity in genocide.

ARTICLE 3
Crimes against humanity

The International Tribunal for Rwanda shall have the power to prosecute persons responsible for the following crimes when committed as part of a widespread or systematic attack against any civilian population on national, political, ethnic, racial or religious grounds:
  (a) Murder;
  (b) Extermination;
  (c) Enslavement;
  (d) Deportation;
  (e) Imprisonment;
  (f) Torture;
  (g) Rape;
  (h) Persecutions on political, racial and religious grounds;
  (i) Other inhumane acts.

ARTICLE 4
Violations of Article 3 common to the Geneva Conventions and of Additional Protocol II

The International Tribunal for Rwanda shall have the power to prosecute persons committing or ordering to be committed serious violations of Article 3 common to the Geneva Conventions of 12 August 1949 for the Protection of War Victims, and of Additional Protocol II thereto of 8 June 1977. These violations shall include, but shall not be limited to:
  (a) Violence to life, health and physical or mental well-being of persons, in particular murder as well as cruel treatment such as torture, mutilation or any form of corporal punishment;
  (b) Collective punishments;
  (c) Taking of hostages;
  (d) Acts of terrorism;
  (e) Outrages upon personal dignity, in particular humiliating and degrading treatment, rape, enforced prostitution and any form of indecent assault;
  (f) Pillage;

(g) The passing of sentences and the carrying out of executions without previous judgement pronounced by a regularly constituted court, affording all the judicial guarantees which are recognized as indispensable by civilized peoples;

(h) Threats to commit any of the foregoing acts.

The Contributors

Mary Albon
   Program officer for the Project on Justice in Times of Transition from its founding in 1991 until 1993. Extensive work in the nongovernment sector promoting democratization and civil society in Central and Eastern Europe and the former Soviet Union following the collapse of communism.

Donna Axel
   Instructor, New School for Social Research. Former Projects Coordinator and cofounder of the Women's Caucus for Gender Justice in the International Criminal Court; former program associate at the Coalition for an International Criminal Court; graduate of the City University of New York School of Law.

M. Cherif Bassiouni
   Professor of law, director, International Criminal Justice and Weapons Control Center, DePaul University; president, International Association of Penal Law; President, International Institute of Higher Studies in Criminal Sciences; vice-chairman, U.N. Preparatory Committee on the Establishment of a of a Permanent International Criminal Court; former chairman and rapporteur on the gathering and analysis of the facts, Commission of Experts established pursuant to Security Council Resolution 780 (1992) to investigate violations of international humanitarian law in the former Yugoslavia.

Bill Berkeley
   Journalist and senior fellow at the World Policy Institute. Has reported extensively on civil conflicts in East, West and Southern Africa for the *Atlantic Monthly, The New Republic, The New York Times Magazine* and many other publications, and is currently writing a book about ethnicity and conflict in Africa.

Stephen Breyer
   Associate Justice of the Supreme Court of the United States.

Alison Des Forges
   Consultant to Human Rights Watch since 1991 and its specialist on Rwanda and Burundi. Ms. Des Forges chaired the International Commission of Investigation into the assassination of President Melchior Ndadye in Burundi and subsequent massacres in 1993 and co-chaired a

similar commission of inquiry into human rights abuses in Rwanda from 1990–1993. She is serving as an expert witness for the International Criminal Tribunal for Rwanda.

Benjamin B. Ferencz

Benjamin Ferencz, a graduate of Harvard Law School, was involved in liberating the concentration camps after World War II and the investigation of Nazi war crimes. In 1946 he became executive general counsel of the Nuremberg Military Tribunal and later chief prosecutor of one of the subsequent U.S. trials, the *Einsatzgruppen* trial. He is an adjunct professor of international law at Pace University and has written widely on international law.

Jennifer Green

Staff attorney at the Center for Constitutional Rights. Member of the team of private and public interest lawyers representing the plaintiffs in *Doe v. Karadzic*, the suit in New York court against Radovan Karadzic.

William W. Horne

Lawyer, former senior writer and editor for *The American Lawyer* magazine. Now a freelance writer living in Leesburg, Virginia.

Jörg Friedrich

Historian and journalist based in Berlin; has published widely on postwar German history and military history.

Neil J. Kritz

Senior Scholar on the Rule of Law, United States Institute of Peace. Mr. Kritz is the editor of a three-volume work, *Transitional Justice: How Emerging Democracies Reckon with Former Regimes* (1995), and conducts ongoing research, writing and consultation on the question of how societies deal with a legacy of past abuses. He has provided advice and organized conferences on war crimes and mass abuses in Rwanda, South Africa, Cambodia, Guatemala and Bosnia.

Peter Maguire

Historian; has taught at Bard College and Columbia University. Mr. Maguire served as historical advisor for a documentary film entitled "Nuremberg: A Courtroom Drama" and as advisor to Spiegel TV in Germany on the documentary "The Lessons of Nuremberg."

Bernard D. Meltzer

Edward H. Levi Distinguished Service Professor Emeritus of Law at the University of Chicago Law School. Professor Meltzer served as assistant trial counsel for the United States Prosecution at the International Military Tribunal in Nuremberg.

Julie Mertus

Assistant professor of law at Ohio Northern University. Has published widely on human rights and war crimes issues. Editor, most recently, of *The Suitcase: Refugee Voices from Bosnia and Croatia* (1997).

Madeline Morris

Professor of law, Duke University. Advisor on justice to the president of Rwanda, 1995–97. Special consultant to the secretary of the U.S. Army, 1997, co-director of Duke Law School Pro Bono Project for Research Support to the Office of the Prosecutor, International Criminal Tribunal for former Yugoslavia and Rwanda.

Diane F. Orentlicher

Professor of law, Washington College of Law, and director of the War Crimes Research Office at American University in Washington, D.C. Professor Orentlicher has written widely on human rights issues and has provided legal opinions to the prosecutor for the International Criminal Tribunals for the former Yugoslavia and Rwanda. In 1996 she served as an investigator in the former Yugoslavia for the ICTY prosecutor.

Timothy Phillips

Founding co-chair of the Project on Justice in Times of Transition, established in 1991 by the Foundation for a Civil Society. The aim of the project is to assist states emerging from repression or conflict to engage in dialogue across ethnic, religious and ideological boundaries to help heal the wounds of the past and work constructively to secure peace and democracy.

Tina Rosenberg

Member, editorial board of *The New York Times*. Winner of the 1996 Pulitzer Prize and the 1995 National Book Award for her book *The Haunted Land*, on problems of transitional justice in Eastern Europe.

Beth Stephens

Associate professor of law at the University of Rutgers Law School-Camden and a cooperating attorney at the Center for Constitutional

Rights. Published *International Human Rights Litigation in U.S. Courts* (Transnational Publications, 1996), with Michael Ratner. Member of the team of lawyers representing the plaintiffs in *Doe v. Karadzic*.

Ruti Teitel

Professor of law, New York Law School; former Senior Fellow, Orville H. Schell Jr. Center for International Human Rights, Yale Law School. Author of numerous articles on human rights and constitutionalism. Her forthcoming book, entitled *Transitional Justice*, will be published by Oxford University Press. Member, Steering Committee, Human Rights Watch/Helsinki.

Patricia Viseur Sellers

Legal advisor to the prosecutor for gender related crimes at the International Criminal Tribunals for the former Yugoslavia and Rwanda.

Edward M. Wise

Professor of law and director of the Comparative Criminal Law Project at the Wayne State University Law School in Detroit. Author of numerous books on comparative and international law and criminal law.